Practical Applications of
PSYCHOLOGY

Anthony F. Grasha
University of Cincinnati

Winthrop Publishers, Inc.   Cambridge, Massachusetts

© 1978 by Winthrop Publishers, Inc.
17 Dunster Street, Cambridge, Massachusetts   02138

10   9   8   7   6   5   4   3   2

Interior design by Amato Prudente.
Cover design by Phil Carver & Friends, Inc.

Library of Congress Cataloging in Publication Data

Grasha, Anthony F
    Practical applications of psychology.

    Bibliography: p.   Includes index.
    1. Psychology, Applied. I. Title.
BF636.G577   158   77–16297
ISBN 0–87626–704–5

To
Carol, Kevin, Eric, and my parents
who encouraged me to pursue things that interested me

Contents

List of Exercises

Chapter 1

Chapter 2

Chapter 3

Chapter 4

Chapter 9

Chapter 10

Preface

I have always thought that psychological principles had a high potential for helping people deal more effectively with their environments. This book covers several areas of the field and illustrates how to use such principles in daily living. The concepts discussed come from the areas of psychological research; perception; learning theory; attitude, motivation, and personality theory; interpersonal communication; group processes; problem solving; and personal adjustment. Within each chapter, applications are stressed which will help you understand yourself better, change your behaviors if needed, and enhance your interactions with other people. A major assumption underlying the text is that the transition from theory to practice cannot be made simply by reading about applications. Consequently, the book is explicitly designed to encourage applications. Each chapter has an experiential component built into it. Exercises are used to illustrate particular concepts and to personally involve you with the information. The thrust is always on "how you can use this information in your daily affairs."

While the book stresses application, it also attempts to help you understand many of the major aspects of human behavior that psychologists study. The content was selected from psychological research, the experiences of practitioners, popular literature on psychology, and the experiences of the author. An integration of such information is made, and the reporting of individual research data is kept to a minimum. The goal is not to present the theoretical controversies in the field. Rather, the book provides you with information regarding reasonable principles which are found in the major areas of psychology.

In one sense this text is a cookbook. It has a decidedly "how to" flavor. Yet the application information is developed from relatively well-established conceptual or theoretical points of view. Care has been taken to make sure that you not only know how to use the information but that a perspective on where the information comes from is maintained. To do this, the text is organized around ten concerns that psychologists have raised in studying human behavior. Each concern is addressed in one of the ten chapters. The concerns and the chapters that relate to them are listed below:

Concerns	*Chapter*
1. The concern with objective data.	Chapter 1. Research Principles in Daily Living.
2. The concern with sensory and perceptual processes.	Chapter 2. Perceptual Processes and Our Daily Interactions.
3. The concern with human learning.	Chapter 3. Acquiring New Behaviors.
4. The concern with behavior modification.	Chapter 4. Modifying Existing Behaviors.
5. The concern with individual variations in behavior.	Chapter 5. Needs, Values, Attitudes, and Our Behavior.
6. The concern with interpersonal communication.	Chapter 6. Interpersonal Communication.
7. The concern with communication skills.	Chapter 7. Developing Personal Communication Skills.
8. The concern with group processes.	Chapter 8. Group Dynamics in Daily Life.
9. The concern with problem solving.	Chapter 9. Individual and Group Approaches to Problem Solving.
10. The concern with personal adjustment.	Chapter 10. Adapting to a Complex Environment.

Accompanying the text are a *Student Guide* and an *Instructor's Manual*. The *Student Guide* provides a format for you to self-test your knowledge of content, to enhance your understanding of key concepts, and to facilitate your work on the application exercises in each chapter. By providing ample space for your responses, the guide also serves as a record of your reactions to the text content and will help you to review and study the information. There are five sections for each chapter: a self-test on the content objectives; short-essay questions; observing selected chapter concepts in daily events; exercise worksheets; and suggested answers.

The *Instructor's Manual* discusses in detail both teacher and student concerns in teaching applications in psychology. Classroom procedures for involving students are discussed, as are suggestions for coordinating classroom procedures with the text. Sources of additional information to supplement the text are presented, and a listing of suggested films focuses on those emphasizing practical applications. Exam items (multiple-choice, fill-in, and short essay) are given for each chapter.

Many people contributed their support to this project. I appreciate the encouragement of my colleagues at the University of Cincinnati, my wife and children's patience with my long hours at the typewriter, the thoughtful comments of my reviewers, my secretarial staff, Diane Askew, Jane Keller, Linda McCabe, and Lee Stone for typing the manuscript, the comments and questions of Nancy Kaminski, and the support, assistance, and advice of Paul O'Connell, John Covell, and Bill Sernett at Winthrop, and my students who got me started on this project in the first place.

CHAPTER AIMS

A. **After reading this chapter, the reader should be able to explain:**

1. Five common ways in which numbers are often used deceptively in the types of data we encounter daily.

2. Three ways in which the words "average score" are used.

3. Why a correlation between two things does not mean that one of them caused the other.

4. Five questions we should ask of any piece of research to determine how good the information actually is.

5. Two problems we are likely to encounter when comparisons are made between two or more issues in information others give us.

6. Three things we can do to obtain a representative sample of people and products.

7. How extraneous variables—factors that are not specifically under study—can influence the outcome of a research study.

8. The meaning of probability and what it tells us about how consistently events occur.

9. How the assumptions we make about behavior influence the types of questions we ask and the answers we obtain.

10. How to ask questions about a behavior using different assumptions about its causes.

11. The advantage of stating our questions about behavior in the form of a hypothesis or "educated guess" regarding an answer.

12. Three things we do to attend to particular aspects of our environments and to ignore other aspects.

B. **The reader should be able to use the information:**

1. To solve the problems posed in the exercises used in the chapter.

2. To better interpret information they deal with daily and to begin asking questions about the causes of behavior in a more objective manner.

1

Research Principles in Daily Living

GLOSSARY

Correlation. A tendency for the measures taken on two events to vary together. When increases in scores on event A are associated with a corresponding growth in event B, this is called a positive correlation—for example, when the scores students get on a midterm are similar to the scores students receive on a final exam. When an increase in the scores on event A is associated with a decrease in the scores on event B, this is called a negative correlation. An example would be the finding that as the number of policemen walking a beat on certain streets increases, the number of crimes committed on those streets decreases.

Control group. A comparison condition in a research study. A control group has all the attributes of the people or products under study except that it does not receive the variable under study or it receives it in different amounts.

Dependent variable. The measure that we use to assess the effect of the variable or factor under study. In a study in which the variable we are testing is the presence or absence of a gasoline additive, the dependent variable could be the distance a car traveled.

Experimental group. In a research study, the group that gets the variables or factors the experimenter wants to manipulate (for example, gasoline additive, amount of time studying course content).

Extraneous variables. Unwanted factors in a research study that could interfere with the variable under study or produce the same effect as that variable.

Hypothesis. An educated guess as to the answer to a question we may have. The purpose of gathering information is to check if our hypothesis is correct.

Independent variable. The variable whose influence is under study. In a study of the amount of practice on speed of learning, the independent variable would be the amount of practice.

Mean. The sum of all the individual scores in a distribution divided by the total number of scores.

Median. The score in a distribution that has 50 percent of the other scores above it and 50 percent of the other scores below it.

Mode. The most frequently occurring score in a distribution.

Probability. The likelihood that an event will occur.

Random sample. The selection of people or products to study from a larger population without any known biases for selecting particular people or products.

Selective attention. A tendency to focus on particular aspects or characteristics of our environments and to ignore others. A person who only hears the positive things that people say to him or her and discredits or ignores the negative is using selective attention.

Statistically significant. A term used to describe two events that are assumed to differ because of factors other than chance. If we can assume that the observed difference would occur fewer than five times in 100 due to chance, then we say it is statistically significant.

Data Givers and Data Seekers

"Step right up folks. I've got something for each of you. It's guaranteed to make you feel better and live longer and it will not cost you a week's pay. For one little dollar, the amazing benefits of Mother Hubbard's Secret Snake Oil Tonic can be yours. I don't need to remind you that this is no ordinary product. Nine out of ten people tell me that after one sip they feel absolutely marvelous. Three out of four doctors recommend Mother Hubbard's Secret Snake Oil Tonic when everything else fails. No wonder it's the leading snake oil tonic on the market today. Now I ask you folks, can you afford not to have this tested product in your home?"

Have you ever bought a jar of snake oil? Probably not by that name. But each of us has bought some product or service or made some decision based on the information or data someone else gave us. Similarly, each of us has sought information to answer some question we have had about the factors which influence our lives. In my role as a researcher, this is often done within a laboratory setting. Outside the laboratory, I am no different from anyone else in wanting reliable and accurate information to understand my environment and to make day-to-day decisions. Yet how can each of us tell if the information others present to us is accurate? How can we obtain useful information on our own? This chapter will help answer these questions by exploring the applications of principles derived from psychological research to our daily affairs.

Research Activity and Your Life

Perhaps you have not thought about it very much, but you are asked to make decisions based on research data every day. The news media, advertisers, and even the textbooks you read make claims or support arguments with such data. Such claims are often designed to influence your thoughts and behaviors. How can you tell if their interpretations are accurate or if the procedures used to collect the data were appropriate? It is often a good idea to develop a critical attitude toward data. Facts and figures should not be accepted at face value. In many instances they are not as logical as they appear. Consider the following statements which you have probably encountered. As with many of the examples in this book, some of the details have been altered slightly to protect the guilty.

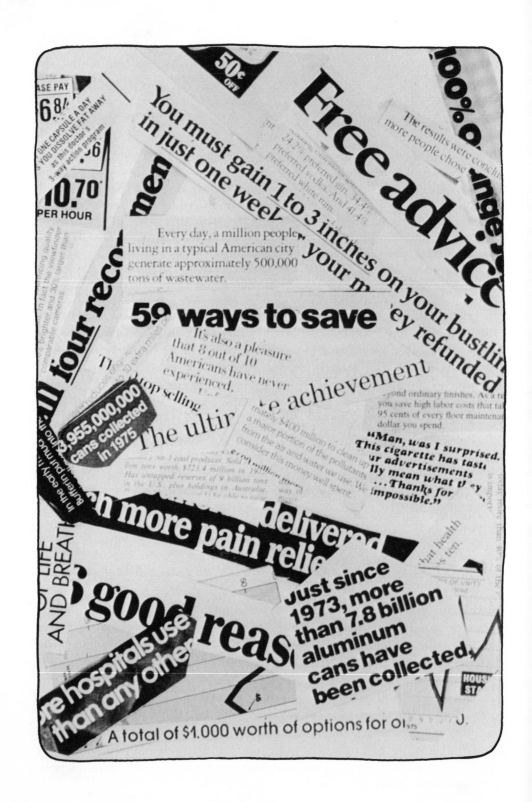

4

1. "Seventy-five percent of the women interviewed recommended new Sudsy for cleaning dishes, pots and pans, and the kitchen walls." Should you run out and buy a box of Sudsy as the announcer suggests?
2. "A spot check of 20 welfare recipients selected from 20,000 files in the welfare office showed that 5 were cheating the state." Does this mean that 25 percent of all welfare recipients cheat and that cutbacks in welfare aid are justified?
3. "A recent survey commissioned by the mayor's office estimated that 2 million rats (animal kind) live in our city." Would you support a new tax levy to exterminate rats, as the mayor suggests?
4. "During the recent rail strike, the city Association of Commerce and Industry estimates that the city lost 40 to 60 million dollars a day through lost freight revenues, store sales, and hotel and restaurant business." Would you be willing to write a letter to the union leaders protesting the hardship that has been inflicted upon your city, as the advertisement suggests?
5. "During the past holiday weekend, the Safety Council reported that a record number of highway deaths occurred." Would you be willing to assume that we are progressively becoming a nation of extremely poor drivers?
6. A statistician in a large city reported that as the sales of ice cream bars increased during the summer, the number of burglaries increased. Should ice cream bars be banned during the summer months? Should people who buy a lot of ice cream bars be considered potential thieves?
7. A newspaper recently reported on the wage negotiations between the union and management of a small company. The hourly wages for the nine workers were: $2.00, $2.50, $3.50, $3.50, $4.50, $4.80, $5.00, $10.50, and $15.00. The union representative argued that an increase in wages was justified since the average wage was $3.50 an hour. Management replied that the average wage was $5.70 an hour. Consequently they proposed a smaller hourly wage increase than the union wanted. Who is actually correct in this situation? Is a large or small wage increase justified?

EXERCISE 1-1: ANALYZING DATA FROM DAILY EXPERIENCES

How logical do you think these statements are? How would they affect your thoughts and behaviors? Think of at least one problem with each example. List the things you think are issues concerning each statement. Please do not read ahead until you have done this.

Did any of the following things occur to you?

Statement 1: While 75 percent of the women interviewed recommended new Sudsy, how many women were interviewed? The number is often left out of such claims and this presents a problem. What if only four women were interviewed? Would you be willing to try a product that three out of four women in the country recommended? How were the women selected? What would you say if they were wives of soap company executives? Whenever percentages are reported, you should be concerned about the number and type of people tested. Otherwise, an inappropriate decision or interpretation might be made.

Statement 2: If 20,000 people in a city are on welfare, then how representative of welfare recipients is a spot check of 20 from the files in the welfare office? With such a large number of people on welfare, it is unlikely that such a spot check is representative. You should also question *who* did the spot checking and the particular method used. What if a group in favor of cutbacks made the sample? This group is likely to be biased. If there are 200 file drawers with records and only one was chosen, then there may be something unusual about the people whose records are kept in such a file. Consequently, it is premature to assume that 25 percent of all welfare recipients cheat.

Statement 3: A flat statement that there are 2 million rats in a city is likely to be in error. The method that was used to survey or estimate the number of rats needs to be examined. How would someone count or estimate precisely that 2 million rats existed somewhere? In addition, the agency or people who did the survey should be taken into account. What would you say if the leading pest control company in the city conducted the survey? In the final analysis, tax dollars should be spent wisely and not on the basis of this kind of data.

Statement 4: Before you complain to the union leaders, you might ask what happened after the strike was over. In many cases, the majority of such losses are made up once a strike ends. Stockpiled freight is delivered and after the strike people will usually buy the previously unavailable items they had planned to buy. Businesses will recoup lost revenue through a general increase in sales to the public and through the rescheduling of conventions and other postponed activities.

To best assess the effect of a factor that operates to hold something back or retard its growth (e.g., the effect of strikes on sales, the effect of a wage price freeze on inflation), ask yourself what the situation is likely to be once that factor is removed. This helps to provide a clearer perspective on such data.

Statement 5: An increase in the *number* of traffic-related deaths on holiday weekends is relatively unimportant data (unless someone close to you is one of the people involved in an accident). It is unimportant because it may not reflect a decline in driving habits. What is left unsaid in such reports is that the number is related to population increases and the wider use of automobiles. Given these considerations, the important data are the *proportion* of deaths on one weekend compared to other weekends, not the *absolute number.*

When holiday weekends are viewed on a percentage-of-death basis compared with other weekends, the fatality rate is usually just as high on the other weekends. When small differences do occur in percentages, holiday weekends have an edge since they are a little longer than normal weekends. The important point is that the use of absolute numbers often makes comparisons among events difficult. This is particularly true when one of the two events has a greater or lesser chance to occur (e.g., accidents occurring on a normal weekend in a city when 10,000 cars are on the road versus on a holiday weekend when 25,000 cars are on the road).

Statement 6: The situation cited is an example of a statistical *correlation* between two events. A correlational analysis allows us to describe what happens when two things change together. When both show an increase (e.g., increments in ice cream bar sales during the summer and a growth in the number of burglaries), this is described as a positive correlation. When the incidence of one event increases and a second decreases (e.g., a rise in the number of polio inoculations over a 10-year period and a drop in the incidence of the disease), this is called a negative correlation.

We need to be careful when we see information that suggests a correlation. Just because two events are correlated *does not necessarily mean* that one caused the other. To determine that ice cream sales caused the growth in the number of burglaries, we first need a good reason for this causation and we need to eliminate other possible causes. In this case, it is hard to think of good reasons why eating ice cream bars would influence burglaries. More likely, as the summer months continue, more people take vacations and leave their homes and businesses vulnerable to theft. Unemployment often increases during the summer, and some of the unemployed may feel a need for "easy" money. All these factors occur simultaneously with increases in sales of ice cream bars.

How would you assess the likelihood of a cause and effect relationship if there were a high positive correlation between (a) drug sales and crime, (b) cigarette smoking and lung cancer, (c) suicides and unemployment.

Statement 7: Actually, both management and the union are correct. The problem is that there are three ways to represent the "average" score. This fact is not known by most people and often leads to misunderstanding and at times devious practices on the part of people presenting data. A rule of thumb is that when someone tells you what the "average" score is, ask them which one they mean. If we look at the three types of average scores, the reason for asking this question will become clearer.

Arithmetic mean. The *mean* is simply the sum of all the individual scores divided by the total number of scores. To obtain the mean wage, simply

divide the total hourly wages of the employees by nine. You should get $5.70 per hour, which is the "average" that the company's management quoted.

Median. The *median* is the score that has 50 percent of the other scores above it and 50 percent of the other scores below it. In the wage distribution, the hourly wage that meets this criterion is $4.50 per hour. The union might have used this "average" because it was smaller than the mean. They did not, because there is a third "average" score that is even lower.

Mode. The *mode* is the most frequently occurring score in a distribution. A wage of $3.50 per hour is earned by two employees and therefore is the modal wage. This is the "average" the union used because it best suggests that the employees are underpaid.

This type of situation is often repeated in news reports of wage negotiations, the cost of doing business, the average number of clients served by an agency, and the reading or other abilities of students in a school system. As you can see, everyone can quote the "average" and each is to some extent correct. Perhaps you are wondering how you can tell which "average" is better. In practice, the mean and median have certain advantages and each is used most appropriately in certain situations. The median is best when there are several very extreme scores in a distribution in which the others tend to cluster together. For example, a distribution on one of my recent exams was 99, 99, 98, 91, 89, 88, 87, 86, 85. Here, the median (89) is a better estimate than is the mean (91.3). The extreme scores affect the mean more than they do the median. The arithmetic mean would become a better choice if my scores clustered together more and there were not any large deviant scores (e.g., 99, 98, 97, 97, 96, 93, 92, 90, 88). In this case the mean (94.4) is a fair estimate of the "average" score.

The mode is seldom a really good estimate of the "average" for two reasons. Often you will find distributions that have more than one score that occurs equally often. It is a problem to decide which one to pick. Furthermore, the mode is not very stable. A change in one score can drastically affect the mode. If I used the mode as my average of the test scores, I would have a problem if I scored one exam incorrectly. If one of the 99 scores in the first set presented an error and it were changed to an 85, then my "average" will really fall. A change in one score will not affect the mean or median as much.

Overall, the seven statements represent a sample of several common problems in data that are presented to you daily. The factors that were discussed do not represent the only things that are problems with each statement. They do illustrate, however, the need for care in interpreting data that is designed to influence your thoughts and behaviors.

Five Questions to Ask Regarding Research Data

Fortunately, there are some things that you and I can do when confronted with data that will assist us in determining their validity. The answers to the following five questions will give us the information we need:

1. What is being compared and is the comparison a fair one?
2. Is the sample of people or products studied adequate?
3. Were representative test conditions used?
4. Were extraneous variables controlled?
5. How consistently did the event occur?

Before accepting any data from any source, we ought to have answers to each question. To aid in discussing the important points regarding each question, let us first apply the questions to a research design that you have probably seen in the mass media. The design is presented in Table 1-1.

1. *What is being compared and is the comparison a fair one?* In doing research certain factors are manipulated by the experimenter. These factors are called *independent variables*. The measures we take of their effects are called *dependent variables*. To assess whether any independent variable (e.g., presence of a gasoline additive, use of a new cigarette filter, amount of practice) has an effect on the dependent variable (distance traveled, amount of tar and nicotine, speed of learning) we need to compare it to something else. Comparison conditions in research are called *control groups*. The group in which the independent variable is manipulated is called the *experimental group*.

Control groups help us determine whether the independent variable actually made a difference. An adequate control group has all the attributes of the people or products (e.g., cars, televisions, radios, cigarettes) under study except that it does not receive the independent variable or it receives it in different amounts. In the latter case, it is known that the absence of the independent variable would produce no effect. In a study of how much practice it takes to learn to use a power tool or to speed read, a zero prac-

Table 1-1

A Mass Media Research Design

Exhibit A. Two scientific-looking individuals appear on your television screen. You immediately recognize them as scientists because they are dressed in white coats and carry clipboards. They walk toward two identical cars that are parked on an airport runway. The announcer's booming voice says that the experiment is designed to determine which one of the two identical cars will travel farther than the other under the influence of a gasoline additive. The announcer's voice challenges you. "Will car A running on Super-ZOOM *with* S-100 outperform car B running on Super-ZOOM with the S-100 removed?" One test run is shown right before your eyes. Car A travels farther than car B. "Now I ask you, folks," the announcer confidently says, "shouldn't you run down to your nearest Super-ZOOM station and purchase the only product we sell, Super-ZOOM with S-100?"

tice condition is not necessary. It is unlikely that the task would be mastered without practice.

An important exception to this generalization is the study of the influence of drugs. Telling subjects that they are receiving a drug, regardless of dosage, might influence their ability to learn, recover from a disease, or otherwise accomplish a task. Consequently, a *placebo* or neutral substance (e.g., sugar pill) is given to participants in the control group to control for the "expectation" in the experimental group that the drug will work. Thus, it is necessary in drug studies to have a group that receives a placebo.

We are likely to encounter two problems with control groups in our daily experiences. They may be absent or they may not be appropriate for what is under study. In the latter case, they usually have characteristics that are not included in the other conditions. Consequently, they are not fair comparisons for other conditions. A "research report" on television recently said that 60 percent of the children using Decay Away toothpaste showed no cavities. We really do not know if this performance is better or worse than in those using another brand or even not brushing at all. A control group was not used. Several years ago a new brand of window glass was advertised as far superior to its competitors in visual clarity. Unknown to the public at that time, comparative pictures of this brand with others on the market were deceptive. The panes that supposedly had the new glass in them were empty. It is no wonder that the other brands were not as clear. The comparison conditions certainly had characteristics that were not included in the experimental condition.

Let us apply this information to Exhibit A in Table 1-1. Based on what you have just read, answer the following questions before reading further.

a. What is the independent variable in Exhibit A?
b. What is the dependent variable in Exhibit A?
c. Is a control condition used?
d. Do you think that it provides a fair comparison for testing the effects of the additive? If not, why do you feel the way you do?

The description in Exhibit A appears to include several of the elements mentioned in these questions. The independent variable is the presence of the gasoline additive and the dependent variable is the distance each car travels. The control or comparison condition is the car without the additive. Is this a fair comparison?

On the surface, the Super-ZOOM comparison may seem appropriate because two identical cars were used. They apparently differed only in that one had the additive and the other did not. However, a "mild" deception is involved here. In reality there is no place where you can buy a tankful of Super-ZOOM without the additive. The manufacturer hopes that the viewer will assume that Super-ZOOM without the additive is like the other, competitive premium gasolines on the market. This assumption, of course, is not necessarily valid. To test adequately whether Super-ZOOM with S-100 is better than its nearest competitor one needs to have another car running with a competitive gasoline in its tank. Even though a control condition was included, we should question how fair a comparison it allowed.

2. *Is the sample of people or products studied adequate?* One intent of most data collection is to be able to make statements that apply to a large number of people. If a razor only shaves the actors on the screen or a political preference only applies to the 100 people interviewed, we cannot generalize. The people questioned or otherwise studied and the products tested should be representative of a larger population. They should not be biased toward a particular point of view or result. If I am interested in what people in this country feel about the Democratic party candidate for president, I should question other people besides registered Democrats. Similarly, an all-purpose, all-weather tire that only hinders subcompacts from skidding is hardly an all-purpose tire.

There are two general ways to get an adequate sample. One is to select randomly the people or products that will be tested. The other is to select them with regard to certain predetermined characteristics. A *random sample* is analogous to picking names out of a hat. Based on a larger sample of names or products, those that will be studied are picked *without any known biases* for our selection of them. One method for doing this is to assign a number to the names in a telephone directory or to the products produced. To select people or products randomly, a sample of numbers is drawn from a container that has all the possible numbers in it. In practice when large samples are needed, this is usually done by a computer.

A second method is to select people or things because they have certain characteristics of interest. In testing a hair dye that gradually reduces grayness, only people with gray hair would be of interest. Consequently, a sample could be randomly selected from the general population of people with gray hair.

A variation on the last technique is to select a small group of people who represent certain characteristics of segments of the population. They are then repeatedly interviewed or observed for their reactions to products, current events, and even television shows. This technique is called a research panel. The A. C. Nielsen Company uses a panel technique to gauge the television viewing habits of people. They use 1200 families who make up .0018 percent of the total viewing audience. An electronic device attached to the television set called an Audimeter records the show to which the set is tuned. On the basis of the viewing habits of people in these 1200 homes, the fate of a television program is decided. What you and I are able to see depends upon what these families consider important. Obviously a great deal of care must be taken in selecting such a panel and recording information.

Based on the information we are given, we should try to determine if the sample shown is adequate. That is, could we generalize to other people or similar products? With regard to Exhibit A in Table 1-1, is the sample of cars shown representative of automobiles in general? Yes_____ No_____. Please specify one reason for your response.

Only two cars of the same make were shown. Therefore, a representative sample was not tested. Although two cars of the same make and size were tested against each other, in order to generalize a range of compacts, intermediates, and luxury cars ought to be used. In this way we could determine if the additive works with different size engines and models.

Of course, if one attempted to test every make and model against every other make and model, the experiment might never end. We could randomly select a small sample of compact, intermediate, and luxury cars on the market. Automobiles from the same or different manufacturers that had similar body sizes, engines, body weights, and prices could be tested. The intent is to obtain a representative sample of automobiles from the population of those manufactured. If this is done well, the findings can be generalized to a wider variety of automobiles than just the ones tested. Because this was not done in the television commercial, the results may hold only for the make and model tested.

3. *Were representative test conditions used?* It is important to generalize not only to other people or products but to nontest situations as well. We are not likely to be pleased with the performance of a product or a person or with a person's opinions if they occur only under the conditions tested, particularly if the conditions are not typical of what we normally do in our daily lives. We should be interested in defining the normal limits or conditions under which people or the product performs. Test conditions should relate to such limits or conditions. An all-weather tire that is shown stopping on dry pavement or a food additive that produces cancer in rats when given at 10,000 times the normal daily consumption level for six months hardly represents normal conditions.

There is no set rule for determining a set of normal conditions. The first step, however, is to clarify the intent of the study. If it is to demonstrate that an all-weather tire stops faster than competitive brands on various road surfaces, then various road surfaces should be shown. If the intent is to show that a drug retards learning, then it is fair to ask how much of the drug is needed and what types of learning are retarded. If it is to indicate vote preference for candidates, then how any one compares to each of the others is information we need to have.

Review the test description in Exhibit A. Are the conditions under which the test was made representative of normal driving? Yes_____ No_____. Please give one reason for your answer.

We might want to know, for example, how the gasoline performed on highway driving conditions, city driving, in the desert, in rain, in snow, or in conditions of extreme cold. After all, automobiles are driven in a variety of road and climate conditions. In fact, they are hardly ever driven on airport runways as shown in the commercial. A test of a variety of conditions cannot be done in any one experiment. But such data are valuable. Otherwise, we might have an effect that only occurs under ideal driving conditions.

4. *Were extraneous variables controlled?* A good research design will allow us to assess if what occurred was due to the independent variable studied. To do this, *extraneous* or unwanted variables need to be controlled. Extraneous variables are factors that could interfere with the variable under study or could give us the desired result even if the independent variable were not used. They are considered controlled if they affect all the people or products tested equally or if we eliminate them before the research project begins. As an example, several students recently

told me that they tried to study the effects of marijuana on their ability to prepare for an exam. They told me they had stayed up most of the night before, studying together and smoking pot. They wondered if the marijuana in any way influenced their subsequent poor exam scores. It is hard to tell. I think that their having to study everything at the last minute, staying up late the night before and, I would assume, having a party atmosphere present affected their performance. Each of these factors is an extraneous variable. It is unlikely that they were present for all the other students in class. Each alone or in combination could have produced the poor exam scores. Smoking marijuana may have had nothing to do with the students' scores.

Turn back to Exhibit A in Table 1-1 and answer the following questions to test your understanding of extraneous variables:

1. List two things that *could be* extraneous variables in this situation.
2. How well do you think that each of the factors you listed were controlled?

Besides the gasoline additive, there are other things that might lead one car to go farther than the other. Such things as the size and horsepower rating of each engine, whether the cars were recently tuned, the amount of air in the tires, and whether the windows in both cars were closed to reduce air drag are all examples of extraneous factors that could influence the results. For example, if car A was recently tuned and car B was not, or if car A had more air in its tires than car B, or if car A had its windows closed and car B did not, then car A might go farther than car B regardless of the type of gasoline additive used. The point to remember is that we should not conclude that the gasoline additive was effective unless we know that extraneous factors were controlled.

We cannot determine whether these factors were controlled on the basis of the data that were presented. Such things are seldom shown. However, since most advertisements are trying to influence you and sell you on a product, their test procedures are not always unbiased. Thus it is helpful to think of some factors that could have produced the effect shown.

5. *How consistently did the event occur?* When looking at data, it is helpful to ask how often the event under study occurred. If it occurred consistently, then we are in a better position to say that the independent variable produced the effect. How can we tell if 5 out of 10 consumers selecting a particular brand of coffee or 9 out of 10 dentists choosing one brand of toothpaste represent a consistent preference? A general understanding of the concept of *probability* can help us make this decision.

When we say that one event is *more or less likely* to occur than another, we are dealing with probability. Before you walk out of your house in the morning you probably assess the likelihood of rain, or you may listen to a weather report that says there is a 90 percent chance of rain in your neighborhood. Of course, sometimes even with this forecast it will not rain. A probability statement does not guarantee anything. It is merely our best estimate or guess of the chances for some event to occur. One way to define the probability of an event is to first assess how often the event could occur. Then divide this by the total number of events that are possible. Be sure that each possible event has an equal opportunity to occur—that is, that no bias exists to favor one event over the other (e.g., loaded dice, marked cards) .

For example, what is the probability of obtaining a head when you flip a coin once? A head can occur only once per flip, but the total set of possible related events is a head and a tail. Thus, one head divided by two possible related events (one head and one tail) gives us a probability or likelihood of 50 percent or .50. To test your understanding of this logic, work the problems in Table 1-2 before continuing.

When we say that the probability of a head is .50, we are saying that on the basis of chance or blind luck, we would expect to get a head about 50 percent of the time. Therefore, if I flipped a coin 100 times and got a head 90 percent of the time, then I might suspect that chance was not operating. A head occurred an additional 40 percent as often as I would expect on the basis of chance. Therefore, I would want to look for explanations besides chance to explain this. Perhaps the coin is top heavy or I have learned to put just the right number of spins on it to get a head each time. I would account for this result in terms of the coin's weight or my skill in flipping it.

This same logic applies when we are given data in our daily lives and must assess whether the factor under study really makes a difference. We must first remember that everything in this world has a probability of occurring on the basis of chance. There is a probability that purely on the basis of chance the floor you are sitting or standing on will collapse, that the next plane ride you take will end in a crash, and that you will lose a large sum of money on the sidewalk in front of your home. Unfortunately for me, there is even a probability that a single monkey could have written this book by chance. See Table 1-3 for the rationale behind this last statement. Fortunately for all of us, each of the above probabilities is quite small. We need not worry too much that a floor will collapse, that our next plane ride will end in disaster, or that we will lose a large sum of money. Nor should we get overly excited and buy a monkey to write our term papers or books. We also should not buy cigarettes, automobiles, coffee, aspirin or deodorants just because some preference seems to be established. We need to determine whether the data represent a nonchance event.

Table 1-2

Probability Problems

Please answer each problem and check your response against the answers and rationale for each answer at the bottom of the table.

1. What is the probability of drawing an ace of spades from a deck of normal playing cards?
2. What is the probability of obtaining an ace on a single draw regardless of its suit?
3. What is the probability that someone will select brand X if they are asked to pick among three brands (brands X, Y, and Z) ?
4. A women is asked to taste two cups of coffee. She is then asked to indicate whether she preferred the first cup with brand A or the second cup, containing brand B.
5. An honest coin is flipped four times and four heads occur. What is the probability of obtaining a tail on the fifth toss? another head on the fifth toss?
6. The probability that shoppers in a supermarket on any day will select brand C soap bars from among the competitors on a shelf is .25. If 600 bars of soap are normally stocked each day, how many brand C bars would you expect to be selected?
7. What if an advertising campaign for the soap bars were run and on the corresponding day a week later shoppers selected 150 of the bars. Would this represent a consistent preference? What is the new likelihood that they would select Brand C?

Answers

1. There are 52 cards in a deck and one ace of spades. The probability is 1/52 or .019.
2. There are four aces and 52 cards. The probability is 4/52 or .076.
3. There are three brands and one brand X. The probability is 1/3 or .33.
4. There are two cups and, assuming the woman was not told beforehand what brand was in each cup, the probability is 1/2 or .50.
5. The probability of a tail on the fifth toss is .50 and the probability of another head is .50. Any other conclusion is an example of the gambler's fallacy. Although we might expect 50 percent of the tosses to be heads in the long run (e.g., a thousand tosses), in the short run it is quite possible to get a string of heads or tails occurring. Remember that a probability does not guarantee anything. It is our best estimate of what could occur if the situation is not biased. We have no reason to expect a change in fortune just because several events did not conform to the likelihood that they would occur.
6. We would expect 150 of the bars selected to be brand C. There are 600 bars of soap and 25 percent of the time a brand C bar is selected. $600 \times .25 = 150$.
7. They have selected just as many as they did the week before. Thus there would not appear to be any additional preference established by the advertising campaign.

Table 1-3

Probability of One Monkey Writing This Book

There are approximately 1,400,000 letters and spaces in this book. My typewriter has 50 keys on it including the space bar. The chance that a monkey would hit the correct key is 1/50. To write the book the monkey would have to select the correct key consecutively 1,400,000 times. The probability of doing this is 1/50 or .02 raised to a power of 1,400,000. To get some idea of how rare this event is, remember that: $.02^2 = .0004$, $.02^3 = .000008$, $.02^4 = 00000016$, and .02 raised to the 1,400,000 power would be a figure that had a decimal point followed by enough zeros to fill every space on every page in this book.

See, it is virtually impossible for a monkey to have written this book—I hope!

There are at least four ways to do this:

1. Remember that things that occur with a high degree of frequency are often not due to chance. A brand of soap that is picked from among its competitors 80 percent of the time by a large sample of people is most likely a consistent and nonchance preference.

2. Try to figure out how often the event would occur on the basis of chance. When people are making choices among products or other things, use what you already know from Table 1-2 to determine the chance expectation. See if the data shown exceed or fall below chance. If people are asked to tell which of three coffee brands tastes best and 33 percent of them say Brand X is best, such a preference does not exceed chance. Similarly, if 52 percent of the people sampled preferred one of two presidential candidates, we should not get overly excited. While above chance, the latter data are only 2 percent above chance. As a *general rule of thumb,* you probably should accept only a difference of 10 percent or more as representing a significant preference. Better yet, use the procedure described below.

3. If the data are reported in terms of a certain number or proportion of people in one condition who said or did something differently than those in another, there are statistical tests which can help us. They will allow us to determine rather precisely whether or not the variations between two or more groups exceed chance. If 60 percent of the people sampled liked Brand X or political candidate A and 40 percent liked Brand Y or political candidate B, how could we tell for sure if these differences are not likely to have occurred on the basis of chance?

Unfortunately, we can never tell *for sure.* Remember that everything in the world can occur on the basis of chance. This includes both large and small differences among groups. The best that we can do is to find the probability that the difference was due to chance. Most social scientists use statistical tests to help them make such judgments. They are willing to reject chance if the test shows that the difference is likely to occur less than five times out of 100 (.05) on the basis of chance. This is called a *statistically significant* finding. We should then be willing to assume that this represents a time when factors other than chance produced the effect. The reference section of this chapter lists two introductory statistics books which can show you how to use various statistical tests.

4. This is not so much a formal procedure as some advice my grandfather once gave me. He asked me to consider whether I would bet my life's savings that the event was not due to chance. His point, of course, was that placing money on the line has a tendency to make us conservative. It is only after adopting such a cautious attitude that we should make decisions about data. This will at least force us to examine the data carefully for anything suspicious. Most of the time we may lose only a dollar or two in purchasing something, but people have lost thousands in buying automobiles or stock in a company that did not live up to the data in their advertisements. We should at least look carefully before making a decision based on the data we receive daily.

Let us look again at Exhibit A in Table 1-1. Answer the following questions before reading further:

1. How consistently did the event occur?
2. Do you think this exceeds chance, and why?
3. What if car A with the additive travelled farther in 90 percent of the tests? Do you think that this would represent a result that was not due to chance? Yes_____ No_____. Why do you feel this way?
4. What if 10 tests were run and each resulted in a tie?
5. What if after 10 tests in which both cars won occasionally, we found no difference in the total distance each car travelled?

The television advertisement showed only a single test. The fact that car A travelled farther this time is not evidence for a consistent effect of the additive. Assuming that both cars are equal in all other respects, we would need several tests to see if car A with the additive is superior. If it beat car B 90 percent of the time, this result probably did not occur on the basis of chance. If the additive had no effect, we would expect the two cars either to each win about 50 percent of the time, to tie each time, or to show a zero difference in total distance travelled after 10 tests.

A final point to remember is that just because some event exceeds chance, it is not necessarily true that the factor under study produced it. Keep in mind our discussion about the representativeness of the sample, whether or not an appropriate comparison or control condition was used, and the extent to which extraneous variables were controlled. We should not decide that the effect we observed is due to the factor under examination unless we can answer appropriately each of the five questions on page 10. It may not always be possible to obtain a definite answer to each question based on the data given, and it is important to treat a partial confirmation cautiously.

Questioning Your Environment

Not only are we asked to interpret the data from the questions that others ask, but you and I also ask questions about the things in our environments that affect and influence us. For example, I recently asked some of my students to list the questions they recently had about human behavior. Some of the things they said were: "I wonder why my uncle Fred attempted suicide?" "What were the reasons that Alice had for quitting school?" "Will spanking my child affect his emotional development?" "I often make funny remarks at meetings, does that mean that there is something wrong with me?" "How many really good teachers are there on this campus?" "Why do people cross the street when a 'Don't Walk' sign is showing?" "I wonder what my customers think about the quality of the merchandise and service in my store?" "Are students really in favor of closing the student union at noon on Saturday?"

With most of our questions we would not think of using elaborate research designs to obtain satisfactory answers. Yet the way we seek answers to our questions has elements of the research process in it. We state questions, we gather information or "data" that relate to it. We form an answer based on the information and we often have to defend our answers (e.g., in discussions with friends, exams, term papers). Several principles related to the practice of psychological research can assist us in obtaining the best possible answers to our questions. We can then avoid some of the common problems associated with gathering and interpreting information from our environment. The remainder of this chapter describes some of these principles and how they might assist you in answering the questions you ask daily.

Be Clear about the Assumptions You Make
Regarding Behavior

How we ask questions reflects our assumptions about human behavior and what influences it. "I wonder why Mary decided to quit school?" "I wonder what the school did to force Mary to quit?" Both questions relate to the behavior of Mary leaving school. The first, however, makes the assumption that personal choices and decisions are important parts of that process. The second implies that external forces made Mary quit. Both, of course, may be important in understanding why Mary left school. Yet if we state the question in either one of these ways, we are unlikely to obtain information regarding both factors. Rather, we are more likely to seek information that will reflect one or the other point of view. We will have an answer that relates either to our assumption that personal choice and decisions are important or to the role of external forces in causing behavior.

Because our questions reflect the assumptions we make about behavior, they guide us toward certain types of answers. There are both advantages and disadvantages to this process. One advantage is that it enables us to develop a consistent set of beliefs about why certain things happen to us and to others. We are able to explain things without appearing to be uncertain in our approach. On the other hand, we may close ourselves off from alternative explanations and points of view. We may find ourselves drawn into arguments about the cause of some behavior only to discover that the source of the conflict is different assumptions. Discussing each of our assumptions first can often help us reach a mutually agreeable solution on an issue.

EXERCISE 1-2: BASIC ASSUMPTIONS

People do not make the same assumptions about behavior. Nor do they often think about those assumptions that are implicit in the types of questions they ask or the behaviors they engage in. The following exercise will help to clarify some of these issues for you.

1. Listed here are six general assumptions about human behavior. Use the following rating scale to rate the degree to which you agree with each statement. (1 = strongly agree; 2 = moderately agree; 3 = neither agree nor disagree; 4 = moderately disagree; 5 = strongly disagree.)

    _____Human behavior is predictable.

    _____Human behavior is caused by observable factors within the individual and the environment.

    _____The factors that cause behavior can be measured.

    _____A person is responsible for the choices and decisions he or she makes.

    _____The external environment forces people to choose and decide things.

    _____Only a limited number of factors cause any behavior to occur.

2. List one to three other general assumptions you make about human behavior.
3. Write a brief description to explain what you think caused the following things to occur.
   a. Lee Harvey Oswald to kill President Kennedy
   b. Former president Nixon to leave office
   c. Your enrolling in this course
   d. A mother to care for her child
   e. The rise in the price of a product after it becomes popular
4. How consistent are your explanations with the importance of the assumptions you rated and listed in the previous questions? In what specific ways were these assumptions reflected in your descriptions? Were your assumptions consistent across each of the five situations?
5. Compare your responses with those of a friend or classmate. What are the similarities and differences between your explanations and the assumptions that underlie them?

Ask Questions from the Perspective of Different Assumptions

Our goal in seeking answers to questions is to increase our understanding of behavior. The assumptions we make lead us toward certain answers or viewpoints about our daily lives. To broaden our perspective on the factors that influence behavior, sometimes it is helpful to ask questions that reflect an assumption contrary to accepted beliefs (e.g., If the concept of mental illness is myth, then why are people put in mental institutions?) or that combine two or more assumptions that are not necessarily compatible (e.g., How do people make personal decisions that take into account the influences of the environment?). We might then obtain insights that enrich our understanding of behavior and that give us different solutions to our questions. One of my personal experiences shows what can happen when this is done.

When I was in Vietnam several years ago, I accompanied a medical team to a primitive village located in the central highlands of the country. Because of water pollution, the villagers were experiencing upset stomachs and diarrhea. When we arrived in the village we noticed that the people had the equivalent of a local medicine man. He was delighted when we told him the problem was due to their water. He knew exactly what to do. He placed a large container of water on the ground. He then began to pray and play soft music from an instrument that resembled a flute. He was going to drive out the "evil spirit" that was temporarily in the water. The following conversation occurred through an interpreter between the physician on our team and the medicine man.

PHYSICIAN: That is not going to help much. It is not an "evil spirit" but a microorganism that causes the illness.

MEDICINE MAN (*staring blankly into space*): What is a microorganism?

PHYSICIAN: Well, you know, it's something that is quite small and you cannot see it. It is invisible, yet it causes you a lot of harm.

MEDICINE MAN: Just like evil spirit. I know how to treat evil spirits.

It was obvious that two different assumptions about the causes of the illness were being made. The physician and I thought that the occurrence of this illness was predictable and due to observable factors in the environment. The medicine man felt the occurrence could not be predicted and was due to an "evil spirit" that happened to occupy the water supply at that time. I realized we would get nowhere arguing about whose set of assumptions was correct. There is actually nothing wrong with either. Most scientists would not make the same assumptions as the medicine man. However, the assumptions did allow him and others in the village to make sense out of their world. It gave them consistent answers to their questions about the causes of things.

I decided to make the medicine man's assumption and see where it got me. I told myself that the disease was not caused by a microorganism but by an "evil spirit." After all, according to the physician's description, the two had many characteristics in common. I then thought about how to eliminate an "evil spirit." Praying and playing the flute would help, but I also wondered if heat would drive the spirit out of the water. I asked the medicine man and he agreed that heat was sometimes used to drive an "evil spirit" away. We left the village with the medicine man praying and playing music in front of containers of water that were boiling in an open fireplace. The problem with the "evil spirit" was solved.

EXERCISE 1-3: CHANGING ASSUMPTIONS

The following exercise will demonstrate some of the things that can happen when you make assumptions contrary to those usually accepted or that combine one or more assumptions that are not necessarily compatible.

1. Some people can become severely depressed for extensive periods of time. They may sit around doing nothing, they may cry a lot, and their interactions with others are affected. Some psychiatrists and psychologists would diagnose such symptoms as a clinical "depression." The people might be given drugs, confined to a hospital, or placed in psychotherapy. The assumption is that there is an illness within the individual that needs treatment.
   a. Pretend that these people are friends of yours. *Assume that they are not suffering from an illness called "depression"* but they are sad and unhappy. What would you do that might be helpful to them? How does it differ from what was suggested in the last paragraph?
   b. Do you think you would ask different questions about the cause of their behavior if you assumed they were "sick" rather than sad and unhappy. How would the questions be the same or different?
2. Listed here are several pairs of statements about the same behavior. They are stated as opposites of each other. For each statement, list one question it evokes about behavior. Assume that both parts are true when you ask your question. How do the types of questions differ? I have done the first one for you.
   a. Our attitudes produce changes in our behaviors. Our behaviors produce changes in our attitudes. What effect does radio and television advertising have on getting people to like certain products? What is the effect of giving people free samples of products on getting them to like the product? As you can see, if I were a manufacturer, I would take two different approaches to getting people to like my products.
   b. People who hold racial prejudices dislike other people. People who dislike other people hold racial prejudices.
   c. People who talk to a guidance counselor will begin to develop changing ideas about personal and career choices. People who begin to develop changing ideas about personal and career choices will talk to a guidance counselor.
3. For each situation previously described in question 3 of Exercise 1-1 on basic assumptions, think about assumptions that are contrary to the ones you made. How does this affect your understanding of each situation? Did it give you any new insights?

Try to Expand Your Questions into a Hypothesis about Behavior

Most of us ask questions about behavior in a rather casual or general manner. For several examples of this tendency, review the questions that were presented on page 20. Most are in the form of "I wonder," "Why did," or "Will something occur?" This does not mean that they are less than legitimate questions or that they are uninteresting. In fact, such general questions are needed to get us thinking about what influences behavior. However, by themselves they do not give directions about the specific type of information that will answer them. Whenever possible, expand a general question in such a way that you might suggest one or more possible answers. "I think Uncle Fred attempted suicide because his business failed and because his wife left him." The information we obtain will then confirm or not confirm our potential answer. It will also save us time in getting information. We will know what specific aspects of the behavior interest us. When we make such an educated guess about the answer to a question, we are forming a *hypothesis*.

One of my students had a friend who was seriously injured while crossing a street near the university. Her friend crossed when the "Don't Walk" sign was on. Her initial question was quite general: "I wonder why people do something like that?" She then formed several educated guesses or hypotheses about why this occurs. She thought that people might be more inclined to disobey a "Don't Walk" sign if a police officer were not present, if an older respected model (e.g., a professor) did it, if there were social pressure to conform (e.g., a large crowd started to walk against the light) or if the environment encouraged such behavior (e.g., it is going to rain at any minute). She spent several minutes each day for two weeks watching people at crosswalks. Based on her observations she concluded that social pressure to conform and the absence of any authority figure were important causes of the behavior.

There are two constraints we should place on our educated guesses or hypotheses in our daily lives. The hypotheses should be statements that we are capable of answering without elaborate techniques. They should also lead us to focus on observed behaviors to confirm them. The following are interesting hypotheses, but they do not easily meet either of these criteria: "People can have misfortune if other people think bad thoughts about them." "A full moon affects the way that I and other people feel." It is not clear whether these are hypotheses that can be easily answered. Nor is it clear what specific behaviors we should focus on to confirm them. It is important to form questions about behavior in ways that permit you to obtain a personally satisfactory answer to them. Each of us is curious about the behaviors around us. Few of us, though, have the time and energy in our daily lives to use elaborate measurement and research techniques to answer our questions. If you do, however, there is certainly nothing wrong with exploring your questions in such detail. Many psychologists on a campus do this as part of their research activity. Perhaps you could assist one of them with a project.

EXERCISE 1-4: HYPOTHESIS FORMING

1. Several general questions about behavior are listed below. I have stated one hypothesis and a method that focuses on observed behaviors to try to confirm the hypothesis. Write an additional hypothesis and a method that focuses on observed behavior to try to confirm your hypothesis.
    a. Why do some people seem to worry about taking classroom tests?
    Hypothesis 1. This is more likely to be the case with students who have low grade point averages. A poor course grade might mean they will have to drop out of school. I could talk to several of the good and poor students in each of my classes and ask questions about their feelings toward exams. Their responses should help me confirm or disconfirm my hypothesis.
    Hypothesis 2.
    b. I wonder what it takes to get a good grade in the tough class I'll be taking next term?
    Hypothesis 1. People who do well in that course probably have to have their answers on their exams well organized. I know some of the people who have finished the course. I'll ask them to tell me which factors are most important (organization of an answer, using lecture material in an answer, using content from the book on exams, class participation).
    Hypothesis 2.
    c. Why do some people not use their automobile turn signals when switching lanes or turning a corner?
    Hypothesis 1. People are more likely to use their turn signals if the car in front of them has just done so. As I drive around town this week, I'll watch for people who do and do not use their turn signal. I'll try to count the times that each does and whether or not the people in front of them have just used theirs.
    Hypothesis 2.
2. Take one or more of the hypotheses you wrote and actually see if you can confirm it. If you want, you might see if any of mine are accurate.

Try to Avoid Misinterpreting the Information You Obtain for Your Questions

Earlier in this chapter we reviewed several principles that will assist us in interpreting correctly the information and data that others present. We also need to exercise care in the conclusions and decisions we make with regard to our own questions. My experiences suggest that it is usually easier to be critical about information that someone else is presenting. We often trust and accept the information we have sought without critically examining it. Think of the number of times that someone found a hole in an answer you gave to a problem or question. Were they ever right?

To restate the discussion in the earlier sections of this chapter, we must make sure that our personal conclusions and decisions regarding our questions are based on: (a) having an adequate sample of information, (b) the consistency with which the things we observe occur, (c) whether we have eliminated other possible factors as explanations, and (d) whether we have misused any numerical information. To evaluate each of these considerations accurately, we need to become aware of and overcome a tendency people have to attend selectively to particular aspects of their environments. Descriptions of several common types of *selective attention* and how they affect our conclusions and decisions follow:

1. *The focus on data that fit our belief system.* We have already discussed how our assumptions lead us to ask questions that predispose us toward obtaining certain types of information. Although this is a problem, a greater source of concern is that we actively ignore, forget, or otherwise inhibit information that *does not fit* our belief system. Not only do we seek certain types of information, but we often ignore contradictory evidence. Ralph K. White has called this process "selective inattention." He has shown that once an activity is under way, people tend to retain only those thoughts and ask only those questions that are in harmony with it. He believes that this process affects a range of minor and major decisions we make. In fact, he indicates that the operation of "selective inattention" is a major cause of nations going to war. National leaders are not able to examine evidence that goes against the good image of themselves and the diabolical image of another nation. This happens in part because they usually are surrounded by advisors who help support and encourage a particular set of beliefs.

2. *The focus on restricted samples.* Few of us encounter a truly broad sample of people or events in our daily lives. On the job, in school, or in our social groups, we do not meet people or engage in activities that are a representative sample of a larger population of people or activities. My university colleagues are not a representative sample of people in the general population. Their educational backgrounds, salaries, and interests are not typical. Nor are the few hobbies and outside interests I have a representative sample of such things. The problem is that I often forget this fact. I find myself in other situations making decisions and drawing conclusions

based on information from my experiences with this restricted sample. The answers to many of my everyday questions are hard data-based and fairly logical, and usually I cite an outside authority. I am dismayed to find that local politicians, church leaders, and homemakers are not usually influenced by this approach.

In a similar way, I tend to underestimate the chances of my home getting broken into. I live in a low crime area, and thus I assume that it will probably not happen. On the other hand, several local police officers who live in the neighborhood overestimate the chances of a break-in occurring. They deal with thieves daily and they perceive that thieves are everywhere. The police officers are overly cautious and take elaborate precautions to protect their homes. Both of us are basing our decisions on information from the restricted samples of people and events we normally encounter. We assume that the samples we experience are typical of everyone or everything.

EXERCISE 1-5: REDUCING SELECTIVE ATTENTION

1. Check the statement regarding an aspect of selective attention that is *most* like you. Check the statement that is *least* like you.

    a. _____I tend to focus on data that fit the way that I believe and feel about things.

    b. _____I forget sometimes that the people I know well and the activities that I engage in are not typical of everyone else.

    c. _____I tend to form generalizations without seeking as much information as possible.

    d. _____I tend to trust numerical data and seldom question the numbers I see.

2. List recent examples from your behavior that illustrate each of the statements you checked. What problems did the factor that is most like you create? How can you avoid such problems?

3. What problems did the factor that is least like you allow you to avoid? What are things that you do to keep this factor from influencing your life?

SUMMARY

We are often asked to make a decision or change our behaviors based on information or data that someone else has given us. Similarly, each of us has sought information to answer some questions we have had about the factors that influence our lives. When assessing information or data that another person or source gives us, it is often a good idea to ask the following five questions about it:

1. *What is being compared and is the comparison a fair one?* In any research project certain things are manipulated (e.g., presence or absence of gasoline additive, amount of practice). These factors are called independent variables. The measures we take of their effects are called dependent variables (e.g., distance a car travels, speed of learning). To assess whether the independent variable has had an effect, we need a comparison or control group. There are two problems we may encounter with comparison or control conditions in our daily lives. First, they may be absent in the data we are asked to assess. Second, they may not provide a fair comparison because they have characteristics that are not included in the other group (s) under study.

2. *Is the sample of people or products studied adequate?* One intent

of collecting data is to be able to make statements that apply to a large group. The people questioned or otherwise studied and the products tested should be representative of a larger population. There are several ways to accomplish this aim. One is to randomly select a sample of people or products from a larger population. Sometimes it is necessary to have a sample that has certain characteristics (e.g., a particular political preference and age combination). Thus, a random sample can also be made of people or products with certain characteristics. Finally, a research panel might be formed. This is a small number of people who are matched carefully to reflect the characteristics of a larger group of people.

3. *Were representative test conditions used?* It is also important to generalize to situations in our daily lives. We are not likely to be pleased with a product or people's opinions or their performance that occur only under the conditions tested. To decide if the conditions were representative, we need to understand the intent of the study. Then we can decide if the conditions tested are those that represent the normal, everyday situations we are likely to encounter.

4. *Were extraneous variables controlled?* Extraneous or unwanted variables need to be controlled. Extraneous variables are factors that could give us the desired result even if an independent variable were not used. They are considered controlled if they affect all the people or products tested or if we eliminate them before the research project begins.

5. *How consistently did the event occur?* If some event under study occurs consistently, then we are in a better position to say that the independent variable produced the effect. One way to assess if the event is consistent is to determine whether the probability or likelihood of it occurring exceeds chance. Statistical tests are available which will allow us to do this rather precisely. Overall, we need to maintain caution when determining if the occurrence of an event exceeds chance.

In addition to interpreting data that others present to us, we ask questions about the things that affect and influence our behaviors. Although we may not be interested in doing elaborate research projects to answer our questions, several principles related to the practice of psychological research can assist us in obtaining the best possible answers to our questions.

1. *Be clear about the assumptions you make regarding behavior.* The way we ask questions reflects our assumptions about human behavior and what influences it. Consequently, our assumptions guide us toward certain types of answers. Although this helps us to appear consistent in our answers to questions, it also leads us to ignore alternative explanations.

2. *Ask questions from the perspective of different assumptions.* To broaden our perspective on the factors that influence behavior, sometimes

it is helpful to ask questions that reflect an assumption contrary to accepted beliefs. We can often obtain insights into our understanding of behavior.

3. *Try to expand your questions into a hypothesis about behavior.* We often begin to ask questions in a rather general way. Whenever possible, we should try to form an educated guess or hypothesis about an answer. This will help give our search for information some direction. Our answers to questions will then either confirm or not confirm our hypothesis.

4. *Try to avoid misinterpreting the information you obtain for your questions.* To avoid this, we need to overcome a tendency to attend selectively to particular aspects of our environments. We are selective when we tend to: (a) focus on data that fit our belief system and ignore other things, and (b) focus on the restricted samples of people and activities we normally encounter daily and the information they give us.

THINGS TO DO

1. Develop a list of the "top ten" best pieces of research data you've encountered in your daily life. Develop a similar list of the ten worst examples you've encountered. Share them with your classmates. Discuss your reasons for including them in your list. Why not send a copy of your report to the "guilty parties"?

2. Look through your favorite magazine or watch television for an advertisement that makes claims based on research data. Analyze the data using the five-question procedure outlined in this chapter. Having done this, redesign the experiment so that it is improved. Have your instructor and/or classmates comment on your design.

3. Discuss some of the problems with the following piece of research. Share your ideas with some of your classmates.

   The mayor of a large city is interested in giving himself a better public image. Through party funds and the influence of his office a three-month image campaign is begun. The mayor increases his public appearances, requests news coverage for all city hall events, gets public officials to praise him in public, issues a weekly report at a news conference on the good deeds of his office, and sets up a campaign against crime and pollution. At the end of this three-month period he sends a team of ten interviewers into the streets of the downtown area to interview people regarding their general image of the mayor. The interviewers find that when people are asked to rate the mayor on a scale from 1 (poor image) to 8 (excellent image), the mean score is 6.0. The interviewers conclude that the public relations campaign has increased the amount of good feeling toward the mayor.

4. Design an experiment to determine whether or not cramming for a test is effective. That is, do people who cram do worse, better, or is there no signifi-

cant difference between people who cram and those who study systematically over a period of time? Have your instructor and others in the class critique your design. Get a couple of your classmates to help you run the experiment.

5. Pick a question that you have about behavior. Using the material discussed in this chapter, design a procedure for answering questions. If more than one person is interested in doing this, why not hold a class symposium at the end of the term for people to present and discuss their studies.

6. Select a current issue on your campus. It can be something that affects either students, faculty, or both groups. Working with three or more of your peers, develop a questionnaire that asks for opinions on the issue. Select a representative sample of the campus population to answer your questionnaire. Don't keep the results to yourself. Why not have the school newspaper publish them?

7. Ask your instructor to give you the distribution of scores on a recent test (names withheld, of course). Calculate the mean, mode, and median. Which one do you think is most appropriate for the data and why? Which one did your instructor use?

8. Select a research panel of four or five students to help the instructor evaluate the course. The students selected should be representative of the different types of students in the class. Some characteristics to consider are age, major, GPA, race, and degree of interest in psychology. The instructor should meet ith the panel four or five times during the term. At the end of the term, the instructor and panel members might discuss the advantages and disadvantages of this approach.

REFERENCES AND OTHER INTERESTING THINGS TO READ

CAMPBELL, S. K. *Flaws and fallacies in statistical thinking.* Englewood Cliffs, N.J.: Prentice-Hall, 1974.

EVANS, R. I. Predicting consumer behavior. *Forum,* January, 1957, 23–26.

GUTTENTAZ, M. The relationship of unemployment to crime and delinquency. *Journal of Social Issues,* 1968, *24* (1), 105–114.

McCOLLOUGH, C. *Introduction to statistical analysis: A semiprogrammed approach.* New York: McGraw-Hill, 1974.

McCOMBS, M. Editorial endorsements. A study of influence. *Journalism Quarterly,* 1967, *44* (3), 545–548.

NORBECK, E. The interpretation of data: Puberty rites. *American Anthropologist,* 1962, *64,* 463–485.

SENTER, R. J. *Analysis of data: Introductory statistics for the behavioral sciences.* Glenview, Ill.: Scott, Foresman and Company, 1969.

"The Science and Snares of Statistics." *Time,* September 8, 1967, p. 29.

Skedgell, R. A. How computers pick an election winner. *Transaction,* 1966, *4,* 42–46.

Swingle, P. G. *Social psychology in natural settings.* Chicago: Aldine, 1973.

Weaver, W. *Lady Luck (The Theory of Probability).* New York: Doubleday Anchor Original, 1963.

Webb, E. J., Campbell, D. T., Schwartz, R. D., and Sechrest, L. *Unobtrusive measures: Nonreactive research in the social sciences.* Chicago: Rand McNally, 1966.

White, R. K. *Nobody wanted war: Misperception in Vietnam and other wars.* New York: Doubleday, 1970.

Williams, E. P., and Raush, H. L. *Naturalistic viewpoints in psychological research.* New York: Holt, Rinehart and Winston, 1969.

CHAPTER AIMS

A.   After reading this chapter, the reader should be able to explain:

1. Perception as a process in which sensory inputs are assigned meaning.

2. How the meanings we assign to sensations influence our actions.

3. The role the total context of sensations plays in our perceptions.

4. How assigning labels to people interferes with our relationships, and two things we can do to overcome this problem.

5. One way that we can use a frame of reference to improve our ability to make comparisons among people, objects, and events.

6. Three things that we can do to improve our ability to attend to parts of our environment.

7. How producing changes in stimuli and focusing on things in unusual ways enhances our ability to attend to various parts of our environment.

8. The way that judgment errors and our impressions of individual and situational responsibility influence our perceptions of the causes of other people's behaviors.

B.   The reader should be able to use the information:

1. To complete the exercises in the chapter.

2. In applications to relevant situations in his or her daily interactions.

2

Perceptual Processes and Our Daily Interactions

GLOSSARY

Figure-ground relationship. The relationship of the part to the whole in any sensations or cognitive ideas to which we attend. Examples include picking out a blue shirt in a pile of white shirts or relating your thoughts and feelings about a given course to other courses you have taken. Two parts are included in this relationship: a figure (i.e., item observed or idea thought about) and the background in which the figure occurs (e.g., the white shirts or thoughts and feelings about other courses).

Frame of reference. Another name for the background in the figure-ground relationship.

Judgment errors. Factors that lead to inaccurate judgments of people, objects, or events on our part. They include a tendency to rely on initial impressions, relying on overall impressions, assuming that certain traits go together (e.g., that courteous people are also highly intelligent) or being needlessly lenient in assessing someone.

Perception. The process in which sensory inputs are assigned meanings to help us identify and interpret the similarities and differences among people, objects, and events in our lives.

Perceptual set. Fixation on things in our environment that are important to us or that we expect to see. Thus we notice our physician's receptionist, the office hours, and the number of people in the waiting room. We may fail to see a piece of modern art displayed on the wall.

Sensory adaptation. A tendency not to notice the intensity of a stimulus to which we are exposed for long periods of time. Thus a cold or warm room does not seem quite as cold or warm after we experience it for a while.

Stereotype. A tendency to develop preconceived ideas about what characteristics other people, objects, and events possess. Familiar examples include the beliefs that women are not fit for hard work and are highly emotional, and that white people are untrustworthy and racist.

Basic Characteristics of Our Daily Perceptions

"I was really scared. Those shadows from the street light made it seem as if there were someone waiting for me in the alley." "We are traveling 55 miles per hour, but this car feels as if it's standing still." "It's funny, but the sounds, smells, and colors in this room give me the creeps." "It's only 4:00 P.M. and I'm feeling hungry." "After working alone in the office all day, I appreciate having some people around me." "Your perception of the world situation is too optimistic; I think we are in for some rough times over the next ten years." "You could tell by the way she looked that she was angry." "Everyone who works for that corporation dresses and behaves in the same way."

Do any of these statements sound familiar? You have probably said or thought similar things. They illustrate that our *perceptions* cover a wide range of events in our daily lives. Broadly defined, perception is a process whereby various sensory inputs are assigned meanings to help us identify and describe parts of our environment. Max Wertheimer, Donald Snygg, and Arthur Combs indicate that our perceptions are not simply the result of sensory inputs to our nervous system. There is also a cognitive component which gives meaning to such sensations. For example, the shapes on this page are more than just individual groups of letters which stimulate our visual systems. You and I also take these groups of letters and interpret the words they form. Similarly, sensations from the objects in a room are more than just paints, dyes, textures, or pieces of fabric. Each of the objects is understood in terms of the meaning it is given. Their meaning may range from "table" to "That is a table my grandmother gave me before she died." Let us look at several basic characteristics of this broad approach to perception and the implications for our behavior.

Figure-ground relationships are the basic units from which our perceptions develop. As noted in the last paragraph, our perceptions consist of some organization of physical stimuli and the interpretations we give to them. We can thus identify and describe the similarities and differences among parts of our environment. To do this well, we must remember that any sensation occurs in a context with other sensations. This context always includes a figure (the item observed) and a ground or *frame of reference* (the background in which the figure occurs). This relationship of the part to the whole is called the *figure-ground relationship*. You are already familiar with figure-ground relationships although you may not have used that name. Have you ever:

- tasted the salt on a piece of meat or a french fried potato after placing it in your mouth?
- tried to find the rough spots on a surface by running your fingers over it?
- focused on the music from a single instrument in a band?
- detected a foul odor in the air?
- watched an airplane fly through a blue sky?
- complained about a toothache?
- favorably compared the current United States president to his predecessors?
- judged a particular ball player as the best on the team?

Our ability to identify and interpret events accurately depends upon our paying attention to the total context in which something occurs. You and I are able to identify and describe a particular taste, touch, sound, smell, sight, or pain because it is somehow different from other things in the background. Salt, for example, has a taste different from a steak, and a foul odor is noticeably different from the fresh air you normally breathe. It is also important to remember that figure-ground relationships are not related to our ability to identify and describe physical stimuli only. According to Arthur Combs, figure and ground do not always represent physical stimuli. They may also be ideas. In the examples of the last paragraph, the judgment that a particular president or ball player is better than others is made with regard to a background or *frame of reference* of thoughts and feelings regarding other presidents and ball players. The background has a great deal to do with the interpretation events are given. A french fry will not taste as salty if the steak is also salty. A foul odor will not seem quite as bad if the air we breathe is normally foul. A particular ball player or president may not look as good if compared to the best ball players or presidents who ever lived.

Our actions are related to the meanings various sensations are assigned. Most of you drive an automobile. Imagine yourself approaching an intersection. What makes you decide to slow down, stop, or continue at the same rate of speed? One set of factors is the total sensation from the traffic light, cars in front of you, and context of other vehicles in the intersection. Your neural system is affected by the pattern of stimulation you experience. The pattern may consist of the light turning red, cars in front of you coming to a halt, and vehicles on streets that cross the intersection beginning to move. You then attach some meaning to important parts of this pattern. Based on your past experience you might describe this pattern as indicating "caution," "danger," or "an unsafe condition." As a result, you slow down and bring your car to a halt. What are some ways in which the combination of sensory inputs and meanings attached to your teacher's behaviors, dark clouds in the sky, a fire alarm, and your favorite beverage influence your actions?

Variations in how people interpret the same sensations cause differences in their behaviors. Two or more individuals are likely to see, taste, or hear the same stimulus and yet react differently. It is often the differences in how they interpret sensations that result in these different behaviors. Recently, a friend of mine and I were walking to the office. He is a retired U.S. Army Colonel and a very patriotic citizen. In a field about 150 yards away, a group of young people were milling around a bonfire. They were tearing up pieces of a red, white, and blue material and throwing it into the fire. It looked to me as though they were simply burning large sheets of colored paper. All at once my friend said, "My God, those little #$%*¢&@ are tearing up an American flag and burning it. I'll show them!" He rolled up his sleeves and ran in the direction of the bonfire. I followed to try to stop him from doing something drastic. About 25 yards from the fire we both stopped. The red, white, and blue material was simply large, multi-colored posters left over from a Fourth of July celebration. Both of us experienced the same sensory stimulation from the material. Our interpretations of it varied and this produced the variations in our reactions.

Different reactions to the same sensory stimuli are a fairly common occurrence. Have you ever had such an experience? Such things often happen because of differences among people in attitudes, opinions, preferences, and other learning experiences. Listed here are several rather common examples of instances in which this occurs. Read each item and think of one or two specific reasons the variations in perception might have occurred. Can you think of other examples from your personal experiences?

- You read a review of a movie. You attend the movie only to find that the reviewer was "wrong." You either liked or disliked it more than the reviewer did.
- You are invited out to dinner. Your host serves you a dish and remarks, "This is really great; wait till you get your teeth into it." You have just the opposite opinion.
- A policeman tells you that he saw you exceeding the speed limit. You disagree and tell him you were not going so fast.
- A friend recommends a certain teacher as a great instructor. You take the course and find out that this is not the case.

Broadly defined, perception is a process in which sensory inputs are assigned meanings. Our interpretations of stimuli influence our actions and help to account for the variations in behavior among people. The remainder of this chapter will examine several principles associated with our ability to identify and interpret stimuli. Particular attention is paid to those things that will benefit you in your daily interactions.

Our Perceptions of Similarity among People, Objects, and Events Influence the Way We Relate to Them

Our ability to identify and describe a cluster of objects as people, automobiles, or chairs or to categorize them as anything else depends in part upon the characteristics that each shares. Similar attributes help us distinguish people, objects, and events from their background. That is, we are able to differentiate one thing from another or to separate a figure from its background. Familiar examples of this include: looking from the stage of a theater and identifying the people against a background of chairs and carpet; watching two football teams line up and distinguishing the members of one team from the other; noting that two wines or menthol cigarettes taste and smell the same; perceiving that two popular songs contain the same musical chords.

As we grow and develop, we are taught to assign one label to similar things. The label may be something like "basketball team," "men," "women," "trees," "teachers," "automobiles," or any number of other descriptions. Such labels help us identify a particular person, object, or event from its background. Labeling also helps us know a great deal about something based on limited information. If I asked you to tell me something about policemen, alcoholic beverages, history courses, mothers, or automobile races, you could do this with ease. Each label would probably key a response regarding the common characteristics of objects with each label.

Although our ability to identify and label similar attributes is often helpful, sometimes it produces problems for us in interpersonal relationships. We may begin to *stereotype* or to develop preconceived notions of the similar characteristics that people, objects, and events possess. Let us focus on the implications of this stereotyping for how we relate to other people. Before reading further, please complete the following exercise. It will help to identify some of the problems with stereotyping.

EXERCISE 2-1: THE EFFECTS OF USING STEREOTYPES

1. Think about a "lemon" for a few moments. List five to eight characteristics of lemons.
2. Pick a number from one to nine. Look at Figure 2-1 and study the picture of the lemon that corresponds to that number for 30 seconds. Concentrate only on that picture. Try not to look at the other pictures as you examine the lemon you picked.
3. Close your eyes for 30 seconds and think about the characteristics of the lemon you selected.
4. Look at Figure 2-2 and *try to find your lemon.* The pictures have been rearranged. Check the number of the picture in Figure 2-2 that you think corresponds to the lemon you studied with the answers given in Table 2-1.
5. Were you able to find your lemon? If you could find it, how helpful were the characteristics that you listed earlier in assisting you to do this? If you were not able to find it, what are some of the reasons?

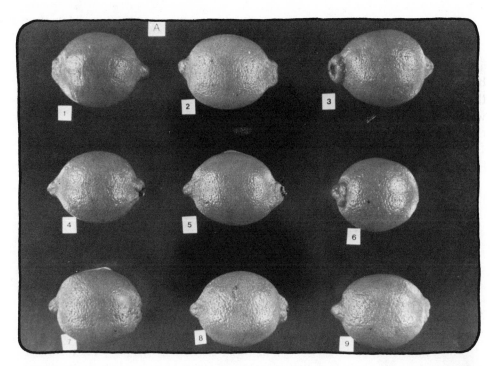

Figure 2-1

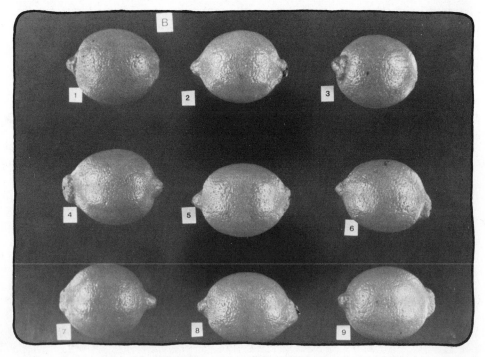

Figure 2-2

Table 2-1

Correct Responses to Lemon Exercise

After selecting the number of the lemon in Figure 2-2 that you think corresponds to the lemon you studied in Figure 2-1, check your response below. The number of the same lemon in Figure 2-1 appears in the second column.

FIGURE 2-2 POSITION	FIGURE 2-1 ORIGINAL POSITION
1	7
2	4
3	6
4	3
5	9
6	8
7	1
8	5
9	2

The exercise illustrates several things about the use of labels to stereotype and the problems this process presents. *Labels often force us to overgeneralize.* We then tend to see everything as similar. About 35 percent of the people who try the exercise are not able to find their lemon. One of the reasons they give is that "all lemons look alike to me." They know what lemons are like and they have a hard time seeing the differences that exist. The same thing occurs, for example, when we stereotype racial and religious groups. How often have you heard the phrase, "All blacks [or all whites or all Jews] are alike"?

Labels may lead us to feel as if something is not very important. As a result we spend little time trying to find out more about someone else. Several of my students tell me that thinking of lemons in general terms made them feel as if lemons were not very important objects. They showed little interest in something that was termed "sour," "yellowish," or "oval." Consequently, they spent very little time and energy trying to "get to know" their lemon. The same thing happens when we label people as "lazy," "stupid," "thieves," "crafty," or "untrustworthy."

Labels affect our behaviors toward other people. An interesting demonstration of this principle was conducted by Harold Kelley. He had a guest lecturer appear in his class and passed out a written biographical sketch of this person to the students. The description half the students received referred to the lecturer as "a rather warm person," and the other half of the class read that he was "a rather cold person." After the presentation, students rated the guest lecturer on several traits. People who were told he was "a rather warm person" rated him as much more informal, sociable, popular, good natured, and humorous than did the students who were told he was "a rather cold person." Furthermore, the students who were informed that he was "a rather warm person" interacted more with the instructor during the class session than did the others.

To overcome the problems we have described, we must force ourselves to focus on the specific characteristics of people. There are two things that we must do. We should always ask, "What is unique about this person?" Then, we must spend time and energy trying to determine what is unique. Otherwise, the general characteristics associated with the label will guide our thoughts and actions in less than helpful ways. The general characteristics of lemons (e.g., oval, yellow, bitter tasting, used to make lemonade) are not helpful in finding a given lemon. Such characteristics are also not useful in discovering what other people are like.

Do you find yourself using labels to overgeneralize and thus having your thoughts and actions about other people affected adversely? Do you look for the unique qualities in other people? How do labels affect your thoughts and feelings about other objects and events in your life (e.g., certain foods, sports, music, stores, movies)? Can you think of one thing you can do tomorrow to begin to overcome this problem?

Our Ability to Make Comparisons among People, Objects, and Events Is Enhanced if We Think about the Frame of Reference We Are Using

"How well does Mr. Jones organize his lectures?" "What do you think of the history exam we just took?" "Does the United States have the best possible president running it?" "What do you think of this dance?" I am sure that you have asked similar questions. Each of these questions is asking someone to make a comparison. The comparison may be between Mr. Jones and other teachers in the college, a given history test and other tests you took, or the current president and past presidents. Mr. Jones, a history test, and the current president are all ideas that exist in a background of other thoughts and feelings regarding other teachers, tests, and presidents. In each case, some background or frame of reference of thoughts and feelings exists for making the judgment. Unfortunately, people often respond to such questions without carefully stating or thinking about the frame of reference they used. They may respond by saying, "I think Mr. Jones does a good job," "That test was terrible," or "The current president is fine." There are two problems with this type of response. *Unless we consciously focus on some frame of reference for our response, we are likely to make judgments that are superficial or otherwise not well thought out.* Other people may then stop asking us for our opinions. *Furthermore, the individual asking the question can better evaluate our reaction if he or she knows the frame of reference we are using.*

To clarify and illustrate the last two points, please turn to Table 2-2. Before reading further, rate your instructor in this course on the rating scale that is shown. The way you responded to such questions is one example of how easy it is to evaluate someone without thinking about the context. You

Table 2-2

An Instructor Rating Form

Please rate the ability of your instructor on each of the items below using the following rating scale. Place your rating in the blank space next to each item.

1	2	3	4	5	6	7
Excel-lent	Very Good	Good	Satis-factory	Fair	Poor	Ter-rible

_____ 1. Discusses points of view other than his (her) own.
_____ 2. Contrasts implications of various theories.
_____ 3. Communicates clearly.
_____ 4. Evidences careful preparation for class.
_____ 5. Encourages class discussion.
_____ 6. Invites students to share their knowledge and experiences.
_____ 7. Shows a genuine interest in students.
_____ 8. Shows friendliness toward students.
_____ 9. Appears dynamic and energetic.
_____10. Encourages students to pursue further study in the field.
_____11. Demonstrates knowledge of subject matter.
_____12. Creates a friendly and open atmosphere in the class.
_____13. Organizes the course well.
_____14. Presents ideas which provoke careful thought and discussion.
_____15. Adapts course presentations and requirements to my level.
_____16. Challenges me to do my best.
_____17. Encourages students to learn from each other.
_____18. Helps me to build my interests in the field.
_____19. Presents issues as well as concepts and information.
_____20. Shows patience.
_____21. Receives questions and challenges openly.

probably had no trouble in assigning ratings of "excellent," "good," "poor," or any of the others to your instructor's behavior. However, did you ask yourself, "What is my instructor excellent, good, or poor in relation to?" In several research studies, I have found that students actually use a number of frames of reference to judge their instructor's ability. They include: "how an ideal teacher would teach," "the best instructor (s) they ever had," "the worst instructor (s) they ever had," "the average ability of all their current teachers," and even "how they would instruct if they were the teacher." *Unfortunately, many people do not use them unless they are told to do so.* Did you remember using one or more of these frames of reference? Are you likely to rate your instructor differently if you compare him or her to the "worst" or "best" teacher you ever had?

Think about the effect of considering one or more frames of reference before making an assessment. How would your instructor react if you said, "Compared to how I would teach, you are good," versus, "Compared to the best teacher I ever had, you are good"? To make either statement, you had to consider your evaluation carefully. Your teacher may appreciate the latter statement more but in either case, your instructor knows from your response where he or she stands in relation to someone else. Such judgments are much more specific than simply saying "you are good" and are likely to be appreciated more and listened to more carefully.

Based on the information in this section, there are several things you can do to improve your ability to make comparisons about other people, objects, and events. The next time someone asks you to make a comparison, *think about several frames of reference that might apply. Then pick the one that you think best applies to the judgment you must make.* When responding to another person, include the context you used in your answer. This can be done by saying, "Compared to _____ I think the following." *Finally, when someone else makes a comparison about something, encourage him or her to share the frame of reference used.* You can do this by asking questions like: "When you said I didn't do a good job, what is that in relation to?" and "I'm not sure what you mean; what is that compared to?" Asking questions in this manner helps you gain additional insights and information about the response the person is making. Act on these suggestions the next time you are in a conversation in which something is compared.

How might you respond if someone asked you to give an assessment of this textbook, your automobile, the clothes you are wearing, a movie you watched, or a sporting event you observed?

Our Ability to Attend to Important Parts of Our Environment Is Improved by Our Becoming More Vigilant, Producing Changes in Stimuli, and Focusing Our Attention in New Ways

"Honey, stop! Didn't you see that red traffic light?" "I am a little concerned that no one seems to notice what I say or do." "I know we are traveling at 600 miles per hour, but this plane feels as if it is standing still." "Even though there are people talking around us, it doesn't bother me and it hasn't interfered with our conversation." "My, look at that arrangement of apples. I don't think I've seen them displayed in such an unusual way." "Sitting here and looking at that piece of art was good for me. It really cleared my head out and I feel a bit more relaxed."

As noted earlier, one of our tasks as perceivers is to identify and interpret sensations which exist against some background. To do this, we must focus our attention on various stimuli. Without our ability to focus our attention, everything would become a blur of sensory patterns. The statements in the last paragraph are reactions I have heard from people that reflect some of the things that may happen when our attention is focused. They illustrate that:

1. Our attention drifts, e.g., we fail to see the traffic light, we find ourselves daydreaming during a lecture.
2. Our ability to interpret accurately sensations we attend to is sometimes deceptive, e.g., we fail to notice we are traveling at a high rate of speed, we cannot discriminate between our "favorite" cigarette and another similar brand after two or three puffs.
3. We tune out stimuli that interfere with other things we are doing at the same time, e.g., we don't hear what other people are saying as they talk in the same room, we don't hear the radio playing as we study.
4. Our tendency to notice things is influenced by changes in stimuli, e.g., how certain food products are displayed, movement or changes in color in a television commercial.
5. Focusing our attention in new and different ways may have beneficial effects, e.g., clearing our heads, helping us to relax.

Can you think of examples from your own experiences that also illustrate each of these five points? Let us take a closer look at several applications related to three of these five aspects of attention.

Our attention drifts. Most of us are able to concentrate on almost any stimulus for short amounts of time, but seldom do we give our undivided attention to anything for extended periods. We daydream, briefly entertain another thought, take a break, perform another task, or otherwise allow our attention to drift periodically. In the course of writing this section, I stopped to think about a family problem, had a short meeting with my secretary, and made a telephone call to a friend. What are some of the things you did after sitting down to read this book?

Factors like fatigue, a low interest in the task, feeling it is not very important, or just a need for a change in stimulation will cause us to shift our attention. Most of the time such shifts are without consequence. We return to reading the book, typing, working on the laboratory assignment, or some other task. On the other hand, there are times when such things can have negative consequences. What are some of the effects of shifts in attention for: (a) an air traffic coordinator watching a radar scope, (b) a soldier standing guard duty at a top secret military installation, (c) a student listening to a teacher review the content for an exam, (d) a lifeguard at a pool, (e) a person driving a car, and (f) a doctor monitoring life signs during an operation?

As you can see, the consequences can be quite serious. Research by Joel Warm, Roy Davies, and Jane Mackworth suggests these principles which can help us remain vigilant or keep our attention focused on a task:

1. Consciously force yourself to increase the frequency with which you will monitor the stimuli associated with the task.
2. Give yourself feedback on how well you are doing.
3. Reward yourself for paying attention.
4. Take a break periodically. Twenty to thirty minutes seems to be the optimal time period for concentrating on anything without increasing the chances for errors.

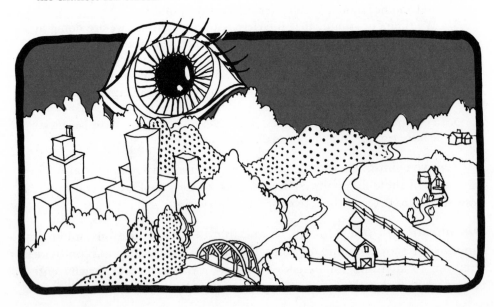

EXERCISE 2-2: INCREASING OUR ABILITY TO PAY ATTENTION

Most of us drive a motor vehicle and attend presentations in school or elsewhere. A drift in attention may have negative consequences. For the situations listed here, think of one additional way in which each of the four principles for remaining vigilant can be used. Two examples are given for you under each principle. Discuss your responses with a classmate. *Why not try the things you came up with?*

1. *Driving a Motor Vehicle*
   a. Consciously force yourself to increase the frequency with which you will monitor the stimuli associated with a task.
      — Try to look at the instrument panel once every thirty seconds.
      — Will assume that a "radar" speed trap is set up every four miles and will search the road for one.
   b. Give yourself feedback on how well you are doing.
      — Will try to drive exactly at the speed limit. Will look at the speedometer every thirty seconds to see if I am maintaining that speed.
      — Will look at the speed of other cars to help me judge my speed.
   c. Reward yourself for paying attention.
      — Will play the radio only if I continue to do what I said I would do in a and b. Otherwise, radio will not be played until I improve my performance.
      — Will tell myself what a good job I am doing at least once every hour.
   d. Take a break periodically.
      — Will stop car and take a stretch break every thirty minutes.
      — Will stop for coffee every two hours on long trips.

2. *Paying Attention to a Presentation*
   a. Consciously force yourself to increase the frequency with which you will monitor the stimuli associated with a task.
      — Will take notes to summarize what is said.
      — Will make two comments during the session which show the implications of what is said to a related topic.
   b. Give yourself feedback on how well you are doing.
      — Will privately answer any questions someone asks the presenter to see how well I understand the information. Will check my response with what the presenter says.
      — Will check my notes with a classmate after each session to make sure I did not miss anything.
   c. Reward yourself for paying attention.
      — Will treat myself to a soft drink after the session if I feel I listened well.
      — Will tell myself how well I am listening every fifteen minutes.
   d. Take a break periodically.
      — Will schedule my classes so that I have an hour break between them.
      — Will take a deep breath and relax my muscles every fifteen to twenty minutes.

Our tendency to notice things is influenced by changes in stimuli. Have you ever wanted to get someone else's attention. Stop and think for a few seconds. Were there two to three occasions during the past week when you wanted to get someone to notice what you said or did? In my own experiences, I wanted my students to listen to a presentation I made, my son to cease misbehaving, and readers of a local newspaper to notice an advertisement I ran in the classified section regarding a used humidifier. Each of us has needs for people to focus on what we say and do in a variety of situations. The best way for us to gain this attention is to produce change in the stimulation individuals normally receive.

Change is important because the stimuli we create must compete with other things in the background and because change helps to overcome the problem of *sensory adaptation*. The latter concern represents a tendency to adapt to stimuli that do not change very much. Consequently, we do not notice them as much. You are experiencing sensory adaptation when a piece of chocolate tastes less sweet as you continue to eat it, a warm or cold room appears less so after a period of time, or a teacher's monotone delivery begins to sound like a sequence of dull sounds. The following principles are suggestions for producing change that help to attract attention. As you read them, think of one way that you could use each one in your daily affairs.

1. *Create movement or change the position or color of a stimulus that you want other people to view. Examples:* A colleague was concerned with students paying attention to his lecturing and his writing on the blackboard. Instead of standing behind his lecturn, he started to pace. He also began to use colored chalk on the blackboard. A friend wanted visitors to his office building to find his office quickly. He had his office door painted green. It became the only green office door in the building.

2. *Change the size of a stimulus. Large things tend to attract attention better. Examples:* A restaurant owner had a small typed note in his window advertising for a waitress and replaced it with a sign that was three feet high. A neighbor had a small screen television. Her children showed little interest in watching some of the educational programs until she bought a set with a 25-inch screen.

3. *Vary the intensity of a stimulus. Higher-intensity stimuli are more potent than others within the same sensory modality. Examples:* Visitors to my home had a hard time finding the street number after dark. I replaced an ordinary house number sign with one that had a light in it. A student was concerned that people seldom noticed her at dances. She wore a bright, multicolored dress the next time she went. It became a great conversation piece and was an excellent "icebreaker."

4. *Repeat the stimulation—within limits. Too much repetition may have just the opposite effect. Examples:* I once asked a hotel manager to give me a larger room. He acted as if he had not heard me. I repeated my request four times until he acknowledged it. A friend was concerned that his bosses were not aware of who wrote the memos he sent up the chain of command. He had his name typed in the upper left-hand corner of every page.

5. *Change stimuli that do not meet someone's needs and interests to those that do. Examples:* My nephew was not interested in reading until his mother bought him books on fishing and baseball, which were topics of interest to him. People were not purchasing one of the four brands of sausage a supermarket manager stocked. He cooked a batch and passed them out as free samples to customers while they shopped during the lunch hour. His sales increased.

EXERCISE 2-3: USING PRINCIPLES FOR OBTAINING ATTENTION

1. List at least one problem that you have that relates to obtaining the attention of others.
2. Which of the principle(s) we have discussed might help you solve the problem?
3. Develop a plan to use the principle(s). Try the plan and carefully monitor how well it worked.

Focusing our attention in new and different ways may have beneficial effects. Have you grown tired of your daily environment? Do you feel as if you need a change of "scenery"? Have you ever wanted to just forget about everything and relax? Such thoughts and feelings exist for several reasons. As mentioned earlier, we adapt to stimuli and soon fail to notice or appreciate the changes which occur around us. Such things as a new arrangement of furniture, changes in a room's color schemes, new friends, traveling, and new foods lose their initial interest and excitement over time.

Furthermore, our perceptions are selective. We fixate on things in our environment that are most important to us or that we expect to see. This is called a *perceptual set*. Thus, we notice our physicians' receptionist, the

office hours he or she keeps, and the number of other people sitting in the waiting room. We may fail to see the piece of modern art that is displayed on a wall. We expect our boss to give us negative feedback so we miss hearing the nice things he or she has to say. We expect a friend to be a poor cook so we notice the parts of the meal that are poorly prepared. In the process, we fail to appreciate the parts of the meal that are tasty.

To overcome the feeling that "nothing changes" or that "I've seen all this before" we need to overcome the problems that sensory adaptation and perceptual sets produce. To do this, you and I must focus our attention on parts of our environment in some different ways. *We need to force ourselves to notice and appreciate the sensations we usually take for granted.* Two suggestions for increasing our awareness of the things around us by focusing our attention will be described now.

Treat your senses to an unusual perspective toward your environment. Robert McKim, Harold Cook, Joel Davitz, and David Johnson stress the importance of taking a different sensory perspective toward our environments. Doing this often helps us see how blind we have been to the tremendous variety of different sensations that exist in what otherwise may seem like an uninteresting setting. To accomplish this goal, you and I need only look, hear, smell, taste, and touch stimuli in some different ways. To see how this works, complete the following exercise.

EXERCISE 2-4: INCREASING YOUR AWARENESS

1. Perform each of the following activities to help you discover that there are a number of new things in your environment.
   a. Select a room in your house or apartment that you feel you know quite well—that is, you do not feel as if there is anything in it that you have not seen before. Lie down in the center of the room and view the room from this position. Think about how the room looks to you now. What are some things that you have not noticed before? In what ways is the room different?
   b. Put your nose against the floor and smell the carpet or floor tile. What does it smell like? Have you ever noticed this smell before? Run your fingers very slowly along a two-foot section of the floor. As you do this, pause periodically and rub your fingertips into the floor. What words would you use to describe the texture?
   c. Sit or lie quietly on the floor. Remain perfectly still for 30 seconds. Concentrate on the sounds in the room. What do you hear? What are some things that you have not heard before? Now concentrate on the sounds that your body makes. Besides your breathing, what are some things that you hear?

2. Stand next to some object in your home, classroom, or other location that you see all the time. Put your eyes about one inch from the surface. What do you see that you normally miss when you view the object? Run your fingers along the surface and try to notice changes in the texture. Smell the surface. How would you describe the smell? Put your ear against it. What do you hear?

3. Stand about one foot away from a mirror. Focus your attention on different parts of your body. Concentrate on your eyes, ears, nose, mouth, hands, and other parts. Stare at each part for 20 to 30 seconds. What are some things that you see that you have not noticed before? Step back three feet and do the same thing.

4. Make yourself a cup of coffee or tea or get a glass of a soft drink or some other liquid that you like to drink. Put your nose within one inch of the liquid. Take a deep breath. How does it smell to you? Do the same thing by holding it six inches away from you. What differences do you notice in the smell? Sip it and hold it in your mouth. Swish it around a bit. Think about the taste of the liquid. Where do you taste it—on the front part of your tongue, the middle part, or can't you taste it until you swallow it?

5. The next time you are in a situation and become bored, explore it with your senses using some of the methods described. Remember that our environments hold a lot of new experiences for us. We only need a different perspective to increase our awareness about such things.

Try meditating. Meditation is a second way to focus our attention and, subsequently, to become aware of things we are not normally able to experience. In recent years, this has become a rather popular way for people to increase their awareness of their inner processes and experiences. The success of Maharishi Mahesh Yogi and his transcendental meditation movement suggests that each of us has a need to go beyond our everyday experiences. According to Leon Otis, meditation has benefits which include feeling less tense, becoming more alert, and increasing one's energy and creativity. Although the claims may be somewhat exaggerated, it is clear that meditation is a helpful relaxation device, a good way to hold one's concerns in abeyance for a few minutes, and an easy method for "tuning out" some of the stimulation from our environments. Most of us have a need to do such things at one time or another.

The various meditation methods all offer a chance for someone to sit in a comfortable position for 10 to 20 minutes and to relax by breathing slowly and focusing attention on something other than external sensations. This usually involves concentrating on an inner process like breathing or silently repeating a word to oneself. Exercise 2-5 is one technique that you can try to obtain some idea of what it is like to meditate. If you would like to pursue it further, the advice and guidance of an experienced meditator or teacher is often helpful. You might want to try to find such a person in your community.

EXERCISE 2-5: LEARNING TO MEDITATE

1. Select a place in your home, apartment, or elsewhere where it is quiet and you are likely not to be disturbed for 20 minutes.
2. Sit in a chair or on the floor in a comfortable position. Try to keep your back straight. Take several deep breaths and try not to tense your muscles.
3. Close your eyes and try to clear your mind of any thoughts that you might have. Make your mind as "blank" as you can.
4. Breathe normally. Concentrate on your breathing. Try not to think of anything else. If you have trouble doing this, count each breath up to 20 and then start over again. You may stop counting after you feel you can concentrate on your breathing. Try to do this for 5 or 10 minutes.
5. Repeat this procedure every day. Increase the amount of time that you spend each time. You might want to add one minute to your time each day until you reach a meditation period of 20 minutes.
6. A variation on this procedure is to concentrate on a word that you silently repeat to yourself for the entire meditation period. To try this, select a word that makes a sound that you like. Instead of concentrating on your breathing, repeat this word silently to yourself for the amount of time that you meditate. Concentrate on the word and try to think about and feel the sound that it makes within you.

Our Perceptions of What Other People Are Like Are Influenced by Judgment Errors and Our Impressions of Situation versus Individual Responsibility for Their Behavior

"Ed just slipped on the ice outside; he's such a clumsy person." "The way those tough-looking people crowded around Pete, he had no choice but to run. I don't think he is a coward." "I like people who are polite. Sally impresses me as a rather courteous person. I bet she is also friendly and very intelligent." Have you ever made similar statements?

Other people observe our actions and we, in turn, observe theirs. Our observations may be used simply to identify some stimulus (e.g., That's Ed who slipped on the ice), or we may evaluate or otherwise make inferences about what we observed (e.g., That's Ed, he slipped on the ice. He's such a clumsy person). Fritz Heider and Harold Kelley note that we are usually not interested in simply observing the actions of others. Rather, we want to understand the reasons for their actions. Since we cannot directly perceive the thoughts and desires of individuals, we make inferences about them. You and I make such judgments every day. We interpret the actions of others and they, in turn, do the same to us. *This process often helps us determine how we will interact with them and they, in turn, with us.* If I accurately infer that their behaviors show that they like me, then I will probably show my appreciation. If I accurately infer that their actions show them to be greedy or untrustworthy, then I may avoid close interactions.

Unfortunately, our inferences are not always accurate. We misinterpret the actions of others and they, in turn, do the same to us. This often produces problems in our relationships with people. Ed may slip on the ice, but does this mean that he is basically a clumsy person? If you believed this, how might that information affect your relationship? Sally may be courteous. However, does it necessarily follow that she is also very intelligent? What might happen if you trusted her with a job that demanded a high degree of intellect and she disappointed you? Have people ever watched you do something and then made incorrect inferences about why you acted as you did? How did this affect your later interactions?

Whether or not they are accurate, the meanings you and I attach to the behaviors of others have a great deal to do with our social relationships. Consequently, we are better off if we improve our ability to make such judgments. Let us examine several factors which affect our ability to perceive the causes of other people's actions accurately.

Judgment Errors

You will remember from our earlier discussion that perception involves the sensations we observe and the meaning we attach to them. In forming impressions of people, certain ways that we assign meaning to objects interfere with our ability to judge the individuals accurately. Such factors are called *judgment errors*. Let us look at several of the more common errors and how they affect the impressions we form of other people.

Relying on Initial Impressions

You might think that the view you have of others, and they of you, is formed gradually over time. However, this is often not the case. The perceiver's first impression of another person has an enormous impact on later judgments. If you walk into a meeting at which new people are present and spill coffee over yourself, you may indeed get "tagged" as sloppy and careless. The initial information creates a frame of reference in which later behaviors are judged. Does this surprise you? You remember from our discussion of figure-ground relationships that any stimulus is judged with regard to a certain background. If you have observed a person's behaviors for the first time, or he or she observes yours, an adequate background does not exist. That first set of observations establishes a frame of reference. Consequently, later behaviors are assessed in terms of that initial context, so much so that new information is often distorted so that it fits with the initial frame of reference. Have you ever felt unfairly judged because someone relied on a first impression?

"Halo Effect"

This is a tendency for us to evaluate someone on a number of characteristics based on an overall good or poor impression we have of them. A professor who likes a student may assess the quality of his or her essay test as higher than it is. Or the professor may rate the second, third, or fourth question higher because the first question was answered well. Of course, a different outcome could occur if the teacher did not like the student or the answer to the first essay question. The overall impression we have of people, and they of us, is an important determiner of the judgments made. That is why it is sometimes important to try to forget an overall impression when you need to assess an action objectively. Otherwise, you may have your observations influenced by the belief that the individual "can do no wrong" or "does everything wrong." Can you think of an instance in which a "halo effect" has worked in your favor? Against you?

Logical Error

To assume that certain personal traits occur together, and therefore to assume that they are all present in a particular individual because you have observed some of them, is to make a logical error. I recently attended a meeting at which one of the members took a rather aggressive stand on an issue. The person sitting next to me said, "Wow, he really held his ground. Not only is he aggressive but I bet he has a strong character, is powerful, and has a lot of energy for debating." Making such broad statements without adequate evidence is an example of the logical error. Because of it, you or I might assign characteristics to others, or have them assigned by others to us, that are not actually present. If such attributes are positive, then this process probably will not hurt us. On the other hand, if they are negative, we might experience some difficulty in our relationships. It's harder to interact with someone who, we think, has characteristics we do not appreciate. Have you ever made a logical error? Were you ever the "victim" of this error on the part of someone else?

Leniency Error

This is a tendency for us to make many positive judgments and to avoid negative ones—that is, we give people the "benefit of the doubt." This is particularly noticeable when we must publicly state what we have observed. Most of us have a hard time telling people that we do not like something they have done. Look at the ratings you gave your teacher in the exercise in Table 2-2. How many were really negative? If you had to face your teacher and give feedback on each item, would you tell your instructor how you really feel?

Our Perceptions of Situational versus Individual Responsibility for Actions

Thus far we have seen that observing the actions of others leads us to evaluate and to assign certain characteristics to their behaviors. In addition, we also try to determine if the behavior was caused by internal or external factors. For example, did Sally laugh at the teacher's joke because she thought it was funny or because she knows the teacher likes people to laugh? Whether we or others judge the person or the situation to be responsible is important. *We are more likely to forgive someone if we think that the situation caused them to behave as they did. We will blame them more if we feel that their actions were self-determined.* An acquaintance of mine was fired from his job. He told me that the boss had no choice. The company was losing money and people had to be let go. He was one of the last people hired. Thus, he was not angry with his boss because he focused on factors in the situation. How do you think he would feel if he thought his boss simply wanted to get rid of him?

Based on the work of Fritz Heider and Harold Kelley, several factors are associated with whether we attribute the causes of some action to the individual or to the situation. *The less freedom of choice we or others think a person has, the more likely it is that the situation will be blamed.* After getting fired from his job, my friend looked for factors in the situation because he saw his boss as having no other option. *Behaviors that seem to conform to what other people are doing in that setting are seen as caused by the situation.* A child who begins to tease another child is less likely to make a parent mad if other children are also teasing at the same time. *Actions that deviate from what other people are doing are perceived as internally caused.* A person who gets angry and walks out in the middle of a meeting is likely to incur the wrath of other members. They will not feel as if they contributed to the anger. Instead they are likely to see that person as uncooperative, a quitter, or simply as having a poor disposition. *Unusual occur-rences are seen as due to internal factors.* People who spill coffee all over themselves are likely to be seen as clumsy. Similarly, someone who unin-tentionally slights another is often perceived as hostile. *When in doubt, causes are attributed to the person and not the situation.* It is generally harder for us to find some factor in the situation that can be seen as causing a behavior. It is much easier to blame the person. When causation is at-tributed to the person, what happened can be attributed in an absolute way to a single origin. You and I are more likely to feel satisfied with such an outcome. Withholding judgments until situational factors are found is much harder to do.

Based on our discussion of judgment errors and attributing causes to the situation or the person, I am sure that you realize that the potential for inaccurate evaluations, assigned traits, and causes is quite high. This is a problem particularly when the errors are made by others about our own actions. The following are some things that you can suggest doing to insure that you are not unfairly perceived.

Call attention to what caused your behavior. Remember that other people are inferring causes based on what they see. Only you know what caused you to behave in a particular manner. Get into the habit of saying such things as: "I'm sorry I dropped the tea cup. My fingers were pinched in the door yesterday and since then I can't seem to hold anything well." "I hope you don't think we hate each other. We always argue about the best way to play this game. It's all very friendly."

Maintain an impression by pointing out an error or perhaps joking about it. In this way, you become a competent person who has committed an error. It also lets the other person know that the error is not typical of your be-havior. "What a terrible meeting I ran. I should never have let Sam and Jane talk for so long. I don't think I have ever managed things so poorly." "I'm so tired lately that I'm forgetting things. I hope I'm not becoming an absent-minded professor."

Let people know that you have changed. Ask them to give you a chance to show them what you can do. As you will remember from our discussion of first impressions, there is a tendency for people to maintain that impression. You have to be very open and direct to get them to see you in other ways: "Look, Phil, I know that I have not handled that client well in the past. I've been doing my homework lately and I know things will be different this time. How about a chance to show you that I'm a much better sales-person today than I was three months ago?"

EXERCISE 2-6: PERCEIVING THE CAUSES OF BEHAVIOR

There are times when we misjudge others, or they us. As you have seen by reading this section, it can lead to problems in our relationships. The following set of tasks should help you see what affects our judgments and, in turn, what you might do to overcome the inaccurate judgments of others.

1. Think of one example from your experiences during the past month of a situation in which you evaluated, assigned a trait, or suggested a cause for some behavior in others. Describe the situation in a few sentences.
2. Think of one example from your experiences during the past month of a situation in which you feel you were evaluated or assigned a trait or someone felt you did something for a certain reason and they were inaccurate. Describe the situation in a few sentences.
3. For the two situations you have just described, pick any relevant judgment errors or factors that determine a cause as internal or external that might have played a role in each judgment. Describe how each factor affected each judgment.
4. Based on the principles discussed in this section, what are some things you could have done to increase the accuracy of your own perceptions and/or overcome the errors in judgment that you or someone else made? A completed exercise by a student appears in Table 2-3.

SUMMARY

Broadly defined, perception is a process by which various sensory inputs are assigned meanings to help us identify and describe parts of our environment. Thus, our perceptual processes include a sensory and a cognitive component. Several basic characteristics are associated with this approach. They include the observation that *figure-ground relationships are the basic units from which our perceptions develop.* Our perceptions occur in a context in which a figure (the item observed) is viewed in relationship to a ground (a background in which the figure occurs). Figure-ground relationships range from tasting the salt on a piece of meat after placing it in your mouth to judging that a particular person is the best student in class. As such, figure-ground relationships exist in our senses and in the various cognitive judgments we make. Furthermore, *our actions are related to the meanings that various sensations are assigned.* Based on our past experiences, we interpret the sensations we receive. Such interpretations influence a variety of our daily behaviors, ranging from stopping our cars at an intersection to deciding what clothes to wear together. Finally, *variations in how people interpret the same sensations cause differences in their behaviors.* Two people are

Table 2-3

A Sample of a Completed Exercise

1. Think of one example from your experiences during the past month of a situation in which you evaluated, assigned a trait, or suggested a cause for some behavior in others.
   - I told my best friend Ed that he played a super game for our basketball team. I thought he played a good game with the other team members and didn't try to "showboat" his talents. I think that he is basically a person who is not very selfish and is generous in his relations with others.

2. Think of one example during the past month of a situation in which you feel you were evaluated or assigned a trait or someone felt you did something for a certain reason and they were inaccurate.
   - I turned in a draft of a term paper to my teacher for review. My friend Sally had typed it and I didn't have time to proofread it before turning it in. He told me that I must be a sloppy typist with so many errors in the paper. When I turned in a corrected draft my teacher took it and said, "I wonder how many typos there will be this time."

3. For the two situations you have just described, pick any relevant judgment errors or factors that determine a cause as internal or external that might have played a role in each judgment. Describe how each factor affected each judgment.
   a. Since Ed is my best friend, I suppose a "halo effect" might have influenced how I see his performance. In reality, he only scored six points and maybe I overemphasized his contribution because I like him so much.
      - In saying that he is a person who is not very selfish or greedy I might be making a logical error. It doesn't necessarily follow that a person who is unselfish is also generous. Even though he might be this way on the basketball court, there is no reason he has to be that way off the court.
   b. My teacher relied on a first impression of my typing to say what he did about the second draft. Also, a poor "halo effect" must have influenced his last statement to me. Finally, blaming me for the typos and calling me a sloppy typist is probably due to the principle that "unusual occurrences are seen as due to internal factors."

4. What are some things I can do to increase the accuracy of my own perceptions and/or overcome the errors in judgment that I or someone else made?
   a. I think I need to recognize that the judgment errors affect my behaviors and to be more careful next time. Perhaps I can withhold forming opinions until I look at the facts.
   b. I think that using the principles "calling attention to what caused the behavior" and letting people know that you have changed, would help. I should tell my teacher that I don't do my own typing and that there were so many errors the first time because I didn't have time to proofread the paper and that he should give me a chance to show him that I can turn in neat papers.

likely to see, taste, or hear the same stimulus and yet react differently. It is often the differences in how they interpret sensations that influence such behaviors.

Several principles that affect our daily interactions are related to this broad approach to perception. They are:

Our perceptions of similarity among people, objects, and events influence the way we relate to them. Similar attributes help us distinguish people, objects, and events from their backgrounds. As we grow and develop, we are taught to assign the same labels to similar people, objects, and events. Labels help us identify things easily, and they let us know a great deal about something based on limited information. This both helps and hinders us in our relationships with others. The negative aspect is that labels lead us to stereotype, or develop preconceived notions of what other things are like. When we stereotype people, we are likely to have problems in our relationships with them. We might overgeneralize the characteristics of a given group to individuals or feel that someone is not important because of the label. To overcome this problem, we must force ourselves to focus on the specific attributes of people.

Our ability to make comparisons among people, objects, and events is enhanced if we think of the frame of reference we are using. In making judgments that one person is the best or that a test was difficult, we must remember that a background of thoughts and feelings exists for making such judgments. We should state the frame of reference we use because it helps our judgments become less superficial and it gives others additional information for evaluating our reactions.

Our ability to attend to important parts of our environment is improved by becoming more vigilant, by producing changes in stimuli, and by focusing our attention in new ways. One of our tasks as perceivers is to identify and interpret sensations that exist against some background. To do this, we must focus our attention. Focusing our attention is sometimes difficult because our attention drifts and sensory adaptation makes it less likely that we will notice changes. To overcome such problems we must force ourselves to pay attention. This process is often made easier by taking rest breaks from monitoring stimuli, giving ourselves feedback on how well we are doing, and rewarding ourselves for attending to something. Furthermore, producing changes in stimuli captures our attention and that of other people. Such changes can be produced by creating movement, varying the size and intensity of a stimulus, repeating it (within limits), and changing it so that it better meets the needs and interests of people. Finally, focusing our attention in new and different ways may have beneficial effects for us. We can do this by treating our senses to an unusual perspective of our environment and by meditating. An unusual perspective is accomplished by such things as looking at a familiar setting from an unusual position, viewing it at close range, or simply quietly listening for things we typically fail to hear. Meditating helps us become aware of things we are normally not able to experience. It is a popular way to increase our awareness of inner processes and experiences.

Our perceptions of what other people are like are influenced by judgment errors and our impressions of situational versus individual responsibility for their behavior. Other people observe our actions and we, in turn, observe theirs. We often want to understand the reasons for the actions taken. Since we cannot directly perceive the thoughts and desires of individuals, we make inferences about them. This process often helps us determine how we will interact with people, and they in turn with us. To make such judgments accurate, we must avoid judgment errors and accurately determine whether the situation or the individual is responsible. Judgment errors interfere with our ability to infer accurately the causes of certain behaviors. They include tendencies to: rely on initial impressions; evaluate someone based on an overall good or poor impression we have of them; assume that certain personal traits go together; and make many positive judgments and avoid negative ones.

Whether we feel the situation or the individual is responsible for certain actions affects our relationships. We are more likely to forgive someone if we think that the situation caused the person to behave in that way. We will blame the person more if we feel that the actions were self-determined. To avoid getting mislabeled we must call attention to what caused our behaviors, let people know when we have made an atypical error, and ask people to give us a chance to show them we have changed.

THINGS TO DO

1. Read the following pairs of labels. As you read each one, try to think of one or two ways you or someone else might act if they consistently used one or the other description.
   a. Referring to a person as a:
      • "cracker" vs. "Caucasian"
      • "nigger" vs. "Afro-American"
      • "dago" vs. "Italian"
      • "politician" vs. "statesman"

- "ex-con" vs. "citizen"
- "student radical" vs. "socially concerned student"
- "mental patient" vs. "person with problems"

   b. Referring to an object as:
- "a thorny bush" vs. "a rose bush"
- "old furniture" vs. "an antique"
- "a disorganized painting" vs. "modern art"
- "outrageously priced" vs. "expensive"

   c. Referring to some event as:
- "a freak show" vs. "a rock concert"
- "ding dong school" vs. "teacher education classes"
- "a real grind" vs. "a demanding course"

2. What frames of reference do you think are appropriate for a:
   a. judge to sentence a criminal or levy a fine?
   b. teacher to grade a student?
   c. boss to promote an employee?
   d. storekeeper to price products?

3. The following statements are based on the research literature regarding stereotypes. Think of one or two specific examples from your personal experiences that support each statement.
   a. Stereotypes help us enhance our status by seeing others as inferior.
   b. Stereotypes give insecure people a chance to scapegoat others and actually get rewarded for it.
   c. Groups that are stereotyped isolate themselves, cut off effective communication channels with outside groups, and allow rumors about themselves to go unchecked.

4. Based on information in this chapter, what is some advice you might give to the following people to improve their ability to pay attention?
   a. an airplane pilot
   b. a night watchman
   c. a tennis player
   d. a bus driver
   e. a traffic police officer

5. Think of five things that caught your attention today. What were they and why do you think this happened? Can you relate this information to principles discussed in the chapter?

6. Turn off all the lights in your bedroom. Put cotton in your ears and lie in bed with your eyes closed for one hour. Don't fall asleep but think about what it feels like not to have some of the sensations you are used to having. After an hour, turn on the lights and take the cotton out of your ears. Do the sights and sounds in your room appear more interesting? What reactions did you have to cutting off the stimulation you normally experience for an hour?

7. Think of several ways that the information in the chapter regarding our perceptions of the causes of people's behaviors might influence:
   a. the decisions a jury reaches.
   b. a promotion and tenure committee deciding to promote a professor.
   c. a fraternity or sorority deciding to accept a new member.

REFERENCES AND OTHER INTERESTING THINGS TO READ

CARVER, R. P.   Speed readers don't read; they skim. *Psychology Today,* August, 1972.

COMBS, A. W., RICHARDS, A. C., and RICHARDS, F. *Perceptual Psychology.* New York: Harper & Row, 1976.

COOK, H., and DAVITZ, J. *60 Seconds to Mind Expansion.* New York: Random House, 1975.

DAVIES, D. R., and TUNE, G. S. *Human Vigilance Performance.* London: Staples Press, 1970.

DEMBER, W. N. *Psychology of Perception.* New York: Holt, Rinehart and Winston, 1965.

ELKIND, D. Perceptual development in children. *American Scientist,* 1975, *63,* 533–541.

GARFIELD, P. *Creative Dreaming.* New York: Simon & Schuster, 1974.

GOLEMAN, D. Meditation helps break the stress spiral. *Psychology Today,* February, 1976.

GRASHA, A. F. The role of internal instructor frames of reference in the student rating process. *Journal of Educational Psychology,* 1975, *67,* No. 3, 451–460.

HEIDER, F. *The Psychology of Interpersonal Relations.* New York: John Wiley and Sons, 1958.

JOHNSON, D. W. *Reaching Out: Interpersonal Effectiveness and Self-Actualization,* Englewood Cliffs, N.J.: Prentice-Hall, 1972.

JONES, E. E. How do people perceive the causes of behavior? *American Scientist,* 1976, *64,* 300–305.

KELLEY, H. H. The warm-cold variable in the first impressions of persons. *Journal of Personality,* 1950, *18,* 431–439.

KELLEY, H. H. Attribution theory in social psychology. In D. Levine (Ed.), Nebraska Symposium on Motivation. Lincoln: University of Nebraska Press, 1967.

MACKWORTH, J. *Vigilance and Attention.* Baltimore: Penguin Books, 1970.

MAHARISHI, M. Y. *Transcendental Meditation: Serenity Without Drugs.* New York: Signet, 1968.

MARKS, L. E. Synesthesia: The lucky people with mixed-up senses. *Psychology Today,* June, 1975.

McKIM, R. H. *Experiences in Visual Thinking.* Monterey, Calif.: Brooks-Cole, 1972.

OTIS, L.   If well integrated but anxious, try TM.   *Psychology Today,* April, 1974.

REGISTER, R.   In touch with feeling.   *Human Behavior,* July, 1975.

ROGO, S. D.   Strange journeys of the mind.   *Human Behavior,* April, 1976.

SNYGG, D., and COMBS, A. W.   *Individual Behavior: A New Frame of Reference for Psychology,* New York: Harper & Row, 1949.

SUEDFELD, P.   The benefits of boredom: Sensory deprivation reconsidered. *American Scientist,* 1975, *63,* 60–69.

WARM, J. D., KANFER, F. H., KUWADA, S., and CLARK, H. L.   Motivation in vigilance: Effects of self-evaluation and experimenter controlled feedback. *Journal of Experimental Psychology,* 1972, *92,* 123–127.

WERTHEIMER, M.   Laws of perceptual form.   In W. O. Ellis (Ed.), *A Source Book of Gestalt Psychology.*   New York: Harcourt Brace Jovanovich, 1939.

A.   After reading this chapter, the reader should be able to explain:

1.   Why taking into account individual differences in rate of learning and learning styles are important for developing learning environments.

2.   How paying attention to information we want to learn and actively practicing it increases our ability to learn.

3.   The effects of spacing our practice on things we want to learn over a period of time versus doing the same amount of practice in less time.

4.   How the stimulus and response components of one task can facilitate or interfere with our ability to learn a second task.

5.   How positive reinforcers, negative reinforcers, and knowledge of results operate to influence our ability to learn.

6.   The different effect that occurs when unpleasant stimuli are used as a negative reinforcer as opposed to when such stimuli are used to punish behavior.

7.   The flow of information we receive from a sensory register to short- and then long-term memory.

8.   How overlearning, providing a meaningful context, and using mental imagery can improve our ability to learn and remember.

B.   While reading this chapter, the reader should be able to use the information:

1.   To complete each of the demonstrations and exercises.

2.   To begin to think of ways to apply it to situations in life in which such principles could be helpful.

3

Acquiring New Behaviors

GLOSSARY

Distributed practice. Spacing the total amount of practice on a task over a period of time. For example, studying six chapters over a six-week period to prepare for a test.

Knowledge of results. The feedback we get from other people and events in our environment when performing a task and our ability to evaluate our own performance. Its purpose is to help us reduce the number or degree of errors we make.

Learning. The relatively permanent changes that occur in our skills and knowledge as a function of our experiences.

Learning styles. The typical strategies we use or prefer in learning situations. Students often use or prefer learning styles that include competitive, collaborative, independent, dependent, participant, and avoidant behaviors.

Long-term memory. The part of our memory system in which information is stored for extensive periods of time.

Massed practice. Extensively practicing a task within a short amount of time—e.g., studying six chapters in three hours the night before the exam to prepare for a test.

Mental imagery. Our ability to form images of the things we are about to learn.

Mnemonic. A device for helping us to remember something. Such devices often use something that has a known image content and associate it to images of things we want to learn.

Negative reinforcers. Aversive stimuli (e.g., shock, pain, loud noise) that increase the probability of responses which are successful in removing them from a situation.

Overlearning. Reviewing or repeating information beyond the point at which we feel we have mastered it. Reviewing our notes three additional times before an exam even though we feel we know the material is an instance of overlearning.

Positive reinforcers. Stimuli (e.g., food, praise) that increase the probability of a response when they are added to a situation immediately following the response.

Punishment. The use of aversive stimuli to eliminate or decrease the probability of a response that is considered undesirable. The aversive stimulus (e.g., beating, loud noise) is given immediately after the response occurs.

Transfer of training. The tendency of a prior task to facilitate or interfere with the learning of a new task. Positive transfer occurs when the prior learning facilitates and negative transfer occurs when the prior learning interferes with a subsequent task.

Sensory register. The part of our memory system that receives information from the environment and retains it as a visual image. The image is produced by stimulation of the rods and cones in our eyes. This image usually lasts for less than a second.

Short-term memory. Information in immediate memory is condensed, analyzed and interpreted for interest or importance and transferred to short-term memory. It usually remains in short-term memory for a few seconds to several minutes.

Learning Outcomes

What is the best way to study for an exam? How well do we understand classroom content when we cram for exams? Should we punish criminals to help them learn better behaviors? What is it that people learn when they are punished by imprisonment? What do babies learn when they get picked up for crying? Your answers to these questions will, in part, reflect what you think makes for effective learning practices. More than likely, some of your friends will give answers that you will find are different from yours. People usually disagree on how learning variables should be used and what it is that gets learned. Some students feel they memorize information only by cramming the night before exams. Other students space their exam study time over several days or weeks and consequently feel they understand it better. Many people think that imprisonment is a good punishment to teach criminals not to commit crimes. Others argue eloquently that imprisonment only teaches people how to become better criminals. One parent feels that picking up a child every time it cries teaches it to cry more. Another parent feels the child learns that mother is a constant source of affection and comfort.

Our daily behaviors reflect the ideas we have about the process of learning. That disagreement exists on what factors are important and the effects they produce indicates the variety of principles and assumptions that are possible. We will examine several of the more widely shared views on learning in this chapter. I use the term *widely shared* because even psychologists differ in their beliefs concerning the importance and relevance of many learning variables and practices.

We Learn at Different Rates

Learning is a relatively permanent change in our skills and knowledge as a function of our experiences. With sufficient experiences, we can acquire a new response or modify an existing one. The learning of most new responses looks similar to the graph in Figure 3-1. Here the mean number of correct responses of a group of 100 individuals is plotted. They were asked to perform a relatively easy learning task: learning a list of 10 nonsense syllables in the order presented. A nonsense syllable is a consonant-vowel-consonant construction (e.g., VIG) which does not form a word in English. Because nonsense syllables are unfamiliar to people, it is possible through the use of them to gain insights into how people acquire new responses. As you

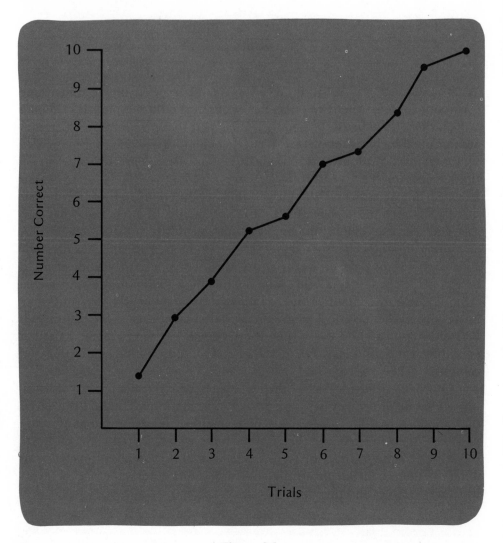

Figure 3-1

A learning curve for 100 individuals for learning 10 nonsense syllables in order.

can easily see, a few correct responses were initially made and gradually the group's correct responding increased. This gradual increase with practice is a characteristic of how we learn a new response.

Figure 3-1 represents the mean response of a number of people. It does not show the many variations in the rate of learning that occur within and between individuals. A fundamental principle of learning is that not everyone learns in the same way or at the same rate. Ideally, any learning environment should allow for individuals to learn in different ways and at different rates. Unfortunately, many of our learning environments (e.g., classrooms) attempt to treat everyone as if such variations did not exist. What are some exceptions to the latter statement in your experiences?

EXERCISE 3-1: LEARNING A NEW RESPONSE

Let us take a closer look at individual differences in learning by means of the following exercise. In it you will be asked to learn a set of new responses. This exercise should give you several insights into the process of learning a new response. To gain the most benefit from the exercise, please follow the instructions as they are presented.

1. Take two sheets of paper. On the first, prepare a worksheet like that shown in Worksheet 3-1. Cut along the vertical lines so that you have 10 separate sheets. On the second sheet, cut a rectangle about ½″ × ¼″ so that a hole appears in the middle of the paper.
2. Now turn to Table 3-1 and immediately cover the page with your second sheet of paper so that the five asterisks above the list of nonsense syllables appear in the rectangle.

Table 3-1

A List of 10 Nonsense Syllables
*****
GAX
VEH
WOJ
XIQ
YUJ
JIC
TEC
CEF
MEF
VUK
*****

3. The paper now covers the 10 nonsense syllables in the table. Your task will be to learn to write the entire list of 10 syllables in the correct order from memory.

Worksheet 3-1

	Trial 1	Trial 2	Trial 3	Trial 4	Trial 5	Trial 6	Trial 7	Trial 8	Trial 9	Trial 10
1.										
2.										
3.										
4.										
5.										
6.										
7.										
8.										
9.										
10.										
	Score___	Score___	Score___	Score___	Score___	Score___	Score___	Score___	Score___	Score___

4. To learn the list use the following procedure. Please read the whole procedure before beginning.

   a. Move the rectangle down the table until it exposes the first nonsense syllable. Repeat each letter of the first syllable aloud quickly and then move the rectangle down to the second nonsense syllable and repeat each letter aloud. Do this for each of the 10 items in the list. Say each letter in the syllable only once.

   b. After you have done this, take the piece of worksheet paper labeled Trial 1 and try to write the list as best you can in the correct order. *You may write the list in any way that you think is appropriate* (i.e., starting at the beginning, the end, or some other way).

   c. After your first attempt, turn over the first sheet of paper and repeat steps a and b. Use the sheet labeled Trial 2 to record your response for the second trial. Do not peek at the table or at your answers from the previous trial. Repeat this procedure for a total of 10 trials.

   d. Try to improve your performance each time. After you have completed the 10 trials, read the next instruction.

5. Now that you have completed the task, please do the following three things before continuing with your reading.

   a. On each sheet of paper, check your response with the correct items in Table 3-1. Give yourself one point each time you placed the correct syllable in the correct position.

   b. On Figure 3-2 plot the number of correct responses for each trial in the empty graph on the right-hand side of the figure. Compare your performance to the two people from my class whose data are in the left-hand side of the figure.

   c. Check with one or more of your classmates and plot their data on your graph if this is convenient.

The exercise illustrates that acquiring a new response is quite variable. We learn at different rates because the same learning factors do not affect each of us in the same way. Compare your performance to a student in one of my classes or to a classmate of yours. Note the differences in performance after the same amount of practice. After five trials, the fast learner in my class is performing almost 50 percent better than the slow learner. Everyone did not benefit from the same amount of practice equally. This is often the case with variables which affect our learning. One application of this finding is that we should make allowances for such differences when designing learning environments. Slower individuals should be given enough time to complete a task. They should not be expected to perform at the rate of the fastest learner. How do you think this principle can be used in classrooms, in raising children, and in learning a new skill (e.g., tennis, driving a car)?

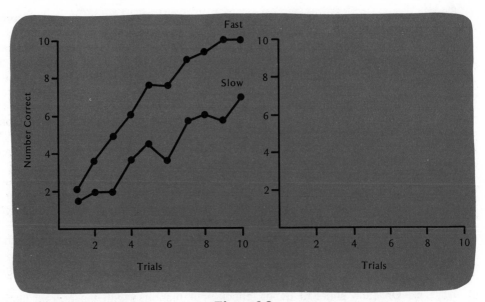

Figure 3-2
A learning curve for a fast and slow learner on the 10 nonsense syllables.

We Use a Number of Different Learning Strategies or Styles. They Change as We Develop and with Variations in Our Learning Environments

A rather simple learning strategy is to memorize information. However, most of our everyday learning requires that we do more than this. We organize information, develop concepts, test hypotheses, and otherwise take a more active role in our learning. As people grow older or as their learning environment changes, they begin to adopt different and more complex learning strategies. Research in this area by Jean Piaget, Jerome Bruner, and Tracy Kendler shows that as we age, changes occur in the cognitive processes we use to learn. We progressively acquire the ability to use abstractions, to become more logical in our thinking, and to formulate more complex concepts and hypotheses regarding the solutions to learning tasks. For example, preschool children have a tendency to rely on learning by association and have difficulty generalizing beyond the task at hand. With age, we become more concerned with formulating rules for relationships in our environment that will allow us to generalize our learning to other situations.

Our environments also influence the formation of and changes in our learning styles. To illustrate this influence, let us identify several learning styles that characterize how individuals approach classroom learning environments. In Table 3-2 you will find descriptions of six learning styles Sheryl Riechmann and I have identified in classrooms. They were developed from interviews with faculty and students and subsequent research with the Grasha-Riechmann Student Learning Style Scales.

Table 3-3 presents the names associated with each style and the types of classroom activities that students who score high on each style prefer. Do you feel you have preferences for classroom activities similar to those of the learning styles that you identified as most like you (i.e., those you ranked as 1, 2, and 3)? Do any of the classes you are currently taking provide activities that are compatible with your preferred learning styles?

An example of the influence on learning styles of changes in our learning environments is a study I did investigating changes in the Grasha-Riech-

Table 3-2

Descriptions of the Grasha-Riechmann Student Learning Styles

Student Learning Styles

___ A. This response style is exhibited by students who learn material in order to perform better than others in the class. They feel they must compete with other students in the class for the rewards of the classroom, such as grades or teachers' attention. They view the classroom as a win-lose situation, where they like to win.

___ B. This style is typical of students who feel they can learn the most by sharing ideas and talents. They cooperate with teachers and peers and like to work with others. They see the classroom as a place for social interaction as well as content learning.

___ C. This response style is typical of students who are not interested in learning course content in the traditional classroom. They do not participate with students and teachers in the classroom. They are uninterested or overwhelmed by what goes on in classes.

___ D. This style is characteristic of students who want to learn course content and like to go to class. They take responsibility for getting the most out of class and participate with others when told to do so. They feel that they should take part in as much of the class-related activity as possible and little that is not part of the course outline.

___ E. This style is characteristic of students who show little intellectual curiosity and who learn only what is required. They see teacher and peers as sources of structure and support. They look to authority figures for guidelines and want to be told what to do.

___ F. This response style is characteristic of students who like to think for themselves. They prefer to work on their own, but will listen to the ideas of others in the classroom. They learn the content they feel is important and are confident in their learning abilities.

EXERCISE 3-2: ASSESSING YOUR LEARNING STYLES

Each of us has more than one style that describes our classroom attitudes and behaviors. For the descriptions of the learning styles in Table 3-2, rank order the degree to which each description is like you in the space provided (1 = this style is most like me to 6 = this style is least like me). Identify the two styles that you feel are most and least like you first. Then rank order the others (i.e., 2, 3, 4, 5) in terms of how you feel they fall between the styles that are most and least like you.

mann Student Learning Styles. I observed that students in traditional lecture-oriented classrooms tended to approach the learning situation with competitive, dependent, and avoidant learning styles. Consequently, I programmed classroom environments to include group activities, individual projects, and requirements for extensive student participation. It was then possible to show that people adopted more collaborative, participant, and independent learning styles. Part of our flexibility as learners is an ability to acquire or use a number of learning styles as situations change. Do you feel that your classroom learning styles change from class to class?

Table 3-3

The Names of Each Style and the Classroom Activity Preferences of
Students Who Score High on Each Style

A. *Competitive.* To be a group leader in discussion or when working on projects. . . . To ask questions in class. . . . To be singled out for doing a particularly good job on a class-related activity. No real preference for any one classroom method over another (e.g., lectures, seminars) as long as the method has more of a teacher-centered focus than a student-centered focus.

B. *Collaborative.* Lectures with class discussion in small groups. . . . Small seminars. . . . Student-designed and -taught courses and classes. . . . Doing group rather than individual projects. . . . Peer-determined grades. . . . Talking about course issues outside of class with other students. . . . Instructor-group interaction.

C. *Avoidance.* Generally turned off by classroom activities. Preferences include no tests . . . self-evaluation for grading . . . no required readings or assignments . . . blanket grades where everyone gets a passing grade. . . . Does not like enthusiastic teachers. . . . Does not prefer well-organized lectures. . . . Does not like instructor-individual interactions.

D. *Participant.* Lectures with discussion. . . . Opportunities to discuss material. . . . Likes both objective and essay type tests. . . . Class reading assignments. . . . Likes enthusiastic presentations of material. . . . Prefers teachers who can analyze and synthesize material well.

E. *Dependent.* Teacher outlines or notes on the board. . . . Clear deadlines for assignments. . . . Teacher-centered classroom methods.

F. *Independent.* Independent study. . . . Self-paced instruction. . . . Problems which give the student an opportunity to think for himself. . . . Projects which the student can design. . . . Prefers a student-centered classroom setting over a teacher-centered one.

Active Practice Is a Necessary Condition for Our Learning Effectively

Actively practicing and otherwise paying serious attention to information we want to learn is an essential component of effective learning. We learn very little in a passive manner. Many of you have heard rumors about or know people who seemingly learn complex things quickly and with little effort. On the surface their learning appears casual. When in college, a friend of mine claimed such an ability. He said he never studied outside of class. His reputation grew until late one night he was caught frantically studying in his room for an exam. Needless to say, his reputation as a "genius" soon disappeared. Learning is not a process in which we absorb

HERE'S JOE'S ROOM. WHAT A GENIUS! HE NEVER STUDIES!

information in a relatively passive manner. Unfortunately, many people fail to use this principle. Research on student study habits, for example, shows that one-half of high school and college students study late at night lying in bed with their pajamas on. Obviously, these are not conditions that are conducive to an active review of course content. Take a closer look at this principle by completing Exercise 3-3 before you read further.

Before you get angry at me for tricking you, let's look at what the demonstration tells us about the learning process. This was an incidental or passive learning situation. You did one thing (counted letters) and then were tested for how much of the list you had learned. I diverted you so that you paid less attention to the items and were not able to practice them adequately. In spite of this, you were able to remember some of the items. Your score should be higher if you disregard whether the order is correct. Students in my classes get about 3 to 5 points if the correct position is counted. They usually obtain 5 to 8 points if the correct position is ignored. The fact that you were able to get any right shows that small amounts of learning occur in passive learning situations. However, compared to when your attention is focused on the task and active practice of the content takes place, passive learning runs a poor second.

If the principle of active practice were not true, we could play a tape recorder at night and teach ourselves while we slept. Many of our waking hours spent in learning might then be used for other activities. In fact, re-

Before reading further, follow the instructions listed here.

1. Look at Table 3-4 and count the letters in each item; write the number of letters in the space next to each item.
2. Cover Table 3-4 with the sheet of paper that has the rectangle in it.

Table 3-4

A List of 20 Items	
*****	
Railroad	_____
Monkey	_____
Automobile	_____
Book	_____
Wallet	_____
Scissors	_____
Watch	_____
Key	_____
Journal	_____
Light	_____
Picture	_____
Carpet	_____
Basket	_____
Pen	_____
Blanket	_____
Institution	_____
Yard	_____
House	_____
Door	_____
Camera	_____
*****	

3. *Write the 20 words in Table 3-4 in order from memory.*
4. Check your answers with those in the table.
5. Give yourself one point for each word in the correct position. Now rescore your answers and give yourself one point for a correct word regardless of whether it's in the correct order. Which score is higher?

search does exist on learning while asleep. Needless to say, the research is not very positive. In a few cases small amounts of learning have been observed. A closer examination of the data shows that the learning that did take place most likely occurred when the participants drifted out of a deep sleep and listened to the material being presented.

In Learning Complex Tasks, the Distribution of Practice Can Affect Our Learning

The way we space our practice in learning is often extremely important. Should we practice a task in a concentrated manner for short periods of time, or should we space the same amount of practice over a longer period? Students often ask me whether it is best to cram the night before an exam or to study and review over a period of days or weeks preceding the exam. *Massed practice* is equivalent to cramming the night before, and *distributed practice* is equivalent to studying the same amount over a longer time.

Reviews of the research on massed versus spaced practice in verbal skills by Benton Underwood and in motor skills by the late Edward Bilodeau suggest that the issue is not conclusively settled. A generalization from the

literature is that relatively easy tasks show little effect due to massed or distributed practice. With more difficult tasks, distributed practice usually leads to better learning. This information should not surprise you, as a major disadvantage of massed practice is that fatigue builds up quickly and makes information processing more difficult. In cramming for an exam late at night, the joint effects of fatigue due to massed practice and remaining awake makes it difficult to learn. Studying for exams is a rather complex undertaking. Some distribution over time of reading, reviewing, and committing the information to memory is advisable. How would you describe the distribution of practice in your current study habits? How do you think massed or spaced practice would affect your ability to learn: a sport like golf or tennis; a foreign language; chess; to shoot a rifle or bow and arrow?

Practice on a Prior Task often Affects Our Ability to Learn a New Task

The first experience can facilitate or interfere with our performance on a second task. If it facilitates, then we say that positive *transfer of training* has occurred. If it interferes, then we say that negative transfer of our prior training has occurred. An experience I had as an undergraduate should help clarify this distinction. I drove a small "Good Humor" ice cream truck during the summer. I found it quite easy to learn to drive the truck. Like my car, it had a standard transmission, brakes, and steering. Friends of mine who drove automobiles with automatic transmissions, power steering, and power brakes experienced problems learning to drive the truck. They initially thought the clutch was a brake, they pressed too lightly on the actual brakes and they did not turn the steering wheel enough around corners. They experienced negative transfer from their car experiences to the truck. With practice, these problems were eventually overcome.

EXERCISE 3-4: TRANSFER OF TRAINING

This exercise is designed to illustrate several principles associated with the transfer of training that will be discussed in the next couple of paragraphs. Try to work as fast and as accurately as you can.

A.   Each of the letters listed below has a number beneath it. Take a few seconds to become familiar with the letters and corresponding numbers. Your task will be to fill in the blank spaces next to each of the letters in Part A with the corresponding numbers as fast and as accurately as you can. Be sure to write the time that you started (e.g., *Hour* 9 *Minute* 10 *Second* 15) and the time that you completed Part A. Then read the instructions for Part B and complete the second task.

A	B	C	D	E	F	G	H	I	J	K	L	M
1	2	3	4	5	6	7	8	9	10	11	12	13

N	O	P	Q	R	S	T	U	V	W	X	Y	Z
14	15	16	17	18	19	20	21	22	23	24	25	26

PART A: *Start Time* (Hour_____ Minute_____ Second_____)

Begin: W__ Q__ E__ R__ T__ A__ S__ Y__ D__ J__ M__ X__ G__ L__
V__ C__ O__ I__ U__ Z__ B__ K__ M__ D__ P__ R__ Q__ J__ X__ D__
Z__ H__ F__ A__ U__ K__ C__ X__ Z__ L__ J__ H__ G__ F__ D__ S__
A__ P__ O__ I__ U__ Y__ T__ R__ E__ W__ Q__ H__ G__ J__ K__ F__
L__ D__ S__ Z__ A__ X__ C__ W__ V__ R__ E__ M__ T__ P__ O__ U__
Y__ T__ R__ E__ W__ Q__ J__ K__ L__ M__ V__ S__ A__ F__ C__ Z__
T__ M__ P__ A__ X__ L__ V__ W__ T__ R__ S__ F__ H__ Z__ B__ Q__
D__ Y__ E__ G__ T__ Y__ S__ K__

Finish Time (Hour_____ Minute_____ Second_____)

Check your responses and count the number of times you made a mistake and corrected it (No._____) and the number of times you made a mistake and did not correct it (No. _____). (Total errors _____)

B. The letters listed below have been assigned new numbers. Take a few seconds to become familiar with the letters and corresponding numbers and complete Part B. Work as fast and as accurately as you can.

A	B	C	D	E	F	G	H	I	J	K	L	M
23	14	18	26	13	1	9	15	11	17	14	2	4

N	O	P	Q	R	S	T	U	V	W	X	Y	Z
25	22	5	8	7	20	21	3	19	24	12	10	6

PART B: *Start Time* (Hour_____ Minute_____ Second_____)

Begin: W__ Q__ E__ R__ T__ A__ S__ Y__ D__ J__ M__ X__ G__ L__
V__ C__ O__ I__ U__ Z__ B__ K__ M__ D__ P__ R__ Q__ J__ X__ D__
Z__ H__ F__ A__ U__ K__ C__ X__ Z__ L__ J__ H__ G__ F__ D__ S__
A__ P__ O__ I__ U__ Y__ T__ R__ E__ W__ Q__ H__ G__ J__ K__ F__
L__ D__ S__ Z__ A__ X__ C__ W__ V__ R__ E__ M__ T__ P__ O__ U__
Y__ T__ R__ E__ W__ Q__ J__ K__ L__ M__ V__ S__ A__ F__ C__ Z__
T__ M__ P__ A__ X__ L__ V__ W__ T__ R__ S__ F__ H__ Z__ B__ Q__
D__ Y__ E__ G__ T__ Y__ S__ K__

Finish Time (Hour_____ Minute_____ Second_____)

Check your responses and count the number of times you made a mistake and corrected it (No._____) and the number of times you made a mistake but did not correct it (No. _____). (Total errors _____)

In designing educational and training experiences, we often want to have a positive transfer of learning from one situation to another. Charles Osgood has shown that the stimulus and response components of different learning tasks are important to understanding positive and negative transfer. *If two tasks have highly similar stimulus and response components, what we learn on one will facilitate our learning the second task.* Once you have learned to drive a full-sized car of one manufacturer, you will not have difficulty in learning to drive the same type of car from another manufacturer. Both the stimulus and the response components are highly similar. *However, if the stimulus and/or response components are different across tasks, we are likely to experience varying degrees of interference or negative transfer from one task to the other.* A pilot who learns to fly a single engine Piper Cub airplane will initially experience some negative transfer in learning to fly a jet airliner. The stimulus and response components are not entirely the same. The exercise you just completed is an example of what can happen when the stimuli are the same but the responses across tasks differ. Interference or negative transfer will occur. You probably found that Part B took more time to complete and that you made more copying errors than in Part A. The stimulus and response associations you learned in Part A interfered with your performance on Part B. How would you explain the negative transfer that occurred in the ice cream truck example cited earlier?

Reinforcement and Knowledge of Results Are Necessary for Us to Learn

Little learning would occur without incentives for wanting to learn and for continuing a task once it is begun. This is the role reinforcers play in learning. In everyday terms, *reinforcers* refer to the rewards and punishments our behaviors receive. Reinforcement traditionally has been studied in terms of the motivation processes associated with learning. The study of *knowledge of results* (*KR*) has emphasized the role of feedback in learning. The specific types of guidance and direction that we need to reduce our errors is the domain of *KR* research (e.g., "increase your response by nine inches"; "you are short of the target"; "you misspelled that word, the correct spelling is . . ."). Let us take a closer look at both types of processes.

Reinforcement can come from both internal and external sources. We have the capacity to monitor and regulate our own behaviors. Thus, we use internal reinforcers to praise or chastise ourselves when our behavior meets or deviates from the standards we have set (e.g., "I really did a good job";

"What a mistake that was"). Some external sources are grades in school, money from the boss, praise from friends, a slap on the hand, and even the food we eat if it is used to assist our learning. In most learning situations, both internal and external sources of reinforcement are present. I can remember as a student having my efforts at studying rewarded with a good exam grade. Yet the teacher was not the only source of reward. I patted myself on the back for doing a fine job and usually found friends who congratulated me on a good mark.

As we develop, internal sources should become more important. Parents often say, "I wonder when she will learn to stop doing that without my having to act as a policeman." Such a parent is in reality wondering when internal sources of control will begin to substitute for the external reinforcers. Fred Kanfer has shown that it is our experiences with external reinforcers that allow us to develop internal systems of control. As we grow older, we develop the capacity to transfer some of our dependence on external rewards to internal sources (e.g., self-praise). Robert Havighurst suggests that this process of using internal rewards begins to increase between the ages of 5 and 10. However, we never completely stop responding to external reinforcers.

Reinforcers are classified as positive or negative. Both produce effects on our behaviors. *Positive reinforcers* include such things as money, food, praise, and even a chance to watch a favorite television program. *When presented following a behavior, they increase the probability of the behavior's occurring again.* If a young child is praised after putting her toys away, she is more likely to repeat this behavior in the future. Positive reinforcers are most effective in increasing a desirable response if they are given immediately after the response occurs. If they are delayed or withdrawn, there is a tendency for the response to weaken, not to be learned at all, or to stop occurring. The young child is not likely to associate praise with picking up toys if the praise is given three hours later. Similarly, we would stop working if our boss stopped paying us.

Negative reinforcers are aversive stimuli that increase the probability of a response when they are removed from a situation. Aversive stimuli are things that are unpleasant to us, such as pain, loud noises, and electric shocks. When such stimuli occur in our lives, we often try to remove them. Responses that are successful in removing them will increase in frequency. Fastening our seat belts to stop the buzzer, feeding or changing a baby to stop its crying, and closing a window to shut out street noise are examples of behaviors we have learned to remove aversive stimuli. When such stimuli function to increase the frequency of a response, they are classified as negative reinforcers.

Aversive stimuli can also be used to decrease the frequency with which a response occurs. To decrease response frequency, an aversive stimulus must be added to a situation immediately after a response occurs. We call this procedure *punishment*. The goal of punishment is to eliminate a response or decrease the probability that it will occur in the future. Slapping a young child's hand to stop him from touching the television knobs or misbehaving are examples of punishment. B. F. Skinner has argued that punishment is a rather weak form of behavior control. It tends to suppress undesirable behaviors only temporarily and often leads to frustration and anger within the individual. If there is no constructive alternative response available, the undesirable behavior is likely to return. Skinner suggests that if punishment is used, it should be followed by the rewarding of a desirable alternative response. A child whose hand is slapped for touching the television might then be handed a toy to play with and praised for using it.

We will discuss in more detail in Chapter 4 several of the ways in which positive and negative reinforcers are used to change behaviors. The activities in the next two exercises are designed to check on your understanding of the concepts of positive and negative reinforcers and punishment. Please complete them before reading further.

EXERCISE 3-5: IDENTIFYING POSITIVE OR NEGATIVE REINFORCEMENT AND PUNISHMENT

For each situation listed, complete each statement by indicating if it represents an example of positive reinforcement, negative reinforcement, or punishment.

1. A young child complains of a headache. He is given aspirin. The next time he gets a headache he asks his mother for aspirin. The headache is an example of _____.
2. Ellen is trying to teach her dog to sit. Everytime she says sit she forces the dog to sit and praises it. Eventually the dog will sit on its own when she commands it to. Praising her dog to sit is an example of _____.
3. Tom asks his mother if he can go to the movies. She says no and he begins to cry. His mother then says that he can go. Tom's crying is an example of _____.
4. Ed parks his car in a no-parking zone to run into a store for a few minutes. He returns three minutes later and finds a police officer writing a parking violation sticker. Giving Ed a ticket is an example of _____.

EXERCISE 3-6: EVERYDAY EXPERIENCES WITH REINFORCEMENT AND PUNISHMENT

1. List one example from your experiences of a positive reinforcer, a negative reinforcer, and punishment in the following situations.
   a. A classroom.
   b. A restaurant.
2. Think of the things you did last week. What are some examples of positive and negative reinforcers and punishment in those situations? Check some of your responses with a classmate.

Appropriate responses to Exercise 3-5 and Exercise 3-6 appear on page 86.

Knowledge of Results

Learning any simple or complex skill would be impossible without feedback. Each of us has relied on feedback in learning tasks ranging from swimming to writing a paragraph. The primary purpose of feedback is to reduce the extent to which we will make errors. We use both external and internal sources of feedback. External sources include *KR* that we receive from, for example, teachers, supervisors, and the speedometer on an automobile. Once we begin to learn a task, we also begin to self-monitor and regulate our performance without a heavy reliance on external feedback. Our internal perceptions regarding our performance based on cues we receive from our bodies and how well the task is progressing allow us to correct errors. When I was learning to drive a car, my instructor initially said things like "turn the wheel just a bit more to the left"; "Press down on the brakes harder"; "You missed the curb by six inches." Initially I relied on his feedback to assist my driving. As I became more familiar with driving, I learned to make essentially the same judgments myself. Of course, I could not have done this without his initial assistance. My ability to provide internal feedback depends upon experience with external sources.

Two general principles emerge from the research on *KR*. As with reinforcement, the more immediate the feedback the better our performance will be. Ina Bilodeau has shown that this is particularly true for tasks in which similar responses need to be made in quick succession. Everyday examples of this type of task are learning to drive a car, to swim, to type, or to shoot a rifle. For an exam, immediate feedback is necessary only if further exams will rely on knowledge and skills tapped by earlier exams. In many content areas, this is not the case. Subsequent exams tend to be relatively independent of earlier ones in content tested (e.g., tests cover different historical periods, different readings). In such cases there is no strong effect due to a delay in feedback.

The more specific and detailed the *KR*, the better our performance. In learning to write a good paragraph, you will perform better if the teacher makes detailed comments rather than saying "That's good" or "That's poor." More helpful would be comments like "The comma belongs here"; "The correct spelling of that word is . . ."; "The lead sentence is too long by three to five words." It is important to remember this point regarding feedback. In my experience, I've noted that people often give feedback that is too general. Always ask yourself if the individual could make at least one specific correction based on the feedback. If so, then it is most likely detailed enough.

EXERCISE 3-7: KNOWLEDGE OF RESULTS

The following exercise will illustrate the effects of specific versus general *KR* in assisting your learning of a motor skill.

1. You will need two blank sheets of lined paper, a blindfold, a pencil or pen, a 12-inch ruler, and a friend, classmate, relative, or neighbor who is willing to assist you.
2. Place the blindfold over your eyes so that you cannot see. It is important that you not see during the demonstration. Have your partner sit across from or next to the hand *you will not use to draw* and lay the ruler across one of the lines near the top of the page. The straight edge of the ruler should face you. Have your partner hold the ruler firm. Place your pen at the left edge of the ruler. Your task will be to draw a three-inch line blindfolded. Move the pencil until you think you have made a three-inch line. Tell your partner to say "on target" if the line is within ¼ inch (in either direction) of a three-inch line. Have your partner say "too short" if it is more than ¼ inch shorter than the target and "too long" if it is more than ¼ inch longer than the target. Repeat this procedure until you are "on target" for two consecutive trials. Count the number of trials it took to reach the criterion of two consecutive trials on target.
3. Now switch roles. Your partner will now attempt to draw a three-inch line. You will give specific feedback. Simply give the amount of error in inches as feedback. Consider your friend on target if he or she is within ¼ inch of the three-inch mark. Feedback should be given to the nearest ¼ inch—for example, "You are 1¼ inches too short."
4. How many trials did it take to reach the criterion of two consecutive trials on target? How does this compare to your performance with general feedback? What do you think are the advantages or disadvantages of specific versus general feedback?

Suggested Answers to Exercises 3-5 and 3-6

Exercise 3-5

1. Negative reinforcement
2. Positive reinforcement
3. Negative reinforcement
4. Punishment

Exercise 3-6

1.
    a. Classroom:
    Examples of *positive reinforcers* include: praise from the teacher for good work on an exam or paper; recognition from your friends for making a good point in a discussion; a smile from the teacher or class-mates for saying something funny; the feeling that you are making progress in learning a new skill.

    Examples of *negative reinforcers* include: a fear of failing an exam (and so you study hard for it); the frown on a teacher's face before you respond to a question (a correct response will remove the frown).

    Examples of *punishment* include: taking a quiz and immediately getting a poor grade; giving an answer in class that the teacher says is incorrect; having people disagree with an idea that you just presented in a discussion.

    b. Restaurant:
    Examples of *positive reinforcers* include: good food; a pleasant atmosphere; friendly remarks from a waiter; reasonable cost of the meal.

    Examples of *negative reinforcers* include: an empty table next to a noisy kitchen which you refuse to sit at; loud talking in the restaurant by others, which makes you eat faster to get out of there; a date who ignores you only when you talk about your family.

    Examples of *punishment* include: a waiter who tells you the food combinations you selected will not taste good; a nasty remark from the waiter for leaving a small tip; eating food that is not well prepared.

Before leaving the topics of reinforcement and *KR*, some similarities between the two must be mentioned. Psychologists have formally studied reinforcers and knowledge of results separately. I suspect that the two classes of events are not in principle that much different. In learning something, the feedback you receive gives you information about your performance. It also helps by giving you an incentive for continuing the task. The more accurate we become, the better we feel and the more likely we are to complete the task. Thus, feedback cannot be entirely divorced from its motivational qualities. Similarly, reinforcement cannot be divorced from the information it gives us. Students who receive verbal praise from the teacher not only are rewarded but also are given information that their response errors were low. *KR* and reinforcement are not entirely independent events.

Our Learned Responses are Best Viewed as Relatively Permanent Changes in Behavior

Our learning does not necessarily imply a constantly available set of responses. Because of situational factors and forgetting, it is better to view what we learn as a relatively permanent change in behavior. Situational factors that affect our ability to show what we know include interpersonal conflicts, poor working conditions, fatigue, and the effects of drugs. Once these factors are corrected or removed, our performance is able to return to normal.

Difficulties in recalling information previously learned are another problem. Problems in remembering are related more to our ability to process information than to factors in our environments. But forgetting is not always a bad thing. I suspect that if all our experiences were easily remembered, our functioning would be adversely affected. Having constantly available everything we ever learned would interfere with our daily interactions. On the other hand, there are probably few things that we forget entirely. Research has shown that previously learned skills and concepts can be learned in less time than it took to learn them originally. For this shortened relearning to occur, we must have retained some of the information. In most cases, the concepts and skills that we have easy access to are those most frequently used in our daily lives, those most recently learned, or things that are important to us for personal reasons (e.g., the phone number of our best friend) .

Your data and that of your classmates should demonstrate that the longer the time interval between original learning and the retention test, the larger the retention loss. Furthermore, considerable savings in the amount of time needed to relearn the list should have occurred. Did your personal data deviate in any way from these two expectations? How long do you think you remember the content from a course you have completed?

EXERCISE 3-8: CHARACTERISTICS OF FORGETTING

Before reading further, let us do a short exercise that illustrates several characteristics of forgetting.

1. Prepare another worksheet like Worksheet 3-1, and cut it into 10 pieces.
2. Write in order the list of 10 nonsense syllables that you learned earlier. Guess if you are not sure.
3. Score your response the same way you did earlier. Compare your responses to those made after the last trial the first time you learned the list.
4. Approximately how much time has elapsed since you did the exercise the first time? Check to see if other people in class did this at a different time than you did. How did they score?
5. Try to relearn the list in order using the procedure outlined when the exercise was presented. How many trials did it take you to relearn the list? You should have a considerable amount of savings in the time needed to learn the list the second time.

Can you remember events in your life, 5, 10, 15 years ago? Which events are easiest for you to remember?

The Information We Learn Passes Through a Sensory Register, Short- and Long-term Storage System

How does information enter our memory system in the first place? The work of George Sperling, Jane Mackworth, Nancy Waugh, and Donald Norman suggests that three processes are involved. Initially, information from our environment enters our eyes and what is called a *sensory register*. The rods and cones in our eyes begin to send a pattern of nerve impulses along the optic nerve to the visual centers of the brain. This pattern forms a visual image or copy of the stimulus which usually lasts for less than a second. To demonstrate the existence of this image, take out a sheet of paper. Quickly look at the following visual patterns one time:

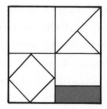  

Close your eyes immediately and see if you can still see them. *Cover the patterns with a sheet of paper before reading further.*

Your brain begins to analyze the information for importance and meaning. It condenses the information, keeping the major details and coding it so that you can retrieve it verbally, in writing, or by drawing it. When this condensation occurs, the information has now entered *short-term memory*. Please complete the following:

1. What word or words would you use to describe each figure?
2. Draw each of the three figures from memory.

How accurately do you think the words you used described each figure? What did you forget to include when you drew each figure? Were you able to reproduce the major details?

Research suggests that our short-term memory has a limited capacity. That is, we remember things only for from a few seconds to several minutes in short-term memory. Furthermore, it cannot hold more than five to nine items of the same stimulus class at any one time. We need to practice or rehearse information to retain it longer in short-term memory. Think of what you do after you read a new telephone number and have to walk a short distance to a phone. I repeat the number so that I can keep in it my short-term store.

Arthur Melton indicates that anything we remember longer than five minutes is considered to be in *long-term memory*. If information is important to us or if we rehearse it properly, it will be transferred to long-term storage. We will find ourselves able to remember it for periods of time which range from hours to years.

The description of the three parts of memory suggests that information we learn moves from one container to another. However, a word of caution is needed here. It is not entirely accurate to think of our ability to recall information as simply selecting bits of it from one of the containers. With the exception of reading information from the sensory register, it is more accurate to view retrieval as a more dynamic process. Although the sensory register maintains the information in the same format in which it was presented, short- and long-term memory depend upon transforming it into a simpler format. We thus establish memory codes for the information. When we are asked to recall something, we need to reconstruct, reproduce, or recreate the original information from its memory code.

This process is most noticeable when we try to reconstruct informaton from long-term memory. To illustrate this point, think of your last Christmas or Hanukkah holiday and answer each of the following questions.

1. What are four things you did that day?
2. What presents did you receive? Who gave them to you?
3. What presents did you give? To whom did you give them?
4. Whom did you spend your time with that day?
5. What did you discuss?
6. Where did you have dinner?
7. What did you eat for dinner?
8. What are two ways that this Christmas or Hanukkah holiday differed from the one before it?

In answering these questions you probably found yourself reconstructing that day and the events in it. Were events rather hazy and incomplete at first? Did you find yourself remembering a few important details and then having others begin to occur to you? Rather than passively selecting isolated bits of information from a container, you used your knowledge and creativity to actively reconstruct what happened.

Overlearning Information, Providing a Meaningful Context, and Using Mental Imagery Can Assist Our Learning

The previous two sections have demonstrated some of the factors associated with forgetting. We should not feel that there is nothing we can do to improve things. Rather, *overlearning* information, placing it into a meaningful context, and using *mental imagery* can help us retain information longer. Let us review each of these factors.

Overlearning Information

To overlearn something, you continue to practice it beyond the time that you feel you "really know it." In research studies overlearning is easy to accomplish. Participants learn a task to a particular learning criterion (e.g., 100 percent correct responses). They are then given additional practice opportunities amounting to from 25 to 200 percent of the amount of practice they needed to master the task initially. Particularly with verbal material, the amount of material retained is directly related to the amount of overlearning that occurred. That is, the more people overlearn, the more they remember when tested later.

Think of the last time you studied for an exam. Did you continue to review the information once you "knew it"? Overlearning is something you can do while studying. Simply review the information beyond the point at which you feel you have mastered it. One to three additional repetitions is usually sufficient to improve our long-term retention of the information.

Provide a Meaningful Context

The more meaningful the context in which you learn, the better your chances for retaining the material. One example of this principle is that our past experiences make some things more meaningful than others. Because of it, you should be able to learn and remember the first 10 items in Table 3-3 better than the 10 in Table 3-1. Based on past experiences, you should find words more meaningful than nonsense syllables. Sometimes, however, we must explicitly create a more meaningful context. In many courses, textbooks, outside readings, and lecture notes must be mastered. To create a more meaningful context, it is often necessary to reorganize the lecture notes, abstract the outside readings, and pull out major points from the text. This information can then be combined to form a more meaningful integration of the content (e.g., events leading up to the Civil War, problems in American society after the war, the impact of the Civil War on the twentieth century). Research has shown that establishing such relationships can increase information retention.

One important aspect of establishing meaningful relationships is our ability to categorize information. Categorizing helps because it provides a context for information and because it enables us to overcome limitations in our information processing system. George Miller suggests that limitations are built into our capacity to process information. When presented with a series of single items (e.g., those in a number string, such as 583569247658) and asked to repeat all of them immediately after a single presentation, we are able to produce an average correct response of seven items, plus or minus two. Our immediate retention span is limited to five to nine single items of information. Miller says that one way to overcome this problem is to "chunk" information—that is, to form relevant categories for what we learn. The number string presented is remembered better if instead of thinking of it as 5, 8, 3, 5, 6, etc., we think of it as 583, 569, 247, 658. Such chunking or categorizing enables us to overcome problems with our immediate retention span and facilitates retention. To test this for yourself, take each of the number sequences that follow this paragraph. Read the first one quickly and then try to write the sequence from memory. Then do the second and third sequences in the same way. Now go back and redo each sequence by chunking the information as we have described.

476398723458   160489342673   854920157384

The Use of Mental Imagery

Before we acquire language, we undoubtedly categorize our environment in terms of mental images. Familiar things are recognized because they match some internal representation of them. At age two, my son was able to tell me the colors of all the buildings and cars in a train set he had received for Christmas. He had not seen the set since he was 16 months old, or 8 months earlier. As we grow older, we place less emphasis on images in learning. The use of words becomes more important because of the stress on verbal learning in our society and school systems. To some extent we are taught not to rely on images.

This does not mean that mental imagery is not important to us as adults or that we cannot make use of it. Gordon Bower argues that information is processed by adults with both a verbal and an image component. The verbal process helps us to deal with abstract information; imagery allows us to deal with more concrete concepts. In learning theoretical equations or information that contains relatively abstract words (e.g., *anxiety, attitude, intelligence*), we undoubtedly use the verbal component more. In attempting to learn how the flow of electricity is analogous to a water plumbing system or in using information that contains concrete concepts (e.g., *tree, children, table*), we rely on the imagery component more. Research has shown that concrete information is learned faster and retained better than is abstract information. The stronger use of images in processing concrete concepts is thought to make the difference.

There are individual variations in the way we normally use images. At one extreme are individuals who have eidetic or photographic memories. Such people are able to remember all the details of a photograph or visual scene and even whole pages of a textbook. Most of us are probably able to use mental imagery to a lesser extent. One way to increase our use of imagery is to force ourselves to form images in our learning. When meeting a new person, try to form an image using his or her name. The infamous John Doe gets transformed into an image of that person with a deerlike face. Concepts like the flow of electricity, the structure of molecules, and historical events can be transformed into real or imaginary images. Use your imagination to do this. I have often used some fairly bizarre images to learn concepts, but they have worked.

Another popular way to use imagery is to use *mnemonic devices*. The basic process of a mnemonic system consists in taking something which has known imagery content and then beginning to associate to it images of things to be learned. Such devices are used by stage magicians to learn the names of people sitting in the audience. A person good at this procedure can learn the names of 100 people after hearing them only once. The famous Roman orator Cicero was the inventor of an early system called the method of loci. He used the images associated with walking to different parts of his garden to learn the order of ideas in his speeches. He made up images of key words in the speech and associated them to images of things in his garden. You might use this technique by thinking of the images of the first 10 things you do every day on your way to school. You then would take 10 things you must learn and try to form an image that combines the daily event and the information to be learned.

When I was in the Army, I used this technique to memorize my lectures. As instructors, we got good ratings if we did not use notes. I would first take the list of concepts I had to teach and then form categories. In a class on the causes and characteristics of guerrilla warfare, concepts like the use of hit and run tactics, the occurrence in lands of rising expectations, and the necessity of the support of local people for success were major points I needed to make. Each category had a number of examples and ideas associated with it. I found that if I could recall the major point, the others were easy to reconstruct. My first location on my way to work was a guard post and I imagined a gorilla standing in front of it (guerrilla warfare). The second was a mess hall, and I imagined a baseball game on its roof (hit and run tactics). An open field was my third location, and I imagined people standing around watching a pillar of money grow (land of rising expectations). I used as many locations as I had categories to learn. I was both delighted and surprised at how easy it was to learn and remember information this way.

EXERCISE 3-9: USING A MNEMONIC DEVICE

Perhaps you are still somewhat skeptical of the use of images. The following demonstration should give you some personal data for deciding whether such techniques are useful to you. *Please read the four instructions* before proceeding.

1. For this demonstration we are going to use the words in Table 3-5.
2. Take out the sheet of paper with the rectangle cut in it. When I tell you to do so, you will expose each word in the list in order. Each word is a natural association for a number from 1 to 20. Colleagues of mine, Jay Persensky and R. J. Senter, developed the list for some research they were doing in mnemonics. The rationale for each item in the list is rather obvious except perhaps for the following: two = pair of dice; eight = eight ball in a set of pool balls; thirteen = baker since 13 is a baker's dozen; fourteen = heart since February fourteenth is Valentine's Day; fifteen = pool balls since there are 15 pool balls in a set; sixteen = girl since sweet sixteen is often used in that context; nineteen = a calendar since every year in this century begins with 19; 20 = cigarettes since there are 20 cigarettes in a pack.

Table 3-5

A List of Twenty Items

Dollar bill	_____
Dice	_____
Tricycle	_____
Four-leaf clover	_____
Hand	_____
Six-pack	_____
Seven-up	_____
Eight ball	_____
Baseball team	_____
Bowling pins	_____
Football team	_____
Dozen eggs	_____
Baker	_____
Heart	_____
Pool balls	_____
Girl	_____
Magazine	_____
Golf course	_____
Calendar	_____
Cigarettes	_____

Courtesy of J. J. Persensky, Ph.D., now at the National Bureau of Standards, Washington, D.C.

3. Expose each word and try to form a mental image of the item. You might imagine one-dollar bills as wallpaper in your room or a giant tricycle sitting outside your home. As soon as you form your image, go on to the next item. Try to be creative in forming images.
4. As soon as you are finished, write the list of words in the order in which they occurred. Give yourself one point for each item that is correct in the correct position.

How many of the items were you able to write in the correct position? After one practice trial, 20 percent of my students can write 15 to 20 items in their correct positions, 70 percent are correct on 10 to 14 items, and the remainder have between 5 and 9 items correct. A group that is simply shown the list and not given the imagery instructions is able to recall approximately 4 to 6 items in their correct positions. What do these data suggest to you about the influence of imagery on learning?

The twenty items can now be used as a mnemonic system. As with the

Figure 3-3

Use of the 20-item mnemonic list to form images with the items in Table 3-5. Images can be as bizarre as you care to make them.

Cicero technique, simply form images of the concepts to be learned with as many of the 20 items as you need. The 20 items can be used over again for the same or for different subjects. If you have more than 20 items, combine items to form their numbers. A combined image of a pair of dice and a tricycle (e.g., a tricycle resting on a pair of dice) can be used for the number 23. All that you need do is set up a personal system for numbers above 20. To reap the benefits of this or any other mnemonic system, you need to first practice and train yourself to use it.

Figure 3-3 gives an example of the use of this mnemonic to help learn a list of items. Why not try to learn that list using the images that are suggested?

EXERCISE 3-10: THE USE OF LEARNING PRINCIPLES TO IMPROVE YOUR STUDYING

A number of ways to use learning principles have been suggested in this chapter. Now we will combine them with some additional information into a format to help you improve your studying. Analyses of study habits makes it clear that transmitting principles for improving these habits is not enough. People must want to change, and they need a structure that will facilitate their learning. The procedure we will now outline is such a structured format. You might want to try the procedure to gain personal experience with the application of learning principles as well as to improve your study habits.

Five Steps Toward Improving Studying

The procedures listed should begin at least two to three weeks before your next exam. To gain experience with them, it is best to use them with one or two courses initially. Once the procedures become integrated and their personal advantages and disadvantages noted, their use can be expanded to other courses. With experience, you may also want to modify the procedures somewhat to better meet your personal needs. Familiarize yourself with each step before beginning.

Step 1. Use a blank study habit log sheet like the one used for the example in Figure 3-4 to record your responses.
    a. List the activities that you need to perform to get ready for this exam (e.g., outside readings, textbook chapters to read, special projects or assignments to be completed, review of notes). *List them in the order in which they must be accomplished.*
    b. Determine the number of days that remain between now and the exam. Assign a specific deadline for completing each activity.
    c. Determine the approximate number of hours that you will need to complete each activity.
    d. Allocate the number of hours that you need for each activity over the days that are available. This preparation schedule should be made on a daily basis. The minimum amount of time scheduled should be

Course: Principles of Psychology

Exam Date: 4/26

ACTIVITY	DEADLINE	HOURS NEEDED	PREPARATION SCHEDULE			
1. Read & Outline Chap. 5	4/1	3	3/25 8:30-9 PM	3/26 9-10:00PM	3/27 8-9:00 PM	3/28 8:30-9 PM
2. Read & Outline Chap. 6	4/7	3	4/2 6-7:00 PM	4/4 6-7:00 PM	4/6 4-5:00 PM	
3. Review Lecture Notes	4/9	1	4/8 3-4:00 PM			
4. Read & Outline Outside Reading	4/12	2	4/10 8-9:00 PM	4/11 4-5:00 PM		
5. Integrate chapters, outside Readings & Lecture Notes	4/20	6	4/12 7-9:00 PM	4/13 8-9:00 PM	4/15 3-5:00 PM	4/18 6:30-7:30
6. Develop Mnemonic System for Erikson's Personality Stages	4/22	1	4/21 4-5:00 PM			
7. Final Review	4/26	4	4/24 3-5:00 PM	4/25 8-10:00 PM		
8.						
9.						
10.						
11.						
12.						

Figure 3-4
Study log sheet.

97

half an hour. *Be specific. For example,* on Saturday October 5, I will spend one hour on reading Chapter 5 of the textbook, half an hour on one of the outside readings and half an hour reviewing my notes.

Step 2. Answer the following:

    a. Is your study area conducive to thoughtful studying? That is, can you really get something done? Yes_____ No_____. If *no,* choose a more appropriate time and/or place to study and prepare material.

    b. List 8 things that are rewarding to you (e.g., cola, potato chips, watching television).

    c. List five things that are aversive to you (fines, not watching a favorite television show, denying yourself a reward, etc.). Try to be specific.

Step 3.

    a. Begin to prepare and study in the time periods designated in Step 1. At the end of each half hour's worth of activity, give yourself a reward. After using this procedure for three or four days, gradually increase the amount of time you spend on an activity before you reward yourself. You might raise the time interval in 15-minute increments (i.e., 30, 45, 60, 75, and 90 minutes). Ninety minutes should be the maximum amount of time between rewards. Some students find it helpful not to take the reward they have earned immediately. Rather, they keep records of what they owe themselves and save their rewards for a block of time when they simply indulge. Use whatever works best for you.

    b. Administer a punishment if you fail to complete an activity as you scheduled it or if you fail to do it in a satisfactory manner. Having done this, perform or schedule an appropriate alternative response immediately and give yourself a reward for performing or scheduling the alternative response. You might want to schedule a new time to perform the activity or redo it so that it is now satisfactory.

    c. At the end of the week, take 10 to 15 minutes to review your progress with regard to your schedule. Make any sensible modifications.

Step 4. Select the learning principles and study tips listed below and use those that most interest you.

    a. *Overlearn the material.* That is, when you are sure you know it, review it at least one more time just to make sure.

    b. *Actively review notes and textbooks.* Don't try to read the textbook or review your notes in a passive manner. Underline key passages, ask yourself questions as you read, and think of how your reading relates to other information in the course. A good way to do this is suggested by Francis Robinson. First, survey what you must read. Then, for each section you read, ask yourself a question before beginning. Try writing the question down. Read the section to answer the question. Now recite to yourself the answer to the question. Review all the sections after finishing by restating your questions and recalling each answer. If you write the questions and answers down as you go, this review process is easier.

    c. *When preparing for an exam, summarize or paraphrase* in your own words the material to be learned.

d. *Chunk units* to be learned into revelant categories. Try to figure out what the relevant categories are for the material you must learn. Group the information that relates to that category together. Categories should combine material from the text, readings, and class notes. This will assist in providing a meaningful context for the information.

e. *Space your practice and avoid cramming.* To do otherwise invites fatigue, which interferes dramatically with your ability to process information.

f. *Use mental imagery whenever possible.* Sometimes it is helpful to think of the types of images that certain types of content present (e.g., a molecular structure, a behavioral model). A formal way to do this is to use mnemonic devices whenever possible. Often information that can be chunked or categorized can be converted to images or lends itself to the use of mnemonic devices.

g. *Stress understanding rather than rote repetition.* A good strategy is to prepare for an exam as if you were going to make a presentation on the material to a group of people—that is, where you will be the expert and they will have the opportunity to ask questions. In such a situation, you would not have only a rote memorization knowledge of the material.

h. *Study in a relaxed, pleasant atmosphere and avoid studying when tired or fatigued.* If you are too tired to learn, a nap beforehand, or even getting up early to study is an extremely good idea.

Step 5. Thinking about what you did, how would you improve this procedure the next time you used it?

SUMMARY

Learning represents relatively permanent changes in our skills and knowledge as a function of our experiences. In trying to understand the factors that influence learning, one finds that people differ on the importance in their learning of any one variable. However, certain basic principles seem to hold across different viewpoints regarding the learning process. They

We learn at different rates and use a variety of learning strategies. Individual differences occur in how fast we learn and in the approach we take to learning. Students show learning styles labeled as competitive, collaborative, independent, dependent, participant, and avoidant. A well-designed learning environment should allow for individual differences in learners.

Our learning strategies or styles change with our development and with changes in our learning environments. As we grow older our learning strategies change. We increase our ability to use abstractions, to be more logical in our thinking, and to formulate complex hypotheses regarding solutions to problems. Different learning tasks and situations can force us to adopt new strategies or to change existing ones.

Active practice is a necessary condition for our learning effectively. We learn very little in a passive manner. Attention to the task and active practice of it are prerequisites for effective learning.

In learning complex tasks, the distribution of practice can affect our learning. Practice can sometimes have negative effects on learning. One way is for fatigue to build up and consequently affect our performance. With complex learning tasks it is better to distribute the amount of practice over time.

Practice on a prior task often affects our ability to learn a new task. One goal of most educational efforts is for the training to transfer to other situations. Depending upon the stimulus and response relationships across tasks, positive or negative transfer can occur. In general, the higher the degree of stimulus and response similarity, the greater the chances for positive transfer.

Reinforcement and knowledge of results are necessary for learning to occur. Little learning occurs unless individuals have incentives for wanting to learn and for continuing with a task once it is begun. Reinforcers are classified as positive or negative. Positive reinforcers (e.g., food, praise) increase the probability of a behavior when they are added to a situation following a response. Negative reinforcers (e.g., loud noise, pain) increase the probability of responses which remove them from a situation. Punishment occurs when we immediately follow a response with an aversive stimulus. Knowledge of results acts to provide us with feedback so that we can reduce the extent of our errors in learning.

Learned responses are best viewed as relatively permanent changes in behavior. Because of situational factors and forgetting, we are not always able to demonstrate what we have previously learned. The greater the amount of time between learning and our attempts to recall the information, the greater the retention loss.

The information we learn passes through a sensory register, short- and long-term storage system. Information enters our memory system by first entering a sensory register for a fraction of a second. Our brains analyze the information for importance and meaning. It is condensed and coded so that it can be retrieved verbally, in writing, or by drawing it. When this condensation occurs the information is now in short-term memory. If the information is important to us or we rehearse it properly, it will enter a long-term storage. We will be able to remember it for periods of time which range from hours to years.

Overlearning information, providing a meaningful context, and using mental imagery can assist our learning. Each of these factors can help us overcome our tendencies to forget information. To overlearn something, we should continue to practice it one or more additional times beyond the point at which we feel we have mastered it. To create a more meaningful context, it is often necessary to integrate diverse pieces of information. Our ability to categorize information can help us here. Trying to form images of the things we must learn is often helpful. A formal way to do this is to use a mnemonic device: take something which has imagery content and begin to associate images of the things we want to learn to it.

THINGS TO DO

1. Pick a situation or problem in your life for which learning principles might be useful. Describe the problem in some detail, including the background to it, the key actors, and the type of changes that must occur. Develop an action plan for solving the problem using one or two of the learning principles discussed in this chapter. Keep a diary of your attempts to solve the problem. Note the changes that occur and try to assess the influence of the learning principles on the solution.

2. Think about what happened to you yesterday. In what ways was your behavior affected by positive and negative reinforcers? What kinds were used? Who used them? Did you have the feeling of being manipulated? If appropriate, share your reactions with a classmate.

3. Pick a course that you are now taking. What should the next related course contain to maximize positive transfer? Think in terms of the content that it might cover and the types of responses it would require of students. What if your current course were a theory course and the next one emphasized applications of the theory? Would positive transfer necessarily occur? What might be some conditions under which initially the transfer would be negative?

4. If people in class have not already done so, have them assess their individual student learning styles as discussed in Table 3-2. Develop a composite ranking of the learning styles found in class. Discuss how compatible your cur-

rent classroom activities are with these student styles. What are some changes that must occur to bring the classroom activities more in line with the styles?

5. Use one of the mnemonic systems described in this chapter to learn: (a) a list of concepts or names for an upcoming test, (b) a grocery or shopping list, (c) the major points in a speech or talk that you must give, (d) the names of people that you have a hard time remembering, (e) the names of new people that you meet at a party or meeting.

REFERENCES AND OTHER INTERESTING THINGS TO READ

ASIMOV, I. I remember, I remember. *Is Anyone There?* New York: Doubleday, 1967.

ATKINSON, R. C. Mnemotechnics in second language learning. *American Psychologist,* 1975, *30,* 821–828.

BILODEAU, E., and BILODEAU, I. Motor skills learning. *Annual Review of Psychology,* 1961, *12,* 243–280.

BILODEAU, I. Information feedback. In Bilodeau, E. (Ed.), *Acquisition of Skill.* New York: Academic Press, 1966.

BOWER, G. H. Analysis of a mnemonic device. *American Scientist,* 1970, *58,* 496–510.

BRIGGS, R. D., TOSI, D. J., and MORLEY, R. M. Study habit modification and its effect on academic performance. *Journal of Educational Research,* 1971, *64* (8), 347–350.

BRUNER, J. S. The course of cognitive growth. *American Psychologist,* 1964, *19,* 1–16.

GRASHA, A. F. Observations on relating teaching goals to student response styles and classroom methods. *American Psychologist,* 1972, 27, 144–147.

HAVIGHURST, R. Minority subcultures and the law of effect. *American Psychologist,* 1970, *25,* 313–322.

HULSE, S. H., DEESE, J., and EGETH, H. *The Psychology of Learning.* New York: McGraw-Hill, 1975.

KANFER, F. H. The maintenance of behavior by self-generated stimuli and reinforcement. In A. Jacobs and L. B. Sachs (Eds.), *The Psychology of Private Events.* New York: Academic Press, 1971, 39–59.

KENDLER, T. Development of mediating responses in children. In J. C. Wright and J. Kagan (Eds.), Basic cognitive processes in children. *Monographs of the Society for Research in Child Development,* 1963, Serial No. *86,* 33–47.

KRAMER, R. What we're learning about learning. *New York Times Magazine,* June 11, 1967.

LURIA, A. R. *Mind of a mnemonist.* New York: Harper & Row, 1968.

MACKWORTH, J. R. The duration of the visual image. *Canadian Journal of Psychology,* 1963, *17,* 62–81.

MELTON, A. W.   Implications of short-term memory for a general theory of memory. *Journal of Verbal Learning and Verbal Behavior,* 1963, *2,* 75–85.

MILLER, G. A.   The magic number seven plus or minus two: Some limits on our capacity for processing information. *Psychological Review,* 1956, *63,* 81–97.

MILLER, G. A., GALANTER, E., and PRIBRAM, K.   *Plans and the Structure of Behavior.*   New York: Holt, Rinehart & Winston, 1960.

MURDOCK, B. B., Jr.   *Human memory: Theory and Data.*   Potomac, Md.: Lawrence Erlbaum Associates, 1974.

OSGOOD, C. E.   The similarity paradox in human learning: A resolution. *Psychological Review,* 1949, *56,* 132–143.

PERSENSKY, J. J., and SENTER, R. J.   An experimental investigation of a mnemonic system in recall.   *Psychological Record,* 1969, *19,* 491–499.

PIAGET, J.   *The origins of intelligence in children.*   New York: International Universities Press, 1952.

ROBINSON, F. P.   *Effective study.*   New York: Harper & Row, 1946.

SKINNER, B. F.   *Beyond Freedom and Dignity.*   New York: Bantam, 1971.

SPERLING, G.   The information available in brief visual presentations. *Psychological Monographs,* 1960, *74* (Whole No. 498).

UNDERWOOD, B. J.   Ten years of massed practice on distributed practice. *Psychological Review,* 1961, *68,* 229–247.

WAUGH, N. C., and NORMAN, D. A.   Primary memory. *Psychological Review,* 1965, *72,* 89–104.

A. **After reading this chapter, the reader should be able to explain:**

1. How operant conditioning explains our ability to learn.

2. The importance of defining target behaviors before undertaking a plan to modify a particular behavior.

3. How to record information on a behavior, both before we begin to change it and after our plan to change it is in operation.

4. Two reasons negative reinforcers and punishment are not recommended for producing long-term changes in our behaviors.

5. Four things that we can use as positive reinforcers to assist us in modifying a behavior.

6. Two procedures for administering positive reinforcers when we undertake a plan to change some behavior.

7. The importance of considering the effort it takes to make a response before deciding how much of a reinforcer we need to use in a behavior modification plan.

8. The way that avoidance and escape responses to unpleasant stimuli in our environment develop.

9. How classical conditioning explains our ability to learn.

10. How systematic desensitization, a procedure for reducing an emotional reaction, can be used to lessen our fear of a situation.

11. One way to use images to enhance our emotional reactions to an event.

B. **While reading this chapter, the reader should be able to use the information:**

1. To solve the issues raised by each of the exercises.

2. To begin to develop a change plan to modify a behavior based on behavioral learning principles.

4

Modifying Existing Behaviors

GLOSSARY

Antecedent stimuli. Stimuli that occur before a response. Some antecedent stimuli may directly elicit a response (e.g., a hot burner causes you to lift your hand).

Avoidance response. An action we take to avoid an aversive event (e.g., taking the long way home to avoid traffic jams).

Behaviorism. A theoretical approach to human behavior which attempts to break our behaviors into stimulus and response components. Our actions are then explained in terms of how various stimuli affect these responses.

Classical conditioning. A learning procedure for developing a particular response to a stimulus that normally does not elicit that reaction (e.g., salivating at the sound of a bell).

Consequent stimuli. Those stimuli that occur after a response. Some consequent stimuli can reinforce a behavior (e.g., pulling a lever on a candy machine and obtaining a piece of candy).

Cost/benefit ratio. People derive certain benefits from positive reinforcers. However, in deciding whether to repeat a response they usually assess these benefits against the effort it took to obtain the reward.

Discrimination. The process of learning to perform a response in the presence of some stimuli and not in the presence of others (e.g., stopping at an intersection when the light is red).

Discriminative stimulus. A stimulus that occurs before a response and signals that a particular action will be reinforced (e.g., the sight of a movie theater signals that buying a ticket will allow one to watch a favorite movie).

Escape response. An action we take to terminate an unpleasant stimulus once it occurs (e.g., fastening our seat belts to stop a buzzer).

Extinction. Taking away a reinforcer that controls some behavior. The usual result is for the behavior eventually to stop occurring. Ignoring a child who shows off to get your attention is one example of extinction.

Intermittent reinforcement schedules. The presentation of a reinforcer on a less-than-continuous basis. We might reinforce only after a certain time interval or after a particular number of correct responses.

Interval schedules. The administration of a reinforcer after a variable or fixed amount of time. An example is getting paid after a fixed amount of time (e.g., every two weeks) or receiving "pop quizzes" in a class after variable time intervals.

Operant conditioning. A learning procedure that emphasizes the role of positive and negative reinforcers in controlling our behavior.

Operants. Behaviors that are usually considered to be subject to our conscious control. Examples include eating, walking to school, and answering the telephone.

Ratio schedules. The administration of a reinforcer after a fixed or variable number of responses. An example is getting a bonus for selling a fixed number of products or winning at poker after a variable number of hands played.

Respondent. Behaviors that occur in response to certain antecedent stimuli. They are usually considered to be associated with the autonomic nervous system, include the movements of our internal smooth muscles, and are highly similar from person to person. Our reflexes and emotional responses fall into this category.

Shaping. A process of learning a behavior where each successful attempt at making a part of or the complete response is rewarded.

Stimulus generalization. A process in which a stimulus with characteristics similar to another produces the same type of reaction. Our ability to stop our cars at red lights which are slightly different shades of red is an instance of stimulus generalization.

Systematic desensitization. A process developed by Joseph Wolpe to help reduce emotional responses. It involves learning to relax while we form images associated with and including a situation that we might fear.

Target behaviors. The specific behavioral outcomes or goals that we are working toward. Reducing our smoking by 10 cigarettes a week for 10 weeks is an example of a target behavior.

Token reward. A symbolic reward that is given after a desirable response. One example is the use of plastic chips to reward a grade school child's performance. The chips can be traded in at a later time for other rewards (e.g., better seats in class, more playground time).

Designing Learning Environments

The fifth-grade teacher looked at Ellen and smiled. "Your English paper was the best in the class. I'm going to give you four plastic chips for the fine job you did." Ellen was delighted. Including those chips earned in her other subjects this week, she had a total of 15. She was now assured of a good report card. More importantly, she could use 10 of the chips to buy a seat in the soft chairs at the front of the school auditorium. A magician was scheduled for a school assembly next week. Ellen knew how much more she would enjoy the performance with a preferred seat. Students who had earned fewer than 10 chips could not purchase such a good seat. They would sit farther back in the auditorium.

In Ellen's school, the teachers use behavior modification procedures based on the learning principles of B. F. Skinner. Children earn plastic chips or *token rewards* for completing class assignments and behaving in ways that are not disruptive. The chips buy privileges which range from good seats in the auditorium to extra time in the playground. Because desirable behaviors are rewarded on a systematic basis, they occur quite frequently. These good behaviors help to create a learning environment which students and teachers typically enjoy. A key to the success of this procedure is that a well-thought-out plan exists for managing the classroom environment.

Could such a system be used in one of your current classes? Which one? What kinds of token rewards might be used? What behaviors could they be used to reward? What privileges would they buy? Do you think you would enjoy such a system? Does the current reward structure in your classes have anything in common with the token reward system described? Why not ask several of your classmates what they think about these issues?

Each of us at one time or another has wanted to change some aspect of our own or someone else's behavior. We may have been interested in giving up smoking, losing weight, speaking more confidently in public, teaching someone a job-related skill, or helping one of our children develop good table manners. To do any of these things, we need to design experiences for ourselves and others that will produce relatively permanent changes in behavior. Yet these experiences must be helpful and must not harm or embarrass ourselves or others. This goal can best be achieved if we have a well-developed plan for the changes we are interested in producing.

What should such a plan include? Two elements seem to be important. First, learning environments must be designed based on principles and assumptions regarding learning. We need to know why we are doing certain things. Second, the assumptions should lead to methods and procedures which will ensure a certain degree of success. We need strategies for action that are likely to produce the changes we desire. This chapter will present principles and assumptions regarding learning based on the *behaviorist* influence in psychology. Several behavioral change methods and procedures based on these assumptions will be examined. This information should assist you in developing personal plans for behavioral change.

Behavioral Approach: Operant Conditioning

This approach to learning has its roots in the work of B. F. Skinner. It emphasizes how stimuli that follow our responses are able to control and influence them. Such stimuli are called *consequent stimuli,* and you are already familiar with them. Positive and negative reinforcers, described in Chapter 3, are examples of stimuli that follow our responses and help to control and maintain them. The responses such stimuli control are called *operants,* because they operate or produce effects in the environment. Operants are responses that we voluntarily emit. Familiar examples include selecting a television program, walking to a restaurant, and turning on a room air conditioner when we are hot.

Operants make up a large part of our daily responses. Have you ever thought about how we are able to learn such responses? This learning process is called *operant conditioning,* and four basic elements must be present for it to function. They are: (a) stimuli in the environment that help us know that certain responses will be reinforced, called *discriminative stimuli* (S^d); (b) a response that we can select to meet the demands of a situation; (c) an appropriate reinforcer that will increase the probability of the response's reoccurence; and (d) time to practice so that each of the first three components can become associated and the response can increase in frequency and accuracy.

To illustrate how these elements function in our lives, let us look at an experience I had as a five-year-old child. My father used to take me to the movies. Part of the treat for me was to eat popcorn or candy or to have a soft drink. On several occasions, in the middle of the movie I told my father I was thirsty. He did not want to leave the movie, so he gave me money to buy a soft drink. Unknown to my father, I initially did not know how to use the machine. It was a mystery to me. There were so many openings and buttons that I was not sure what to do. I dropped money into holes which led to the compressors. I pressed buttons without putting money in or after putting money into the wrong slots. On more than one occasion I had to settle for a drink of water. One day I hit the jackpot. I put money into a hole that was just the right size for it. I pushed a selection button and received a soft drink. That was one of life's memorable experiences for me. I was able to work the machine with hardly any errors after that.

Let us look at this experience in terms of the operant learning procedure mentioned earlier. The components are diagramed as follows:

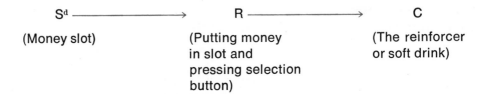

Initially I was faced with making the correct response sequence in the presence of quite a few openings and buttons in the machine. With practice, which cost me a little bit of money, I discovered that placing money in the slot designed for it was the first part of the correct response sequence. The money slot became a discriminative stimulus because it helped me to know that making a certain response in its presence would eventually lead to a reinforcer. (Other everyday examples of such stimuli include restaurants, movie theaters, or the building in which your favorite class is taught.) I had several responses that I selected to try to solve the problem of obtaining a soft drink. The only ones that worked were placing the money in the correct slot and then pushing the selection button. Obtaining a soft drink as a reinforcer did two things for me. It helped to increase the probability that I would repeat the same response sequence the next time. In addition, I learned which stimuli on the machine to pay attention to the next time I wanted a soft drink. In a similar way, eating a delicious meal, watching a good movie, and having an interesting class reinforce the behaviors of entering restaurants, buying movie tickets, and attending class, respectively. Reinforcers also teach us which stimuli (e.g., restaurants, movie theaters, classroom buildings) we must orient our behaviors toward to obtain additional reinforcers. Reinforcers help to develop and maintain a correct response, but they also help us focus our responding on those parts of our environments that are likely to lead to reinforcers.

We must have time to practice the correct responses in order to reduce our errors. How much time we need depends upon the difficulty of the response. Once the right sequence of events was discovered, the soft drink machine was easy to master. This is not the case with other operants. Playing golf, driving a car, and studying for exams are examples of operants that are not as easy to acquire.

Can you think of things you have learned through operant conditioning? Do you see examples of this type of learning in the classes you take, the sports you practice, the job skill you acquire?

Behavioral Approach: Operant Applications

During the last 20 years, methods for using operant conditioning principles to develop or modify behaviors have become very popular. These methods have been used in areas ranging from developing and changing skills associated with losing weight, reducing smoking, and improving studying to personal adjustment problems. This section will show you how to use such principles to acquire or modify a variety of behavioral skills. The process presented is simply an elaboration on the basic elements of operant conditioning presented in the last section.

1. *Identify specific target behaviors.* To modify behavior we need specific behavioral goals or outcomes that a change process will allow us to achieve. The behavioral goals or outcomes that we want to reach are called *target behaviors.* To begin to think about target behaviors, it is sometimes helpful to first state them in general terms. Friends and neighbors of mine have said to me that they wished they could "reduce their cigarette smoking," "lose some weight," or "play golf better." Colleagues of mine have often said they want their students to "learn the content," "have good attitudes," or "act creatively in the classroom." Such statements represent good ways to initiate thinking about behavioral changes we might want in ourselves or others. However, we need to elaborate on our thinking. Such statements are too general for us to design learning experiences that will allow us to achieve the changes. We must be more specific about how many cigarettes we want to stop smoking, how much weight we want to lose, and what content we want to be learned and to what degree. We might say, "I want to reduce my smoking by a total of ten cigarettes a week." "I need to lose fifteen pounds." "I want my students to be able to list ten famous events in history between 1800 and 1870."

EXERCISE 4-1: LISTING TARGET BEHAVIORS

Listed following this paragraph are five behaviors that a friend of mine wanted to achieve. Restate each one so that specific target behaviors are suggested. Since there is usually more than one way to achieve a general goal, try to generate two to three specific alternatives for each statement. I have done the first for you. Check your responses with those on page 112.

a. I need to be more sociable.
   I should hold a party at my house once a month.
   I need to have four friends over each week to watch television with me.
   I need to play cards with close friends three times a month.
b. I need to get more exercise.
c. I wish my son would not keep his room so messy.
d. I need to become better informed about current national news events.
e. I want people on my assembly line to reduce their absenteeism on work days.

To obtain a better understanding of the subsequent steps in this process, pick two behaviors that you want to modify. At least one of the two should represent a choice that you want to make in your own behavior. First state each target behavior in a general manner. Then make it as specific as you can. Try to consider two or three alternative ways to state specific target behaviors for each general goal.

---

2. *Identify how much of the target behavior currently exists.* Thinking about a specific goal obviously is our first step in acquiring a new behavior or modifying an existing one. Target behaviors indicate some alteration in our responses. To measure any change, we need information about the current state of our behavior. When we do this, we are gathering *baseline data.* Baseline data can answer such questions as: "How many cigarettes do I currently smoke?" "How many calories do I consume in a day?" "How far do I jog each day?" and "How much content do I require my students to learn about a particular topic?" Once we have this information, we can begin to monitor our progress toward achieving a target behavior. It gives us a performance level from which to monitor changes in our behavior.

How do we obtain baseline data? A good way to start is to keep records related to our target behavior. For behaviors that occur on a daily basis, it is helpful to keep such records for a period of five to seven days. In some instances, we may want to modify a behavior that occurs less frequently. It might be something that occurs in a weekly business meeting or social group. Baseline data should be obtained for one to three sessions or until you are satisfied you have assessed its normal occurrence. For example, if the problem relates to your use of "OK," "you know," or some other figure of speech at a weekly business meeting, you may need only one to three meetings to assess its frequency of occurrence adequately. The only time we do not need to gather baseline data is for a target behavior that you have never performed before.

What apsects of the behavior should we record? We are usually interested in how frequently a behavior occurs, how much time it takes, or the amount of something a behavior consumes. We might be interested in the number of cigarettes smoked per day, the time it takes to punt a football, or the amount of calories we consume at a meal. Depending upon our target behavior, we might want information on one or more of these measures. For example, I might want to modify both the number of textbooks I read daily and the time I spend reading each one.

Table 4-1 shows several formats for recording baseline data for some of the target behaviors listed in the answers to Exercise 4-1. Having examined these sample formats, design a baseline recording format for each of the behaviors that you identified earlier. *Please do not begin to record baseline data until you have read the rest of the chapter.*

3. *Try not to set target behavior goals that are too high.* A risk we run in attempting to change behavior is that we might fail. One of the causes of failing is a tendency to try to accomplish too much. There are two things we can do that will lessen the chances of our failing.

a. *Work with a single behavior.* Exercise 4-1 identified two or three specific target behaviors for each of the statements. We are usually confronted with alternative ways of obtaining our goals. Any one of the alternatives in Exercise 4-1 is probably desirable. It is difficult, however, to develop and use behavioral change plans for everything at the same time. It is much better to pick one alternative. An easy way to do this is mentally to rank order your alternatives in terms of importance. That is, you establish priorities among your options and select the one that is most important to you. For the two general behaviors you identified in Exercise 4-1, think of the specific targets you identified for each one. Select your most important specific target behavior in each case.

b. *Think of the specific behavior as composed of several interrelated units.* A mistake that is often made with even a single target behavior is to try to change all of it immediately. I might want to jog a mile each day. I might want my son to pick up all his toys each day. However, it is unlikely that I will be able to get either to happen all at once. I might look at the task of jogging as composed of 1/4-, 1/2-, and 3/4-mile subunits. Similarly, picking up 12 toys could have subunits of 3, 6, 9, and 12 toys. Being able to analyze a response into its component parts is important for the process of reinforcing behaviors. We will later examine how to reinforce behaviors using information about their components. For now, it is important that

---

---

you be able to analyze a response into reasonable subunits. Review the specific targets in Exercise 4-1. What are several components of each target? Do the same thing for the two personal target behaviors you selected in the last paragraph.

4. *Use positive reinforcement to change behavior.* Our goal in modifying behavior is to achieve a specific target behavior. Based on previous discussions, you are already aware of the important role that reinforcers play in our behavior. By reinforcing the occurrence of a target behavior, we will strengthen it. The research literature suggests that whenever possible we should use positive reinforcers to influence behavior.

Why should we stress the use of positive reinforcement? There are several things we ought to consider in answering this question. One is that the use of aversive stimuli as negative reinforcers or to punish behaviors can present legal, moral, and ethical issues. There is always the possibility of harming ourselves or someone else, particularly if strong aversive stimuli are used extensively. A few years ago, several of our prisons were criticized by authorities for the use of behavior modification principles based on negative reinforcement and punishment. In one case, Wayne Sage reports that prisoners were given the drug ampomorphine for lying or swearing. This drug induces uncontrollable vomiting for fifteen minutes to one hour. Do you think this is an appropriate way to influence desirable behavior? What are some feelings that prisoners are likely to have toward those trying to "help them" learn desirable behaviors?

Table 4-1

Recording Baseline Data Formats

Target Behavior: I need to spend three hours (180 minutes) per week in the library reading news magazines.

Recording Start Date: May 10

Current Level of Behavior:

	Day 1	Day 2	Day 3	Day 4	Day 5	Day 6	Day 7
Minutes reading	20	20	0	0	60	15	20

Target Behavior: I need to invite four friends over each week to watch sports events or the movies on television with me.

Recording Start Date: October 20

Current Level of Behavior:

	Day 1	Day 2	Day 3	Day 4	Day 5	Day 6	Day 7
Number of people whom I invite to watch television with me	0	0	0	1	0	1	0

Target Behavior: I want my son to pick up the toys in his room at the end of a day.

Recording Start Date: November 14

Current Level of Behavior:

	Day 1	Day 2	Day 3	Day 4	Day 5	Day 6	Day 7
Number of toys on floor at end of day	10	12	9	12	7	10	12

Target Behavior: I want people on my assembly line to reduce their absenteeism on workdays.

Recording Start Date: April 1

Current Level of Behavior:

	Week 1	Week 2	Week 3	Week 4	Week 5	Week 6	Week 7
Number of people absent per week	10	12	9	10	11	12	10

A second problem with aversive stimuli is that emotional reactions of anger, frustration, and anxiety are associated with them. Thus, we may find ourselves learning responses that allow us to avoid or escape from the stimuli that produce such reactions. However, this does not mean that we have learned a desirable response. More often than not, we learn to suppress temporarily the undesirable response or we learn behaviors that are on the border between desirable and undesirable. The following two examples illustrate these points.

A colleague of mine teaches a foreign language. He ridicules and harasses his students when they make a mistake. His philosophy is that the students will learn better when they are punished for their mistakes. The majority of students do not like this approach. They simply cut classes or withdraw from classroom activities (see the Avoidant student style in Chapter 3). His classes also have the smallest enrollment of any of the language classes. The development of this avoidance response is diagramed as follows:

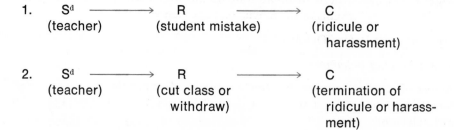

1. S^d ⟶ R ⟶ C
     (teacher)   (student mistake)   (ridicule or
                                            harassment)

2. S^d ⟶ R ⟶ C
     (teacher)   (cut class or   (termination of
                  withdraw)   ridicule or harass-
                                          ment)

As you can see, the first step in the development of an *avoidance response* is the use of a punishment procedure. Some students simply avoid punishment by not coming to class or by withdrawing from its activities. To be fair to my colleague, there are students who remain in the class and try to do well. They have learned to avoid the punishment by not making mistakes. Yet I have not met one of them who reported that he or she was comfortable in class. In varying degrees, they were afraid but decided to stick it out. Thus, the harassment and ridicule acted as a negative reinforcer to strengthen two different behaviors. Have you ever had similar reactions to a class?

Automobile manufacturers under pressure from the federal government began to install seat belts on cars. Several systems based on operant principles were designed to encourage people to use them. Initially, the manufacturers used a buzzer as a noxious stimulus to punish the behavior of not fastening the belts. The car would start but the buzzer remained on until you fastened the belt. You developed an *escape response* to the buzzer. This is diagramed:

   S^d ⟶   R ⟶   C ⟶   R ⟶   C
(seat belt)   (not fastening)   (loud buzzer)   (buckle belt)   (buzzer off)

Experience showed that people after one or two experiences with this system learned an avoidance response. They fastened their belts before starting the car. Unfortunately, more than a few simply fastened the belts and sat on them. To overcome this problem, the system was designed so that the car would not start and the buzzer would sound if the belt was unfastened. In order to ensure that they were fastened around our bodies, the belts had to be pulled out an appropriate distance before the system worked. Again humanity's creativity in the presence of aversive consequences rose to the occasion. Some people simply heeded the safety intentions of the system and fastened their belts. Others fastened them around the car door and window levers, had the system illegally disconnected at a service station, or wrote angry letters to members of Congress, senators, automobile manufacturing executives, and newspaper editors. Because of the latter efforts such interlock systems are no longer required by law.

When used on other people, aversive consequences do not necessarily initiate desirable behaviors. In addition to the effects we have discussed, they can produce problems in our interpersonal relationships. People are likely to rebel against us or reject us if we develop a long-term change plan using aversive consequences. In addition, they produce similar problems when used to modify our own behaviors. My experience is that people generally tire of behavioral change procedures and see them as less effective if they are based on aversive consequences. Overall, we are likely to be much better off if we use positive reinforcement.

5. *Select positive reinforcers that are likely to influence the behavior you want to change.* There are four types of positive reinforcement that we might consider employing. They occur through: (a) our social interactions with others, (b) the things we do to reduce our physiological needs, (c) the stimuli in our environments that we find attractive and pleasant, and (d) our ability to reinforce ourselves verbally. Examples of each type are presented in Table 4-2.

A reinforcer should be selected that is appropirate for the behavior you want to modify. No one reinforcer is likely to work in all situations. Praising people who work for us for getting reports finished on time can be effective. However, people still expect a paycheck for the overall job they do. Praise is unlikely to sustain their total job performance. Think about the two specific target behaviors you identified earlier. Select a positive reinforcer that you think is appropriate for each response.

6. *Reinforce a behavior immediately after it occurs.* The best time to use a positive reinforcer is immediately after the response occurs. The

Table 4-2

Examples of Four Types of Positive Reinforcement	
A. *Social*	
Approval of another person's behavior	"That was a nice job you did."
	"I appreciate the time and energy you took to do this."
Paying attention to another person	"That looks interesting; can you show me how it works?"
	"I'd like to have the other people see what you are doing."
Giving affection	"I like you."
	"Let's spend more time together."
B. *Physiological needs*	*Food:* potato chips, peanuts, pretzels, cookies, favorite meal.
	Liquids: water, soft drinks, beer, wine, milk shakes, ice cream sodas.
	Sex: sexual relations with another person.
C. *Pleasant or attractive environmental stimuli*	Going to a movie, attending a concert, sunbathing, taking a drive in the country, buying a new set of clothes.
D. *Verbal self-reinforcement*	"I did very well on that problem."
	"I think that I'm performing extremely well."
	"That was a neat thing I just did."
	"I'm really doing a good job."

association between a behavior and the reward is easily made at this time. Because of the task, however, a delay between the response and the reinforcer is sometimes desirable. A teacher may find it difficult to give each child an M&M candy every time he or she responds correctly. There may be too many who deserve a reward at the same time, or it might be close to lunch or dinner. In a similar way, I might want to reward myself with a soft drink after I jog a certain distance. It is possible that I might not be thirsty enough, or a soft drink may not be conveniently available. One way to deal with this problem is through the use of token rewards, or by simply keeping records of how many reinforcers have been earned. The teacher might give the students plastic chips, and I might simply keep a record of rewards I owe myself in a notebook. In this way, a symbolic reward is given immediately and the actual reinforcers can be obtained at a later time.

An example of such a system used in a colleague's classroom is shown in Table 4-3. Different classroom activities are assigned points, and the grade depends upon the number of points earned. Each activity is reinforced with a certain number of points when it is satisfactorily completed. The points are then "cashed in" for a grade at the end of the course.

Think about the two target behaviors you want to change. Is there any way the information about tokens, earning points, or record keeping can be used? If so, design a procedure for doing this. Why not have your instructor comment on it?

7. *Do not demand too much effort for too little reward.* Positive reinforcers are effective because we and other people derive certain benefits from them. Research shows that we assess these benefits against the effort it took us to obtain a reinforcer. William F. Whyte calls this the *cost/benefit ratio.* If the benefits the reward provides are not worth the effort (i.e., do not provide satisfaction) we are not likely to work for the reward. Giving an 11-year-old child a nickel every week for cleaning his room each day is probably expecting too much. The reward is not likely to be adequate. Any reward has to be worth our time and energy to pursue it. Failing to heed this principle often leads to failure in the use of positive reinforcers. Recently, a major credit card company offered $10,000 a year to a man they suspected of counterfeiting their cards. He was quite clever in hiding the evidence that could convict him. The man refused. He was apparently making $40,000 a year with the phony cards. Ten thousand dollars was simply not enough of an incentive for him to stop counterfeiting.

Answer the following questions for each of the two behaviors you wanted to influence.

1. What do you have to do or what does the other person (s) have to do to obtain a reinforcer?

Table 4-3

An Example of a Classroom Point System

Activity	Points Earned
90–100 on each exam	50
80–89 on each exam	40
70–79 on each exam	30
69–lower	0
Design and implement a laboratory project.	50
Design a laboratory project.	20
Write a book report on as many outside reading books as you want.	20 each report
Run a class session on a special topic.	40
Write a term paper.	50
Classroom attendance.	2
Points needed for a grade.	A = 350 or above
	B = 275–349
	C = 220–274
	D = No Ds or Fs given. Each student must earn at least a C.

2. How would you assess the amount of work needed to obtain a reinforcer in relation to its value? Try to imagine yourself performing the response.
   a. The reinforcer is probably inadequate.
   b. The reinforcer is probably adequate.
   c. The reinforcer is probably too much for the response.
3. If the reinforcer is inadequate or too much for the response required, what adjustments do you need to make?

   8. *When first beginning to change a behavior, reinforce each successive approximation to your target behavior.* In Chapter 3, we saw that learning takes place gradually over time. A change in behavior is seldom completely

correct the first time we or someone else tries it. A reinforcer may be adequate for the target behavior, but we need not wait until the complete response occurs before reinforcing it. Components of the total response should be rewarded. This helps develop the target behavior because each of our little successes is reinforced. This process is called *shaping* a behavior.

Let us review three approaches we can take to shaping a response. Point 3.b. in this chapter examined possible subunits associated with our target behavior. To learn the target behavior, each subunit should be reinforced until it is mastered. Jogging a mile might be viewed as composed of ¼-, ½-, and ¾-mile subunits. I would reinforce myself with the total reinforcer each time I completed a component of the target behavior. I would allow myself a soft drink for jogging one quarter of a mile or some other appropriate subunit in the sequence of responses. When I had mastered that unit, I would reinforce myself only after I completed the next unit. I might then earn a soft drink only after jogging one half of a mile. One method for shaping a response is simply to give a reinforcer for mastery of a subunit. Obtaining further reinforcement then depends upon mastering the next component.

A second way to shape a behavior is to administer a portion of the total reinforcer for completing a part of the target behavior. The point system in Table 4-3 is one example of this method. The instructor is interested in shaping everyone's behavior to at least a C grade. For those who desire a higher grade, each of their successes toward the better grade is reinforced. A target behavior of a child picking up his toys each day might also be shaped using this technique. I might get the child to agree to pick up his toys each day for a total reward of 84 cents per week. If four toys are typically left lying around, he would receive three cents per day for each toy. The money could be given immediately, or tokens could be used or records kept for the week. With this system, we must be careful that the part of the total reward received is seen as worth the effort expended. A good test of this point is whether your system is producing the desired result.

A third way to shape a target behavior is to reinforce and learn the final response in a sequence of related actions before we reinforce and learn the earlier responses. This procedure is often used by animal trainers. I am sure you have seen animals perform tricks on television or at a circus. Recently I saw a chicken receive a reward only after it entered the stage, climbed a platform, opened a door, walked into a cage, rang a bell, walked to a small flagpole, and pulled a string to raise a flag. This is a very complicated set of responses for a chicken to learn. To teach this trick, the trainer first reinforced the chicken for pulling a string until it learned to raise the flag. Next it was rewarded for learning to walk between the bell and the flagpole. Then it was rewarded only after walking from the bell and pulling the string on the flagpole. All the other parts of the trick were taught in a similar fashion. Eventually the bird was reinforced only after the entire sequence was correctly performed.

For certain responses this procedure is often helpful. In toilet training young children, the first thing to reinforce and learn would be to sit for a few minutes on the "potty." Normally this is the last response in the sequence of using a toilet. The children would then be taught to pull their pants down and to sit on the toilet. Eventually each aspect of the sequence of notifying a parent, walking to the bathroom, undressing, and sitting on the potty is reinforced. Remember that all this training is achieved by reinforcing and learning responses later in the sequence first. How would you use this method to teach a young child to dress? How could you use this method to teach a worker to assemble an automobile engine or typewriter? Can you think of other responses for which the procedure might be appropriate?

Review point 3.b., where you listed the subunits of your target behavior. Take the reinforcer that you decided to use for each behavior in point 5 and develop a system for shaping the subunits of your target behavior. Why not check your plan with your instructor?

9. *Once the target behavior is acquired, a shift from continuous reinforcement should be made.* Obtaining a reinforcer each time we complete a target behavior is not always practical or possible in our daily lives. We initially continuously reinforce behaviors because they are then learned more quickly. Our goal should be to bring the behavior under self-control or under the influence of reinforcers that occur naturally in our environments, or both. That is, we might continue jogging because it makes us feel good or because other people admire us for being athletic. The child needs to clean his room because it is his household responsibility or it makes his parents happy. At some point, we need to stop performing a behavior only to acquire a soft drink or to earn money.

It is not recommended that you abruptly stop using the reinforcer. When this is done, *extinction* is likely to occur. Withdrawing a reinforcer on a permanent basis often leads to a cessation of the response. This is particularly true if the behavior is still under the control of the reinforcer.

It is much better to change the reinforcement schedule so that a reward is obtained on a less-than-continuous basis. Such schedules are called *intermittent reinforcement schedules.* We are quite able to continue responding if we learn that we can expect to receive a reward at least occasionally. Most of us get paid on an hourly or weekly basis, but we do not directly receive the money in our hands each day or week. We may learn to expect it once every two weeks or at the end of the month. Switching to an intermittent schedule decreases the chances that extinction will occur. It helps maintain the response and allows self-control or the influence of other natural reinforcers to develop.

Psychologists have developed several methods for giving reinforcers on a less-than-continuous basis. They are based on reinforcing behaviors after certain time intervals or after a certain number of responses. Those based on time are called *interval schedules* and those based on a certain number of responses are called *ratio schedules*. Each is described in Table 4-4, along with several everyday examples of its use.

When shifting to an intermittent schedule, it is best to do so gradually. If I wanted to use a fixed ratio schedule, I might first use it so that 75 or 80 percent of my responses were still reinforced. Once an adjustment was made to this schedule, I could increase the number of responses needed for a reinforcer. The important point is not to shift too rapidly to a schedule that produces only a few reinforcers.

Think about each of the two target behaviors you selected. Imagine that each one has been learned. It is now time to switch to an intermittent schedule. For each behavior determine what type of schedule you will use and how you will start the schedule. Why not check your responses with a classmate or your instructor?

10. *Monitor and record on a daily basis the behavior you are interested in acquiring or modifying.* Earlier in this chapter, we examined several ways to record baseline data. Not only baseline data are important; we need to record our progress toward achieving a target behavior as well. Behavioral changes take time, and monitoring our progress will allow us to assess if our plan is working. We can then determine what, if any, adjustments should be made. To keep such records, you need only extend in time the procedure you used for the baseline data. A suggested way to do this appears in Table 4-5.

A little common sense is applicable here. There may be responses that are difficult for us to keep monitoring alone. A friend of mine wanted to improve his golf swing. He had determined that the length of his backswing, the position of his wrists, and his hip movement needed to be corrected. He could not monitor his movements and still swing the club. Monitoring only made things worse. He solved the problem by asking one of his playing partners to watch each component for him. He was then able to keep accurate records. There may be times when another person can assist us in monitoring our behaviors.

Based on our discussion to this point, develop a recording procedure for monitoring and recording your progress toward achieving each target behavior.

Table 4-4

Common Reinforcement Schedules

Continuous:	A reinforcer is given each time a response occurs. It is the fastest way to establish a response.
Fixed Ratio:	A reinforcer is given after a certain number of responses occur. Examples include getting salary based on producing a fixed number of units of a product on an assembly line or a sales bonus based on the number of units sold. If the number of responses needed to obtain a reinforcer is high, a pause in an individual's responding will occur after the reward is given. To eliminate such pauses, the number of responses required for a reinforcer should be kept low. Think about what happens to your studying behavior immediately after an exam. The decrease most students experience is an example of the pause.
Variable Ratio:	A reinforcer is given after a variable number of responses. That is, an individual may receive a reinforcer for every tenth, fifteenth, or twentieth response. In laboratory situations, attempts are made to give the reinforcer for an average number of responses (e.g., an average of every tenth response). In our daily lives we encounter variable ratio schedules when we play golf, poker, or slot machines. Every response is not reinforced, nor is the reinforcement given after a predetermined number of responses. A high-handicap golfer usually has few "rewarding" shots. Their occurrence is somewhat erratic since it is hard to predict when a good shot will be made.
Fixed Interval:	A reinforcer is given after a fixed interval of time, provided the response has occurred at least once during that interval. This can be hourly, weekly, or even monthly. Your pay at work and the grades you receive in school occur on a fixed interval schedule. People tend to increase their responding just before the reinforcer is given and to decrease it afterward (e.g., cramming before an exam and relaxing afterward).
Variable Interval:	A reinforcer is given after variable intervals of time. As with the variable ratio schedule, the reinforcer is obtained after an average interval of time (e.g., an average of every 10 minutes). This is not a typical schedule for human beings. An instructor who gives "pop quizzes" is using a variable interval schedule.

Behavioral Approach: Classical Conditioning

This approach to learning had its beginnings in the work of Ivan Pavlov and John Watson. It emphasizes how certain stimuli which precede our responses are able automatically to cause them to be emitted and to control them. Such stimuli are called *antecedent stimuli.* Your mouth watering at the sight of food, closing your eyes when a gust of wind hits your face, and removing your hand from a hot burner are examples of behaviors that are automatically controlled by antecedent stimuli. The responses such stimuli control are called *respondents,* because they occur in direct response to these stimuli. Our reflexes and emotional responses fall into this category. Examples of respondents you are familiar with include your mouth watering, blinking your eyes, removing your hand from a hot burner, and feelings of anger, fear, and love.

Most respondents occur to stimuli that we would normally expect to elicit them (e.g., food, hot burners, sharp objects). However, there are occasions when such responses occur to stimuli which do not, under normal conditions, elicit them. A recent experience of mine illustrates this last point. I recently stepped, in my bare feet, on a needle embedded in the rug of my living room. I shouted out in pain and was somewhat anxious because the needle was stuck in my foot. Both the pain and the fear responses were directly elicited by the needle. However, for a few days after that experience, I was cautious and felt somewhat anxious whenever I stepped on the rug. Why should the rug, which previously had no unpleasant feelings associated with it, cause me to act anxiously?

Table 4-5

A Record-Keeping Format

Target Behavior: I need to spend 3 hours (180 minutes) per week in the library reading newsmagazines.

		Days							
		1	2	3	4	5	6	7	Total
Recording Start Date: May 10									
Reinforcement Began: May 17	5/10	20	20	0	0	60	15	20	135
Type of Reinforcer: For	5/17	20	0	30	60	20	0	20	150
every 30 minutes of reading, I will be able to eat a	5/26	20	10	30	50	30	0	20	160
favorite snack (e.g., ice cream cone, cola, or potato chips).	6/2	30	20	30	30	30	20	0	160
	6/9	30	30	30	20	30	20	0	160
	6/16	30	30	30	30	30	30	0	180
Minutes reading	6/23	30	30	30	20	30	20	20	180

Target Behavior: I want people on my assembly line to reduce their absenteeism on work days by 50 percent.

		Weeks							
		1	2	3	4	5	6	7	Total
Recording Start Date: April 1									
Reinforcement Began: May 15	4/1	10	12	9	10	11	12	10	74
Type of Reinforcer: A	5/27	9	9	8	8	6	5	5	50
lottery will be held at the end of each week. A	7/1	7	8	8	9	6	6	6	50
$25.00 prize will be given to the winning five-digit	8/19	8	8	7	7	8	4	4	46
number. Each day a worker gets a number	10/9	6	6	6	5	5	6	6	40
as he or she shows up for work.	11/29	5	5	6	5	6	5	6	38
Number of people absent per week.	1/28	5	6	5	5	5	6	5	37

A learning process called *classical conditioning* can help us understand how this and other respondents develop to stimuli that do not normally elicit them. There are three basic stages to learning a response in this manner. Each stage is diagramed in the steps that follow.

1. A stimulus that naturally elicits the response is identified. The stimulus is called an *unconditioned stimulus* or *UCS*. The response is called the *unconditioned response* or *UCR*.

    UCS —————————→ UCR
    (needle)   (pain/anxiety)

2. A neutral stimulus is then associated with the UCS. This neutral stimulus is called a *conditioned stimulus* or *CS*. The two are paired together a number of times.

    CS
    (rug)

          UCS —————————→ UCR
          (needle)   (pain/anxiety)

3. Through association with the UCS, the CS begins to elicit a response that is similar to the UCR. This response is called a *conditioned response* or *CR*. A CR is not necessarily the same response as a UCR. It may differ in degree or it may represent one part of a more complicated UCR. In this example, I did not experience the pain when stepping on the rug but it did make me feel anxious.

    CS —————————→ CR
    (rug)   (anxiety)

EXERCISE 4-2: CLASSICAL CONDITIONING COMPONENTS

As a test of your understanding of classical conditioning, complete the three-stage process for the development of the following response. Label the CS, UCS, UCR, and CR in each example. Check your answers with those on page 128.

Situation: An eleven-month-old child is playing with a toy near an electrical outlet. He sticks part of the toy into the outlet. He gets shocked, becomes frightened, and begins to cry. For several days after that experience, he shows fear when his mother gives him the toy and he refuses to play with it.

```
1.  UCS ─────────────>          UCR
    (      )                    (      )

2.  CS
    (      )

        UCS                     UCR
        (      )                (      )

3.  CS                          CR
    (      )                    (      )
```

Can you think of something you learned through classical conditioning? Have you ever observed someone else learn a response through this procedure?

Behavioral Approach: Respondent Applications

The observation that many of our emotional responses develop through classical conditioning has led to several practical applications. To understand one such application, we must first understand *stimulus generalization*. Stimulus generalization occurs when a stimulus that has characteristics in common with the conditioned stimulus (CS) elicits a similar reaction. An early example of stimulus generalization and its effect on an emotional response was described by John Watson. An eleven-month-old boy showed no fear of animals. However, he was afraid of loud noises. A white rat was paired with the loud noise using the same procedures we have described. Eventually, the rat, when presented alone to the boy, elicited a reaction similar to that of the noise. The boy acted afraid and cried when it was presented. His fear, however, was not confined to the rat. Any white furry object, including the sight of a rabbit and the white beard on a man, had the same effect.

Fortunately, such reactions to similar stimuli do not last forever. What makes them lessen or disappear leads us to a practical application. To understand this application better, consider what happened to a close friend and to my son. My friend once fell off the roof of his house. Not only did subsequent experiences on his roof cause anxiety, but he felt uneasy and anxious above the ground floor of any building for some time after that experience. My son learned that a frown on my face meant that I was feeling angry with him. Unfortunately, because of her facial muscles and bone structure, his first teacher in school constantly had such an expression. For several weeks, he was very concerned that his teacher was angry with him.

Both had emotional reactions that generalized from the stimulus that originally caused them.

Both my friend and son eventually lost their reactions to the other stimuli. They did this by associating positive reactions to the upper floors of buildings and the teacher, respectively. My friend made several big sales on the upper floors of office buildings. My son enjoyed the activities the teacher provided. Pleasant emotions were learned to be associated with the stimuli that originally produced unpleasant reactions. In principle, the same process should work with the original stimulus as well. My friend would relax on his roof if he could have several uneventful experiences there. My son would not fear my frown if he had several pleasant experiences with me when I had such an expression.

Joseph Wolpe developed a procedure for losing our fears based on learning a more pleasant emotion to the fear-producing situation. This process is called *systematic desensitization*. The components of desensitization to reduce a response of fear include: (a) a situation that normally produces the reaction, (b) stimuli associated with the original situation that produce the reaction to a lesser degree, (c) the ability to form images of each stimulus, and (d) the learning of a response to each image that is more pleasant than fear.

One pleasant response that can be associated to fear-producing stimuli is our ability to relax. Edmund Jacobson showed that it is relatively easy to learn to relax, and he developed a number of procedures for helping people

Answers to Exercise 4-2

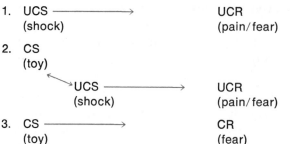

1. UCS ⎯⎯⎯⎯⎯⎯→   UCR
    (shock)   (pain/fear)

2. CS
    (toy)
    ⟋ UCS ⎯⎯⎯⎯⎯⎯→   UCR
        (shock)   (pain/fear)

3. CS ⎯⎯⎯⎯⎯⎯→   CR
    (toy)   (fear)

Note that the UCR to shock is a combination of pain and fear. The CR does not have the pain component.

---

to do so. Systematic desensitization uses relaxation as the response that is then associated to the fear-producing images.

To see how this process works, let us assume that you and I fear a final examination in an American history course. We are sure that despite our studying, we will not do well. The professor has a reputation as a hard grader and asks tough questions. Our initial step is to list in writing the things we fear associated with the exam. Our goal is to form a hierarchy which begins with some event or situation associated with the exam that is neutral and then proceed to list in order those that we most fear. An example of such a list appears in Table 4-6. List any other items that you think might be included and indicate where they would fall in the hierarchy.

Having listed our hierarchy, we would desensitize our fear by learning

Table 4-6

A Hierarchy for Desensitizing a Fear of a Final Exam

1. Reading about the American history course in the college catalog.
2. Standing in line to register for the course.
3. Sitting in class the first day.
4. Reading the syllabus containing the reading assignments and final exam date.
5. Listening to the professor announce the date of the final exam in class.
6. Seeing a copy of the grade distribution from last year's final.
7. Sitting in your room studying for the exam.
8. Walking to class the day of the final.
9. Entering the classroom.
10. Watching the professor pass out the exams.
11. Reading the questions on the exam.
12. Writing answers to the questions.

to relax while thinking about each event or situation. Relaxing is a response that is opposite to our normal association of fear to these stimuli. To carry out this procedure, we need a comfortable setting where we can lie down. A bed, couch, or soft rug is perfectly adequate. A suggested procedure for relaxation is presented in Table 4-7. Once relaxed, we would form an image of the first, neutral event in our list. This helps to get us started. We would think about it for 15 to 30 seconds. We then form an image of the least feared event or situation on the list. We continue to do this until we are comfortable thinking about it. We then move to the next item in our hierarchy. If at any time we feel the slightest fear, we should back up to an image that involves no fear at all. We should repeat this procedure until we can work through the hierarchy without any fear. It is best to spend 20 to 30 minutes per day performing this task. Research shows that over time, people are able to face and cope with the actual situation better having first used a desensitization procedure.

Systematic desensitization is used to reduce an emotional reaction. However, there may be situations in which we need to increase the range of our emotional reactions. Friends and acquaintances occasionally tell me that they seem to feel emotionless when they ought to be happy, sad, or delighted about some event. Often they are too tired, feeling depressed, or thinking about other things and cannot really get involved in a situation. My next door neighbor was recently promoted. The night before his boss gave him the good news, he worked on his income tax return until 4 A.M. Consequently, he was tired and haggard looking when he met with his boss. All he could say was a tired "Thank you." His boss asked him several times

---

EXERCISE 4-3: PRACTICING RELAXATION AND DESENSITIZATION

To test your understanding of the concepts we have discussed, please do the following.

a. Practice the relaxation procedure suggested in Table 4-6. Did it help you to relax? What modifications might you make to meet your own preferences for becoming relaxed?

b. Pick a situation in your own life that you are afraid of or that makes you anxious. Develop a hierarchy similar to the one in Table 4-7. Once you have established the critical events or situations in your list, put each item on a separate sheet of paper or an index card.

c. Try the desensitization procedure for 10 days. At the end of that time, try to think about what value it has for you. Could it be used for other emotional reactions (e.g., controlling anger to certain stimuli)? With what types of fears is it likely not to be helpful?

Table 4-7

A Suggested Procedure for Relaxing

1. Select a quiet area where you can lie down. Lie in a comfortable position on your back. Place your hands at your sides. Close your eyes and take a deep breath slowly.

2. Clench the fist of your preferred hand. Increase the tension in your arm as much as you can. Think about how this feels. Concentrate on your arm. Now, relax your arm and let your fingers straighten out.

3. Repeat the same procedure with your other hand.

4. Take a deep breath and exhale slowly. Make your body feel as limp as you can.

5. Place your hands on the surface you are lying on. Push down as hard as you can. Concentrate on your hands, chest, and back, as these are the areas you will feel tension in. Notice the tension in both arms. Relax your arms so that the tension is released. Repeat this step once.

6. Take a deep breath and exhale slowly. Make your body feel as limp as you can.

7. Frown and close your eyes as tightly as you can. Think about how tight your face feels. Hold this expression for five seconds and then relax. Repeat this step once.

8. Take a deep breath and exhale slowly. Make your body feel as limp as you can.

9. Clench your teeth as hard as you can. Concentrate on the tension in your jaws. Do this for five seconds and then relax. Repeat this procedure once.

10. Take a deep breath and exhale slowly. Make your body feel as limp as you can.

11. Shrug your shoulders until you feel the tension in the top of your shoulder and the back and sides of your neck. Think about the tension you feel and hold this for five seconds. Relax and repeat this procedure once.

12. Take a deep breath and exhale slowly. Make your body feel as limp as you can.

13. Tighten the muscles in your stomach. Hold them in this position for five seconds and then relax them. Repeat this procedure once.

14. Take a deep breath and exhale slowly. Make your body feel as limp as you can.

15. Tighten the muscles in your legs and concentrate on the tight feelings in your leg muscles. Increase the tension and hold it for five seconds. Repeat this procedure once.

16. Take a deep breath and exhale slowly. Make your body feel as limp as you can.

17. Breathe regularly and try to relax each part of your body. Think about your legs, stomach, arms, shoulders, neck, face, and jaws as you do this. Imagine that all the tensions are leaving your body. Try to stay completely inactive for one to two minutes.

18. Begin to think about the first item in the hierarchy.

that day if he was feeling all right or if he (the boss) had done something to make him look so depressed. A colleague of mine was angry at a student for missing class. He called the student into his office and said in a low monotone with no expression on his face, "I'm not happy with your class attendance." The student remarked to me later that my colleague was not very convincing about his concern for the student's absence.

People often expect certain reactions from us. When we do not deliver, they may wonder if we really appreciate them, if we really mean what we say, or about any number of other concerns that can affect our relationships. A technique for eliciting a broader range of emotions based on respondent principles was developed at the Actors' Studio by Lee Strasberg, its director. Michael Schulman reports that actors are taught to use certain stimuli so that, on cue, they will give a proper emotional response. The Actors' Studio teaches people to give a response by forming an image of a situation that would elicit the reaction. If a fear reaction is needed, they might imagine a deadly snake crawling up their arm. To act joyful, they might imagine the most pleasant event in their life. Images are used as stimuli to elicit an emotional response.

There are probably times when you and I need to increase the range of reactions in how we are feeling. I recently used this technique when an uncle visited my home and gave me a new watch unexpectedly. I had not seen him in years and he was never known for his generosity, so I was quite surprised by the gift. However, I also knew he would be disappointed if I did not show my appreciation. Having accepted the gift, I formed an image of a shower of money filling my living room. This made me feel quite delighted, and I expressed my delight by commenting on the new watch.

EXERCISE 4-4: ELICITING EMOTIONAL RESPONSES

To try this technique, do the following exercises in front of a mirror. If you are satisfied with the results, try using the procedures in one or two situations in your life.

a. Think about a situation involving another person in the last month in which you were *not satisfied* with the feelings you expressed. Face the mirror and pretend that the other person is looking at you. React as you remember that you did.

b. Form an image of a situation or stimulus that would allow you to react with the feelings you wanted to express. For example, if you were angry at that individual, imagine that person breaking a favorite possession of yours or think about some other event in your life when you were angry. If you were happy, form an image of a situation involving that person or someone else when you were happy. Perhaps it was the first formal dance you attended.

131

c. Look at the mirror and replay the situation. This time use some of the reactions that you would make to the image you formed. How do you think you came across this time? Was it better than the first time you did this? Did you seem unnatural or was your reaction phony?

d. The next time you are in a situation in which you have to express an emotion, try this technique and assess its effects on yourself and other people.

SUMMARY

Each one of us has wanted to change some aspect of our own or someone else's behavior. This must be done in ways that are helpful and that do not harm or embarrass ourselves or others. To do this well, learning environments must be designed that are based on sound principles and assumptions regarding learning. A behaviorist orientation to learning provides one type of system for modifying behavior.

Behaviorism emphasizes observable stimuli and responses as the basic units of behavior. Stimuli are seen as controlling our responses. Behaviorists differ, however, on how stimuli produce their effects. Some, like Ivan Pavlov and John Watson, emphasized how stimuli that precede certain responses control and influence them. Others, like B. F. Skinner, have placed the control and influence of behavior on stimuli that occur after a response. Stimuli that precede a behavior are termed antecedent stimuli. The responses they elicit are called respondents. Our emotions and reflexes are examples of respondents. Stimuli that occur after a response are called consequent stimuli. Reinforcers are examples of consequent stimuli which control our behavior. The responses such stimuli influence are called operants. Operants are the daily behaviors that we voluntarily choose to make.

Respondents can occur to stimuli that do not normally elicit them. A learning procedure called classical conditioning is used to explain their elicitation by previously neutral stimuli. A stimulus that naturally elicits the response is identified. The stimulus is called an unconditioned stimulus (UCS) and the response an unconditioned response (UCR). An example would be the smell of food eliciting a salivation response. A previously neutral stimulus is associated with the UCS. This could be a bell, a table or chair, or a cookbook. This neutral stimulus is called a conditioned stimulus (CS). The CS and UCS are presented together a number of times. When the CS is subsequently presented alone, it will elicit a response similar to the UCR. Salivating at the sound of the bell, the sight of the table or chair, or the sight of the cookbook is an example of a conditioned response (CR).

Operant conditioning is used to describe how an operant is acquired. We learn to associate responses we make in the presence of particular stimuli as leading to a reinforcer. Discriminative stimuli (S^d) are stimuli that signal that a particular action will lead to a reinforcer. The money slot on a vending machine signals that a response of placing money in it will be reinforced with something to eat or drink. The reinforcer is a consequent stimulus that increases the chance that we will repeat the response in the future. Operant conditioning involves acquiring through practice the relationships among a discriminative stimulus, a response we initiate, and a reinforcer.

A 10-stage process for applying operant principles includes the following components.

1. Identification of specific goals or target behaviors.
2. Recording how much of the target behavior currently exists.
3. Working with a single behavior and thinking of it as composed of several interrelated units.
4. Using positive reinforcement to change behavior rather than relying on negative reinforcement or punishment.
5. Selecting a positive reinforcer that is likely to influence the behavior you want to change.
6. Reinforcing a behavior immediately after it occurs.
7. Not demanding too much effort for too little reward.
8. Reinforcing each successive approximation to the target behavior.
9. Shifting from continuous reinforcement once the target behavior is acquired.
10. Monitoring and recording the behavior we are interested in acquiring or modifying as we use a behavioral change plan.

Since our emotional responses develop through respondent procedures, two applications of this information are possible. A process called systematic desensitization allows us to reduce an emotional reaction like fear to a situation. It involves learning to relax while we think of situations which lead up to and include the stimulus we fear. We condition a reaction that is the opposite of being afraid to these stimuli. This allows us to unlearn our feeling afraid. It is also possible to increase the range of our emotional responding. A technique to train actors to elicit an emotional response on cue is often helpful. An image is formed of a stimulus or situation that would normally elicit the desired emotion for us. We then use the reactions we would have to the image to enhance our actions in the real situation.

THINGS TO DO

1. Let your imagination run wild. Pretend that you are in absolute control of your school. Students, professors, and administrators will do whatever you tell them to do. Design a college environment that is based on principles associated with operant and respondent learning. Pay particular attention to such things as: (a) faculty salary schedules, (b) grades that students receive, (c) discipline problems, (d) classroom organization, (e) administrative organization, and (f) graduation requirements.

2. Based on what you know about classical conditioning and stimulus generalization, how would you explain (a) why a teenage boy blushes whenever he sees a girl whom he likes and (b) a child showing a fear of any appliance that has an electrical cord showing.

3. There is a tendency for some people to feel that they are "bribing" another person when they use positive reinforcers. "I'm not going to bribe them to get what I want" is something more than a few parents, teachers, and business managers have said. Based on your understanding of information in this chapter, how would you respond to someone who said that?

4. How would you use operant learning principles discussed in the text to (a) get shoppers to return shopping carts when they take groceries to their cars, (b) get people to use parking meters at the end of a block rather than in the middle, (c) increase the number of people who use a mass transit system, (d) encourage married couples to have no more than two children, (e) reduce the number of people who are on welfare, (f) get readers of an advertisement to send in names of possible people who might be contacted by a salesperson to buy a product?

5. Think about the classes you have taken this term. What are several examples of respondent and operant behaviors that occur in your classroom? Which behaviors tend to facilitate the teaching/learning process and which impede it?

REFERENCES AND OTHER INTERESTING THINGS TO READ

CLAIBORNE, R. Behavior modification and its positive aspects. *The New York Times,* April 28, 1974.

ESTES, W. K. Reinforcement in human behavior. *American Scientist,* 1972, *60,* 723–729.

HAMBLIN, R. L., BUCKHOLT, D., BUSHELL, D., ELLIS, D., and FERRITOR, D. Changing the game from "get the teacher" to "learn." *Trans-action,* 1969, *6,* No. 3, 20–25.

JACOBSON, E. *Self-Operations Control.* Philadelphia: J. P. Lippincott, 1964.

LICHTENSTEIN, E.   How to quit smoking. *Psychology Today,* January, 1971.

MCINTIRE, R. W.   *For Love of Children: Behavioral Psychology for Parents.* Del Mar, Calif.: CRM Books, 1970.

MILLER, G. A.   Ivan Petrovich Pavlov—Physiologist.   In Michael Merbaum and George Stricken (Eds.), *Search for Human Understanding: A Reader in Psychology.*   New York: Holt, Rinehart and Winston, 1971.

PAVLOV, I. P.   *Essential Works.*   New York: Bantam Books, 1966.

SAGE, W.   Crime and the clockwork lemon. *Human Behavior,* September, 1974.

SCHULMAN, M.   Backstage behaviorism. *Psychology Today,* June, 1973.

SKINNER, B. F.   Operant behavior. *American Psychologist,* 1963, *18,* 503–515.

SKINNER, B. F.   Teaching science in high school: What is wrong? *Science, 159,* 704–710.

WATSON, D. L., and THARP, R. G.   *Self-directed behavior: Self-modification for Personal Adjustment.*   Monterey, Calif.: Brooks/Cole, 1972.

WATSON, J. B.   *Behaviorism.*   New York: Norton, 1930.

WATSON, J. B., and RAYNER, R.   Conditioned emotional reactions. *Journal of Experimental Psychology,* 1920, *3,* 1–14.

WHYTE, W. F.   Skinnerian theory in organizations. *Psychology Today,* April, 1972.

WILLIAMS, R. L., and LONG, J. D.   *Toward a Self-Managed Life Style.*   Boston: Houghton Mifflin, 1975.

WOLPE, J.   *The Practice of Behavior Therapy.*   New York: Pergamon Press, 1969.

CHAPTER AIMS

A. **After reading this chapter, the reader should be able to explain:**

1. The role of needs, values, and attitudes in guiding and directing our behaviors.

2. The way that Abraham Maslow has organized the types of needs that influence our behaviors.

3. Why certain of our basic physiological and safety needs must be met before we can attempt to satisfy other needs.

4. How our needs for achievement, affiliation, and power influence our behaviors.

5. How the stories we write reflect some of our needs and motives.

6. Why information about achievement, affiliation, and power motives can help us predict the likelihood that nations will go to war or experience an economic recovery, or the things that people are likely to die from.

7. The way our personal values influence some of our personal preferences and our goals, perceptions, and emotions.

8. One way we can distinguish between a value and an attitude.

9. Two reasons our attitudes do not always appear in our actions.

10. How information about cognitive dissonance, social pressure, and our needs can help us understand changes in our attitudes.

B. **The reader should be able to use the information:**

1. To work the exercises in the chapter.

2. To understand better the reasons for the types of activities and goals that are pursued in people's daily lives.

5

Needs, Values, Attitudes, and Our Behavior

GLOSSARY

Achievement need. A learned need that is characterized by behaviors directed toward becoming successful, performing better than others, and trying to accomplish something unique.

Affiliation need. A learned need that is characterized by behaviors directed toward forming friendships and working closely with other people.

Attitude. A relatively durable organization of thoughts and positive and negative feelings toward specific objects and situations. The statements "I like late movies on television," "I think that Ed will make a good presidential candidate," and "I like instant coffee" are examples of attitudes.

Cognitive dissonance. A state of tension or displeasure caused when we receive information that disagrees with an attitude we have or when we behave in ways that are contrary to it. A smoker who reads an article on the dangers of cigarette smoking is likely to experience dissonance. Similarly, a person who is asked to debate the positive aspects of some topic he or she is basically negative toward will experience dissonance.

Need. A lack or deficit of factors within us. It is often used as a synonym for motive. Our needs may have a physiological base (e.g., needs for water and food) or they may be learned (e.g., needs for recognition, status).

Personality. The organization of the various characteristics which describe each of us.

Power need. A learned need that is characterized by behaviors which reflect a high degree of interest in controlling and influencing other people and in competing with others.

Projective test. A device for measuring some of our personal characteristics. It requires us to react to stimuli which are actually neutral or ambiguous. Consequently, the interpretations that we give must reflect some of our personal attitudes, values, and needs.

Reactance. A tendency to resist the attempts of other people to modify our thoughts or behaviors by thinking or behaving just the opposite of how they want us to. Relates to our need to maintain our personal freedom and options and to resist attempts to take such things away from us.

Self-actualization need. Identified by Abraham Maslow as the highest-order human need. It is characterized by behaviors that have a personal growth focus and that allow the individual to extend interests beyond those of ordinary, everyday experiences.

Values. The important and stable ideas, beliefs, and assumptions that underlie and are observed in our behaviors across a number of different situations. They represent the general ideals that we strive to meet in our life, such as collaboration, creativity, dignity, and justice.

Our Needs, Values, and Attitudes Are Personal Characteristics Which Help Guide and Direct Our Behaviors

After a bank robbery, several people talked to newspaper reporters. This is what they said:

BANK GUARD: I saw the whole thing. He came into the bank, pulled this gun out and shouted, "This is a robbery." He then had the tellers fill a laundry bag with money. I've seen two other robberies in my career at the bank and this one was no different. You could almost see the greed in his eyes as he left the bank with the money. The manager told me that he probably had it in for us since we refused to give him a loan several weeks ago.

MOTHER OF THE ACCUSED: Jim has had a lot of tough things happen to him lately. He has been unable to find work for the past nine months. He has a wife and three children to support and it's tough to do. He didn't see welfare as any help because they never gave him enough money to live on. I think he was really hurt that he was unable to provide for his family.

MINISTER: I've known Jim and his family for 15 years. He has always been a law-abiding citizen. This is the first time he has ever done anything outside the law. I don't think he was simply looking out after his own interests in robbing the bank. Jim has always been unselfish and that helps to explain why he gave about half of what he took to families that were worse off than he was. To understand that action, you have to see that he is basically a decent person who made one big mistake in his life.

POLICE OFFICER: I've never met a person like him. I mean, after we arrested him he acted kind of funny. He kept asking me questions like "Do you think it's right for society to force people to live in poverty?" "Do you think that people who have a lot of wealth should share it with those that don't?" It's almost like he believed that what he did was justified because he thought that certain things were right.

Why did Jim rob the bank? Do you think he did it because he was a greedy person by nature? Was he motivated out of a concern for providing for his family or did his feelings about social conditions in our country influence him? As you can easily see, his reasons are rather complicated. This is often the case when we try to understand why we or anyone else does something. There is seldom a single reason for any behavior. Most explanations will include factors in the immediate environment (e.g., rewards, demands of other people) as well as some of our personal characteristics. Both are important for understanding our behaviors.

Perhaps you are wondering what some of these characteristics are. The study of *personality,* or our personal characteristics, has shown that people are similar and different on a large number of qualities. While no pun is intended, the range does include everything from anxiety to zest. There are several uses for such information. We can use it to describe the relatively stable qualities that each of us has. Based on tests that are designed for this purpose, we might find that we are best described as sensitive, imaginative, and emotionally stable. Furthermore, such qualities may be used to describe the style in which we interact with others. When this is done, we might find that we are shrewd, outgoing, or suspicious. Finally, we can use various personal characteristics to help us understand why our behaviors are guided and directed toward certain activities and goals.

Three general categories of characteristics can help us understand how our behaviors are guided and directed in certain directions. They are our *needs* or motives, our *values,* and the *attitudes* we have toward specific people, objects, and events in our environments. A need or motive is a lack or deficit of some factor within us. When we are hungry, our behavior is directed toward obtaining food. The specific foods we seek, however, are often related to our values and attitudes. Values are the very stable ideas and beliefs that underlie our behaviors across a variety of situations (e.g., beliefs in freedom, equality, and collaboration). They are the general ideals that we try to achieve in our lives. If we value "personal health," we may seek nutritious foods that do not contain food additives to satisfy our hunger. We may shop at health food stores, eat in restaurants that specialize in wholesome meals, and perhaps read magazines and books that describe ways to prepare foods to retain their nutrients. The specific brand of health food (e.g., Brand X or Brand Y) and the specific foods (e.g., tomatoes, spinach, eggs) we select have a great deal to do with our attitudes about particular brands and products—that is, the specific thoughts and feelings we have about such things.

The remainder of this chapter will examine in more detail the role of personality characteristics, needs, values, and attitudes in our lives. Each is an important part. We can understand our own actions better and those of other people by paying attention to such factors.

The Role of Needs or Motives in Our Behaviors

"I'm hungry; I had better get something to eat." "Sally, these locks should keep our house safe from burglars." "I really want to join your club. The people in it have so much fun." "You know, Bill, I did a pretty good job with that project. I hope the teacher gives me a good grade." "If I could get that job, it would represent the best opportunity for my growth and development that I have ever had." I am sure that you have heard yourself or other people say things that are similar to these statements. They show that the needs we have are often reflected in what we say and do. Our needs may have a physiological base (e.g., needs for food and water) or they may be learned through our experiences in the world (e.g., needs for personal recognition and status). What needs do you think are shown in the statements at the start of this paragraph? The range is quite diverse and includes needs for food, keeping ourselves safe, belonging to social groups, gaining recognition for our work, and trying to realize our full potential as human beings.

Abraham Maslow suggests a way to view how a variety of motives operate in our lives. He proposes that our needs can be arranged in terms of how far they allow us to rise above a basic level of existence. Consequently, we can arrange different needs in a hierarchy based on their relative importance for our survival. A description of this hierarchy appears in Table 5-1.

According to Maslow, there are two types of motives. One set consists of needs that relate to deficiencies in our lives. They are things we cannot live for long without and include our physiological, safety, social, and self-esteem needs. The second set is oriented toward our personal growth; these needs are called *self-actualization* needs. Our attempts to gratify them allow us to rise above a basic level of existence. They help us enhance the quality of our lives.

An important part of Maslow's thinking is that needs lower in the hierarchy must be satisfied before we try to fulfill those above them. For example, our physiological needs must be met before we are likely to pay attention to those above them. When we are very hungry or thirsty, our thoughts and behaviors are directed toward obtaining food or something to drink. Other things are relatively unimportant until our hunger or thirst is satisfied. In a similar manner, we are not going to spend a great deal of time in activities that enhance our self-esteem if there is a threat to our physical safety. Regardless of how much status or recognition it gives, a politician is unlikely to speak to a group while knowing that assassins are present in the audience. In such a case, concern for safety becomes more important than personal status or recognition. If they are not satisfied, needs lower on the hierarchy will influence us more than higher-level motives.

There are, of course, exceptions to these principles. Each of us has the capacity to withhold the satisfaction of particular basic needs or to ignore them if circumstances demand it. People have entered dangerous situations

Table 5-1

Maslow's Need Hierarchy

Listed are five categories of needs identified by Abraham Maslow. They are arranged from low to high in terms of the extent to which they allow us to rise above a basic level of existence. Thus, physiological needs are considered lower-order needs and self-actualization needs are of a higher order.

I. *Physiological:*
   Examples of needs included in category
   - Hunger
   - Thirst
   - Sex
   - Sleep
   - Rest
   - Exercise

II. *Safety:*
   Examples of needs included in category
   - Shelter
   - Protection from immediate or future danger to physical well-being
   - Protection from immediate or future threat to psychological or economic well-being

III. *Social:*
   Examples of needs included in category
   - Love and affection
   - Friendships
   - Associations with others
   - Affiliation

IV. *Self-esteem:*
   Examples of needs included in category
   - Self-confidence
   - Independence
   - Achievement
   - Competence
   - Knowledge
   - Status
   - Personal recognition
   - Respect

V. *Self-actualization:*
   Examples of needs included in category
   - Realizing one's own potential
   - Self-development activities
   - Behaving creatively
   - Problem-centered orientation to life
   - Identifying with the problems of humanity
   - Acceptance of self and others

Data from "Hierarchy of Needs" in *Motivation and Personality*, 2nd Edition by Abraham H. Maslow, Copyright © 1954 by Harper & Row, Publishers, Inc. Copyright © 1970 by Abraham H. Maslow.

in combat zones or during a natural emergency and risked their lives to save other people. Why would people place another person's survival above their own? Many talented artists, musicians, actors, and actresses are not able to meet their basic physiological and safety needs adequately. Despite few jobs and a lack of money, they put a great deal of energy into satisfying the self-esteem needs associated with their professions. Such exceptions do not fit easily into Maslow's system. However, as a *general orientation* to the relative importance of various motives in most of our lives, his system is a fairly accurate description of our needs.

Each of us spends different amounts of time trying to satisfy the various needs in Table 5-1. Sometimes our personal circumstances lead us to spend much time and energy on our physiological and safety needs. Consequently, we would spend relatively little of our time fulfilling higher-level needs. One consequence is that we would be unlikely to have experiences that would increase our feelings of confidence, personal worth, and adequacy. Our higher-order needs are important for our overall development. We cannot afford to ignore them for long. We must be concerned with trying to fulfill as many of our needs as possible.

What needs in Table 5-1 do you currently fulfill? Which ones would you like to spend more time on? What is preventing you from doing this? What are some things that you can do about this problem? How would solving the problem enhance your daily life? The following exercise is designed to help you answer each question. Please complete it before reading

further. The response of one of my students is presented as an example for you on page 144.

EXERCISE 5-1: MASLOW'S NEED HIERARCHY IN OUR DAILY AFFAIRS

A. Identification of time spent on each need. Before planning any changes in how you spend your time and energy, you should have some idea of what you currently do. Think of the activities you were involved in (i.e., your major thoughts and behaviors) during the past four weeks. Review the specific examples of motives under each need category in Table 5-1. For each category, *list several of your major thoughts and behaviors during this time period.* This will help you locate your thoughts and behaviors in terms of the need category to which they belong. Having done this, estimate as well as you can the percentage of time you spent on each of the categories. *Your percentage of time estimates should add to 100 percent.*

B. Satisfaction with fulfilling each category of need. Most of us have different feelings about how well we are able to fulfill each of the needs that Maslow identified. Before reading further, rate the extent to which you are contented with your present attempts to fulfill the needs in each category of the hierarchy. Use the following rating scale: 1 = completely unsatisfied; 2 = somewhat unsatisfied; 3 = neither unsatisfied nor satisfied; 4 = somewhat satisfied; 5 = completely satisfied. Place your rating next to the name of each need category.

Maslow believes that the average person is most satisfied with things they do to fulfill their physiological needs and least satisfied with things they attempt at self-

143

actualization. Safety, social and self-esteem needs are often ranked second, third, and fourth respectively. Did your ratings conform to what Maslow said?

C. Enhancing your ability to fulfill needs identified in the hierarchy. Pick the need category(ies) to which you gave the lowest rating. Ask yourself the following question: What can I do to increase my current level of satisfaction with the things I do to fulfill this need? Develop and implement an action plan to answer this question. The following are three suggestions for where to start thinking about a plan of action.

- Consider the strengths and weaknesses of your current activities in each need category. How can you enhance your current activities so that you will be more satisfied?
- What are two new activities that can help you fulfill that need better?
- Is the fact that some other need in the hierarchy is not satisfied affecting your ability to enhance this one?

Achievement, Affiliation, and Power Needs In Our Lives

Are you interested in becoming the "best that there is" at the things you do? Do you like to meet new people? Are you uncomfortable when you don't have control over what other people are doing? A yes response to each question suggests that *achievement, affiliation,* and *power* motives are present in your behaviors. The things we say or do that reflect a high degree of interest in becoming successful, performing in a highly competent manner, or accomplishing something unique are related to our need for achievement. Thus, a writer who sets out to produce "the great American novel" probably has a high need for achievement. Our need for affiliation is seen in behaviors that are oriented toward forming friendships and working closely with other people. A student who enjoys working in small groups in class and who joins a number of campus organizations is demonstrating a need for affiliation. Behaviors that are designed to allow us to control or influence others or to compete successfully with people will allow us to satisfy our need for power. For example, most politicians and coaches have a fairly high amount of the power motive operating in their behaviors.

An Example of a Completed Exercise 5-1

I. *Physiological:* 4
   Time Estimates: 45%
   Examples of Specific Activities: I've eaten two to three meals a day. Consumed lots of water and fruit juices. Had sexual relations with my girlfriend quite frequently. I sleep about six to eight hours a night. I jog about three times a week.

II. *Safety:* 4

   Time Estimates: 10%

   Examples of Specific Activities: I looked for a new apartment this month. I thought about buying theft insurance when I got the new apartment. I had the brakes fixed on my car.

III. *Social:* 3

   Time Estimates: 25%

   Examples of Specific Activities: I went to two parties this month. Have spent every Wednesday night at a local bar relaxing and enjoying the company of others. I thought about asking a girl I met out for a date next week.

IV. *Self-esteem:* 2

   Time Estimate: 15%

   Examples of Specific Activities: I decided to take a course in Calculus next term. I tried to sell more encyclopedias than I did last month. I studied hard to get a good grade on my history test. I practiced hard so the coach would give me a chance to play.

V. *Self-actualization:* 3

   Time Estimate: 5%

   Examples of Specific Activities: I'm taking a course in carpentry on Saturday morning. It's a skill I've always wanted to have. I started to write a short story for my writing course. I thought about the problems of the people in Africa who are caught up in the fighting there.

   > *Action Plan:* I need to work on fulfilling my self-esteem needs better. In particular, I am concerned about my achieving well and the recognition that I get for what I do. In spite of my efforts, I did not sell more encyclopedias nor did I get a chance to play in a game. It seems that my efforts to do better go unnoticed. I need more information about why this is so. I'm going to talk to my district sales manager and to the coach. I'm going to tell them what I've been doing and seek their advice on why things don't seem to be working out. I think they can give me some good advice on how to do better and they will know that I am concerned about my performance. This should help them focus more on me and hopefully they will recognize my efforts more often.

According to David McClelland and John Atkinson, some of our everyday behaviors are attempts to try to satisfy one or more of these needs. *Depending upon our past experiences and current interests, we engage in a variety of behaviors that might reflect all three needs or that emphasize one motive more than another.* For example, I recently asked several of my students to discuss their career plans with me. I observed that the careers selected and their reasons for choosing certain careers often indicated the importance of achievement, affiliation, and power motives for them. I have listed part of what several of my students said below.

EXERCISE 5-2: IDENTIFYING NEEDS

As a check on your understanding of each motive, read each student's comments and decide which need(s) are reflected in what they said. Give a reason for your response. Check your answers with those on page 148.

Phillip: I'd like to become a member of a management team in a large company. I think I can work well with people and become a part of a group that will help the company grow. I would hope that other people I worked with felt as I do. You know that they will want to cooperate to get the job done. I don't think I would like it much if the people I worked with were only looking out for themselves.

Kevin: I want to follow up with my ROTC training and become a career officer in the Army. I enjoy leadership positions and being in command. There is a certain amount of satisfaction in getting a group of people to get the job done efficiently. I also like the structure a job in the Army requires. You know what is expected of you and other people know what is expected of them. Consequently, the person in charge has fewer problems when he tells someone what to do.

Sally: I've been working part time selling cosmetics door to door. I think I want to continue in sales with the company. Selling is quite a challenge. You get instant feedback on how good you are. I mean if you are not good, your customers will not buy as much. The trick is to keep one step ahead of your customer. You have to know your products, practice your sales pitch, and try to personally improve upon what you did the day before. Eventually, I want to be the best salesperson in the company and work my way up to a district or regional sales manager position.

146

Mary: I'd like to get into the theater initially as an actress. I've always enjoyed performing in public. The personal recognition you get for playing a role well is unbelievable. It takes hard work to be good but seldom are your efforts not rewarded. Later on in my career, I'd like to try directing. I think it would be fun to take a group of people and tell them how to perform their roles. If I do it, I want to be the kind of director that actors and actresses will respect and want to listen to.

In addition to showing that each motive is sometimes present in what we say about ourselves, the examples demonstrate an important distinction between achievement and the other two motives. Affiliation and power needs are interpersonal. They can only be satisfied through our behaviors toward other people. The need for achievement, however, is more individually oriented. People high in achievement needs tend to rely on themselves to get things done. Consequently, they show a high degree of interest in improving the personal skills and abilities which make them successful.

To what extent do these three motives influence your behaviors? One way to gain insight into this question is to analyze your current activities and even your future career plans for evidence of each need. Although this seems straightforward, it may not always work. On occasion, most of us have tendencies to be not completely honest with ourselves. We may deny that certain things influence our actions. I have found people who for different reasons felt that there must be something wrong with them if they saw themselves as having high needs for achievement, affiliation, or power. On the other hand, we may simply not understand all the things our behaviors represent. This, of course, also makes it difficult for us to interpret our actions. Fortunately, there are other, objective although less direct, measures of the presence of various needs within us. Let us take a look at two of them as they apply to our needs for achievement, affiliation, and power.

The first method we will examine is called a *projective test*. Such a test asks us to interpret stimuli that have no clear meaning. Our needs and motives are often evident in the ways we respond to such stimuli. A person who has not eaten for 24 hours might perceive from a distance the number 100D on a door as the word FOOD. The following face might be described as a person who is unhappy or sad by someone who has such feelings.

Suggested Answers to Exercise 5-2

Phillip: Affiliation: This is seen in his desire to work as part of a management team and the importance he places on cooperation.

Kevin: Power: This is apparent from his need to become a leader who can influence what people do and be in control of the situation.

Sally: Achievement: This is evident in the way she talks about becoming a better salesperson. She talks about the need to constantly improve and wants to be the best salesperson in the company.

Mary: Achievement and Power: Both motives are present in her career plans. Her desire to become a better actress by hard work suggests the presence of the achievement need. A need for power is present when she discusses her role as a director. There she talks about showing others how to perform and wanting actors and actresses to listen to her.

In both examples, our needs and feelings are projected into our description of the stimulus.

EXERCISE 5-3: ASSESSING THE PRESENCE OF ACHIEVEMENT, AFFILIATION, AND POWER MOTIVES IN YOUR BEHAVIOR USING A PROJECTIVE TEST

Study the picture in Figure 5-1 for a few seconds. Then write a story about the picture. Be sure to include in your story the following: What is happening? Who are the people and what has brought them together? What has led up to this situation? What are the people thinking and saying? What do you think will eventually happen? Work rapidly and try not to spend more than five to eight minutes writing your story.

Listed below are brief descriptions of the types of things that could appear in your story that would key the presence of each motive. Take each sentence in your story and see if it matches one of the descriptions in the list. Mark each sentence for the presence of each motive. Determine the number of sentences that can be classified according to achievement, affiliation, or power needs. *It is quite possible that none of your sentences or only a few can be classified according to the descriptions in the list. Remember that each need does not occur in everything we do or say.* A sample story I wrote is scored for you on page 152 to illustrate how to do it.

Keys to the Presence of Each Motive in a Story for Exercise 5-3[1]

Score each sentence that you can by putting the number (e.g., Ia, IIc, IIIa) that best describes what is occurring in parentheses at the end of the sentence. Add up the number of sentences that relate to each motive.

[1] From *Motives in Fantasy, Action & Society,* edited by John W. Atkinson, © 1958 by Litton Educational Publishing, Inc. Reprinted by permission of Van Nostrand Reinhold Company.

Figure 5-1

I.   *Achievement:*
   a.   A concern for doing well is shown by an individual(s).
   b.   High standards are set by someone.
   c.   An individual is concerned about getting ahead.
   d.   Someone is interested in accomplishing a long-term goal.
   e.   The story or someone in it is involved in obtaining a unique accomplishment.
   f.   A person wants to be better than someone else.
   g.   A person wants to take personal responsibility for their success or failures.
   h.   Someone in the story wants feedback on how they did.
II.   *Affiliation:*
   a.   An individual is interested in establishing a collaborative relationship with other people.
   b.   A person expresses a need to make friends with someone else.
   c.   Someone is interested in seeing that the needs of other people are met.
   d.   An individual indicates that he or she wants to be liked by another person.
   e.   Someone is interested in joining a club, having a party, or visiting other people.

III. *Power:*
   a. Someone wants to influence or control another person or group.
   b. A strong desire for competition with other people is expressed.
   c. An individual wants to control the flow of information.
   d. A person shows a high need for status.
   e. Someone is interested in the impact of what he or she does on other people.
   f. People engage in activities that lead to stress and conflict. For example, arguing, shouting, demanding, punishing others, or making strong commands appear in the story.

Of interest here is whether your story showed the presence of one or more of the three motives. Did the information you get conform to other things you know about yourself? Did you see in your story any evidence for other needs identified by Maslow in Table 5-1?

Have you ever made doodle or scribble drawings similar to the one shown in Figure 5-2? Perhaps you have made such drawings in notebooks or on scraps of paper to occupy some idle time. This method for assessing the presence of achievement was developed by Elliott Aronson. He used other measures to find out how high or low in the need for achievement participants in his study were. The people were then asked to make scribble drawings. Aronson then looked for differences in the drawings of people high and low in achievement. Before reading further, please complete the following exercise.

Figure 5-2

EXERCISE 5-4: ASSESSING THE PRESENCE OF ACHIEVEMENT MOTIVATION IN SCRIBBLE DRAWINGS

A. Draw a box about 3 inches on a side on a blank piece of paper and scribble draw in the space for two minutes.

B. Based on Aronson's research, several aspects of such drawings are associated with people who are high in the need for achievement.[1] They are:

1. The drawings fill the spaces allocated to them. In particular, relatively small margins are left at the bottom of a page or drawing area.

2. *S*-shaped lines are often present in the drawings.
    E.g.,

3. Very few multiwave lines (two or more crests in the same direction) are used. E.g.,

4. Many figures are made diagonally in the drawings.
    E.g.,

5. Complete or nearly complete geometric figures are present.
    E.g.,

6. Most figures are clear and not fuzzy or hard to distinguish.
    E.g.,

C. The sample drawing at the beginning of this section was made by a person high in achievement.

D. Based on this information, what do you think your drawings say about your need for achievement? Is there any similarity between what you discovered here and in the analysis of your story?

[1] From *Motives in Fantasy, Action & Society* © 1958 by Litton Educational Publishing Inc. Reprinted by permission of Van Nostrand Reinhold Company.

It is possible to measure how much of each motive exists in groups of people as well as in individuals. In a series of rather remarkable and fascinating research studies, David McClelland, John Atkinson, and others have shown that nations can be described in terms of the amount of each motive that is present at different time periods in their history. This is done by analyzing for the presence of each motive the content of such things as children's literature, folksongs, and even the art that is produced in a given period. Figure 5-3 shows the presence of each motive in children's stories in the United States from 1810 to 1950. The stories children read often reflect the

---

The Scoring of a Sample Story for Exercise 5-3

I.	Achievement	IIII	4
II.	Affiliation	II	2
III.	Power	II	2

The men and women are members of a sales department in a business organization. They are meeting to talk about their sales for the year. In past years, their group has had the lowest sales in the history of the company. This year, they have done better than any other department. (*I–a*) Their boss is telling everyone around the table that he expects them to maintain at least the same high performance level next year (*I–b*). He says he is proud to be associated with this group and looks forward to working with them next year. (*II–a*) The woman with her back to the group is about to leave the room. She is angry with the other members of the group for not listening to her. (*III–f*) She thinks they were lucky to have done so well this year and wants them to spend more time realistically talking about the reasons for their success. (*III–c*) The person who is sitting on the edge of the table and talking to the others is telling them how helpful the feedback they gave him earlier in the year on his sales techniques was to him. He wants to know if there is anything else they can tell him now about his selling procedures that will help him next year. (*I–h*) He wants to do even better next year. (*I–c*) In all, the group members are happy and they will want to have a party later on to celebrate. (*II–e*)

---

values that the culture thinks are important. Notice in the figure how achievement reached its peak in our country in 1890, power 20 years later, and affiliation 20 years after that. Can you think of things that our country did at each peak that might account for these data?

An analysis of achievement, affiliation, and power needs makes it possible to predict several things about a nation. A peak in achievement motivation in children's literature predicts that the nation will have its highest level of economic activity within the next 25 to 50 years. Furthermore, when the needs for power and affiliation are studied at the midpoint of a decade, it is possible to predict when a nation will go to war. When the need for power is significantly higher than the need for affiliation, a war is likely to follow within 15 years. Finally, Stanley Rudin has shown that in 17 countries, the 1950 death rate from ulcers, hypertension, murder, and suicide was related to the number of achievement and power themes in children's stories 25 years earlier. Specifically, the level of achievement motivation in

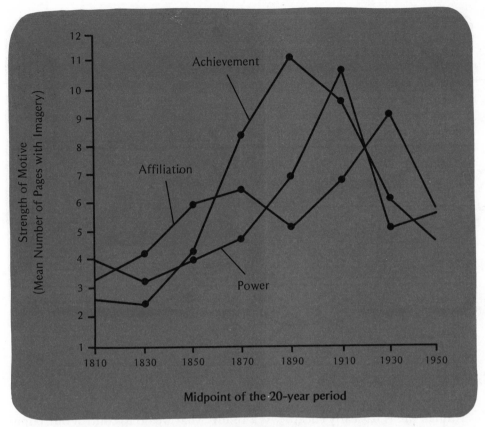

Figure 5-3

Trends in the strength of achievement, power, and affiliation motives in the United States from 1810 to 1950. Motive strength is inferred from content analysis of children's readers. Note how achievement reached its peak in 1890, power 20 years later, and affiliation 20 years after that. (Courtesy of William Dember and James Jenkins. General Psychology: Modeling Behavior and Experience. Englewood Cliffs, N.J.: Prentice-Hall, 1970. Adapted from Rudin, 1965.)

1925 predicted the level of the death rate in 1950 due to ulcers and hypertension. The level of power motivation for this time period predicted the level of the death rate due to murder and suicide.

Can you think of reasons the relationships described in the above paragraph occurred? Since the needs for achievement, affiliation, and power are learned, what are some ways we learn them? Do you think it is possible for one person to train another to develop a higher need for achievement?

The Role Of Values In Our Lives

"Human life is basically cheap. As a result, what we do to control our population should not be based on the dignity or worth of human beings." "Students need opportunities for self-direction in their learning. I don't think that any teacher can teach by telling students everything they have to know." "It's best to assume that people are basically lazy. Management needs to use a carrot-and-stick approach to get people to work." Each of these statements is something I have heard someone say in conversation with me during the past year. Each statement reflects certain values such as "the cheapness of human life," "the importance of self-direction," and "the need for strong controls on people's actions." Values are the important and stable ideas, beliefs, and assumptions that underlie and are observed in our behaviors across a number of different situations. They represent the ideals or desirable qualities that each of us tries to obtain in life. Let us take a closer look at several characteristics of values. In the process, we should begin to gain a better understanding of what they are and how they influence our lives.

Our Values Are Clearly Seen in Our Behaviors

Values are not ideas and assumptions we simply think about or tell others we believe. According to Louis Raths and Sidney Simon, *we act upon the things we value.* As noted earlier in this chapter, our values help to direct our actions, particularly by those behaviors that are directed toward satisfying our needs. Consequently, they play a strong role in a large number of our behaviors. They are seen in our personal preferences, in the goals we select, in our perceptions of the environment, and in our emotions. Let us look at the role that values play in each of these behaviors.

Personal preferences. Our values are seen in our preferences for what we purchase and how we prefer to design activities for ourselves and others. I value what represents, for me, evidence of creativity in art, music, and literature. Consequently, I am very selective in the art, music, and literature I purchase. Unlike some of my friends, I refuse to buy something just because the price is right. I also value collaboration among people. Thus, the classes I design and the groups I organize and lead have a high amount of interaction among participants.

Goal selection. Each of us establishes and works toward obtaining goals in a variety of activities. We pursue goals associated with our careers, schoolwork, and even our social life. Most of us make choices about what goals we will try to obtain. For example, choices might exist between: (a) becoming a police officer versus a grocery store owner; (b) taking a course in personal applications of psychology versus the history of the civil rights movement; or (c) staying at home to read on Friday night versus attending a party. In each case, the goals we choose reflect *in part* our values. In the examples above, important values associated with each choice are: (a) authority versus independence, (b) a concern for self-awareness versus freedom, and (c) privacy versus socializing.

Perceptions of the environment. Our values help us focus our attention on particular parts of our environment. A person who values equality for all people will easily notice restricted housing patterns, segregated schools, and unequal job opportunities for minorities. Someone who values health will pay attention to advertisements for fresh vegetables and vitamins and will read about the dangers of certain food additives.

Emotions. Events in our lives that are in harmony with our values will produce positive feelings. Those that are not in harmony will produce negative feelings. In the examples given in the last paragraph, instances of

155

inequality are likely to make a person who values equality angry. Similarly, attempts by the government to remove food additives from products will be appreciated by a person who places a strong value on health. In both cases, our values are seen in the feelings we show.

Our Values Persist and Occur Across a Number of Situations in Our Lives

Values are not ideas and assumptions we believe in one day and forget the next. They are important and rather durable parts of our personalities. Thus, the same value is often seen in several areas of our lives. A person who strongly values control and authority is likely to say to: (a) *an instructor in school,* "I think it's the teacher's responsibility and not that of other students in the class to make assignments, to tell us what's important, and to assign grades"; (b) *office staff members,* "There are procedures around here for doing things. Based on several incidents this week, I don't think some of you know what they are. You will find a copy of the company's rules and regulations on the bulletin board. I expect them to be followed to the letter in the future"; (c) *his or her child,* "You need to do what I tell you to do. I have a lot of experience in life and I know what is best for you."

Are you aware of several things that you value? Do you know how your values influence your personal behaviors? Are you aware of other values that you might find useful in your life? I suspect that most of us have not given much thought to these questions. However, answers to them often give people a better understanding of why they do certain things. The following exercise is designed to help you gain an understanding of how your personal values influence your behaviors. Completion of this exercise will help you to answer these three questions.

EXERCISE 5-5: VALUE IDENTIFICATION AND CLARIFICATION

A. Look at the words in Table 5-2. They represent some of the values that occur in our society. Read the instructions in the table and select five that represent very important values in your life. Write the five you selected on a sheet of paper.

B. Think about how each value affects your daily interactions. Can you think of at least two different situations or events during the past 30 days in which that value had an effect? Briefly list each situation next to each value you selected, as in the following example.

Value	Situation
Sharing	1. Lent my car to a neighbor two weeks ago.
	2. Talked about the things I did right and wrong at a meeting I had last week with three friends.

Were you able to think of two situations? As we have discussed, values occur in our behaviors across different situations. What does a failure to think of two situations say about how strong that value is for you?

C. Pretend that a "value bandit" wants to rob you of two of the values you listed. You are allowed to select the two that are given away. Which two would you be willing to give away? What reason do you have for your selection? What effect is the absence of each value likely to have on your life? List the two values that you would give away and answer the two questions.

D. Pretend that a "good Samaritan" comes along and finds you without two of your values. This person tells you that you can replace the two values you gave to the bandit with two *new* values. However, you cannot select the two you gave away. Select two of the values listed in Table 5-2 to replace those you gave away. What reason did you have for selecting each new value? What effect is it likely to have on your behaviors?

Table 5-2

A List of Value Words

Listed here are several qualities that are valued by different people in our society. *Read each term and think of what it means to you.* It is important that you have a personal definition of each item. Having done this, select five of the values that are very important to you.

Value Words

Achievement	Dependence	Intelligence	Religion
Aggression	Education	Intimacy	Repression
Alienation	Exploration	Justice	Respect
Authority	Equality	Knowledge	Rigidity
Chaos	Expertise	Life	Rules
Cleanliness	Fairness	Loneliness	Safety
Collaboration	Family Life	Love	Salvation
Comfort	Favoritism	Obedience	Security
Conflict	Fear	Organization	Selfishness
Control	Freedom	Passivity	Self-awareness
Creativity	Happiness	Peace	Self-direction
Competitiveness	Harmony	Pleasure	Self-respect
Community	Health	Power	Sharing
Dignity	Independence	Privacy	Socializing
Disorder	Influence	Purposefulness	Success
Dogmatism	Integrity	Quiet	Wisdom
Dominance			

Why not check with some of your classmates and see how they responded to this exercise? What has this exercise shown you about the role values play in your daily interactions?

The Role of Attitudes in Our Lives

"I think that Corn Crunch is the best cereal on the market today." "I just don't like the foreign policy of the president." "It would be all right with me for a member of a minority group to move into our neighborhood." "In the long run, I feel that smoking is dangerous to my health." I am sure that you have heard similar views expressed. Such statements represent attitudes that people have toward different things. An attitude is a relatively durable organization of thoughts and positive and negative feelings that we have toward specific people, objects, and situations. They represent many of the things we like or dislike and often help us make choices about how we will act toward people, objects, and situations in our lives. To obtain a better understanding of attitudes and the role they play in our lives, let us examine several of their characteristics.

Our attitudes are oriented toward specific people, objects, and events at a given time and place. Milton Rokeach suggests that the same attitude, unlike a given value, does not occur across a wide variety of situations. Attitudes have a much more specific focus than values. A colleague of mine values "independence." As a result, he works alone on research projects, he does not belong to a political party, and he refuses to join social groups. On the other hand, "independence" represents an attitude for me. I like it only in very specific situations. I think that it is a useful skill for researchers to have. However, I mildly dislike people who do not belong to a political party and people who show their independence by not wanting to join social groups.

Our attitude toward something often varies with changes in the situation. Have you ever thought about how your attitudes toward the same person, object, or event become more or less favorable as circumstances change? Listed in the following exercise are some things that each of us has thoughts and feelings about.

Rating scales such as this one are often used to obtain an estimate of the strength of an attitude. Did your attitude change toward each item as the situation varied? Were the changes large or quite small? What do you think accounts for any changes you observed? How would you account for a

EXERCISE 5-6: RATING ATTITUDES

Rate how much you like each of the people, objects, and events listed for each of the situations given. Write your responses on a separate sheet of paper. Try to be as honest and objective as you can. Use the following rating scale.

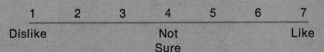

1	2	3	4	5	6	7
Dislike			Not Sure			Like

1. Breakfast cereals for
   a. breakfast
   b. lunch
   c. dinner
   d. late night snacks
2. The president of the United States and his
   a. foreign policy
   b. attempts to help minorities
   c. speeches
3. Basketball games
   a. on television
   b. on the radio
   c. in person
   d. as a participant
4. News reports
   a. in newspapers
   b. on television
   c. on the radio
   d. in magazines

failure to note changes in your attitudes? Why not check with several of your classmates and see how they responded?

We try to organize our attitudes and behaviors in ways that are consistent. Carl Hovland and Anthony Greenwald note that any attitude has thoughts, feelings, and, potentially, certain behaviors associated with it. Sometimes we are successful in making our thoughts, feelings, and behaviors agree with each other. Consider the following statement by one of my students: "I believe in equal housing and would like to have a minority person live in my neighborhood." There are three components to this attitude. The first two are my student's beliefs and feelings about minorities and where they should be allowed to live. The potential behaviors we would expect a person with such an attitude to take are the third component. Thus we might expect him not to resist minorities moving into his neighborhood, to encourage

159

them to do it, or to himself seek housing in an integrated area. In fact, my student has actually taken one of these actions. His attitudes and behaviors are consistent.

There are times when our attitudes do not appear in our behaviors. I know other people who have the same attitude as my student but have not taken any action that related to it. Most people find the fact that our attitudes are not always reflected in our behaviors rather strange. Do *you* think that it is unusual? There are at least three reasons for it. We must remember that our attitudes are thoughts and feelings which suggest certain behaviors we might take. They do not *guarantee* that any specific behavior will occur. We have many thoughts and feelings every day which we fail to take action on. Furthermore, our behaviors toward particular people, objects, or events are often controlled by other factors besides our attitudes about them. Finally, we might tell someone that we have a certain attitude because we do not want to admit how we really feel. Thus, our behaviors appear inconsistent with our publicly stated attitude.

Two of my experiences illustrate the last three points: (1) I tell people that I think that city council meetings are excellent places for citizens to exchange ideas. I also like the fact that they are held frequently and attract a variety of people. However, I never attend such meetings. Two factors influence my behavior more than do my attitudes toward such meetings. My university schedule does not allow me the time to attend, and I am not actively involved in local political issues. (2) Recently, I attended a show of new homes. I was interviewed in front of a large group of people regarding what I thought of the homes. I told the interviewer that I really liked what I saw. In fact, privately I did not feel as positive as I had publicly stated. My attitudes appeared more positive because I did not want to create a negative bias in the minds of the potential buyers who were standing around listening to what was said. I later told the builder that I would not buy one of his homes. Thus, my behavior appeared to him to be inconsistent with my publicly stated attitudes. Both examples show how things in addition to what we tell people we think and feel can influence our behaviors.

We must remember this principle the next time we try to predict someone's behavior based on information regarding their attitudes. We probably should be more cautious than we are normally; otherwise, problems are likely to develop. I have seen manufacturers put products on the market (e.g., the Edsel automobile, atom bomb shelters), business leaders change their organizational structures, colleges add new course offerings, and people run for political office based on the favorable attitudes of people toward such things. The attitudes never surfaced very much in the behaviors of these same people. Consequently, the products did not sell, the organizational changes made little difference in how satisfied workers were, courses were

not well attended, and individuals wasted time, energy, and money running for political office.

Can you think of two examples in your life of cases in which your attitudes and behaviors are consistent? in which they are not consistent? Have you ever tried to predict how someone would behave based on knowledge of that person's attitudes? Were your predictions accurate? In terms of their effect on our actions, how do values differ from attitudes?

Our Attitudes Can Be Modified

"You don't have to take my word for how nice this table will look in your home. Why not take it home and try it for 30 days? If you are not satisfied, return the table and I'll refund your money." "Sally, you can't let us down. We need you to support Phyllis for president of the club. Everyone in our part of town is going to support her." "Why not try this new hair rinse? It will give your hair a sheen that men will just love. Try it and see if you have to sit home on Saturday nights again." Does any of this sound familiar? Deliberate attempts are made by advertisers, salespeople, teachers, ministers, and even our friends to get us to modify our attitudes. Research on attitude change has shown that our attitudes are influenced by a large number of factors. In the following paragraphs, several of the more important factors are discussed. As you read, try to think of situations in your past experiences in which these factors have had an effect. Also try to look for evidence of each factor in your current or future interactions. Such knowledge may help you to resist changing your beliefs needlessly.

Cognitive dissonance.   There are times when we are given information or we behave in a way that is contrary to our attitudes. For example, a member of the Democratic party might read an article by a respected Democrat attacking the party or he might attend a political rally for a Republican candidate. Leon Festinger says that when such things occur, a state of displeasure or tension is produced. Such feelings are called *cognitive dissonance,* and we will engage in thoughts and behaviors to reduce this state.

One way to reduce dissonance is to modify or change an attitude.   The Democratic party member might decide that the information in the article is valid. However, he cannot come to this conclusion and still keep the same level of positive feelings about the party. Thus, he may accept the information and develop a less positive attitude toward the party. Similarly, he has to justify his attending a Republican rally. This action is not consistent with his attitudes about the Democratic party. He could reduce the dissonance by becoming more positive toward the Republicans than toward his own party. This last point is important because it suggests that sometimes our behaviors must change before we will experience a change in our attitudes.

I am sure that you have had experiences in which you reduced dissonance by modifying an attitude. On the other hand, you have probably read information or behaved in a way that was inconsistent with some attitude and the attitude did not change. This is because a modification in our attitudes is not the only way we reduce dissonance. Dissonance does not guarantee a change in our attitudes. It can be lessened also by seeking facts that disagree with the new information—the Democratic party member might read other articles that critique the position held by the author. Furthermore, seeking the support of people who believe as you do will reduce dissonance—the Democrat might get several friends with views similar to his to agree that the author of the article was incorrect. Finally, we might make other excuses for our actions—our Democrat might convince himself that he had nothing better to do with his time that day than to go to the Republican rally.

Have you ever experienced cognitive dissonance? What aroused it within you? Did you reduce it by modifying one or more of your attitudes? Did you reduce it by engaging in some of the other behaviors we have described?

Social pressure.   "Look, George, we can't take a minority position to the board of directors. The rest of us simply don't agree with your views. We must present a united front to ensure that we get what we want. How about changing your mind and joining us?" Surely you have had an experience in which members of a group tried to influence your attitudes and behaviors. We are all influenced by the demands of other people at some time in our lives. Our peers and other people we respect reinforce us for thinking and behaving as they do. They can also make things unpleasant if we resist. Group pressure often causes us to modify an attitude, and it does not necessarily take a large group to do this. Research has shown that as few as three to four people taking a position other than our own is often sufficient to produce a change in attitude.

A study by Theodore Newcomb at Bennington College in 1935 illustrates how pressure from our peers and teachers can change our attitudes. At that time, the prevailing attitude on campus was one of political liberalism. However, the women who attended Bennington came there with rather conservative attitudes. Many of the women over a four-year period became more liberal in their political attitudes. In many cases, such change persisted for years after the women left college. Newcomb believed that the approval of liberal attitudes from faculty and the students' peer group were important factors in modifying their beliefs.

Can you think of any of your own attitudes that have changed since you entered college? What influence did groups of people (peers, faculty, administrators) in your college environment have on changing your attitudes? In what other parts of your life do groups influence the attitudes you have?

Needs

American soldiers, why do you continue to fight this war? Think of your loved ones back home. Can they afford to have you come home in a coffin? Think of the hardships you have suffered here. How many of your friends have been killed or wounded? How many more will you lose before this war is over? When was the last time you had a warm meal and a bed to sleep in? We are not interested in seeing you suffer anymore. This leaflet is a safe conduct pass and will be honored by any member of the liberation front. Use it to free yourself from the danger and suffering of this war.

These statements are taken from a leaflet I found in Vietnam. The leaflet attempts to change attitudes by appealing to some of the needs that each of us has. In this case, our needs for personal safety, food, and shelter are emphasized. Messages such as this were distributed by both sides in the conflict. Although such appeals did not cause many American soldiers to defect, they did have an influence on the Vietnamese who fought on both sides of the conflict. The promise of having basic needs satisfied by coming over to the other side helped to convince several thousands of people a year to defect.

Of course, we do not have to go to war to find attempts to modify our attitudes based on appeals to our needs. Advertisers and salespeople do this all the time. Many times there is an honest and direct relationship between the product and the need it fulfills. Food products are usually tasty and they do satisfy our hunger or thirst. On the other hand, some products are sold with appeals to needs that they have a minimal chance of fulfilling. These appeals are done so well that we sometimes forget the real use of the product we are purchasing. Did you know that: (a) toothpaste is much more effective in cleaning your teeth than it is in getting you dates on Saturday night? (b) coffee is a refreshing drink but has little to do with keeping your spouse or in-laws constantly pleased with you? (c) detergents are much better at taking the dirt out of your clothes than they are at keeping marriages from breaking up? (d) encyclopedias are good reference books but no one has ever received a college degree reading them?

Can you think of three times in the past week when someone tried to modify your attitude about a person, product, or event by appealing to one of your needs? How effective was the appeal?

Obtaining Agreement on Issues

Clever persuaders may influence our behaviors and attitudes if they can first get us to agree with them on issues remotely or closely related to the attitude in question. It becomes harder to disagree after making a number of such positive statements. Let us look at several ways this is done and some reasons the technique works.

Agreement on unrelated issues. Have you ever found yourself agreeing with an insurance, magazine, appliance, or clothing salesperson on things like, "Isn't it a lovely day outside?" "Your children are so well behaved," "You look happy today," or "The price of meat is too high"? You then find yourself tempted to say yes to "Can I have your signature on this sales contract?" The salesperson has first talked to you about a number of issues unrelated to a particular product or service. Ellen Lanzer and Carol Dweck suggest that by getting you to agree, the salesperson has established that the two of you have something in common. You apparently think alike about a number of things. It is harder to resist purchasing a product or agreeing to something someone else suggests when you think alike on so many other things.

Agreement with a small request. John Freedman demonstrated that we are sometimes likely to modify an attitude if another person gets us to agree to help them with a small request. A recent experience of mine illustrates this point. I believe that my annual income is my business and no one else's. Recently, I received a telephone call from a company assessing what television shows people were watching. The questions were phrased as follows: "Do you have a television set?" "How many?" "What hours of the day do you use it?" "Is it currently on?" "What channel are you watching?" "What do you think of the show?" "What advertisements are you aware of watching during the past hour?" "Where do you live?" "What is your occupation?" *"Approximately how much do you make each year?" I answered the questions.* Since I had cooperated with each of a series of small requests for information, it was difficult to refuse answering the last one. I would not have answered if it had been the first question. The same procedure is used by salespeople who try to "get their foot into the door." After all, if you agree to "spend just a minute," "have a cup of coffee or a cigarette," or "let them use your phone," it becomes much more difficult to turn off their sales pitch. One reason is that we do small favors for our friends. Such a person becomes almost like a friend after we comply with one or more small requests. How many of you can fail to do things your friends ask you to do?

Agreement with an analogy. William McGuire has shown that people are likely to modify a view if they agree with another statement that contains similar logic. A neighbor's wife asked me if I would talk to her husband about getting a physical exam. He had not had one in several years, and she thought it was about time for a check-up. In particular, she was concerned about his tendency to overeat and occasionally to feel dizzy. Of course, he told me that he felt fine physically and did not need a medical exam. I asked him if an airline should not check its plane engines if they appeared to run well. He said that this was not true. "Airplane engines may look and sound all right but you need to periodically check them for parts that are beginning to wear." I then asked him if he saw any analogy between his body and the plane engines. He smiled and said, "Of course, there is." He got a medical check-up. McGuire says that this procedure creates cognitive dissonance which is often resolved by a change in attitude.

Agreement through reactance. Jack Brehm notes that each of us tries to exert our personal freedom whenever we feel a high degree of persuasion. A child who feels his parents are trying to get him to eat spinach may decide not to eat it in order to maintain some personal control over what he eats. Similarly, a person is likely to vote against some issue in a meeting if she

165

feels that other members of the group are trying to force her to do something. One of the consequences of trying to change an attitude is that we often think or behave just the opposite of what someone else wants. The process of behaving to maintain our personal freedom to make decisions in the face of persuasive influences is called *reactance*.

Jacobo Varela indicates that reactance can sometimes work against you. Pretend that you are talking to an encyclopedia salesperson who presents you with the following questions and statements: "I bet you are really not that interested in education"; "Have you ever thought that gaining knowledge was a waste of time?" "I bet you spend very little time reading"; "Have you ever thought that reading was a chore?" More likely than not, you would disagree with such statements. In the process, you would begin to agree that "you have an interest in education," "gaining knowledge is not a waste of time," "you spend time reading," and "reading is probably fun." By resisting the statements of the salesperson and saying just the opposite, you begin to agree with the sales presentation. How could you not buy the books after saying that you like to read, you do it often, and it's fun and educational? Can you think of times when one or more of the processes for inducing agreement were used against you? What did you do? What can you do to avoid this influence on your thoughts and actions?

SUMMARY

There is seldom a single reason for any of our behaviors. Most explanations will include factors in our immediate environments (e.g., rewards, demands of other people) as well as some of our personal characteristics. Needs, values, and attitudes are important categories of personal characteristics which help us understand the reasons our behaviors are guided and directed toward particular activities and goals. A need or motive is a lack or deficit of some factor within us. Our needs can have a physiological base (e.g., hunger, thirst) and also can be based on things that we learn (e.g., status, personal recognition). Values are the very stable ideas and beliefs that underlie our behaviors. They are the general ideals that we try to obtain in our lives and include such things as beliefs in freedom, equality, and independence. Attitudes are the thoughts and feelings that we have toward specific persons, objects, and events in our environments. "I like the president and I think that the government spends too much money" are examples of attitudes.

Abraham Maslow suggests that our different needs can be arranged in terms of how far they allow us to rise above a basic level of existence. Our needs can be arranged in a hierarchy proceeding from physiological to safety, social, self-esteem, and self-actualization. *Needs lower in the hierarchy must be satisfied before we try to fulfill those above them.* Because of circumstances, each of us spends different amounts of time and energy satisfying each need. The extent to which we can fulfill our social, self-esteem, and self-actualization needs has a great deal to do with our feelings of confidence, personal worth, and adequacy.

David McClelland and John Atkinson have identified achievement, affiliation, and power as important motives in our lives. Depending upon our past experiences and current interests, we engage in a variety of behaviors that might reflect each need. The things we say or do that reflect a high degree of interest in becoming successful, performing in a highly competent manner, or accomplishing something unique are related to our need for achievement. Our need for affiliation is seen in behaviors that are oriented toward forming friendships and working closely with people. Behaviors that are designed to allow us to control or influence others to compete successfully with them will allow us to satisfy our need for power.

Each motive can be assessed through the stories, songs, and drawings that we and other people create. For example, analyses of the children's literature, folksongs, and art of different cultures show evidence of the presence of each motive. It is then possible to look at the level of each motive at a given time period. A peak in achievement motivation allows us to predict that a nation will have its highest level of economic activity 25 to 50 years after that peak. When the need for power is greater than the need for affiliation in a nation, a war is likely to follow within 15 years. Finally, the level of achievement and power motivation allows us to predict the incidence of death due to ulcers and suicide, respectively.

Values are not ideas and assumptions we simply think about or tell others we believe. According to Louis Raths and Sidney Simon, we act upon the things we value. Values play a role in our personal preferences, our selection of goals, our perceptions of the environment, and our emotions. Unlike our attitudes, the same value will occur across a variety of situations in our lives.

Our attitudes often help us make choices about how we will act toward people, objects, and situations in our lives. We try to organize our attitudes and behaviors in ways that are consistent with each other. There are times when our attitudes are accurately reflected in our behaviors. On occasion, our attitudes are not reflected in our actions. There are three reasons for this problem. First, attitudes do not guarantee that any specific behavior will occur. They often only predispose us toward certain actions. Second, other factors in a situation may influence our actions more than a given attitude. Third, we may publicly state an attitude that does not accurately represent how we privately think and feel.

Our attitudes can be modified. Cognitive dissonance, social pressure, our needs, and a desire to agree with messages related to the attitude have been identified as four variables that are important to attitude change processes. Dissonance is a feeling of tension or displeasure. It is created when we obtain information that disagrees with an attitude or perform an action that goes against an attitude. One way to reduce dissonance is to modify one or more of our attitudes. Social pressure refers to the influence that other people exert on us to think and behave in certain ways. The approval that others give us for thinking as they do is a strong force in modifying our attitudes. Advertisers, salespeople, and others try to modify our attitudes by appealing to the types of needs we have. Attempts are made to have us think, feel, and behave in certain ways toward people, products, and events by showing us how such things will satisfy our various needs. Clever persuaders may influence our attitude if they can first get us to agree with them on issues remotely or closely related to the attitude in question. This persuasion can be accomplished by getting us first to agree to unrelated issues, small requests, and statements analogous to the attitude, or by the use of reactance.

THINGS TO DO

1. Based on your understanding of cognitive dissonance, social pressure, and our needs, think of how the attitudes in the situations discussed here were influenced:

   a. An auctioneer is stuck with four paintings that he has not been able to sell. People just don't seem to like them. At his next auction, he places several of his friends in the audience to bid on the products. He finds that he is able to sell them.

   b. Sue is not a very good guitar player, but she is interested in buying a new guitar. She sees an ad in a music store window which shows members of a popular group using a brand that she has had some reservations about. The salesperson also tells her that members of the popular group are now using the guitar. She decides to purchase the guitar.

   c. A magazine salesman visits Pete's home. Pete feels that he already has too many magazines in the house. However, the salesman tells Pete that the first two months' subscription to three new magazines is paid for by the salesman. At the end of that period, Pete can discontinue them or begin to pay a low subscription fee. Pete takes the two months of free magazines and at the end of that period decides to continue the subscriptions.

   d. An appliance saleswoman quotes a low price on a new refrigerator. Jane tells her that she will purchase it. The saleswoman then goes into her office to get her boss to approve the deal. She comes out and says that the boss will not allow her to sell the refrigerator for the price quoted. However, the boss will approve a price that is $15 above that originally quoted. Jane agrees to the new price.

2. Pick up your favorite magazine and look at advertisements. Try to identify the needs that are present in each of the ads. In terms of Maslow's need hierarchy, what categories of needs are the advertisements aimed at? Which need category appears most often in the advertisements?

3. What values do you think are present in the following: (a) Nazi concentration camps, (b) open admission colleges, (c) welfare programs, (d) scientific endeavors, (e) affirmative action programs, (f) the United States Constitution.

4. Based on what you know about achievement, affiliation, and power needs, which of these needs are likely to be seen in: (a) a police officer, (b) a teacher, (c) a minister, (d) a business manager, (e) a construction worker, (f) a homemaker, (g) a photographer, (h) a salesperson? What reasons do you have for the choices you made?

5. Using the information in Exercise 5-3, analyze the following for the presence of achievement, affiliation, and power needs: (a) a political speech by a candidate that you listened to or read about in the paper, (b) a popular song, (c) several pages from a novel that you are reading.

6. Think of yourself as a product that must be sold on the market. Write an ad about yourself that is likely to appeal to the needs of your reader. Could you use such an approach when looking for a job? If so, how might this be accomplished?

7. Have you ever tried to change someone's attitude about a person, object, or event? How hard or easy do you think it is? In order to find out, do the following: Pick two attitudes that another person has that you would like to try to change. Based on our discussion of attitude change principles, pick one or more principles and develop a plan of action. Try two different approaches for each of the attitudes you want to modify. In one case, try to get someone to change his or her point of view completely. In the other case, simply try to get the person to modify the attitude a little. Assess how successful you were in each case and which was easier to do. What evidence did you use for assessing the change in attitude (that is, variations in thoughts, behaviors, or both)?

REFERENCES AND OTHER INTERESTING THINGS TO READ

ARONSON, E. The need for achievement as measured by graphic expression. In J. W. Atkinson, *Motives in Fantasy, Action, and Society.* Princeton, N.J.: Van Nostrand, 1958.

ATKINSON, J. W. *Motives in Fantasy, Action, and Society*. Princeton, N.J.: Van Nostrand, 1958.

BREHM, J. W. *A Theory of Psychological Reactance*. New York: Academic Press, 1966.

CATTELL, R. B. Personality pinned down. *Psychology Today*, July, 1973.

DEMBER, W. D. Motivation and the cognitive revolution. *American Psychologist*, 1974, *29*, 161–168.

ERICKSON, E. H. *Childhood and Society*. New York: Norton, 1963.

FESTINGER, L. Cognitive dissonance. *Scientific American*, 1962, *207*, 93–98.

FESTINGER, L., RIECHEN, H. W., and SCHACTER, S. *When Prophecy Fails*. Minneapolis: University of Minnesota Press, 1956.

FREEDMAN, J. L., and Fraser, S. C. Compliance without pressure: The foot in the door technique. *Journal of Personality and Social Psychology*, 1966, *4*, 195–202.

GREENE, D., and LEPPER, M. Intrinsic motivation: How to turn play into work. *Psychology Today*, September, 1974.

GREENWALD, A. G., BROCK, T. C., and OSTROM, T. M. *Psychological Foundations of Attitudes*. New York: Academic Press, 1968.

HARRIS, T. G. To know why men do what they do: A conversation with David C. McClelland. *Psychology Today*, January, 1971.

HOVLAND, C., and ROSENBERG, M. J. *Attitude Organization and Change*. New Haven: Yale University Press, 1960.

KORDA, M. *Power! How to get it, how to use it*. New York: Random House, 1975.

LANSER, E. J., and DWECK, C. S. *Personal Politics: The Psychology of Making It*. Englewood Cliffs, N.J.: Prentice-Hall, 1973.

MASLOW, A. H. *Lessons from the Peak Experiences*. In R. E. Farson (Ed.), *Science and Human Affairs*. Palo Alto, Calif.: Science and Behavior Books, 1965.

MASLOW, A. H. *Motivation and Personality*. New York: Harper & Row, 1954.

McCLELLAND, D. C. *The Achieving Society*. Princeton, N.J.: Van Nostrand, 1961.

McCLELLAND, D. C. *Motivational Trends in Society*. New York: General Learning Press, 1971.

McGUIRE, W. J. Resistance to counter-persuasion conferred by active and passive prior refutation of the same and alternative counter-arguments. *Journal of Abnormal and Social Psychology*, 1961, *63*, 326–332.

NEWCOMB, T. M. Attitude development as a function of reference groups. In E. E. Maccoby, T. M. Newcomb and E. L. Hartley (Eds.), *Readings in Social Psychology*. New York: Holt, Rinehart and Winston, 1958.

RATHS, L., HARMIN, M., and SIMON, S. *Values and Teaching*. Columbus, Ohio: Charles E. Merrill, 1966.

ROKEACH, M., and ROTHMAN, G. The principle of belief congruence and the congruity principle as models of cognitive interaction. *Psychological Review*, 1965, *72*, 128–142.

RUDIN, S. A.   National motives predict psychogenic death rates 25 years later. *Science,* 1968, *160,* 901–903.

SIMON, S. B., HOWE, L. W. and KIRSCHENBAUM, H.   *Values Clarification: A Handbook of Practical Strategies for Teachers and Students.*   New York: Hart Publishing, 1972.

SPITZER, R. S.   *Tidings of Comfort and Joy.*   Palo Alto, Calif.: Science and Behavior Books, 1975.

VARELA, J. A.   *Psychological Solutions to Social Problems.*   New York: Academic Press, 1971.

WINTER, D. G.   What makes the candidates run. *Psychology Today,* July, 1976.

CHAPTER AIMS

A. After reading this chapter, the reader should be able to explain:

1. How our interpersonal communications are facilitated and restricted by various communication networks that operate among people.

2. Four advantages and disadvantages of one- and two-way communication patterns as they relate to our interaction with other people.

3. How the perception of differences in psychological size among people can interfere with the process of interpersonal communication.

4. Six things that we do in communicating with others that increase our psychological size and consequently interfere with our interactions.

5. How arrangements of people and room furnishings influence our interactions.

6. The characteristics of the Adult, Child, and Parent components of our personalities and their influence on our interpersonal communication.

7. The way that the things we refuse to share with other people, or our hidden agendas, interfere with our interactions.

8. Two ways that the methods we use to protect our personal space and how we use body language affect our relationships with others.

B. While reading this chapter, the reader should be able to use the information:

1. To solve the problems posed by the illustrations and exercises used in the chapter.

2. To analyze his or her personal interactions in terms of the communication components presented in the chapter.

3. To develop personal action plans to apply the concepts to his or her other daily interactions.

6

Interpersonal Communication

GLOSSARY

Adult. A personality component in transactional analysis theory that enables us to deal with life by solving problems, making decisions, thinking ahead, and anticipating the future.

Body language. Body gestures and postures that convey nonverbal messages to other people. Shaking one's fist in anger, smiling to note happiness, and frowning to show displeasure are examples.

Child. The personality component in transactional analysis theory that replays some of our childhood thoughts and feelings. When a person is angry, curious, or feeling creative or makes statements like "I want . . .," "I wish . . .," or "Mine is bigger," the child component is showing.

Communication. An interpersonal process in which verbal symbols (e.g., words, sentences) and nonverbal symbols (e.g., body postures, facial gestures) are shared and understood by two or more people.

Communication network. The pattern of restrictions that occurs in the flow of messages between people. This inability of people to communicate has implications for their satisfaction, their productivity, and their ability to clarify information and make and accept decisions.

Complementary transactions. In transactional analysis theory, a situation in which two people address each other and the personality components are compatible—for example, when the Parent in one person addresses and is in turn responded to by the Parent in the other person.

Hidden agendas. The unlabeled, private, covered feelings, motivations, attitudes, values, and ideas that we bring with us to discussions. We do not share them with others, but they influence the way we interact.

Latent content. What our words and sentences symbolize about our attitudes, values, feelings, and motivations. A latent analysis represents an in-depth analysis of a communication and attempts to uncover why a statement is made.

Manifest content. The idea or fact that is conveyed in a message.

One-way communication. A pattern of communication in which most of the messages are directed toward the listener. It is a quick way to get a message across but it can lead to misunderstanding, dependency, and frustration in the listener.

Parent. The personality component in transactional analysis theory that develops from characteristics of our real parents that we internalize and use in our daily interactions. When we interact and convey verbal and nonverbal messages of "how to," "always," and "should" and otherwise evaluate or attempt to set rigid standards, the Parent part of our personality is showing.

Personal space. The personal territories or zones we interact in and within which we allow only certain types of behaviors to occur. Examples include our intimate, personal, social, and public zones.

Psychological size. The perceived impact or influence that one person has on another. People who are seen as psychologically big are viewed as having a high potential for influencing and controlling other people.

Transactional analysis. A theory of interpersonal communication that interprets our verbal and nonverbal messages in terms of Parent, Child, and Adult components.

Two-way communication. A pattern of communication in which two or more parties are able to share messages among themselves. It leads to more involvement and interest, and encourages initiative and independence in people. It is more accurate than a one-way pattern.

What Needs to Be Understood?

"I think you are doing a good job, Tony, and I appreciate it." With those words from my boss I turned red, stormed out of his office, and slammed the door behind me. On the surface this looks as though I was not behaving rationally. Let us take a closer look at the situation. As an undergraduate I worked in a steel mill one summer. My boss had given me written instructions on how to repair a piece of equipment. Because of a mistake in the instructions, I ruined an expensive piece of equipment. The plant supervisor was angry and I heard from another worker that my boss blamed me. The plant supervisor was told that I had no business repairing the equipment. I was layed off two days later.

I went to my immediate boss to find out why. He sat behind his desk with arms crossed, a visible frown on his face, and acted nervous. He said that he did not know why I was layed off and that it had nothing to do with the equipment problem. When he then told me how much he had appreciated my efforts, I knew he did not mean it. I really became angry.

Have you ever had a similar experience in which someone said something but you suspected they were not telling the truth? If you have, then it suggests we need to go beyond the words spoken to understand interpersonal *communication*. In our daily interactions there are always messages beyond the words which enhance and modify what the words mean. The situation, our past experiences and knowledge, the tone of voice used, and various facial and body gestures influence the process. Since each of us faces a range of minor and major communication problems in our daily affairs, we probably need to sharpen and extend our understanding of the communication process. This chapter will examine these concerns by assessing (a) how interpersonal networks or patterns of communication, our psychological size, and our environments influence the process and (b) how components of our verbal and nonverbal messages facilitate and retard effectiveness. The communication concepts and principles developed are general enough to apply to information exchanges both between two individuals and among members of a group.

Communication Patterns among People

Our daily interactions differ in the number of ways we send and receive messages. Various *communication networks* or *patterns* develop, and they often influence the nature and quality of our relationships. In a client-therapist relationship there is usually a rather open and direct two-way exchange of ideas and feelings. Both parties can respond immediately to the other's ideas and feelings. This is not the case in a large business organization with which I am familiar. Before reaching the top, messages are often filtered through many layers of the organization. Lower-level managers are expected to communicate in writing with their supervisors. Each successive manager in the chain must then approve the message before it is sent forward. Unlike the therapy situation, the sender does not receive immediate feedback on his or her ideas. The communication pattern is rather impersonal and creates feelings of uncertainty and frustration.

These examples illustrate communication patterns that vary in the ways they facilitate or restrict information exchanges. Research shows communication patterns affect the satisfaction we have in relationships, our productivity, our ability to clarify information, our ability to make decisions, and our acceptance of decisions. Let us take a closer look at several of these issues.

The Identification of Specific Networks

Harold Leavitt's work illustrates the problems associated with inadequate communication networks. He was interested in how people react when their interpersonal communications are restricted. Instead of allowing each member of a group to communicate with everyone else, he created different communication patterns. These are illustrated in Figure 6-1. Note that with the exception of the concom pattern, *two-way communication* between *all* the participants is not possible.

People participating in the Leavitt experiments were given a rather simple problem to solve. Each member was assigned a series of symbols. One and only one symbol was common to every member of the group. By exchanging written messages, the members had to identify the common symbol.

Before reading further, try to think of yourself in each pattern. Which one do you think would produce the *most* number of problem-solving errors: the circle, the Y, the wheel, or the concom? Which one would produce the *least* number of errors? In which two of the patterns do you think people are likely to be most satisfied? What reasons do you have for each of your responses?

The circle arrangement was found to produce the greatest number of problem-solving errors and the Y arrangement the fewest. One reason is that it is hard for *one* person to coordinate a solution in the circle. Because of the opportunities for two-way communication, the circle and concom

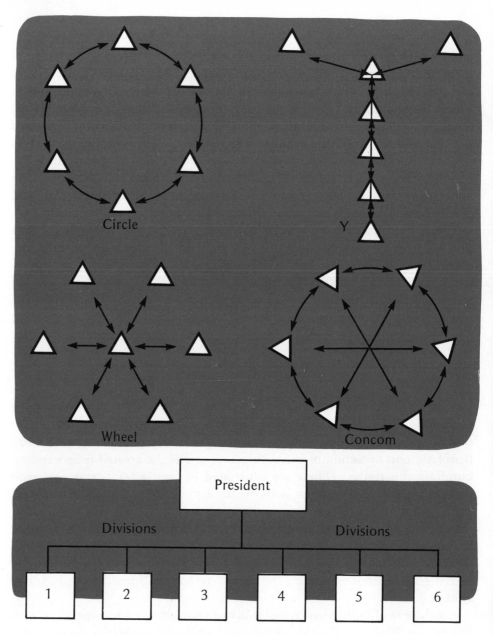

Circle

Y

Wheel

Concom

President

Divisions

Divisions

1 2 3 4 5 6

Alternate Form of Wheel

Figure 6-1

Four communication patterns. The triangles represent people and the arrows show the direction that messages can take among people in the circle, Y, wheel, and concom patterns. An absence of arrows between certain people means that they cannot directly communicate with each other.

members reported more satisfaction with their interactions than members of other patterns. With the exception of the member in the center, people in the wheel had the least amount of satisfaction. The person in the center of the wheel arrangement had the highest satisfaction score of anyone regardless of the communication pattern. A very close second was the member at the junction of the three lines of the Y. This suggests that a person at the center of a communication flow is likely to feel more important and, therefore, better satisfied with his or her role. People in other positions are likely to have less positive feelings regarding the task. How do you think such feelings will affect the quality of the group's product?

Such findings do not occur only in the laboratory. In the lower portion of Figure 6-1 is another way to represent the wheel. Many of you will recognize this as the usual arrangement in most organizations. The example represents an organization in which I once worked. The president of the organization had six division heads. Each functioned somewhat independently of the others and there was an occasional flow of information among them. When a common problem arose the person who enjoyed solving it most was the president. This was because the flow of information was in his direction. He asked for inputs from the division heads but personally made all the decisions. His decision-making style often left the division heads dissatisfied and frustrated because they had only a minor role in the solution.

There is an important implication for working with others in the discussion of networks. When we are in interpersonal situations in which a common task must be solved, it is often a good idea to create as much communication among the participants as possible. A principle of human behavior that is often violated is that *maximum acceptance of a decision occurs only through maximum participation in the decision-making process.* People need to feel ownership of the decisions they are asked to follow. If they do not feel they influenced the decision process, it is possible they will not feel strongly committed to the outcome. A correspondingly poor level of performance is likely to result. Two of my personal experiences illustrate the advantages of a more participatory communication pattern.

A friend of mine runs a small manufacturing plant that produces components for stereo systems. He recently ran into a problem. He had discovered what he felt was a faster method for assembling the components. His employees were simply shown the process and told to use it. Almost immediately the number of rejections by the quality control inspector increased, and frequent complaints about the new assembly process were heard among the workers. A drop rather than an increase in productivity occurred. I suspected that this was a problem more with how the decision to use the new method was made than with the method itself. I suggested that my friend have his foreman and a committee of workers devise a new method. During the course of several meetings, the workers were able to devise a new procedure that combined the best aspects of the old one and the one suggested by the boss. The product quality increased and complaints regarding the system were practically nonexistent.

A neighbor of mine wanted her house kept neat during the week. Every Sunday the family had a meeting and the parents made daily cleaning assignments for their four children. Each was expected to do a particular chore each day. My neighbor was quite surprised at the children's grumbling and the fact that the house was not that much neater during the week. Based on what you have read, what do you think caused the problem? What solution would you suggest?

The Effects of One- and Two-way Communication Patterns in Our Daily Interactions

We can begin to extend the analysis of communication networks to our daily lives if we think of the ways that patterns permit *one-* and *two-way communication*. Each of the Leavitt networks, the groups we meet with daily (e.g., in classes, business and social meetings, dinner parties) , and interactions between two individuals can be characterized by the amount of one- and two-way communication they permit—that is, the extent to which people are able both to send and to receive messages. These are relative distinctions, but in general a one-way pattern occurs whenever one of us dominates a conversation. This does not necessarily mean that a one-way pattern is always bad and that two-way is always good. Each has particular strengths and weaknesses. Which one is used depends on what is needed to accomplish the exchange of ideas.

EXERCISE 6-1: ONE- AND TWO-WAY COMMUNICATION

To begin, let us look at an exercise which demonstrates several of the personal effects of one- and two-way communication patterns. You will need a watch, two blank sheets of paper, and a pencil. There are two parts to the exercise. After following the instructions in the first part, proceed immediately to Part 2.

Part 1: One-Way Communication Exercise

The purpose of this exercise is to demonstrate some of the effects of one-way communication. You will need a blank sheet of paper and a pencil or pen. I want you to pretend that you are sitting in a large classroom or at a meeting in which someone is talking to you. Neither you nor anyone else in the room can ask any questions. Follow the instructions of the speaker as well as you can.

S: Good day. Before we begin I would like each of you to put the time of day in the upper right-hand corner of your blank sheet of paper. Thank you.

S: Today I am going to lecture on the arrangement of five rectangles that I have on the sheet of paper in front of me. I want you to draw the arrangement as I describe it to you.

S: The five rectangles form a rather interesting pattern on the page. The first is to the left of #2 with one of the sides of #2 touching a side of #1.

S: The third rectangle is located at an angle with its long side touching the right end of #2.

S: The fourth rectangle is standing long side up and part of the right side touches the upper left side of #3.

S: To better visualize the pattern thus far, if you extended the right side of the fourth rectangle you would almost form a triangle with part of the lower side of #2 and part of the upper left-hand side of #3.

S: The fifth rectangle is also resting at an angle. The middle of its long right side touches the lower corner of #4.

S: That concludes my talk on the arrangement of the five rectangles. Please put the time of day below the time you wrote when we started. Proceed to the two-way communication exercise in the next table. We will score the one-way exercise for accuracy after we complete the two-way.

Part 2: Two-Way Communication Exercise

The purpose of this exercise is to demonstrate some of the effects of two-way communication. You will need a blank sheet of paper and a pencil or pen. I want you to pretend that you are sitting in a large classroom or at a meeting in which someone is talking to you. People have the opportunity to ask questions and others in the room will do this. The questions they will ask are those that individuals typically ask when doing this exercise. Follow the instructions of the speaker as well as you can.

S: Good day. Before we begin I would like each of you to put the time of day in the upper right-hand corner of your blank sheet of paper. Thank you.

S: The five rectangles form an interesting pattern on the page. The first rests with its long side running parallel to the bottom of the page.

Q: How big is each of the rectangles and where on the page is the first one located?

S: That's a good question. Thank you. The rectangles are each approximately 2½ inches long and 1½ inches wide. The first one sits about two inches from the top of the page. Its short side is located at about the center of the page and begins about two inches from the top.

S: The second rectangle is at an angle with its upper right-hand corner touching the middle of #1.

Q: That's a little ambiguous for me. Do you mean that the upper right-hand corner of #2 touches the middle of #1's bottom line or do you mean that it rests in the center of #1?

S: I wasn't too clear, was I? I meant to say that the upper right-hand corner of #2 touches the middle of the first rectangle's bottom line.

S: If there are no other questions, let's do the third one. The third rectangle is also at an angle, with its short left side touching both the lower right-hand corner of #1 and the lower right-hand corner of #2.

Q: Does that mean that the upper left-hand corner of #3 and its lower left-hand corner join the lower right corner of #1 and the lower right corner of #2?
S: Yes, that's correct. If you do it right, you will have a triangle formed by half of the bottom side of #1 and the short left side of #2 and the short left side of #3.
S: The fourth rectangle is positioned so that its long side touches the bottom long sides of #2 and #3 just past the middle of #2's and #3's bottom line.
Q: Does that mean that the upper left- and right-hand corners of the fourth one touch at the middle of the long bottom side of the second and third one?
S: Yes, that's correct.

S: The fifth rectangle is positioned so that one of its short sides overlaps part of the bottom long side of #4.
Q: Does it touch the right- or left-hand side of #4?
S: It touches the left-hand side of rectangle #4.

S: If there are no other questions, that concludes my talk. Please put the time of day below the time that you started.

After you have completed both the one-way and two-way exercises, look at Figure 6-2 for the correct solutions. Give yourself 1 point for each rectangle that you have correct. Compare the amount of time it took to complete each exercise and the number of rectangles that you had correct. Also try to think about how you felt in both conditions. Did you feel more or less frustrated with the one-way communication? How satisfied do you feel with your performance on each task?

Although this exercise is a somewhat artificial situation, it does show many of the effects of one- and two-way communication. Experience with this exercise shows that one-way communication is faster but is less accurate and tends to make people feel frustrated and less satisfied with their efforts. Two-way communication tends to take longer but is usually more accurate and leaves people feeling less frustrated and more satisfied. To what extent are these results compatible with your experiences with the exercise? If discrepancies exist, why do you believe they occurred? Have you found any of these principles to be true in your daily interactions?

Research by Fred Tesch, Harold Leavitt, and others on one- and two-way communication patterns suggests several other characteristics and applications of these patterns. These are presented in Table 6-1.

Psychological Size

Two-way communication is sometimes difficult because there are status differences between the people communicating. A way to approach this problem is to look at the concept of *psychological size*. This concept is a con-

Table 6-1

Characteristics of One- and Two-Way Communication

One-Way Communication
1. The listener has little or no opportunity to respond immediately.
2. The speaker must make assumptions about the listener's skill level, prior training, and understanding of the material being communicated.
3. It is difficult for a common language to develop as issues are presented.
4. A lack of involvement and interest can occur in the listener.
5. It encourages dependence on the speaker and discourages initiative and independence on the listener's part.
6. Since it encourages dependency, it can also lead to hidden hostility and frustration.
7. It can lead to frustration and anger on the part of individuals receiving one-way communications that are not clear.
8. It takes less time to transmit messages.
9. Compared to two-way, it is often less accurate since people experience difficulty in obtaining clarification of messages.

Two-Way Communication
1. Two-way patterns allow for a better flow of information between and among individuals.
2. Because of the opportunity for immediate feedback, many of the assumptions that one makes about skill level of the listener, prior training, and understanding of the information get tested immediately.
3. It allows for a shared language to develop through discussion.
4. It leads to more involvement and interest on the part of each person in the communication.
5. It can encourage less dependence on the speaker and can encourage more initiative and independence on the part of the listener (s) .
6. It takes more time for a message to be transmitted.
7. It is more accurate than one-way communication and can assist people in developing a better quality product.

venient label for the impact that one person has on another. This impact is usually seen in terms of the potential that one person has for helping or hurting others. People who are perceived as psychologically big have a high potential for influencing and controlling other people. This perception interferes with an open dialogue between people. Figure 6-3 illustrates the concept of psychological size in a business meeting and in an interaction between a student and teacher.

Differences in psychological size have other consequences besides interfering with two-way communication. When someone is perceived as psychologically big, others expect that individual to solve problems, to see that all goes well, to take care of them, to tell them what and how to do things.

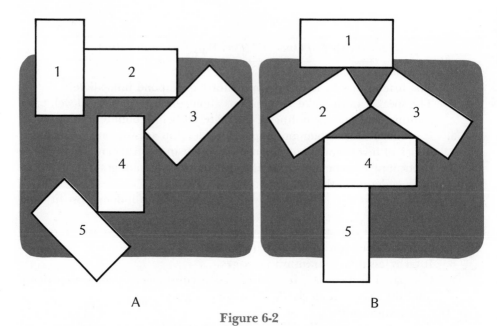

Figure 6-2

Solutions for the one-way (A) and two-way (B) communication exercises.

This dependence can easily lead to apathy and a lack of initiative. Those who are psychologically small may also become resentful and frustrated in interactions. They may feel they must defer to the person who is "big" and thus deny their individuality. Let us take a look at some of the factors that Ronald Boyer and Charles Bolton[1] identify as contributing to psychological size. As you read, try to think of which factors are issues with you or the people with whom you interact.

High status and titles. Many of us forget the effects that our status and titles can have on other people. Consistently using Mr., Ms., Dr., or other titles presents an image of us to someone else of a person who is more competent, somewhat distant, and perhaps even more intelligent than other people. This can cause people to feel less free and open with regard to discussing or contributing their thoughts or ideas.

Use of criticism, sarcasm, ridicule, and humor inappropriately. It is important for us to be sensitive to the way that we criticize another person's work, whether it is written or verbal. While our motivations may be constructive and positive, others may well perceive the criticism as a form of

[1] Part of the material in this section was adapted with permission from a monograph by Ronald Boyer and Charles Bolton, "One and Two Way Communication in the Classroom," Faculty Resource Center Monograph Series, University of Cincinnati, 1971.

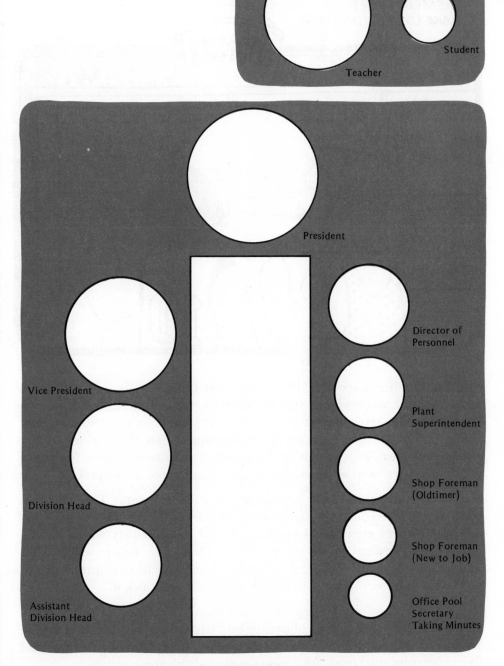

Figure 6-3
The concept of psychological size in a teacher-student interaction
and at a business meeting.

ridicule. Telling someone "That's the worst thing I've seen in my life" is not as helpful as providing specific feedback regarding any inadequacies. Teachers and parents often tell children that some idea is terrible without giving specific reasons. A similar point applies to the use of humor. Although we may wish to lighten the situation or introduce some fun into a relationship, we need to be careful of offending people in the process.

Use of terminal statements permitting no disagreement. This situation often occurs when one-way communication is used. Sometimes we feel that our authority or expertise is challenged, and consequently we try to discourage disagreement. Such statements as "That's fine; let's move on," "I'd like to think of it my way," and "There's no need for us to continue in this way" have the effect of controlling and cutting off a discussion.

Very formal manner. Some people come across in a very formal fashion. Others see them as being rigid and tight. Given this portrait, it is safe to assume that others will have some reluctance or difficulty in being open and free in interpersonal communication situations with these persons.

Use of punishing remarks. Saying things like "That's illogical," "That does not follow," and "How in the world could you do that?" may be perceived as very punishing by others. Such remarks do not serve to improve relationships, and, if they are used too often, people may feel a need to be "more careful" and not "get caught" again.

Display of great amount of detailed knowledge. I am sure you know some-one—a boss, teacher, friend, or neighbor—who delights in how much he or she knows about something. Whether it is the state of the economy, a book, or other topic, this person likes to let you know how knowledgeable he or she is. The effect is that people may not want to say anything to someone with so much knowledge. They do not want to appear stupid or incompetent.

Use of language that is too complicated for the listener. It is important to use good language. If you have an extensive vocabulary or a facility for expressing complex concepts, however, it can be overwhelming for others. Many professional people have this effect when they use the "jargon" of their field extensively with those outside the field. Discussion is facilitated if we bring our words down to a level that we are sure our listeners can tolerate.

Failure to use the name of a person. It is a good idea to get to know the names of people with whom you interact. This personalizes the interaction and breaks down some of the barriers to effective communication. People usually like to interact with someone who acknowledges them as individuals. In my teaching, I have been most impressed at the favorable comments students make with regard to my learning their names. I am sure it makes them feel like more than just objects in a classroom.

Not all the factors that contribute to psychological "bigness" are undesirable. People need to have some degree of expertise and facility with language, for example. Our intent here is simply to indicate that such factors can increase our psychological size and consequent distance from other people. Communication then begins to be less satisfying. We need simply to be aware of this factor in our interactions.

Analyzing an Interpersonal Communication Problem

To begin to get a more personal appreciation of the communication principles discussed thus far, please diagram two situations in your life in which there are problems in communication. The situations do not have to present extremely difficult problems, but they should be situations in which you would like to see some improvement. If applicable, one should involve a group (three or more people) and the other a relationship with only one

Table 6-2

Two Situations Involving Interpersonal Communication Issues

Situation 1. A student in one of my classes comes in to see me periodically to discuss her interpretation of course material. Even though we schedule half-hour meetings, they seldom last more than five or ten minutes. The discussions don't seem to get anywhere. She states what she thinks but, frankly, I have a hard time understanding her. Her thoughts are quite involved and she expects me to respond immediately. When I don't she says that she has another class to get to and leaves.

Diagram of situation:

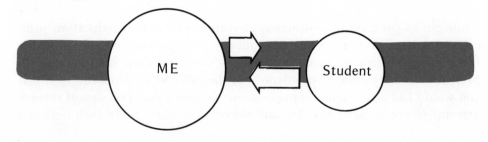

186

Table 6-2 (continued)

The Problem:
There is too much one-way communication. I'm not responding well. The reason is that I do not understand her ideas since they can be quite complex at times.

Action Plan:
The simplest thing I can do is to use principles #2 and #3 in Table 6-3. I'll begin to ask her more questions as she starts to develop ideas. I'll also summarize what she is saying more and ask her to do the same when I comment on an idea she has.

Situation 2. A younger colleague and I are working with a very wealthy, self-made local businessman on a community project. He likes to do things his way and has a hard time accepting advice from others. He often comes back to us to say he did what we suggested, but what he does bear little relation to our suggestions.

Diagram of situation:

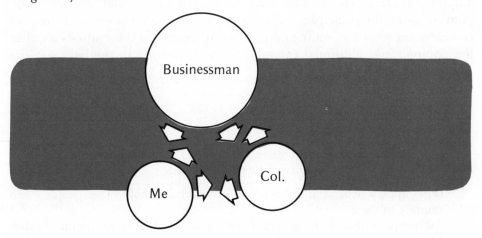

The Problem:
Good two-way communication exists between my colleague and me. Unfortunately it's mostly one-way between us and the businessman. Not only do we need more of an information flow toward him, we need to get him to understand our suggestions.

Action Plan:
He is not really listening to us. Principle #3 could be helpful here. If we begin to model summarizing what he says we should be able to create an atmosphere in which he will do the same. This should help to increase the amount of two-way communication with him.

other person (e.g., a friend, spouse, child, teacher). Diagram the situations as I have two of my personal situations in Table 6-2. Label the people with their initials and indicate their relative psychological size. Use arrows to indicate the relative amount of one- or two-way communication between people. Arrows of equal length indicate a balanced amount of two-way communication; arrows of differing length indicate an imbalance in the pattern.

Having diagramed the situations, pick one or two things in each situation that you feel need to be changed. A few words of caution are in order. Do not try to be too ambitious in a short amount of time. Try to work on one or two things that you can personally influence. A good place to start is with yourself and anything that you might be doing in the situation that is contributing to the difficulties. Remember that changes in interpersonal communication take time and that no one principle is powerful enough to change everything overnight.

Having identified the issue (s) you want to work on, pick one or more principles related to increasing two-way communication and reducing psychological size from Table 6-3. State how you will use them. (See the examples that are given in Table 6-2.) List your problem (s) and an action plan for using the principles. Have a friend or another student in the class comment on what you want to do. We will return to these situations after developing some additional communication principles in the later sections of the chapter.

Table 6-3

*Ten Principles for Increasing Two-Way Communication and
Reducing Psychological Size*

1. Don't appear neutral, indifferent, or unconcerned about other people when you talk to them.
2. Ask people questions to initiate conversations and to clarify points as they talk.
3. Try to get feedback from people on their undestanding of what you said. Ask them to summarize what was said as a check on understanding. Do the same for things that they tell you.
4. De-emphasize your status and title in talking with people.
5. Keep to a minimum any formal mannerisms you may have.
6. Try not to use sarcasm or ridicule in conversations.
7. Try not to make terminal statements when disagreement is possible. Allow time for the ideas and feelings of the listener (s) to be expressed adequately.
8. Avoid making punishing remarks as a consistent habit.
9. Try not to impress people with your use of language or your knowledge.
10. Get to know the names of people and use them in conversations.

Physical Environment

The ways we arrange people and objects (e.g., furniture, rooms, pictures) influence our ability to communicate effectively. Physical arrangements affect our communication by encouraging or discouraging social contact and by their symbolic meaning—the capacity of physical settings to convey messages regarding our status and relative influence.

Social Contact

Physical arrangements have a tendency either to push people together or to push them apart. Robert Sommer reports that chairs placed across a corner of a table were the most effective arrangement for encouraging seated conversations between two people. Chairs arranged across the table from each other were second, and side by side placements were the worst possible arrangement. One reason is that visual contact has a tendency to make people more responsive to each other. They then interact more often.

This principle is violated in many situations in which interaction is desirable. Think of meetings you have attended where the purpose was to discuss issues. Chances are you sat in a front-to-back seating arrangement with the person in charge at the front of the room. Such arrangements encourage one-way communication patterns, since the flow of conversation is

NOW WE CAN BEGIN!

directed toward the front of the room. Thus, only a few people have the opportunity to speak if the group is large. Another popular pattern is to have a rectangular table with one person at each end and the others lined along the sides. The tendency here is for the conversation to flow toward the leader (who usually sits at one end) and toward people sitting opposite each other. People sitting adjacent to each other have fewer communications. Leon Festinger reports that the most desirable physical arrangement for obtaining maximum communication among all individuals is as nearly round a table or seating arrangement as possible.

How do you think the arrangement of people and furniture in your classes, your office, or your home influences interaction? In what ways can the current arrangement be modified to increase interactions?

Symbolic Aspects of Arrangements

The location of objects and their characteristics convey certain symbolic messages which affect our interactions. A few years ago at the Vietnam Peace Conference, discussions did not begin until the participants agreed on the shape and size of the conference table and the height of the chairs. The participants wanted to be seated so that they were all on the same level. The arrangement that best symbolized equal status was a circular table with everyone sitting on the same level. Square and rectangular arrangements were rejected. Why do you think they were rejected?

The office of a professor I once had provides another example of the environment's symbolic value. His office was arranged as shown in Figure 6-4. Note that the only place a student could sit was in the middle between the bookcases. You could not see the professor from the hallway because the bookcases obstructed the view of his desk. He looked as if he were hiding in a barricade of bookcases and filing cabinets. This arrangement conveyed a message that he preferred to be left alone and was not interested in talking to visitors. Sitting in the lone chair in front of the desk was an uncomfortable experience. Conversations were short and they were strictly related to course business. Diagram the office of a professor in which you are comfortable interacting and one in which you are not. How much does the setting contribute to your comfort? How much does the individual?

It is important for us to remember that physical settings seldom act alone to produce their effects. We occupy settings, and it is often our expectations and preferences for particular communication patterns that create and maintain the settings. Our actions and behaviors reinforce whatever implications our environments have for communication. For example, I have been in lavish surroundings with pompous people who were con-

Figure 6-4

An example of a room arrangement which restricts interpersonal communication.

cerned with their status and power, and this hindered communication. On the other hand, I have been in similar settings with people who were quite open and genuine. To focus entirely on the physical layout and the arrangements of people represents an incomplete analysis of the situation.

Table 6-4 lists several principles derived from our discussion of physical space and communication. Take another look at the two situations that you described like those in Table 6-4. Is there any way that one or more of these principles might be useful? If there is, pick a principle (s) from the table and develop an action plan for using it. An example of my use of some of these principles is presented in Table 6-5.

Verbal and Nonverbal Components of the Communication Process

Up to this point we have looked at the effects on interpersonal communication of communication patterns, psychological size, and the physical environment. Let us now look at the verbal and nonverbal components of a pattern

Table 6-4

Principles Regarding the Effects of Physical Space on Communication

1. Communication is affected by the way an arrangement pushes people together or pulls them apart.
2. Seating arrangements across the corner of a table or desk increase visual contact between people and encourage communication. In general, sitting on the same level face to face and close to someone can facilitate communication.
3. For small group discussions, a circular arrangement will maximize the amount of communication among people.
4. Arrange furniture in a room so that people have easy access to you.
5. Build mobility into a space. Try to remove physical barriers (desks, furniture, chairs, partitions) that needlessly isolate particular people or areas. Allow for areas where people can meet in small groups to talk.
6. In meeting areas, use chairs and/or desks that can be moved into different physical arrangements. Try not to think of the furniture as fixed to a given location.
7. Be aware that aspects of physical space have symbolic value which can affect communication. Look at your space and ask yourself, "What does each fixture and its location in the space do to facilitate communication?" If your answer is nothing or very little, think of ways that you could change the setting.

to gain a better understanding of "what is really being said by the speaker." As an example of why this is important, consider the statement from a high school student who says with tears in her eyes and a soft tone, "John did not ask me to the prom." The meaning of the words go beyond the simple fact that she was not asked to the prom. Both the things she said and the way she said it convey feelings of disappointment and rejection. To really understand communication processes we must go beyond the simple meaning of the words and begin to listen for interpretations that deal with the personal and interpersonal concerns of the speaker and listener. Our motivations, values, attitudes, and feelings influence what and how we say things.

A distinction between the *manifest* and the *latent content* of our messages can assist us in understanding this process. The manifest content refers to the idea or fact that is conveyed. For example, "George received a promotion last week," "Mary fell down the steps in the department store," and "Ellen said that she likes the concept of supply and demand in economics" can be interpreted as factual statements. The latent content refers to the things that our words, sentences, and physical gestures symbolize about our attitudes, values, feelings, and motivations. A latent analysis represents a more in-depth analysis. Parts of *transactional analysis* theory, the concept of *hidden agendas,* and an analysis of nonverbal messages can help us to understand latent content.

Table 6-5

Using Physical Space Principles to Improve Communication

Situation 1:   My interaction problem with the student.

The Problem: One-way communication is extensive.   The physical space–related issue is that I think my sitting behind the desk with her in front of it is not helping things.

Action Plan: Principle #2 in Table 6-4 suggests that seating arrangements across the corner of a table or desk should encourage more communication.   Next time she comes in I'll create this arrangement.

Situation 2:   My colleague and I and our interaction with the businessman.

The Problem: There is too much one-way communication and he does not really understand our suggestions.   The physical space aspect of the problem is that we meet in his office.   The symbolic aspects of the objects in it and their arrangement represent a business environment.

Action Plan: Principle #7 suggests that we should try to make the physical area more conducive to informal conversation.   Instead of our meeting around his desk, I'll suggest that we move into an adjoining room which serves as an informal lounge area.   Symbolically I think that the lounge area conveys a more relaxed, informal atmosphere, which is what we need.

Transactional Analysis

This system for understanding communication is based on the writings of Eric Berne and Thomas Harris.[2]   Transactional analysis is a useful tool that can help us interpret both the verbal and the nonverbal messages that occur among people.   Its basic principle is that our personalities have three components, the *Parent,* the *Child,* and the *Adult.*   Since each component influences our daily transactions, it is possible to analyze our daily communications in terms of the contribution of each personality component.   As we will see, determining the extent of influence of the Parent, Child, and Adult in each of two people involved in interaction provides a convenient method of analyzing the communication and enables us to understand why some of our discussions do not go well.

The Parent in our personality develops from characteristics of our real parents that we internalize and use in our daily interactions.   To use a

---

[2] Parts of this section were adapted from Thomas Harris's book *I'm OK—You're OK,* copyright 1967, 1968, 1969 by Thomas Harris, M.D., and used with permission of Thomas Harris, M.D., Harper & Row Publishers, Inc., and Jonathan Cape Ltd.

metaphor, we carry with us tape recordings of the types of feelings and verbal and nonverbal messages associated with our parents. These tapes include not only their nurturing aspects but also the rules they taught us. We were taught what to do and how to do things in particular ways. When we interact and convey verbal and nonverbal messages of "how to," "never," "always," and "should" or otherwise evaluate or attempt to set rigid standards, the Parent part of our personality is showing. Such statements as "George, you must get to school on time," "Ladies and gentlemen, people in this company always do market research in accordance with company regulations," "The term paper should have margins of 1½ inches and it should be double spaced" are verbal messages high in Parent content. Nonverbal Parent messages are often conveyed by such things as wrinkling our foreheads, folding our arms, keeping our hands on our hips as we talk, pointing with the index finger, leaning over someone and wringing our hands.

While we develop and internalize aspects of our parents' behavior, we also have feelings about their behavior. The feelings that develop are often negative. For example, we may come to feel that our parents' behavior signifies "It's my fault," "I can't do anything right," "I'm getting picked on again." It is quite easy to begin to feel frustrated, rejected, or abandoned. We may feel that there is something fundamentally wrong with us. In Eric Berne's terms we are "not OK."

As adults we may find ourselves faced with difficult alternatives or boxed into a corner. We then replay some of our earlier feelings and begin to act angry or depressed. When a person is in the grip of such feelings, the Transactional Analysis theory says that the Child is in control. The Child can be identified by statements like "I want . . .," "I wish . . .," "I guess . . .," and "When I grow up . . .," and by statements that have a quality of bigger, better, best to them—for example, "This sales team is the best in the company" or "My television is a better brand than yours." Nonverbal behaviors like pouting, showing a great deal of anger when speaking, teasing, acting delighted, shrugging shoulders, and laughing are associated with the Child.

The Child is not just a negative state. Creativity, curiosity, and needs to explore and experience the world are parts of the Child. Such behaviors give our lives an interesting dimension. However, it is usually the less positive aspects of the Child that present problems in communication.

Although the Parent and Child begin to develop from birth onward, the Adult is thought to begin developing at about 10 months of age. The function of the Adult is to enable us to deal with life by solving problems, making decisions, thinking ahead, and anticipating the future. It operates like a computer and considers inputs from the situation, the Parent, and the Child. Based on these inputs, it promotes or defers action. The Adult helps us deal with reality in productive and useful ways. The Adult can be found in statements and questions beginning "What," "Why," "Where," "When," "Who," "How," "I think," "I see," and "In my opinion." A listening posture with very little emotion showing represents nonverbal Adult cues.

Interactions between two people are thought to consist of the Parent, Adult, or Child component of one person addressing corresponding components of another. *Complementary transactions* occur when two people cooperate so that each accepts the conditions of the relationship. One form occurs when the communications are on the level of Parent to Parent, Adult to Adult, and Child to Child. Examples are shown in Figure 6-5, in which several interactions between two people are shown. The two parties are addressing each other as equals regardless of the personality components involved.

A second form of complementary relationship occurs when the personality components are not equal but compatible; for example, the Parent of one person addresses the Child of the second and the Child responds back to the Parent of the first individual. Each person is willing to play the role that the other wants. Examples of this second type of relationships are found in Figure 6-6. As long as both parties are willing to stay in their roles, such relationships can continue indefinitely. This does not mean that they are desirable transactions. A boss and subordinates can often engage in complementary Parent-Child interactions, but problems may arise. The subordinates may secretly resent the boss telling them what to do and how to do it. Because they are afraid of the boss (i.e., his or her psychological size), they say nothing that betrays their true feelings. They do as they are told and look to the boss for guidance. The boss in turn might wonder why the subordinates do not take initiative. A solution is to begin to engage in a more Adult-Adult complementary relationship in which people can share their opinions and begin jointly to problem solve.

EXERCISE 6-2: COMPLEMENTARY TRANSACTIONS

To test your understanding of the relationships discussed here, diagram each of the following situations using the same PAC format shown in Figure 6-5. If needed, refer back to the descriptions of each personality component. The correct solutions are found in Figure 6-7.

Situation 1

(1) It's time to go home.
(2) I'm ready; let's go.

Conversations

Parent-Parent

Students do not seem to work hard. They are quite lazy in many respects.

It's simply the way things are today. No one does more than he has to.

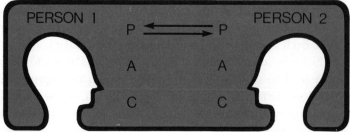

You should never go to that store again after what they did.

You are so right. They will probably always treat me that way.

Adult-Adult

What floor is the furniture on?

It's on the fifth floor.

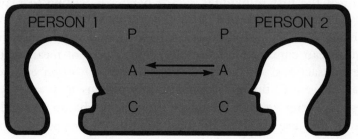

Sue seems to be preoccupied lately.

Let's go and talk to her.

Child-Child

My house is bigger than yours.

But mine has more windows.

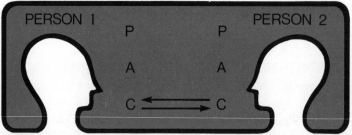

I wish I were the Lone Ranger.

Me too.

Figure 6-5

Complementary transactions in which the two parties are addressing each other as equals.

Parent-Child

You spent too much money for the dress.

But I really wanted it.

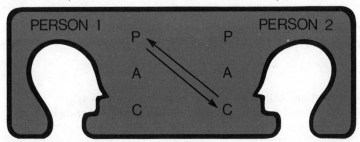

You must do things as I say.

You are always telling me what to do.

Child-Adult

I'm feeling anxious. I don't think I can perform.

In my opinion, you have performed well in rehearsal. Why not try?

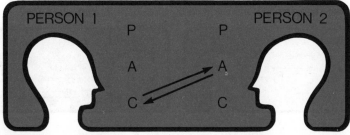

I'm really feeling happy about our new car. In fact, I'm absolutely delighted.

I understand how you feel. What did your brother say?

Adult-Parent

I'd like to quit smoking. Would you help me?

The first step is for you to start chewing gum.

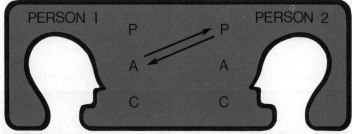

I wonder if I'll ever be any good at painting. Can you give me some tips?

Sure. Just follow the suggestions in the book and do what I tell you to.

Figure 6-6

Complementary relationships, in which one person plays the role that the other wants.

Situation 2

(1) Wow, look at that train set!
(2) Is that ever neat!

Situation 3

(1) You should always wear your heavy coat in the winter.
(2) I don't like that idea but I'll do what you tell me to. (*pouting*)

Situation 4

(1) We ought to lock those criminals up and throw the keys away.
(2) You're right; they should not be allowed on the street. (*hands on hips*)

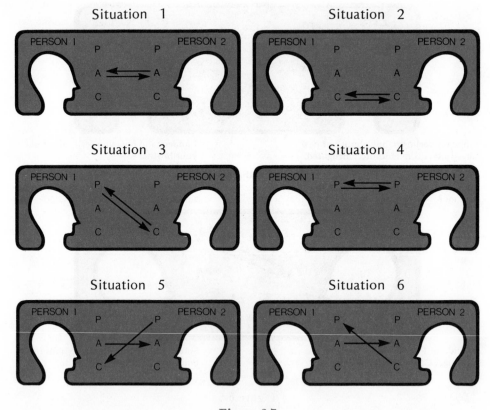

Figure 6-7
*Solutions to the complementary and crossed transaction examples
given in the text.*

I would like to be a fireman.

Don't be silly, you are not strong enough.

Go and clean up the basement.

It does not need cleaning yet. I'll do it when I'm ready. (hands on hips)

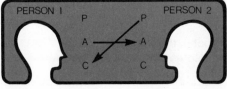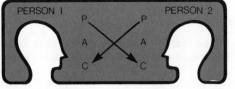

I think that's a nice painting.

You obviously know nothing about art.

That movie is some-thing that everyone should see. When are you going?

I never go to movies that are oriented to mass audiences.

What do you feel are the problems with your paper?

Too many contra-dictions, damm it!

I don't like lettuce. (angrily)

I'm tired of hearing that from you. (angrily)

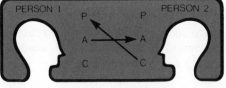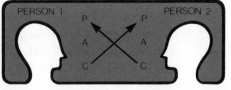

I think that is a good car.

Wow! You are a super person. That is really neat of you.

Why don't you leave me alone? I hate you.

Well, I don't like you much either.

Figure 6-8

Examples of crossed transactions.

Our transactions are not always complementary. Sometimes things do not go well. When this occurs the transactions are crossed. Crossed trans-actions cause arguments to erupt and tension and frustration to occur. They often lead to an end to the conversation. The cause of a crossed transaction is that one person has addressed a personality component of the other (e.g., Parent to Child), but the second individual has responded with a component that was not addressed (e.g., Parent back to the first person's Child). Sev-eral examples of crossed transactions are presented in Figure 6-8.

EXERCISE 6-3: CROSSED TRANSACTIONS

To test your understanding of crossed transactions, diagram the following situ-ations using the same PAC format shown in Figure 6-8. Check your responses with the solutions in Figure 6-7.

Situation 5

(1)   Have you seen my briefcase?
(2)   No, but you should always keep it in front of your desk. *(pointing at the desk)*

Situation 6

(1)   I think that the South is an excellent vacation spot in the winter.
(2)   Don't bother me with your ideas. I wish we could go skiing. *(angrily)*

Communication in crossed transactions is difficult because the parties do not cooperate. When you notice that a communication is crossed there are several things that you can do:

1.   Try to keep the communication pattern between you and another person on a complementary level. Strive for "adult" level interactions. Make several Adult responses to attempt to "hook" the other person's Adult. A less desirable solution would be to respond with the personality component that is being addressed (e.g., Child back to Parent). Although this would make the interaction complementary, it would not be a very viable long-term solution. Anger over having "given in" could occur.

2.   Step out of the situation for awhile. Count to 10 and try to analyze what is going on. Try to mentally diagram the interaction before responding.

3.   Show some restraint and don't respond. Ask yourself if it's worth getting into a discussion on the issue.

4.   Consider compromising on the points at issue.

5.   Try to get the other person into a problem-solving mode. See if you can get him or her to work with you in arriving at a solution. Begin by saying that "our disagreement suggests a problem. I'd like to work with you on finding a mutually agreeable solution." If the other person is not interested it is best to discontinue the interaction.

Take one of the situations that you described analogous to mine in Table 6-2. Think of one to three important interactions that occurred in that situation. Diagram each in terms of the Parent, Adult, Child model. Answer the following questions for each interaction: Was it complementary? If yes, what were the personality components involved? If no, how was it crossed? Which one of the five suggestions we have just presented would enable you to have uncrossed the problem interactions? Consider sharing your responses with a classmate or a friend.

Hidden Agendas

Based on our discussion of transactional analysis, it is clear our messages indicate more than their surface facts and ideas. Developing a habit of looking beyond the manifest content can enrich our understanding of interpersonal communication. Hidden agendas allow us to extend our analysis of latent content. Hidden agendas are the unlabeled, private, and covered feelings, motivations, attitudes, values, and ideas that we bring with us to discussions. They are the things that we know about people and situations *that we do not openly share.* Hidden agendas would include such things as a particular dislike for one or more individuals; an idea for a solution to a problem you want everyone else to accept; having adverse feelings toward a group's goals; and wanting other people to think you are interested in their ideas when you really have little interest. Hidden agendas are the private aspects of us that influence our daily conversations.

There are several things that can indicate the presence of hidden agendas: (a) tension, anger, and frustration in the conversation, (b) long-winded discussions on a given topic that go nowhere, (c) drifting from one topic to another when the announced agenda is to discuss one thing, and (d) conflicts that arise between and among people for no apparent reason. Let us look at an example of a conversation that is affected by hidden agendas.

Situation: A teenage girl is interested in sneaking out on a date with a boy her mother dislikes. She and her mother are discussing her plans for the evening.

TEENAGER: Suzy asked me to spend some time at her house tonight to study for our American History exam on Monday.

MOTHER: That's fine with me, but you should be home around 9:00 o'clock.

TEENAGER: Oh, Mother, we really need the time to study. It's a big exam and I would like to get the top grade. Suzy and I study well together.

MOTHER: You know how I worry when you have to walk home after dark.

TEENAGER: It's perfectly safe outside. We live in a rather good neighborhood. Besides, I'll be home by 11:00 o'clock.

MOTHER: *(somewhat angry)*   Look, we've gone through this a hundred times. Nine o'clock is late enough. Couldn't you study during the day over the weekend?

TEENAGER: Suzy is going to be busy helping around the house this week-end. She won't have any time to study with me.

MOTHER: Couldn't you study by yourself then?

TEENAGER: I like to study with Suzy. She's my best friend.

MOTHER: What if Suzy came here? I'd be glad to drive her home at 11:00 o'clock.

TEENAGER: *(somewhat frustrated)* Her parents are going out this evening and they like someone to be home to watch the house. I don't see any reason why I have to stay here.

Before reading further, think of two ways hidden agendas interfered in this conversation. What is the most likely outcome?

Notice how the daughter's hidden agenda makes the conversation turn into a long-winded discussion. Each party is simply trying to justify her point of view. The problem to be solved is not the study time but how the teenager can see her boyfriend that evening. Her mother is unaware of this and is simply interested in having her home early. The most likely outcome is that bad feelings will result because the real agenda is not getting worked out. The teenager will not appreciate her mother's inflexibility. The mother will not understand why her daughter does not appreciate her attempts at helping to solve the "study time" problem.

One way to understand the context in which hidden agendas exist is to consider a model of interpersonal communication developed by Joe Luft and Harry Ingham.[3] The model is often referred to as the Johari (Joe and Harry) Window. The model is presented in Figure 6-9 and suggests four interrelated aspects to our interpersonal relationships. Each aspect is represented by one of the quadrants in the figure.

Quadrant I is the area of free activity. This refers to behavior and motivation known to ourselves and known to others. It is that part of us that is publicly known. In the teenager example, both the mother and daughter knew that the daughter wanted to stay out later that evening.

Quadrant II represents the blind area. This is where others can see things in us of which we are unaware. The extent to which the mother notices her daughter's rejection of all helpful suggestions without further discussion fits in this quadrant.

Quadrant III consists of things that we know but do not reveal to others. This is the area where our hidden agendas lie. The daughter's hidden agenda, of course, was her desire to see her boyfriend. She did not reveal this to her mother.

---

[3] Parts of the information in this section are reprinted from *Group Processes: An Introduction to Group Dynamics* by Joseph Luft, by permission of Mayfield Publishing Company (formerly National Press Books). Copyright © 1963, 1970 Joseph Luft.

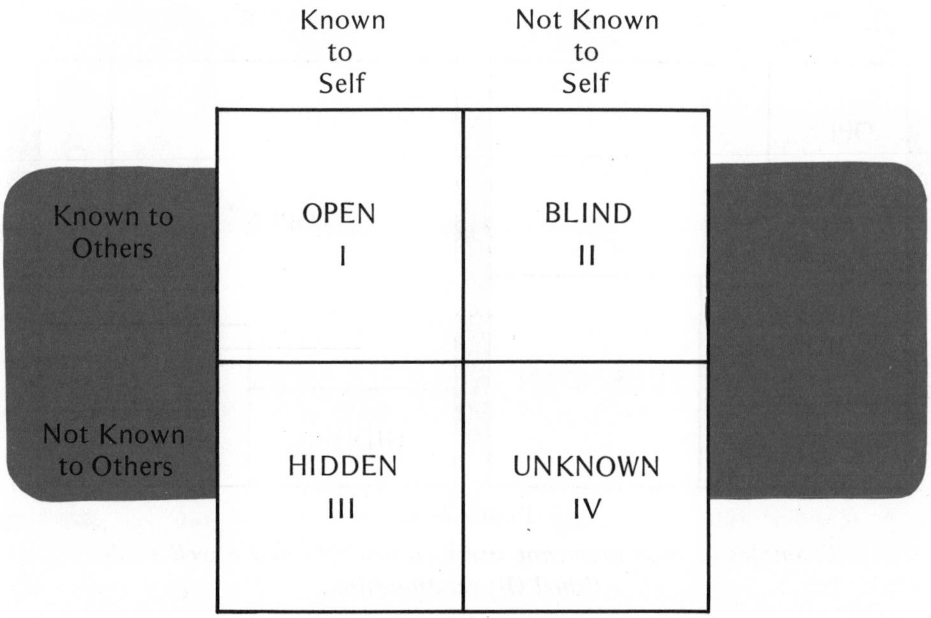

Figure 6-9

The Johari Window. (Reprinted from Group *Processes: An Introduction to Group Dynamics by Joseph Luft, by permission of Mayfield Publishing Company [formerly National Press Books]. Copyright © 1963, 1970 Joseph Luft.)*

Quadrant IV is the area of unknown activity. Neither we nor others are aware of certain behaviors or motives, yet they can eventually become known and then be shown to have influenced our interactions all along. For example, the teenager's attempts to sneak out may be a sign of needs to rebel against her mother's authority. Her mother's concern about hours and her daughter's welfare probably relate to the mother's need for control and authority. Neither one currently sees the problem this way. However, given enough situations like this and some helpful insight and facilitation (e.g., a family therapist) it would be possible for the control and authority issue to surface.

The model suggests that as relationships begin to form, Quadrant I tends to be rather small. As people begin to trust and respect each other's needs and feelings, they become freer to express their true selves and to perceive others more accurately. Thus Quadrant III shrinks as Quadrant I grows. We begin to find it less necessary to hide or deny things we know and feel. Similarly, as trust and respect increase in a relationship, others may not keep as much from us. Therefore, Quadrant II begins to get smaller. To the extent that we become open with others, we might also obtain in-

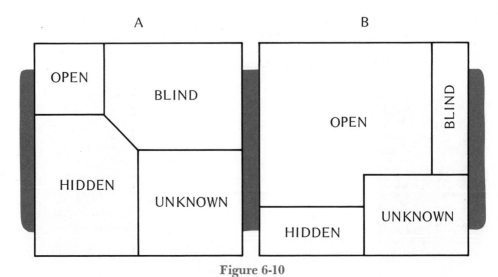

Figure 6-10

*Examples of each quadrant size in a new (A) and a well-estab-
lished (B) relationship.*

sight into the underlying dynamics of a relationship. Fewer things will lie
in the unknown area. Figure 6-10 shows the hypothetical size of each quadrant in a new and in a well-established relationship. Note the reduction in
the blind area and in the area of hidden agendas in the latter.

Take each of the interpersonal situations that you listed earlier and
draw the relative size of each quadrant. Fill in the quadrants with behaviors
that you feel typify each quadrant. Pay close attention to any hidden
agendas that you might identify. Develop an action plan for dealing with
them based on the suggestions listed in the next section.

What to Do about Hidden Agendas

Ideally, any solution should handle the hidden agenda without making the
relationship fail or disintegrate. Leland Bradford has suggested several
methods that can be used in interpersonal situations. One is to diagnose
accurately that a hidden agenda is present. Watching for the cues to the
existence of hidden agendas listed earlier will help. Second, once you are
sure that something is there, take some initiative to bring the agenda to the
surface. You might say such things as, "I'm concerned because we are not
getting anywhere. Let's talk about how we feel about the issue." Another
tack is to say, "I'm concerned about how things are progressing. I have a
feeling that a related problem is . . . What do you think?" When agendas
are laid on the table and discussed, they are often easier to handle. Third,

do not behave in such a way as to make people feel guilty or defensive about hidden agendas. These agendas are legitimate aspects of your relationships with others. As the model shows, we function in relationships at several different levels. Saying such things as, "I can certainly expect that each of us might see things somewhat differently and there is no reason to feel guilty about wanting different things" is often helpful. Recognize that differences in opinions and needs are legitimate. Finally, get in the habit of discussing with others the manner in which you work and interact together. The focus in such discussions is not on the product but on how you arrive at the product. In groups this can be accomplished by scheduling evaluation time or holding special evaluation sessions. In one-to-one situations, simply sit down periodically and talk about how issues were handled. Chapter 8 discusses several personal communication skills that can be helpful here.

Nonverbal Communication Analyses

Our nonverbal behaviors convey certain messages by themselves and enhance the meaning of our verbal communications. For example, pounding one's fist on a table suggests anger without anything being spoken. Holding someone you love close conveys a message that you care. To say, "I don't like you" with a calm voice and relaxed body posture does not convey the intensity of the message. An angry red face, loud voice, and fists waving are nonverbal cues that enhance the message. Let us examine the concepts of *personal space* and *body language* for additional insights into this process.

Personal Space

Edward Hall suggests that we have personal spatial territories or zones that allow certain types of interpersonal behaviors and communications to occur. We only allow certain people to enter or events to occur within a zone. Let us look at how some nonverbal messages can be triggered by behaviors that violate the norms of each zone. The four personal zones identified by Hall are as follows:

1. *Intimate distance.* This personal zone covers a range of distance from body contact to 1 foot. Relationships between a parent and child, lovers, and close friends occur within this zone. As a general rule, we only allow people we know and have some affection for to enter this zone. When someone trys to enter without our permission, they are strongly repelled by our telling them to stay away from us or by our pushing them away. Why do you think we allow a doctor to easily violate our intimate distance zone?

2. *Personal distance.* The spatial range covered by this zone extends from 1 to 4 feet. Activities like eating in a restaurant with two or three other people, sitting on chairs or the floor in small groups at parties, or playing cards occur within this zone. Violations of the zone make people feel uneasy and act nervously. When you are eating at a restaurant, the amount of table space that is considered "yours" is usually divided equally by the number of people present. I can remember becoming angry and generally irritated when a friend of mine placed a plate and glass in my space. As we talked I was visibly irritated, but my anger had nothing to do with the topic we discussed. Has this ever happened to you?

3. *Social distance.* Four to 12 feet is the social distance zone. Business meetings, large formal dinners, and small classroom seminars occur within the boundaries of the social distance zone. Discussions concerning everyday topics like the weather, politics, or a best seller are considered acceptable. For a husband and wife to launch into a heated argument during a party in front of 10 other people would violate the accepted norms for behavior in .the social zone. This once happened at a formal party I attended. The nonverbal behaviors that resulted consisted of several people leaving the room, others looking angry or uncomfortable, and a few standing and watching quietly with an occasional upward glance and a rolling of their eyeballs. What would violate the social distance norms in a classroom?

4. *Public distance.* This zone includes the area beyond 12 feet. Addressing a crowd, watching a sports event, and sitting in a large lecture section are behaviors we engage in within this zone. As is true for the other zones, behaviors unacceptable for this zone can trigger nonverbal messages. At a recent World Series game a young male took his clothes off and ran around the outfield. Some watched with amusement on their faces, others looked away, and a few waved their fists at the culprit. The respective messages were, "That's funny," "I'm afraid or ashamed to look," and "How dare you interrupt the game." What would your reaction be in this situation?

Body Language

Based on the writings of Robert Sommer, Edward Hall, and Julius Fast, it appears that our gestures and postures convey particular messages. A word of caution is needed here. Before interpreting any nonverbal behavior, you need to consider the total context in which the behavior occurs. While some types of behaviors *generally suggest* particular meanings, they should not be considered as universal symbols for these meanings. With these words of caution in mind, let us look at what these authors say about certain body gestures and postures.

Nonverbal messages which include or exclude others.   Certain nonverbal behaviors convey messages that you are friendly and that people are welcome to meet with you.   These include greeting someone with open arms, sitting in a chair with arms relaxed and at your sides, and maintaining eye contact with another person.   On the other hand, not extending your hand to greet someone, keeping your arms and feet crossed when you sit, standing with hands on hips or crossed and folded on your chest, and looking away from a person when you talk could suggest a lack of interest.

Nonverbal messages which suggest involvement, neutrality, or uninvolvement in discussions.   Standing or sitting face to face with someone, nodding your head as they speak, and smiling when they say something humorous are examples of nonverbal messages that suggest that you are personally involved with their message.   Standing or sitting side by side, occasionally nodding your head, or sometimes looking away from them as they speak suggests you are somewhat neutral or mildly interested.   Being listless, silent, and passive suggests that you are uninvolved and not interested in what is said.

Remember that the total communication context must be examined before meaning is given to nonverbal messages.   What were some of the nonverbal components of a recent conversation you had?   Did any of them stem from violations of personal zones?   If so, what zone was violated?   Did any of the nonverbal cues enhance the verbal components?   Were the nonverbal signals incompatible with what was said verbally?

SUMMARY

Interpersonal communication is a process whereby verbal and nonverbal symbols are shared and understood by two or more people.   Several things influence the process.

Communication networks.   In any human system there are restrictions in the flow of messages among people.   Communication networks have implications for people's satisfaction, productivity, ability to clarify information, ability to make decisions, acceptance of decisions, and loyalty to each other and the organization.   As a general rule, it is best to create as much communication among participants in interpersonal situations as possible.   This is particularly true when group decisions need to be made and implemented.

One- versus two-way communication patterns.   One way to characterize communication patterns is in terms of the amount of one- and two-way communication they permit.   Certain trade-offs must be made between the two patterns. One-way is faster but less accurate and tends to make people feel somewhat frustrated and less satisfied with their efforts. Two-way tends to take longer but is usually more accurate, and people feel less frustrated and more satisfied.

Psychological size. This concept refers to the perceived impact that one person has on another. People who are psychologically big are viewed as having a high potential for influencing and controlling people. Some of the causes of psychological "bigness" include high status, a formal manner, the use of punishing remarks, and the display of a great amount of detailed knowledge.

Physical environment. The physical arrangement of people and objects in an environment influences our ability to communicate by means of the types of social contact it permits and the symbolic aspects of the arrangements. Front-to-back seating arrangements and restricted mobility of people and furniture affect social contact. The size and location of the space and the luxuriousness of the furnishings convey symbolic messages which can affect interactions.

Verbal and nonverbal components. What people say and how they say it are important to understanding interactions among people. Messages have a manifest, or everyday, meaning and a latent, or symbolic, content. The manifest content refers to the facts or ideas conveyed, and the latent content refers to the types of things our words and sentences symbolize about our attitudes, values, feelings, and motivations.

Transactional analysis. This is a theory that is quite useful in helping us to interpret the messages our words symbolize. The theory proposes that Parent, Adult, and Child components in our personalities can be identified in our conversations. Parent statements can be identified by words and phrases such as "You should," "Never," and "How to." Adult statements are characterized by "In my opinion," "Why," and "How" and Child messages include "I wish," "I want," and "I guess." When two people address each other and the personality components are compatible, the conversation will continue. When the personality components are incompatible, arguments may evolve and the conversation may cease.

Hidden agendas. These are the unlabeled, private, covered feelings, motivations, attitudes, values, and ideas that we bring with us to discussions. The Johari Window model is often used to provide a context for the understanding of hidden agendas in our relationships with others. It postulates that there are open, blind, hidden, and unconscious areas in our relationships with others. As relationships grow, people become more open in their communications and there is a reduction in their need for personal hidden agendas.

Nonverbal communication. Nonverbal communication can enhance the meaning of our verbal messages or convey certain messages alone. Nonverbal messages can naturally accompany particular verbal messages, or they may be triggered by violations of an individual's personal space. Personal space refers to the personal territories or zones we protect and that allow certain types of interpersonal behaviors or communications to occur. The physical gestures and postures we use can be classified as to whether they include or exclude others and in their suggestion of involvement, neutrality, or uninvolvement with another person. Before interpreting the meaning of any nonverbal behavior, one must be aware of the context in which it occurs. Some types of nonverbal behaviors suggest particular meanings, but they should not be considered as universal symbols for such things.

THINGS TO DO

1. Tape record or videotape a conversation with a friend. Sit down afterward and try to analyze the verbal content in terms of the concepts in transactional analysis. If videotape is available, look for nonverbal cues as well.

2. Hold a nonverbal party. The first hour, all the guests may communicate only nonverbally. No one is allowed to speak.

3. Pick a classroom or other physical space where you spend time communicating. How could you redesign the space to make it more conducive to effective communication? Why not draw a diagram of the changes you would make? Perhaps those who interact with you in the space would be willing to try some of the changes.

4. Based on what you have read in this chapter, what are five things that you could change in your own behavior that would improve your interpersonal communications?

5. List some of the common hidden agendas that you think operate in the following situations: (a) a college classroom, (b) the relationship between a salesperson and a customer, (c) the relationship between a husband and wife, (d) in a legislative body such as the U.S. Congress, (e) the relationship between a coach and the team, (f) in a stockholder's meeting, (g) the relationship between a lawyer and client, and (h) a doctor and patient relationship.

6. A friend of yours stops you on the corner and says that she only has five min-

utes to talk. She wants to know what you think are the three most important things that someone can do to improve interpersonal communication. What would you tell her?

REFERENCES AND OTHER INTERESTING THINGS TO READ

BERNE, E. *Games People Play.* New York: Grove Press, 1964.

BRADFORD, L. The case of the hidden agenda. *Group Development, Selected Readings Series.* Washington, D.C.: National Training Laboratories, 1972.

CHAPANIS, A. Words, words, words. *Human Factors,* 1965, *7,* No. 1, 1–17.

FAST, J. *Body Language.* New York: M. Evans and Co., 1970.

GINOTT, H. G. *Between Parent and Child.* New York: Avon Books, 1965.

HALL, E. *The Silent Language.* Garden City, N.Y.: Doubleday and Co., 1959.

HARRIS, T. A. *I'm OK—You're OK.* New York: Harper & Row, 1967.

HOWARD, J. *Please Touch.* New York: McGraw-Hill, 1970.

LEAVITT, H. J. Some effects of certain communication patterns on group performance. *Journal of Abnormal and Social Psychology,* 1951, *46,* 38–50.

LUFT, J. *Group Process: An Introduction to Group Dynamics.* Palo Alto, Calif.: National Press Books, 1970.

ROSENTHAL, R. Unintended communication of interpersonal expectations. *The American Behavioral Scientist,* 1967, *10,* No. 8, 24–26.

SNYDER, B. R. *The Hidden Curriculum.* New York: Alfred A. Knopf, 1970.

SOMMER, R. *Personal Space.* Englewood Cliffs, N.J.: Prentice-Hall, 1969.

STEELE, F. I. *Physical Settings and Organization Development.* Reading, Mass.: Addison-Wesley Publishing Co., 1973.

TESCH, F., LANSKY, L. M., and LUNDGREN, D. C. The exchange of information: One-way versus two-way communication. *Journal of Applied Behavioral Science, 8,* No. 4, 1972.

A. After reading this chapter, the reader should be able to explain:

1. The function of a source, a receiver, a communication channel, and noise in human interpersonal communication.

2. The importance of reducing uncertainty in our communication through sharing new information.

3. How our skills as speakers can be improved by disclosing our interests and feelings, giving feedback effectively, checking perceptions, and asking open and closed questions.

4. How our skills as listeners can be improved by reflecting the speaker's feelings, paraphrasing and summarizing what is said, asking questions, and receiving feedback in an open manner.

5. How we can improve message clarity by reducing environmental, cognitive, and emotional sources of noise in our discussions.

B. While reading this chapter, the reader should be able to use the information:

1. To solve the problems posed by the illustrations and exercises used in the chapter.

2. To develop personal action plans to use communication skills in their daily lives.

7

Developing Personal Communication Skills

GLOSSARY

Closed question. A question that asks another person to respond with a specific and concise answer. "What is your name?" is an example of a closed question.

Communication channel. The means by which we communicate messages. Human interpersonal communication primarily uses light and sound waves.

Defensive communication. Viewing what another person says or does as a personal attack. We might react by arguing with them, trying to impress them with what we know, or simply not responding.

Feedback. The information that other people give us or that we give them regarding what they do or say. The purpose is to help correct ongoing behaviors.

Information theory. An approach to understanding communication that divides the process into a source, a receiver, a communication channel, and messages, which exist in a noise background.

Noise. The factors in our environments and within our cognitive and emotional systems which interfere with our ability to hear a message clearly. Environment noise includes such things as a loud radio, street noise, or other people talking. Cognitive and emotional noise includes differences in the meaning of words, actions, and tendencies to become defensive when communicating.

Open question. A question that asks another person to state as broad and as extensive an answer as they want. An example is the question "What do you think about the United States?"

Paraphrasing. Putting into our own words the thoughts and feelings of the other person. Helps the other person know that we understand what he or she is saying.

Perception check. Communication skill in which we interpret the nonverbal behavior of other people and ask them if we are accurate in understanding how they feel.

Receiver. The part of the communication process that receives the message. This can be a person or something like a telephone or radio receiver.

Reflection of feelings. Communication skill whereby we describe the speaker's feelings. Helps to show that we understand how the speaker feels.

Self-disclosure. A communication skill whereby we share our thoughts, interests, and feelings with other people. Shows people that we are open and they in turn are likely to share something about themselves with us.

Source. The part of the communication process that initiates the message. This can be a person or something like a radio transmitter.

Summarizing. Communication skill whereby we condense what the speaker says in his or her own words.

Uncertainty reduction. A criterion against which we can assess how much information has been shared. Refers to our gain in new information after a conversation compared with what we knew before it began. In human interpersonal communication, it helps to make conversations enjoyable since people usually appreciate discussions in which they learn something new.

The Importance of Communication Skills

"I wish I had discussed my term paper in a different way with my teacher." How many times have you wondered if a conversation could have been improved? At least half of mine could be more effective. To help me evaluate an interaction, I periodically spend time reviewing what occurred. In doing this, I not only mentally review the components of interpersonal communication to be discussed in Chapter 6, but I examine how I used various personal communication skills. I try to assess such things as: "Did I give feedback that was specific and well timed?" "Did I actively listen to the ideas that were presented?" "Did I reflect and clarify the feelings that were expressed?" "Did I periodically *paraphrase* or *summarize* the conversation to help ensure I understood the issues?" "Did I ask good questions, and were the answers I received clear?"

Communication skills can help us to interact effectively in several ways. They can aid us in making a clear presentation of our ideas and feelings. People are then less likely to misinterpret what we mean. Such skills can assist us in actively listening to and understanding what others are saying. Our interest in the other person's views is certain to be appreciated. When used widely, communication skills will also improve the interpersonal climate for our interactions. We will be able to empathize with the feelings and concerns of other people, to begin to build interpersonal trust, and to gain insight into the effects of our behavior on others.

This chapter will attempt to give you information on how to develop your communication skills and apply them in your life. We will begin with a theoretical framework of the parts of the communication process that these skills will affect. Having done this, we will examine specific actions you can take to make each component more effective.

A Theoretical Framework for Skill Development

Information theory gives us a frame of reference to begin a discussion of communication skills. The theory was developed from attempts by Claude Shannon and Norbert Wiener to describe in mathematical terms the information exchange between a communication *source* and a *receiver*. They were able to quantify the amount of information gained or lost in physical communication systems such as long distance radio and telephone transmissions. By knowing precisely how much information was lost, equipment modifications could then be tested to determine if they increased the amount of information transmitted.

Psychologists were intrigued by information theory because of the similarities between a physical communication system and human communication and information processing. Figure 7-1 presents the similar parts of a physical and a human communication system.

Our interest in this chapter is not in the mathematics of information theory, nor in its many interesting applications within psychology. Rather, the importance to us of information theory is that it provides a criterion for checking our communication effectiveness, and it allows us to identify the parts of the process that our personal communication skills are likely to improve.

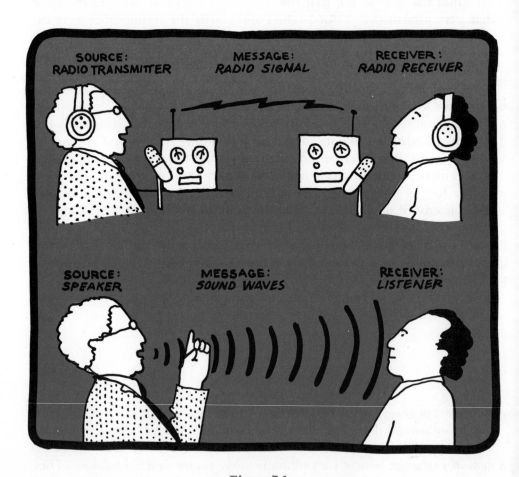

Figure 7-1

The components of a physical communication system and an interpersonal system.

A Criterion for Communication Effectiveness

Have you ever wondered if you learned anything new in a conversation? Communication is not simply the exchange of words between people. According to information theory, the quality of a communication is judged by the amount of new information that was shared. If I am just as uncertain after we talked about your ideas, interests, and feelings as I was before we began, then we had a rather poor interaction. For example, my wife recently handed me a small can of fertilizer and told me to put it on "the rose bush that really needs it." I said, "Do you mean the one on the side of the house?" She nodded and I fertilized one of three rose bushes on the left side of the house. Unfortunately, I had selected an incorrect bush—or, at least, it was not the one my wife wanted fertilized. She came around later and indicated that I had selected the wrong bush. In information theory terms, we did not communicate. I was still considerably *uncertain* about the bush that needed to be fertilized. There was little new information shared in our first conversation. At that point I asked, "Would you tell me precisely which bush you mean?" When she stated, "The small bush on the right side of the house next to the porch," immediately I knew what to do. Compared to our first interaction, the latter one considerably reduced my *uncertainty* about her intention since I was given additional new information.

Why is it important to reduce uncertainty in our daily conversations? Perhaps one reason is that most of us enjoy interactions in which we feel something was accomplished or we learned something new about a topic or the ideas, interests, and feelings of another person. This enjoyment increases our motivation to continue the interaction. If your conversations are anything like mine, they probably vary in the amount of new information that is shared. When I find myself in a situation in which uncertainty is not reduced, I become uncomfortable. I find that it is a good idea to stop periodically and privately assess whether a conversation is leading to anything new. When you find yourself simply exchanging words with people but not sharing anything new about each other's ideas, interests, or feelings, some corrective actions are usually needed. The communication skills discussed in this chapter can help you by suggesting actions that reduce uncertainty by allowing you to maximize the sharing of new information.

The Components of an Information Exchange

A source or speaker, a receiver or listener, a communication channel, and a message were shown in Figure 7-1 as important parts of any information exchange between people. Let us take a closer look at the functioning and characteristics of each part. We will also begin to identify the types of communication skills that enhance their effectiveness.

Speaker and Listener

In any good interpersonal interaction, there is a certain amount of two-way communication. Each of us functions as both a speaker and a listener. We alternate roles and behave based on the topic under discussion and our past experiences, attitudes, values, and emotions. As Chapter 6 showed, any one of these factors can, on occasion, make an interaction difficult. Thus a considerable amount of skill is needed to communicate when issues like our different past experiences and emotions become involved in the interaction. Table 7-1 introduces and describes the types of communication skills that are

Table 7-1

Speaker and Listener Skills

Speaker Skills:

Self-disclosure:	Sharing our interests, thoughts, and feelings with another person.
Giving Feedback:	Giving other people information so that they can modify or change their behavior.
Perception Check:	Interpreting the nonverbal behavior of another person and asking the person if we are accurate.
Asking Open Questions:	Asking questions that allow the other person to respond in a broad and extensive manner.
Asking Closed Questions:	Asking questions that allow the other person to respond with a specific and concise answer.

Listener Skills:

Reflection of Feelings:	Describing the speaker's feelings to demonstrate our understanding of how the speaker feels.
Paraphrasing:	Translating into our own words the ideas and feelings of the other person.
Summarizing:	Condensing what the speaker said in the speaker's own words.
Asking Content Questions:	Asking the speaker to explain or elaborate on parts of the content to check on our understanding it.
Asking for and Receiving Feedback:	Having the speaker give you specific feedback, listening carefully to it, and then taking action to modify your behavior.

important for our roles as speakers and listeners. They assist our interactions in our normal conversations and on occasions when other factors
interfere with the process.

The following situation illustrates several of the points discussed so far.
I want you to pretend that you are a salesclerk in a clothing department of
a major store. You are inexperienced and have been on the job only two
days. Your boss has asked you to rearrange the clothing racks and then returns to check on what you did. After each statement your boss makes,
determine what your response would be. Try to respond as you think you
really would in such a situation.

Boss: You idiot, you put all the clothing in the wrong places!

You:

Boss: I don't want to hear any silly excuses! This is a first-class store and
        I expect perfection.

You:

Here are some typical reactions that my students have in this situation:

Boss: You idiot, you put all the clothing in the wrong places!

My Students: #1. Fix them yourself. I was never really told how to
                    do it.
               #2. You never told me anything that said I could not do
                    it this way.
               #3. What's wrong with this way? The customers
                    haven't complained.

Boss: I don't want to hear any silly excuses! This is a first-class store and
        I expect perfection.

My Students: #1. If this is how you are going to treat me, I quit.
               #2. I'm not trying to be funny, but you are getting
                    excited over nothing.
               #3. I'm beginning to wonder whether or not this is a
                    first-class store.

How similar were your responses to those listed? In what ways were
they different? Was there a sharing of new information regarding the
arrangement of the clothing during the conversation? What role did the
different past experiences of the salesclerk and the boss play in the interaction? How did emotions affect the exchange of information? Do you
think any of the skills described in Table 7-1 would have helped? Let's look
at an instant replay in which the situation is handled somewhat differently

by the clerk. Note how several of the skills described in Table 7-1 are used and how they affect the interaction.

> BOSS: You idiot, you put all the clothing in the wrong places!

> SALESCLERK: Mr. Jones, you really sound angry with me. *(Skill: Reflection of speaker's feeling)*

> BOSS: I am angry, but it's not just with you. Too many people in this store do not seem to care. It seems as if I have to do everything myself.

> SALESCLERK: It sounds to me like having to look after so many details can be overwhelming at times. *(Skill: Paraphrasing the speaker's message to help show understanding)* I want to do a good job. Could you tell me specifically what I failed to do correctly? *(Skill: Asking for specific feedback)*.

> BOSS: What you did is to mix the regular merchandise with the sale items. The fall clothing should be placed next to the outside window and the remainder of the summer clothing moved toward the back of the department.

> SALESCLERK: Thank you. That was helpful. I'll rearrange things immediately.

> BOSS: By the way, I'm sorry for losing my temper.

It is quite easy for such situations to turn into shouting matches. The use of several communication skills by the speaker changed a potentially angry encounter into a fairly positive one. By using the skills of reflecting feelings, paraphrasing the speaker's message, and asking for specific feedback, the salesclerk received a good deal of new information. In the process, the boss began to show positive feelings toward the clerk. We will return to a detailed analysis of speaker and listener skills in a later section.

Communication Channel

The communication channel is the means by which we convey our messages. Human communication uses light waves in sending and receiving written and nonverbal messages, sound waves in speaking and listening, physical contact which affects our skin receptors, and the molecules in various gases which affect our receptors for smell. The majority of our face-to-face communications with other people uses light and sound waves. Our words and voice quality are transmitted by sound waves and our facial gestures and other body movements are delivered by light waves. As important as these two channels are, we must not overlook the fact that messages are also sent by a gentle touch or a delightful aroma from perfume or cologne.

Do you think that the use of more than one channel improves your ability to communicate? There is no easy answer to this question, since it depends upon the situation. Many of you have probably played charades, in which one person must communicate a message nonverbally to others. The communicator engages in different body postures, and those watching try to guess the message. An idea takes longer to communicate visually in charades than if verbal messages are used. I recently spent 10 minutes at a party trying to communicate a book title, *Teaching as a Subversive Activity*. The use of more than one channel would have increased the speed and accuracy of the communication. Unfortunately, the game would not have been as much fun. Its interest depends upon the use of one restricted communication channel.

In other situations more than one channel can be effective. A foreign visitor to Cincinnati recently stopped me for directions downtown. His English was not very good, and he said things like "building," "paint," "frame," and "look." In addition, he made nonverbal gestures which suggested he wanted to stand and look at something. I said, "Do you want to go to the contemporary art gallery?" He smiled and nodded, and I pointed out the building to him. Apparently he understood English better than he spoke it. The use of two communication channels improved our ability to communicate.

Although it is a good idea to use more than one communication channel, a word of caution is needed. Too many communication channels can decrease our ability to process information. We may suffer from an overload of information and actually receive less new information. When I was in the service I listened to a 90-minute lecture that presented two speakers alternating every two minutes, three screens with slides on them in the background, two 10-minute movies, tape recordings to illustrate points, flip charts with major points written on them, a 10-minute "hands-on" practical exercise, a session outline, and a summary sheet. I was exhausted after the presentation. There was just too much information conveyed by too many different channels for me to absorb it well.

In our everyday interactions, the use of one channel as well as the use of too many can present problems. We need to monitor our interactions to ensure that an information overload is not occurring. Skills such as asking closed questions, summarizing what is said, and being sensitive to feedback from others can help us to do this.

The Message

The message is simply the ideas or feelings that we express. In information theory terms, our messages are considered signals which exist in a *noise* background. To be heard, our messages must be stronger than the noise background. In human communication, noise refers to the environmental, cognitive, and emotional factors that interfere with the communication channels between speaker and listener. Have you ever had a telephone conversation with a loud hissing sound or other voices in the background? Have you ever tried to talk with the radio or television blasting away? If your answer is yes, you have experienced environmental noise. Has anyone ever used a word that you did not understand? Have you ever misunderstood the words or intentions of another person? Have you ever felt angry toward a speaker? If your answer is yes, you have experienced examples of cognitive and emotional noise.

If it is strong enough, noise will interfere with our ability to communicate. We have two options for dealing with this problem: We can attempt to make our messages clearer, or we can attempt to reduce the amount of noise. In either case, we want the signal strength to be greater than the noise background. Communication skills related to forming clear messages are: asking good questions about what another person means, summarizing and paraphrasing what is said, and creating an open and *nondefensive communication* climate. Suggestions for achieving these goals will appear in a later section of this chapter.

EXERCISE 7-1: ASSESSING YOUR CURRENT LEVELS OF COMMUNICATION SKILLS

Based on the discussion to this point, you know that important communication skills are those associated with our roles as speakers and listeners and with forming clear messages. Before we take a look at specific suggestions for improving such skills, complete the communication skills assessment questionnaire that follows. Answering these questions will give you insights into specific things that are important in communication and will help you assess which areas you need to develop.

For each of the questions, indicate the frequency with which you engage in the behavior indicated. Do this by placing the number that corresponds to your estimate of frequency in the space to the left of each question. Use the following scale to determine frequency:

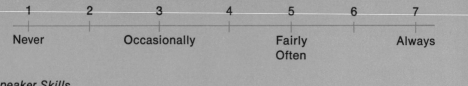

| 1 | 2 | 3 | 4 | 5 | 6 | 7 |
| Never | | Occasionally | | Fairly Often | | Always |

Speaker Skills

_____ I share my ideas, interests, and feelings with my close friends.
_____ I share my ideas, interests, and feelings when meeting new people.

_____I give people feedback on the things I don't like that they do.
_____I give people feedback on the things I like that they do.
_____I ask people if they want feedback before giving it.
_____When I give feedback it describes in detail the specific behaviors I ob-
served.
_____When I interpret the nonverbal behavior of other people, I ask them to
verify whether I am accurate.
_____I ask questions that allow other people to respond in as broad and ex-
tensive a manner as possible.
_____I ask questions that allow other people to respond with specific and con-
cise answers.

Listener Skills

_____I try to describe the feelings that the speaker is showing.
_____When talking with another person, I translate into my own words the ideas
and feelings that are presented.
_____When talking with another person, I condense what is said using essen-
tially the same words the other person used.
_____When I don't understand something, I ask the other person to explain or
elaborate upon what was said.
_____I ask for feedback on my behavior from other people.
_____I try to understand what is accurate about any negative feedback I may
receive.

Message-Related Skills

_____I try to eliminate things in the environment which are distracting when
talking to others.
_____I try to use words that I'm sure the other person understands.
_____I define words that I think are new or that represent jargon when I talk to
someone else.
_____I try to eliminate elements in conversations that threaten other people.
_____I try to listen to different points of view from others on an issue.
_____I try to present different points of view on an issue.

Any response of 4 or less to a question indicates an area that you probably
need to work on. As you come to a section in the chapter that relates to one of
these areas, you might want to spend more time studying and thinking about the
implications for your behavior.

Speaker Skills: Self-disclosure

Self-disclosure is a process of sharing our ideas, interests, and feelings with
other people. Sidney Jourard says that the ability to talk about ourselves
forms the basis for interpersonal communication. It gives other people in-

formation about who we are and helps to put them at ease. More importantly, research on self-disclosure shows that other people are then more likely to disclose their thoughts and feelings to us. This disclosure usually will help reduce our uncertainty about what they know and subsequently move the interaction to a more enjoyable level.

Talking about ourselves is not easy. There is some risk involved. Fears for some people are that the other person may not reciprocate, that what is said might be unacceptable to the other person, or that they may conclude that the other person is not willing to share friendship and love. Have any of these things been of concern to you? I sometimes have such feelings, but I believe that the risk is often less than I think. The advantages of self-disclosure, in my experience, far outweigh the disadvantages. What do your experiences suggest about this last statement?

A related problem is that there is a lack of knowledge about how and what to reveal to other people. A student recently told me, "I just don't know how to make friends." In discussing this problem with her, it became evident that she told other people very little about herself. In addition to some concern for the risk involved, she was not sure what other people would find interesting. What is often interesting to others are things about your personal life, your interests and ideas, and your feelings. Sharing some of these things can be helpful in improving relationships.

How much you reveal about yourself is a personal choice. The next example illustrates some of the problems that occur when there is little self-disclosure.

Situation: Ted is a high school senior who is meeting with the school counselor to discuss career plans. His parents want him to go to college but he wants to join the Air Force, learn a trade, and then decide if he wants or needs higher education. Every time he has raised this idea at home he meets resistance from his parents. He does not want to talk to older people about his interests because of the hassle from his parents. He assumes that the school counselor will not think much of his Air Force interests either.

COUNSELOR: I've just gotten back the aptitude and occupational interest test scores, Ted. Have you had a chance to look over your copy? What do you think about them?

TED: They look OK to me.

COUNSELOR: Could you say a bit more? Did they suggest any areas that you might want to look into after high school?

TED: I'm not sure. What do you think?

COUNSELOR: You seem to have good aptitude scores in the mechanical and electronic areas. If you are thinking of college, Mechanical or Electrical Engineering or Physics might be an ideal major for you.

TED: Yeah. That sounds OK to me.

COUNSELOR: Have you thought about college?

TED: A little.

COUNSELOR: I could give you a list of colleges and universities that have programs in these areas if you would like.

TED: Sure. I'll look them over.

What do you think the implications of Ted's not sharing his career interests are for building an honest and open relationship with the counselor? Is the counselor likely to know what assumptions Ted is making in a career choice? Without some self-disclosure on Ted's part, it is going to be difficult, if not impossible, for the relationship between the counselor and Ted to be anything but superficial. The interaction was certainly not open, and the counselor was not able to give Ted any assistance with his real problem. In fact, by not disclosing some of his interests and ideas, Ted misled the counselor about his career intentions. The counselor was forced to make incorrect assumptions. He thought that Ted was interested in various colleges and universities. If you were Ted, how satisfied do you think you would be with the conversation? Are the same problems likely to occur in other interactions in which one or more people say little or nothing about themselves?

EXERCISE 7-2: SHARING YOUR INTERESTS AND IDEAS

Sometimes a little practice in sharing things about ourselves is needed. This is the only way to test the effects of sharing things on other people. The following activity can assist you in disclosing things about your interests and ideas. You will then be in a better position to assess the advantages or disadvantages of self-disclosure.

1. For each of the statements and topics listed, think of one or two things that you know about them that you have not openly shared with an acquaintance, friend, or relative.
   a. Something that you liked or disliked about a movie, television show, or book that you have experienced in the past four weeks.
   b. Your favorite hobby or pastime.
   c. An interesting person whom you have met during the past three months.
   d. An exciting event that occurred to you in school this year.

e.   An idea or thought that you have about how to make the world a better place to live in.

f.   An important event in your life that occurred during the past six weeks.

g.   An important event in your life that occurred during the last two years.

h.   Something that you are afraid of.

i.   A personal problem.

2.   Think of at least one acquaintance, friend or relative whom you would like to know more about.

3.   Arrange to meet one of these people somewhere. Begin the conversation with a fairly conventional topic, such as the weather, family life, sports, or your course work this year.

4.   Begin to move the conversation so that you can include some of the things you listed for at least two of the topics at the beginning of this exercise. In addition to telling the person what you think, try to get his or her response to the issue. Ask if he or she has had any similar experiences.

5.   After the conversation, think about the following: What effect do you think sharing information about yourself had on the conversation? Do you think the person learned anything new about you? Do you think you were able to learn anything new about the other person?

6.   Share your experiences with a classmate or close friend. Check with your instructor to find out what reactions he or she has to what you observed.

Describing Your Feelings

This process gives the other person accurate information on how you feel. Stating that "the look you gave me made me feel anxious" gives the other person insight into the effect of his or her behavior on you. It can help the

person respond to you differently by changing the behaviors or by discussing the event with you. Rudy Verderber suggests that describing our feelings is one way we teach other people how to treat us. By describing our anger or happiness, we give them clues about how we react to their behavior.

Describing feelings is not the same thing as acting out or expressing how you feel. By only expressing your feelings, it is hard to help the other person treat you differently. This is particularly true with negative emotions because they usually reciprocate. That is, people return your anger with more anger. The following situation illustrates how this occurs:

Situation: Jeff and Mary are neighbors. Jeff likes to borrow appliances but often forgets to return them. He had borrowed Mary's electric mixer and left town for a vacation, and Mary was without her mixer for two weeks.

JEFF: Mary, I've got that mixer I borrowed two weeks ago. Sorry I kept it so long, but I knew you would not mind. We were in such a hurry to leave for vacation that I forgot to bring it back.

MARY: What a stupid thing to do! I've never been so mad in all my life! I had a party last night and I really needed the mixer. (*pounds fist on table*)

JEFF: You should have said something before this! How am I supposed to know your social schedule? (*walks out the door*)

MARY: Oh, just leave me alone.

Mary expressed her feelings rather than describing them. Jeff felt attacked and responded with an angry remark of his own. A better way to handle such situations is to state the behavior you observed and to *describe* the positive or negative emotion it aroused. Examples of this technique include, "George, when you looked at me from the stage, I felt really great"; "Jane, you were 20 minutes late and I was afraid something happened to you"; "Harry, when you overcharged me by $100, I felt angry"; "Ellen, what a delightful thing to say, that really makes me feel happy."

EXERCISE 7-3: DISCLOSING AND DESCRIBING YOUR FEELINGS

Think of some statements that describe and disclose your feelings in each of the following situations:

1. Your cousin has just given you a new watch as a birthday gift.
2. Sally is a neighbor who borrowed your car for "five minutes." Three hours later she returns it with a dent in the fender.
3. Your teacher has just agreed to drop your lowest test score in computing your final grade.

Let us take another look at the situation between Jeff and Mary. Pretend that you are Mary. What could you say to describe your feelings? What are Jeff's responses likely to be?

Jeff: Mary, I've got that mixer I borrowed two weeks ago. Sorry I kept it so long, but I knew you would not mind. We were in such a hurry to leave for vacation that I forgot to bring it back.
Mary:
Jeff:
Mary:
Jeff:

Here is one suggested way of handling the problem:

Jeff: Mary, I've got that mixer I borrowed two weeks ago. Sorry I kept it so long, but I knew you would not mind. We were in such a hurry to leave for vacation that I forgot to bring it back.
Mary: I appreciate your bringing it back, but I'm feeling irritated over not being able to use it for my party last week. I really missed not having it since I couldn't make one of my whipped desserts.
Jeff: Gosh, Mary, I'm sorry for the inconvenience I caused you. I just don't know what to say.
Mary: Oh well, let's not make a big deal out of it. Next time you borrow it I'll just have to let you know when I need it again.

How similar was your approach to the problem?

Speaker Skills: Giving Feedback

There are times in our lives when we need to give other people feedback about their performance. When it is done competently, it can help them make changes in what they do and say. Giving feedback also benefits the speaker. Norbert Wiener suggests that we should treat the feedback process as an error-correcting mechanism that affects both the speaker and the listener. If you change your behavior as a result of something I tell you, I am likely to behave differently toward you. This process can only occur if feedback is given properly. The following principles are helpful in giving feedback.

Try to be as specific as possible. To tell someone who made a mistake while learning to drive, "That just is not the way to do it," is not particularly helpful. The statement probably does not convey anything the driver does not already know, and it is too general. It is hard to make corrections based on the feedback. A better way is to describe the behavior you observed and suggest a specific correction: "Your right front wheel hit the sidewalk when you turned. Try to turn the steering wheel about a third of the way more to the left next time."

Try not to be evaluative when giving feedback. "What a stupid thing to do." "I've never seen such a poor performance." Statements like these are likely to make another person angry. The person will not listen to you. Although it is difficult, it is a good idea to keep the feedback descriptive and behavior oriented. Negative evaluative judgments in particular are likely to get in the way of the feedback process.

Try to give feedback as soon as possible. Feedback is not likely to have as much effect when directed toward behavior that occurred in the distant past. "John, three weeks ago you said that I was not carrying my load at the office. That made me feel angry." A great deal can happen in three weeks, including a change in John's memory of what was said and why. It is best to give feedback as soon as possible after a behavior occurs. The "data" on the interaction are fresh, and the ideas can often be explored in detail.

Try to give positive feedback frequently. My grandfather once told me that "no matter how thin you make a pancake, there are always two sides to it." In our culture we have a tendency to look at the negative side when giving feedback. Certainly this outlook is appropriate on occasion. A problem is that people are "turned off" if all they hear are the negative aspects of their behavior. It is a good idea to give people positive feedback on what you appreciate about them. Even when negative feedback is called for, you should consider preceding it with something positive. "Harry, the way you summarized the client's problem was extremely effective. However, in the future you might want to wait 15 minutes more before closing the interview."

Try to give feedback only when you are sure the other person wants it. If people are not ready to hear what you have to say, they are not likely to learn as much. Before giving feedback, check the other person's readiness for it. "Alice, I'd like to give you feedback on what you did. Can we discuss it now?" "Alice, would you like feedback on what you said?" It also does not hurt to ask the other person to state the specific parts of their actions toward which you should direct feedback. For example, "Fred, what parts of your speech would you like me to comment on?" "Let's see, Ed, how about the part when I mentioned the principles for effective salesmanship?" "What is it that you would like to know about it?" "It would help me, Ed, if you could tell me whether the content was organized and clear. I'm also interested in whether my voice had the right amount of expression in it."

EXERCISE 7-4: FEEDBACK

Let's study an interaction in which feedback principles can be used. You will be given a chance to apply what you have just read. Before proceeding, review the previous section to make sure that you understand the principles on giving feedback.

Situation: A student has written a term paper in a United States history course. The paper was written on conditions in the South leading up to and during the Civil War. The student did a poor job of describing and analyzing the conditions leading up to the Civil War. However, his analysis of the Civil War conditions in the South was extremely good. He has made an appointment with his teacher to discuss the paper. The first interaction illustrates a poor way to give feedback and the consequences of doing it.

> *Teacher:* Your term paper just does not seem to have what it takes. You were not even close to what I consider a good paper.
> *Student:* That's interesting; I worked hard and thought it was pretty good.
> *Teacher:* As I said before, it needs a lot of improvement. I really expect your optional revision to be better. Are you planning to revise it?
> *Student:* No, I don't think so. I guess I'll just take my C and try for an A on the next paper.

What principles of feedback were not used effectively by the teacher? Did the student get any new information? The major problems are that the feedback was too general and highly evaluative and nothing positive was said. Furthermore, the student was not asked to state toward what areas the feedback should be directed. Consequently, the student did not have new information regarding the problems with the paper. The atmosphere created made it hard to be responsive to what the teacher said. Design a dialogue that improves this situation. Try to imagine yourself in the roles of the teacher and the student. What would each party say? *Use the principles for giving feedback in developing your dialogue.* Check your response with one suggested way of handling the situation that appears on page 230. How were your responses similar or dissimilar?

Speaker Skills: Perception Checking

When we talk to others, we elicit a variety of verbal and nonverbal behaviors. Perception checking is a useful way for us to make sure we understand the meaning of the nonverbal aspects of the other person's behavior. Sue and Terry are standing in the hallway when their English teacher approaches them. The teacher stops for a second and tells Sue that she did well on her term paper. Sue smiles and looks pleased with herself. Terry looks at the floor with a lack of expression on her face. Sue says, "I get the impression that you are unhappy. Is that true?" "That's right, Sue; our teacher didn't say anything to me and I think it's because I messed up the term paper." Sue's last statement is an example of a perception check. When using this technique, be sure to let the other person verify its accuracy as Sue did.

Treat a perception check as a hypothesis about how the other person feels. Using statements beginning "I get the impression that . . .," "You look to me like . . .," and "Am I correct in assuming . . ." is a good way to begin a perception check statement. You should not say, "You are angry with me" or "I know you are upset with me." To act this way is likely to sound judgmental. Another person is likely to resent the statement. You might get responses such as "Who said I was angry?" "I don't know what you are talking about," or "You are always looking for the worst in situations." The conversation would not get very far.

EXERCISE 7-5: PERCEPTION CHECKS

Situation: Ed and Harry are discussing a project they are doing together for a class. Ed has not been doing his share of the work.

(1) *Ed:* Hi, Harry. Sorry I'm late.
   Harry: (*looks at Ed with a blank stare on his face*) Yeah, I guess that's all right.

(2) *Ed:* You really understand, Harry. I didn't think you would mind.
   Harry: Did you bring the notes on the reading you were supposed to do?

(3) *Ed:* Well, I really didn't have time to do it. I thought we could talk about what you did instead.
   Harry: (*turns slightly red, stares at the wall, and talks quickly with a great deal of expression*) Sure, let's get it over with fast.

(4) *Ed:* Look, don't get so angry at me. After all, I have a lot of things to do.
   Harry: (*in a loud tone*) I'm not angry, I'm just disappointed with you. Do you think you are the only one who has other things to do?

(5) *Ed:* If you are going to act this way then do the whole project yourself.

Now answer the following questions: Which statements in the conversation do you think would have been helped by a perception check by Ed? What problems would the checks have helped to overcome? Rephrase the second and fourth statements that Ed made in terms of a perception check. Check your response with one of your classmates.

Suggested Answers to Exercise 7-4

The following represents one direction the conversation might have taken if the principles for giving feedback were used.

> *Teacher:*   Thanks for stopping in to discuss your paper. What is it that you would like feedback on? (*Checks to make sure student wants feedback and in what areas*)
>
> *Student:*   Well, I got a C and I was wondering why the paper was so poor. Could you give me some specific reasons? I'd particularly like to know how I handled the Civil War period.
>
> *Teacher:*   I thought you did a good job with conditions in the South during the Civil War. Your analysis was thorough and went beyond the issues raised in the outside readings. (*Gives positive feedback first*) My concern was with the pre–Civil War period. You devoted one paragraph to it and did not mention the issue of slavery and the economic conditions in the South. I thought that it was too short and not complete in that regard. (*Gives specific feedback*)
>
> *Student:*   If I had written a more extensive analysis of that period you would have given me a higher grade. Is that correct?
>
> *Teacher:*   Yes, that's true. I think I've outlined the major shortcoming of the paper. Do you have a clear idea as to why you got the grade and what you could do to improve a revision?
>
> *Student:*   Yes, I do. I'll revise it and expand my analysis of the pre–Civil War period and conditions in the South.

Speaker Skills: Asking Open and Closed Questions

We are often in situations in which we must initiate conversations, keep them going, or probe for additional information. The effective use of questioning techniques is valuable in such situations. Two that we will look at are open and closed questions. An open question is used when you want to give the other person as wide a scope in answering as possible. It is particularly helpful to get a group discussion going and to find out more about another person and his or her ideas. Examples of open questions are: "What do you think about the state of the economy?" "I think the basketball team will do well this year. What thoughts do you have about this?" A closed question forces the other person to respond with specific information about actions, ideas, or feelings. "How much money do you want to spend on a suit?" and "Where did you go last night?" are examples of closed questions. The payoff in asking questions properly is that it shows you are interested in other people and what they think about issues.

EXERCISE 7-6: ASKING QUESTIONS

Often conversations fail because the two types of questioning techniques are not used properly. People ask closed questions when open questions would be appropriate, and vice versa. A good conversation will often have a balance between the two types. Let us take a look at two examples and analyze them for the use of open and closed questions. As you read each question, label it as open or closed.

Situation 1. Phillip is at a cocktail party and wants to find out more about Betty.

> *Phillip:* Hi there! I'm a friend of Ed's. What's your name? (1)
> *Betty:* I'm Betty Jones.
> *Phillip:* Where do you live? (2)
> *Betty:* I live up the street.
> *Phillip:* Did you buy that dress in town? (3)
> *Betty:* Yes.

You should have labeled each question as closed. In each case Phillip asked for specific information. The result was a rather restricted conversation. He did not give Betty the opportunity to respond with a variety of opinions. Consequently, he was not able to find out whether they had much in common. Let us look at a second situation and note the effects of the types of questions asked on the flow of the conversation. Please label each question as open or closed as a check on your understanding of the difference.

Situation 2. A parent has come to school to discuss the homework problems his child is having.

> *Parent:* I got your note, Mrs. Carter, about Bob's not doing his homework this semester. What do you see as some of the problems? (1)
> *Teacher:* It's usually the math, but sometimes he does not know the new spelling words. I don't think he is spending much time with his work after school. It's not that he's not interested in school, but he simply wants to leave his work for class time. It's hard to learn new things that way.
> *Parent:* What did he not do well yesterday? (2)
> *Teacher:* He had five of the 10 math problems incorrect.
> *Parent:* Was there any problem with spelling the new words in the reading as well? (3)
> *Teacher:* No, he seemed to know them.
> *Parent:* Could you suggest some different things that I could do to help at home? (4)

In this situation, questions 1 and 4 were open and 2 and 3 were closed. There was a mix of detailed and general information not present in the first conversation. The parent was able to get information on his child's problem and the teacher was able to express her concerns.

Take what you know about open and closed questions and imagine that you are in the first conversation. Put yourself into the roles of Betty and Phillip. Continue the dialogue that follows using open and closed questions to keep the conversation flowing. Label each of the questions you ask as open or closed. Try to think about the effect that each is likely to have on the other person's response.

Phillip: Hi there! I'm a friend of Ed's. What is your name? (*Closed question*) Would you mind telling me what brings you here? (*Open question*)

Betty: I'm Betty Jones. I met Ed at a tennis tournament last week and he invited me over.

Phillip: Do you play tennis or do you simply like to watch games? (*Closed question*)

Betty: Actually, I enjoy both. Do you play tennis? (*Closed question*)

The Importance of Listener Skills

Listening is a much more complicated process than simply hearing the words the speaker says. I am sure that you have had the experience of explaining something to another person and having the person respond as if he or she never heard what you said. Sometimes words really do go in one ear and out the other. Listening is an active process that allows us to integrate the content and the physical and emotional cues of the speaker. The goal is to search for meaning and understanding behind the words. Theodor Reik refers to this process as "listening with the third ear." To do this, we need to focus our attention on what is said and interpret the inputs. There are four skills that are helpful here. They are reflection of feelings, paraphrasing, summarizing what is said, and asking questions.

Active Listening Skills: Reflection of Feelings

In this process, the receiver periodically verbalizes the sender's feelings. Like the skill of describing our feelings discussed earlier, it is not an easy process. This is because we usually react to another person's feelings with an emotional response. A person gets mad at us and we get angry in response. To promote understanding, sometimes it is helpful to reflect the speaker's feelings. "Pete, you sound as if you are feeling anxious. What is the problem?"

EXERCISE 7-7: REFLECTION OF FEELINGS

One problem I find in working with people is that they are at a loss for words to describe feelings or they use the same words constantly. How many feeling words can you think of besides angry, happy, sad, afraid, or frustrated? How many others do you use? What is likely to be the long-term effect of using the same words all the time?

To begin to practice describing feelings, try to use as many different words as you can. Table 7-2 is a list of emotional words. Use them to complete the reflection of feeling statements used in the following:

Me: Wow! I just can't wait until the Fourth of July comes around. That is going to be some picnic.
You: You sound as if you are feeling _____.

Me: I'm not sure what I have to do to please you. You're always making tough demands on me.
You: You are _____. Is there anything that I can do to change the situation?

Me: This is a pretty tough assignment. I just don't know if I can handle it.
You: It seems to me that you are _____. What are some of the options you have to do the assignment?

Me: That was a really neat movie. I wouldn't mind seeing it again.
You: What was it about the movie that made you feel _____?

Me: Nancy told me that her mother cut off her funds for college. I think I know how that must feel.
You: I can understand your being _____ toward Nancy.

Why not check your responses with those of your classmates and the suggestions on page 234? Could some of these words be used to describe your own feelings?

Active Listening Skills: Paraphrasing

Paraphrasing is a way of checking with the speaker to make sure you understand the idea and feelings as they were intended. When we paraphrase, we put into our own words the ideas and feelings we have heard. In the following interaction between a mother and daughter, note how the mother paraphrases the thoughts and feelings expressed.

DAUGHTER: Suzy has been going to the movies with Alice a lot. She's joining a lot of the clubs which meet after school. Her mother hardly gets to see her anymore.

Table 7-2

Common Emotional Description Terms

afraid	frustrated	loved	shaky
angry	grateful	mistreated	shy
annoyed	happy	nervous	silly
anxious	hated	offended	superior
ashamed	hopeful	optimistic	sympathetic
awed	humiliated	peaceful	tense
bored	hurt	pleased	thrilled
bothered	impatient	precarious	trusting
calm	inferior	protective	uncertain
concerned	insecure	proud	wonderful
confident	irritated	rejected	worried
content	jealous	repulsed	
eager	joyful	sad	
excited	lonely	satisfied	

Suggested Answers to Exercise 7-7

The following represent the types of responses you might make to complete each of the reflection of feeling statements.

1. *You:* You sound as if you are feeling *thrilled, excited, wonderful.*
2. *You:* You are *irritated, bothered, annoyed.*
3. *You:* It seems to me that you are *anxious, concerned, tense.*
4. *You:* What was it about the movie that made you feel *pleased, satisfied, excited?*
5. *You:* I can understand your being *sympathetic, concerned* toward Nancy.

MOTHER: Are you saying that you and Suzy don't do a lot of the same things anymore? *(Paraphrase of content)*

DAUGHTER: That's true; she just does not want to do the things I want to do. I remember how much fun we used to have together.

MOTHER: It looks like she's acting very independent and wants to do things on her own. *(Paraphrase of content)*

DAUGHTER: I'm feeling angry about her attitude. I wish she would begin to act like her old self.

MOTHER: You sound frustrated and want her behavior to become more in line with what you expect of her.   (*Paraphrase of feeling and content*)

DAUGHTER: I wish I knew what to do about it.

MOTHER: Why don't the two of you sit down and talk about the problem? She has always been interested in what you think and seems to respect your opinion.

DAUGHTER: I agree that she respects me and is interested in discussing relationships.   (*Paraphrase of content*)   I'll talk to her next week.

The use of paraphrasing helped both people understand the nature of the problem better.   It also led naturally into discussing a solution of the issue.   How important do you think this skill is in showing other people that you are interested in them?

EXERCISE 7-8: PARAPHRASING

Situation: You are selling life insurance.   This is your first meeting with the customer.   As is usually the case, the customer is skeptical about insurance and feels that he has enough.   You are not convinced this is the case and feel that he is underinsured.   Paraphrase what the customer is saying to demonstrate understanding.   I have added a closed question to lead into the customer's next response.

Customer: I've been thinking about my insurance needs.   I'm not sure that I really need any more.   I've got $10,000 on myself, $5,000 worth of coverage on my wife, and $1,000 on each of the three kids.

1. *You:*   (Paraphrase what was said.)   Could your wife work if something happened to you?

Customer: She used to be a secretary but has not worked in eight years. With jobs the way they are now, she should be able to find a decent-paying position.

2. *You:*   (Paraphrase what was said.)   Who would watch the kids?

Customer: That could be a problem.   I'm not sure if my sister could or would want to do the job.   The $10,000 should buy a lot of babysitting service, I would think.

3. *You:*   (Paraphrase what was said.)   What if it cost $100 per week for a sitter?   Would there still be enough money to feed and clothe them as well as pay off the home mortgage?

Please check your paraphrasing with suggested responses on page 236 and with a classmate.

Suggested Answers to Exercise 7-8

The following represent one way that the customer's statements could be paraphrased.

1. *You:* You are saying that you feel confident your life insurance needs are adequate.
2. *You:* Sounds like your wife could be self-supporting and use some of the skills she learned earlier.
3. *You:* You seem to feel somewhat insecure about the issue of child care.

Active Listening Skills: Summarizing a Message

Summarizing condenses what was said in the same words the speaker used. It is particularly useful when a great deal of information has been given by the speaker. Stopping the conversation periodically to summarize the points ensures a better understanding of the points covered. Consider the following situation.

Situation: Elaine and Steve are both middle managers for a large company. Elaine has just received some interesting information about the company's future.

IF I CAN SUMMARIZE WHAT YOU SAID: I'M NOT FIT FOR THE JOB, YOU CAN'T UNDERSTAND WHY I WORK HERE, I INTERFERE WITH THINGS, BUT YOU'LL RECOMMEND I BE PROMOTED UPSTAIRS.

ELAINE: I've just heard the company is going to merge with United Industries. I'm told that it will make us the second-largest company in
the field. Apparently the deal has been in the works for six months.
So far there is no talk about how the top positions will be affected. I
don't think that you or I need to worry about our jobs. This new
operation will need all the help it can get.

STEVE: Let's see if I understand what you said. Our company has been
negotiating a merger with United Industries for the past six months.
It was approved and things will probably not change much at the top.
We don't need to worry about our jobs. Is that accurate?

ELAINE: Yes, that's correct. All of this sounds exciting to me.

STEVE: I'm just as excited as you are.

EXERCISE 7-9: SUMMARIZING

As a test of your ability to summarize, review the conversation between the mother
and daughter and the insurance-selling situation presented earlier. Summarize
what was said in both situations when paraphrasing was used in the original.
Check your responses with those on page 238. What do you see as the relative
advantages and disadvantages of both techniques? Which one seems to indicate
a better understanding of what was said? Which one forces you to listen harder?
Could a mix of both be used in the same conversation?

Active Listening Skills: Asking Content Questions

In an earlier section, we reviewed the use of open and closed questions to
assist the flow of a conversation and to initiate discussion. Asking questions
can also be a helpful device to assist your active listening. It is often difficult
to follow everything someone is saying or to understand it completely the
first time. Periodically stop and ask a question if you are not following what
was said (e.g., "I'm sorry, I was not able to follow that last point. Would you
please repeat it?"). Sometimes it is helpful to probe for more information
with a question (e.g., "What would happen if that last step were not followed?"). I have found that people who are sharing information appreciate
a good question. To ask a question indicates that you are concerned and
interested in what is being said.

Suggested Answers to Exercise 7-9

The following represent one way that the interactions could use summarizing.

Mother-Daughter Interaction.

1. *Mother:* You are saying that Suzy has not been home much since she's joined several clubs and is going to movies with Alice.
2. *Mother:* I also remember that you and Suzy had a lot of fun doing things together.
3. *Mother:* You certainly sound angry that she is not acting like her old self.
4. *Daughter:* I agree with you that she is interested in my opinion and would sit down and talk to me about it.

Customer-Insurance Salesperson Interaction.

1. *You:* You feel that $10,000 on yourself, $5,000 on your wife, and $1,000 per child is adequate.
2. *You:* Let's see, your wife has 8 years of secretarial experience and could find a decent job.
3. *You:* If I understand you correctly, your sister may not want to babysit but the $10,000 could pay for babysitters.

Listener Skills: Asking for and Receiving Feedback

In your role as a receiver of information, there are times when you will get feedback on your actions or ideas. We have already examined several principles for giving feedback. In this section we will consider two principles for receiving feedback. The intent is to suggest some things that you can do to maximize your benefits from feedback and to ensure that what you receive will be helpful.

Ask for Specific Feedback on Strengths and Weaknesses

There are times when we do not get feedback because someone forgets or thinks we are not interested. Sometimes it is helpful to be active and ask for it. Try to get the person giving you feedback to be as specific as possible and to look at both strengths and weaknesses.

A friend of mine recently began a new job. He was on the job six weeks and was not told how his performance was assessed. His boss hardly ever gave him feedback, and he thought that it was because his performance was poor. I suggested he ask for specific feedback and for information on his strengths and weaknesses. He did, and he reported that his boss appreciated his asking. He learned that his performance was quite good and that a short course at the university could help him in an area in which he was deficient.

Listen Carefully to Feedback

Use the active listening skills discussed earlier when receiving feedback. Paraphrasing, summarizing, and asking questions about the feedback you receive is a good approach to take. It is particularly important when someone is giving you negative feedback. I have found that people are accepting of the good things they hear and resist the negative. When you receive negative feedback, try not to deny it. Assess from your point of view what is accurate about the other person's observations. From someone else's standpoint, there is probably some truth to the comments. Before presenting a legitimate alternative point of view, acknowledge the extent to which the perceptions are accurate. For example: "George, I think this is the third day this week you have been late for work." "That is true, Phil, I was late on Monday and Tuesday. Unless I'm mistaken, I was on time today. I'll watch it in the future." Listening carefully indicates that you are interested in feedback, that you are likely to act on it, and that the speaker need not fear giving you feedback in the future.

EXERCISE 7-10: RECEIVING FEEDBACK

Situation: Ellen is taking a small advanced English course that includes much writing and class participation and many practical exercises, demonstrations, and out-of-class projects. She is wondering how the teacher sees her performance to date.

Ellen: Ms. Jones, I've been wondering how I'm doing in the course. What can you tell me about what I'm doing well and what I'm doing poorly?

Ms. Jones: Your class attendance is good, and your paper was one of the best in the class. Otherwise I don't think you are doing well. Your tests haven't been good and the other people in the class seem to ignore your classroom ideas and inputs.

Ellen: That isn't true. I try hard to do well and I'm sure my friends are listening to me in class. I just do not see how you could feel that way.

Ms. Jones: Well, that's how I see things and if you don't change your behavior you will have problems passing this course.

Based on what you have just read, how well did Ellen ask for feedback? How effectively did she respond to the negative feedback? Imagine that you are in this situation. How would you respond to the negative feedback? Decide what response you would make to each of Ms. Jones's comments. What is Ms. Jones likely to say if you used the principles for receiving feedback well? Check your responses with a friend or classmate.

Improving Message Clarity

At the beginning of this chapter, the idea that a message could be viewed as a signal that exists in a noise background was introduced. Two ways to ensure an adequate signal are to increase its clarity or strength and to reduce the noise background. The communication skills discussed previously will help to ensure that our messages are clear. To reduce the noise background we need to consider factors in our external environment and in our cognitive and emotional makeup.

Reduction of External Noise

External noise is simply the factors in our environments which interfere with our ability to discuss issues. Consequently, it is usually the easiest kind of noise to do something about. Turning off radios and television sets or moving to a quieter room is easy to do. When serious discussions are to take place, a quiet relaxed atmosphere with a minimum of distractions is essential.

Reduction of Internal Noise: Cognitive Factors

An important source of cognitive noise is the difference in interpretation we give to another person's words and actions. All of us do not have exactly the same meanings for words in our vocabularies. To illustrate this, think of the differences in meaning that the following words have for you: "kicking butts," "left wing," "grass," "intelligence," "star," "bank." Have you ever had a conversation in which the meaning was unclear because the words had multiple interpretations or they sounded like jargon to you? A friend recently told me that he would meet me for lunch at the riverside bank. I had to check to make sure he meant a financial institution and not the park on the bank of the river. The best way to deal with this problem is to define any new or ambiguous terms before using them. Analogously, if something is not clear, the receiver should stop the speaker and ask for a clarification.

A related problem is what John Wallen calls the "interpersonal gap." When we say or do something, we often intend to get a specific reaction. Sometimes the effect we get is not what was intended. The reason is that we attach meaning to our own and other people's behaviors from different frames of reference. Both you and I try to understand words and actions based on our backgrounds and past experiences. When our past experiences do not overlap, we run the risk of misunderstanding each other. Neither of our perceptions is necessarily wrong; we simply see things differently. Some examples of this problem appear in Table 7-3. To bridge the interpersonal gap we can use the skills of perception checking, describing our feelings, paraphrasing, summarizing, and asking questions to make sure we understand what was meant.

Reduction of Internal Noise: Emotional Factors

There are times when our behaviors create emotional reactions in other people. This happens because people become threatened by our behavior. They then become defensive and begin to think, feel, and act as if they are under attack. The communication climate changes, and we are no longer trying to understand the other person. Instead, we argue, try to impress the other person with what we know, or simply cut off communication. Research shows that defensive communication climates are characterized by these actions and by a distortion of what is said. The clarity of our messages decreases, because the emotions created interfere with our listening.

Engaging in these behaviors less often will create a less defensive communication climate. Jack Gibb has suggested several additional things we can do. We should convince the other person in our conversations that we

Table 7-3

Examples of the Interpersonal Gap in Communication

The same statement can be interpreted differently by different people.

GEORGE:	"I'd like to take you to my golf club after work."	PETE:	I wonder what he is really up to?
		ELLEN:	That's a really nice thing for him to do.
		STEVE:	I bet he is just trying to impress me again.
		CAROL:	He always seems obligated to include me in what he does.
SUSAN:	"I'm really feeling angry. That's the last time I want to see you do that."	HARRY:	She is always blaming me for things. I wish she would stop.
		JEAN:	It was my fault. She is right. I'll try to do things differently in the future.
		JOE:	I wonder why she is angry. What I did could not be that important.

EXERCISE 7-11: DEFENSIVE BEHAVIORS

Listed after this paragraph are some things that are done during communication that create a defensive climate. Determine which ones you use *at least occasionally* in conversations. As you do this, think about the effect these factors have had on other people. Think of some things that you could do to change your behavior.

- Ordering other people to do something without giving them explanations of why you want it done.
- Threatening people to get something accomplished. Saying such things as "If you don't do this, I'm going to . . ."; "I'm warning you, this is your last chance."
- Using a lot of "shoulds" or "oughts" in your conversation. That is, letting the Parent part of your personality dominate your interactions.
- Criticizing another person without giving specific descriptive feedback on things you are concerned about.
- When a person does something wrong, giving them a lecture on what is the correct way rather than mutually exploring with them a better way to accomplish the task.
- Calling another person "stupid," "idiot," "jackass," or some other summary expression that is likely to anger that individual.

- Harshly interpreting and analyzing the reasons you think the other person did something you disagreed with—saying such things as "I'm sure you did this to spite me," "You are acting just like your brother did," "I'm sure you are doing this because your mother put you up to it."
- Interrogating another person to clarify information or to gain understanding. For example, "Now, I'm not going to ask you again, where did you put the . . ."; "You don't expect me to believe that; what really happened?"
- Withdrawing from the conversation and refusing to discuss the issue anymore.
- Using sarcasm or humor to make fun of what another person did.
- Dispensing blame for what happens on other people. "It's your fault the project failed. I had nothing to do with it."

are flexible in our thinking and willing to listen to different points of view. If other people can see us as willing to explore issues and not take sides on them, we are less likely to create an emotional communication climate. It is important for both parties to approach a conversation with a problem-solving orientation through which both individuals can control what is discussed.

EXERCISE 7-12: INTEGRATIVE COMMUNICATION SKILLS

The following communication skills assessment questionnaire is identical to the one you filled out earlier in this chapter. Based on your reading of this chapter, indicate how often *you would like to use* each skill in the future. Compare your data to the first time you took the questionnaire. Try to be realistic and objective in your assessment.

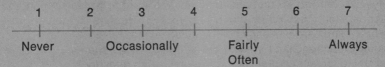

1	2	3	4	5	6	7
Never		Occasionally		Fairly Often		Always

Speaker Skills

_____ I share my ideas, interests, and feelings with my close friends.
_____ I share my ideas, interests, and feelings when meeting new people.
_____ I give people feedback on the things I don't like that they do.
_____ I give people feedback on the things I like that they do.
_____ I ask people if they want feedback before giving it.
_____ When I give feedback it describes in detail the specific behaviors I observed.
_____ When I interpret the nonverbal behavior of other people, I ask them to verify whether I am accurate.
_____ I ask questions that allow other people to respond in as broad and extensive a manner as possible.

_____ I ask questions that allow other people to respond with specific and concise answers.

Listener Skills

_____ I try to describe the feelings that the speaker is showing.

_____ When talking with another person, I translate into my own words the ideas and feelings that are presented.

_____ When talking with another person, I condense what is said using essentially the same words the other person used.

_____ When I don't understand something, I ask the other person to explain or elaborate upon what was said.

_____ I ask for feedback on my behavior from other people.

_____ I try to understand what is accurate about any negative feedback I may receive.

Message-Related Skills

_____ I try to eliminate things in the environment which are distracting when talking to others.

_____ I try to use words that I'm sure the other person understands.

_____ I define words that I think are new or that represent jargon when I talk to someone else.

_____ I try to eliminate elements in conversations that threaten other people.

_____ I try to listen to different points of view from others on an issue.

_____ I try to present different points of view on an issue.

Your earlier responses gave you an estimate of how often *you currently* use each skill. Pick the three skills in which *you have the largest discrepancy* between what you *currently do* and what you *would like to do*. Please do the following.

1. Reread the section in this chapter that relates to each area and think about what you need to do to improve the skill.
2. Pick one to three situations in your life in which you think the skills would be useful. Be sure to select situations that you want to do something about.
3. Describe each situation as it currently exists. Be sure to include what is said and how things are currently communicated.
4. Develop an action plan for using the skill(s) in each situation.
5. After trying the action plan, answer the following questions:
   a. Compared to past conversations, did things improve, get worse, or remain the same?
   b. How well do you think you used the skills you selected?
   c. What would you do to change things in the future?
6. Why not share what you did and the reactions you received with a friend, a classmate, or your instructor?

SUMMARY

The effective use of communication skills helps our interactions by assisting us in clearly presenting our ideas and by enhancing our understanding of what others are saying. Information theory is a useful frame of reference for viewing the communication process. It provides a criterion for communication effectiveness and allows us to identify the parts of personal communication that are likely to be improved by various skills.

The criterion for communication effectiveness is the amount of new information that is shared. If I am just as uncertain about your ideas and feelings after we talked as I was before we began, then we had a rather poor interaction. It is important to reduce uncertainty by new information because this process increases our motivation to continue the interaction. People usually enjoy conversations in which they feel something was accomplished or they learned something new.

The parts of the communication process identified by information theory are a source or speaker, a receiver or listener, a communication channel, and a message. In a two-way conversation, each of us alternates in our roles as speaker and listener. The skills of self-disclosure of interests and feelings, giving feedback, checking perceptions, and asking open and closed questions are important to our roles as speakers. Important listener skills include our ability to reflect the speaker's feelings, paraphrasing and summarizing what is said, asking questions, and receiving feedback in an open manner.

The communication channel is the means by which we convey our messages. Human communication uses light waves in sending and receiving written and nonverbal messages, sound waves in speaking and listening, physical contact which affects our skin receptors, and the molecules in various gases which stimulate our receptors for smell. It is quite possible to overload a communication channel. We need to monitor our interactions to ensure that an information overload is not occurring. Skills like asking closed questions, paraphrasing and summarizing what is said, and being sensitive to feedback from others can assist us in reducing an overload.

The message represents the ideas or feelings that we express. In information theory terms, our messages are considered signals which exist in a noise background. To be heard, our messages must be stronger than this noise background. Noise can come from our environments (e.g., loud radios, people talking, lawnmowers running) or from cognitive and emotional factors. Cognitive noise occurs when our words convey several meanings or intentions. Because the past experiences of each of us are different, we do not always interpret the same things similarly. Emotional factors include a tendency to become defensive or feel threatened by others in conversations. We then begin to distort the messages we hear.

There are several things we can do to reduce the occurrence of noise in communication. Environmental factors can often be lowered at their source (e.g., turning a radio off), or we can remove ourselves to a quieter area. Cognitive noise can be reduced by defining our words and checking our perceptions of what we think others mean. Emotional factors can be handled by monitoring the way we talk to others. We should avoid doing such things as verbally threatening or overly criticizing people, name-calling, and dispensing blame exclusively to other people when things go wrong. Furthermore, we need to show others that we are willing to explore issues and approach situations with a problem-solving orientation.

THINGS TO DO

1. Have each person in the class describe a situation in which he or she has had a problem communicating. List all the different topics on the board. Select the three or four that look most interesting to the class. Appoint each of the people who suggested a chosen problem to act as the director for a skit. They are to select other people in the class to become actors to role-play people in their situations. One of the actors in each skit will role-play the person whose problem was selected. The director should take 10 minutes to outline the problem to the actors and give them some idea of what was said and how it was said. The actors should be given room to improvise.

    Role-play each situation before the class and have class members analyze it for the use of speaker and listener communication skills, factors contributing to communication channel overload, if any, and noise. Class members make suggestions for improving the interaction, and each situation is replayed with the actors trying to incorporate the suggestions. The advantages and disadvantages of the changes are then discussed.

2. Pick a situation in which you do not think you are listening well. Make sure that you select a situation that you want to do something about.
    a. Describe the situation as it currently exists.
    b. What are the major problems as you see it?
    c. Select one or more of the listening skills discussed earlier and develop an action plan for using them.
    d. Compared to past conversations, did things improve, get worse, or remain the same?

3. Pick one class that you enjoy and one that you do not like. Examine each for the presence or absence of the use of speaker and listener communication skills. Try to assess whether there is an information overload and whether environmental, cognitive, and emotional noise factors are present. Do you

think that the two classes differ significantly in any of these factors? In what way do you think this contributes to your enjoying or disliking the class? Are your perceptions shared by other students? Why not share your observations with each instructor?

4. Pick one other interpersonal communication situation in your life that you enjoy and one that you do not like. Repeat the kind of analysis you performed in item 3. If some of the differences are due to problems in communication skills, develop an action plan to work on one or more of the issues.

5. Use a cassette tape recorder to record one or more of your conversations during the next week. Compare your actual use of communication skills in the conversation(s) to your response in the first communication skills assessment questionnaire. How accurate was your assessment in the questionnaire? How does it differ from the reality? What are some additional skill areas that you feel you need to work on?

6. Carefully read the dialogue between characters in a novel or listen carefully to the dialogue between the actors in a television series. Are any of the communication principles and skills discussed in this chapter used? What effect do you think their presence or absence has on the development of the story?

7. Discuss the following personal communication situations in terms of the factors associated with message clarity identified in this chapter. Try to think of the potential sources of environmental, cognitive, and emotional noise and ways they could be overcome: (a) the interrogation of a suspect by a police officer, (b) a prosecuting attorney questioning the person accused of a crime, (c) a television news crew interviewing people on the sidewalk on a current topic, (d) a man proposing marriage to a woman, (e) a student discussing a course grade with a teacher, (f) a mother sitting down to explain the "facts of life" to her daughter, and (g) a salesperson and client discussing business over lunch.

8. In your next conversation with a friend, before you respond to what the person says, paraphrase or summarize it and ask if you were accurate. Tell the person beforehand that you are trying to improve your listening skills and would appreciate cooperation.

   A variation on this project is to use the same technique in a class discussion. Before anyone can talk, they must paraphrase and/or summarize what the other person said to that person's satisfaction. See if your instructor is willing to try this. It often yields interesting data on how well people are listening to each other.

REFERENCES AND OTHER INTERESTING THINGS TO READ

ATTNEAVE, F. *Applications of Information Theory to Psychology*. New York: Holt, Rinehart and Winston, 1959.

FLESCH, R. *The Art of Plain Talk.* New York: Harper & Row, 1946.

GIBB, J. Defensive communication. *Journal of Communication,* 1964, *11,* 141–148.

GORDON, T. *P.E.T. Parent Effectiveness Training.* New York: Peter H. Wyden, 1970.

HANSON, P. Giving feedback: An interpersonal skill. *1975 Annual Handbook for Group Facilitators.* La Jolla, Calif.: University Associates, 1975.

JOURARD, S. *Self Disclosure.* New York: John Wiley and Sons, 1971.

KRUPAR, K. R. *Communication Games.* New York: The Free Press, 1973.

MILLER, G. A. The magic number seven, plus or minus two: Some limits on our capacity for processing information. *Psychological Review,* 1956, *63,* 81–97.

NEWMAN, E. *Strictly Speaking: Will America Be the Death of English?* Indianapolis: Bobbs-Merrill Co., 1974.

POWELL, J. *Why am I Afraid to Tell You Who I am?* Chicago: Peacock Books, 1969.

REIK, T. *Listening With the Third Ear.* New York: Pyramid, 1972.

SHANNON, C., and WEAVER, W. *The Mathematical Theory of Communication.* Urbana: University of Illinois Press, 1949.

VERDERBER, R. *Communicate!* Belmont, Calif.: Wadsworth, 1975.

WIENER, N. *Cybernetics.* New York: John Wiley and Sons, 1948.

A. After reading this chapter, the reader should be able to explain:

1. Why group goals and activities should involve the active participation of the members and be related to their needs to be accepted and recognized and to have an outlet for their skills and abilities.

2. How group norms or standards for behavior affect our actions and perceptions, and the decisions we make in groups.

3. The distinction between a formal and informal group norm.

4. The distinction between conformity and compliance with group norms.

5. Three things that contribute to group members' thinking alike or developing tendencies toward "groupthink."

6. The way that the various roles we play in groups contribute to the interactions that occur.

7. The causes of role conflicts and four things that can be done to eliminate them.

8. How leaders are able to influence other people and the role that expert, referent, legitimate, reward, and coercive sources of influence play in that process.

9. Why it is important for members of a group to be concerned with tasks and the relationship among members.

10. Two ways that the assumptions leaders make about people affect the way that they lead.

11. Why personal characteristics that adequately distinguish between leaders and their followers are difficult to find.

12. The advantages and disadvantages of voting and consensus decision-making processes in groups.

13. Common sources of group conflict, how they affect the group, and three ways that conflicts might be resolved.

B. While reading this chapter, the reader should be able to use the information to:

1. Complete each of the exercises in the text.

2. Begin to think of ways to apply the principles to situations in daily living.

8

Group Dynamics in Daily Life

GLOSSARY

Autokinetic effect. A perceptual illusion in which, when a tiny spot of light is placed on the wall of a dark room, the light appears to move.

Coercive power. Influence over other people derived from an ability to punish them—"Eat your dinner or you will have to stay in the house tonight."

Compliance. The process occurring when an individual follows a group's directions or accepts its opinion or interpretation of an idea or event because it will lead to a favorable reaction from the members.

Conflict. A tendency for a group or individual to have a difficult time choosing among alternative courses of action or to be in opposition to another individual or group.

Conformity. The process occurring when an individual follows a group's directions or accepts its opinion or interpretation of an idea or event because it is personally appealing or rewarding.

Consensus. A decision-making process in which issues are discussed until everyone is in essential agreement with a course of action.

Expert power. Influence over other people derived from one's knowledge or expertise—"I've worked ten years in this area and I suggest we do the following."

Formal norms. Explicit verbal or written standards and guidelines for behavior in a group. They often appear in the form of rules, regulations, or policy guidelines. An army regulation on how to make a bed is an example of a formal norm.

Group. A set of two or more persons who have some observable and definable relationship to each other and who are pursuing a common set of goals.

Group processes. Factors that operate in any group to influence the interactions of members. Examples include goal setting, leadership, the influences of norms on behavior, how decisions are made, the roles members play, and how conflict is managed.

Groupthink. A term coined by Irving Janis to describe a tendency for each member of a group to publicly think alike and exert pressures on others to do the same. The group appears to be unanimous, but some members may privately hold doubts about a decision that they are afraid to share.

Informal norms. The standards and guidelines we follow that are not explicitly stated as rules. Based on our experiences we learn that certain behaviors are allowed. We might find out that students are penalized for missing class or that we are expected to say "good morning" or "good afternoon" when we see our boss at work. In neither case are we specifically told that this is a norm.

Leadership. The process of providing direction and guidance to a group's activity.

Legitimate power. Influence over other people that occurs because of the position an individual holds as the formal head of a group—"As president of the club, I want to have the picnic next Tuesday."

Norms. The ideas that members share regarding what behaviors are appropriate for a situation. They act to set standards and guidelines for our behaviors. When we eat with forks and spoons, address a boss by title rather than by first name, or sit in a particular location we are adhering to group norms.

Referent power. Influence over other people that occurs because a close personal relationship exists—"Ed, we've been friends for a long time. I'd like you to do me a favor."

Reward power. Influence over other people derived from an ability of one person to dispense rewards.

Roles. The parts that each of us plays in our daily lives. Common roles include student, teacher, brother, sister, mother, and father.

Role conflict. Tension and frustration that arise out of our tendency to hold more than one role. It might occur because we have more than one relationship to a person or group or because people give us different messages about how our roles should be played.

Social-emotional maintenance functions. Group member behaviors that assist the group with its internal cohesion and interpersonal relations. Examples include working on conflicts, keeping com-munication channels open, compro-mising, expressing feelings, and recogniz-ing individual contributions.

Theory X. Douglas McGregor's assump-tion about human behavior that suggests people dislike work and need to be coerced, controlled, and directed toward accomplishing a task.

Theory Y. Douglas McGregor's assump-tion about human behavior that suggests people want to take initiative and in-terest in their work and are quite able to exercise self-direction and self-control.

Win-lose conflict. A situation that occurs when two or more people find themselves competing for the same thing. Only one person or group can win. One example is two nations fighting over a common piece of territory.

Basic Processes in Groups

On a hot, humid summer day, the president of the United States and sev-eral of his advisors met to discuss the fate of the world.

CHIEF OF STAFF: Mr. President, it is quite clear to me that based on in-formation from our Intelligence Section, the Soviets are about to launch a hostile action against the United States. We just cannot sit around and let this happen. We need to strike first.

PRESIDENT: I am not sure what to do. But before making a decision, I need to know what some of you other people think.

SECRETARY OF STATE: I would agree with our Chief of Staff. My infor-mation suggests that they are about to initiate some hostile action. Their ambassador has just left town for Mexico stating he was taking a vacation trip. Their armed forces have been placed on alert and there has been a lot of activity around their nuclear missile stations.

NATIONAL SECURITY ADVISOR: With the way things have gone in the Middle East and Africa, they have every reason to see us as a threat. They always interpret our peaceful motives in the wrong way. We ought to strike first before they have a chance to launch an attack. It is our best chance to have peace in the future.

PRESIDENTIAL DOMESTIC AFFAIRS ADVISOR: Mr. President, we need to be careful here. After all, this could be nothing more than an effort to make us nervous because of the crises in the Middle East and Africa. They have done such things in the past. A nuclear war is not the answer to anything.

PRESIDENT: I can understand why you might disagree. I would like to hear how some of you others react to what he just said.

CHIEF OF STAFF: With all due respect to your Domestic Affairs Advisor, Mr. President, he is not in a position to judge the motives of the Soviets. This is quite a different thing than consumer rights, transportation, and housing projects. I've been around too long and I know they always have had hostile motives toward us. This time, they are not fooling around. I am afraid that if we do not get the go ahead within the next hour, that we will lose our first strike capability.

SECRETARY OF STATE: I can only agree with the Chief of Staff. All the critical signs are there. I have never seen or heard of a situation that has been as bad. It certainly is not our fault that things are the way they are.

NATIONAL SECURITY ADVISOR: Mr. President, I feel that it is too late to be cautious as your Domestic Affairs Advisor suggests. We have been too nice in the past. It is now time to get tough.

DOMESTIC AFFAIRS ADVISOR: This is crazy! Surely we can explore other interpretations of their actions first. We can get on the Hot Line and talk to their people. After all, that is what it is there for. That line of communication is still open.

PRESIDENT: I wonder if that idea has merit.

NATIONAL SECURITY ADVISOR: I think it would only tip our hand that we suspected an attack at any moment. We need to act swiftly. The time for talking is over. There is no other way.

CHIEF OF STAFF: I agree.

SECRETARY OF STATE: I agree.

DOMESTIC AFFAIRS ADVISOR: I can't believe this! Please Mr. President, we need more time! There have to be other courses of action.

PRESIDENT: Ladies and gentlemen, based on what I have heard, I have decided to . . .

If you were the president, what would you do? Obviously, this is a difficult decision. As with any decision made in a group context, it will not be reached simply on the basis of the facts presented. A number of processes operate in groups to affect what is said and how decisions are made. Listed are several questions that relate to factors that will influence such interactions. Answer each question as it applied to the example that was presented. Use what you already know about groups based on your past experiences to formulate an opinion.

1. Is more than one person trying to exercise leadership in this group? How is this occurring?
2. What could the president do to provide more effective leadership?
3. What are the sources of the conflict and tension in the group?
4. How do members handle an opinion with which they do not agree?
5. With so many people favoring one course of action, how likely do you think it is that the president will listen to his domestic affairs advisor?
6. How does the group judge its own actions compared with the Soviets?
7. Are people listening to each other's views?
8. Could such a situation ever occur?

After reading this chapter, return to these questions. Based on what you have learned, how would you clarify and extend your responses?

Thinking about these questions probably made you aware of how important a leader's behavior, the management of conflict and tension among members, and the ways in which people influence each other are to a group's functioning. Certainly you and I have encountered such things in the types of groups in which we participate. Our daily group contacts include classrooms, our families, and organizations in which we work and socialize. There are *group processes,* or factors that operate to influence the interactions of people, that are common to the group experiences we have everyday. They include such things as the establishment and attainment of goals, the adherence of members to the *norms* or standards of behavior that members share, the way a leader tries to influence people, the way that decisions are made, and the procedures people use to resolve *conflicts* or differences in opinion. Our knowledge and understanding of such processes can benefit our daily interactions by helping us to develop skills to enhance our participation as group members and giving us information to improve the group's functioning.

Establishing and Attaining Goals

The groups we belong to exist to accomplish certain goals. The goals of such groups vary in complexity. They might range from giving us and other members a chance to socialize, to working on tasks like planning fund-raising efforts or learning about a particular subject in the classroom. Setting and attaining goals are an extremely important aspect of group life. My experiences suggest that there are times when interactions around goals are not very effective. There are two important principles about goals that each of us should know.

Group members should actively participate in the development of group goals and activities. Think of how you would feel if you could not share your ideas regarding goals and the methods for accomplishing them in a group to which you belonged. Is it likely that you would be very committed to the task? Unless we can make inputs into what is going to happen, we are not likely to show interest in the group's goals. This input is important to us and to other members of the group. It is not necessarily true, however, that the membership must develop all group goals and activities. In many existing organizations, certain goals and activities are carried over as a normal part of its functioning. However, the inputs of members are still valuable. Because of its traditions, a college may have a dance every spring. The pre-established goals may be to raise money for student organizations or to promote the college in the local community. But even given these goals, there is still room for inputs regarding direction and activity from the membership.

Is there anything you could do as a group leader or member to ensure that a lack of participation in the development of goals and activities does not occur? Although a total absence of such participation is probably rare, I have observed tendencies for a lack of participation to occur periodically in groups. A helpful suggestion is for the leader or some group member to ask: "What goals are we trying to accomplish with this project or task?" "What are some alternative methods we might use to accomplish our goals?" When responses to both questions are discussed, the sharing of ideas allows for the involvement of people in the development of goals and activities.

Group goals and activities should relate to the task needs of the group and the personal needs of its members. Groups form to accomplish certain tasks. Their goals and activities must correspond to the reasons for the groups' existence. This statement is, of course, somewhat obvious to each of us. What is not always obvious, however, is that goals and activities must bear some relation to the personal needs that we and other members have. Each of us has personal needs met by our participation in groups. Our needs for personal recognition and attention, for affection, and for an outlet for our skills and abilities are satisfied in groups ranging from families and classrooms to work and social organizations. If the group's goals and activities help meet our personal needs, our commitment and satisfaction with its products will increase.

As a group member, is there anything you could do to help ensure that the personal needs of other people are met? When I am a leader of a group, I often ask people to list their interests, skills, and abilities on a blackboard or flip chart, especially in groups in which people do not know each other well. This procedure gives individuals a legitimate opportunity to mention these characteristics and facilitates the assignment of people to tasks based on their interests and abilities. Thus, some of their needs are more easily met. People enjoy doing this, and I have noticed very little resistance to the suggestion.

What personal needs are met by the group's goals and activities in your class and one other group to which you belong?

Group Norms

A group *norm* is simply a shared idea about how particular behaviors should occur. They help us know what is expected of us and what we can expect from others. When I wear a shirt and tie to a formal cocktail party, raise my hand to speak at a meeting, address my parents as mother and father, and hold office hours for my students I am adhering to group norms. Without various guidelines and standards for our behaviors, our lives would become confused and chaotic.

Norms may be formal or informal. According to Richard Schmuck, *formal norms* are explicitly outlined in the verbal or written rules for the group's behavior. They appear in the form of rules, regulations, or policy guidelines of the group or organization. When I was in the Army, formal norms existed for procedures such as making a bed, dressing, and purchasing equipment. Teachers often have strict preferences for the size of margins on a term paper. This is conveyed to students in a written syllabus, or verbally when the rules and procedures of the class are discussed. *Informal norms* are the procedures and routines that we follow but that are not explicitly stated as rules. Based on our past experiences and on-going interactions in a group, you and I learn that certain behaviors are either permitted or not permitted. How to address a teacher (Professor, Mr., Ms., or first name), who is allowed to socialize together (e.g., at lunch or parties), and saying "good morning" and "thank you" are examples of informal norms.

Why do we conform to norms? One reason is that we obtain positive reinforcers from others for conforming, and failing to adhere often leads to aversive consequences for our actions. Based on our discussion of reinforcement in Chapters 3 and 4, you are aware of how positive and negative reinforcers influence the probability of our responding. For example, my stu-

EXERCISE 8-1: NORMS FOR BEHAVIOR

Listed after this paragraph are several norms that exist in my family, in classes that I teach, and in the organization in which I work. As a check on your understanding of the concept of norms, list two to three additional norms for behavior you think exist in your family, this class you are taking, and, if applicable, an organization in which you work. I indicated whether it was formal or informal by placing an *F* or an *I* next to each norm. Please classify each of the norms that you listed as either formal or informal.

My Family:

(F)—Children help to clean the house on Saturday.
(F)—Members call home if they will be late for dinner.
(F)—Dinner is held between 6:30 and 7:00 each day.
(I)—My wife and I usually go out on Friday and Saturday nights.
(F)—Low nutrition foods are not consumed.
(I)—Family members say "good morning" and "good night" to each other.

My Classroom:

(F)—Students are expected to turn assignments in on time.
(I)—Students may call me by my first name.
(F)—Students work in small groups in class.
(F)—Final exams are only held on the announced dates and time periods.
(I)—Students often study for exams together outside of class.
(F)—Students select the final project they want to work on.

My Organization:

(I)—The department head's ideas are often challenged at meetings.
(F)—People attend faculty meetings.
(I)—After a meeting, small groups of people meet to discuss further what was said.
(I)—Faculty consult with each other on the problems they are having with their classes and research projects.
(F)—Faculty must sign a contract for employment every year.
(I)—Senior faculty in the department usually have the largest offices.
(F)—Faculty are allowed to miss an occasional class but they must arrange for a colleague to teach it.

Were there any norms that my family, classroom, or organization had in common with yours? Do you think your instructor or other students in class would agree with the norms you listed? Why not ask them?

dents and department head are likely to positively reinforce me for holding office hours, attending each scheduled class, and turning in grades on time. Similarly, a patient in a therapy group is likely to gain recognition, attention, and praise from the therapist for discussing personal problems in the group. On the other hand, failing to adhere to group norms will lead to negative consequences. If I failed to engage in expected teacher behaviors, I might lose my job or I would certainly have several people angry at me. A recent experience of mine led me to appreciate the effects of violating group norms. I went to see a very popular movie. It was a cold day, and the line was several blocks long. I tried to sneak into the front of the line. People pushed me away, some called me names, and others had angry facial expressions. Needless to say, I retreated. I had violated an informal norm that everyone waits his or her turn at the end of the line. Because of this unpleasant experience, I am likely to follow the norms in order to avoid this incident recurring in the future.

For the norms that you listed earlier, what reinforces you for following them? What would happen if you violated each norm?

Norms affect our perceptions of other people, groups, and objects.

EXERCISE 8-2: EFFECTS OF NORMS ON PERCEPTION

Before reading further, please turn to Figure 8-1. Without directly measuring either drawing with a ruler, your fingers, or any other object, estimate how much longer the straight line in the drawing on the right is than the straight line in the other drawing. Try to judge the difference in eighths of an inch (i.e., 1 inch, $\frac{7}{8}$, $\frac{6}{8}$, $\frac{5}{8}$, $\frac{4}{8}$, $\frac{3}{8}$, $\frac{2}{8}$, $\frac{1}{8}$, 0).

I recently had five of my best students judge the differences in length. They sat together in a small group and each made his or her judgment aloud so that the others could hear. Pretend you are also a member of this group. The estimates of the other five members are:

Len: I would say that there is no difference.
Ellen: No difference.
Carol: Zero.
Ron: I'm not sure but I would say there is no difference.
Linda: No difference.
You: Look at Figure 8-1 again and make another estimate of the difference in eighths of an inch.

In reality both lines are the same. However, they are sometimes perceived to be different. About 25 percent of my students report that they are different. When given the information from other students we have just presented, 70 percent of these will lower their second estimate.

Did you revise your estimate the second time? What reasons did you have for changing your mind? What reasons did you have for not changing your mind? How did several of your classmates respond? Are there differences in people in terms of how much they were influenced?

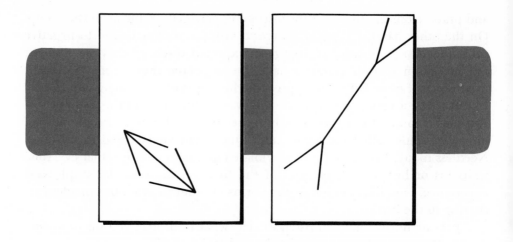

Figure 8-1

*Estimate how much longer the straight line in the drawing on the
right is than the straight line in the drawing on the left.*

Muzafer Sherif and Solomon Asch were able to demonstrate similar
effects of how other people's behaviors affect our perceptions. Sherif used
an illusion known as the *autokinetic effect*. When a stationary pinpoint of
light is placed on a wall in a dark room, it appears to move. You or I could
easily estimate how many inches the light appears to move. However, Sherif
showed that when other people are sitting in the room with us, we are likely
to modify our first estimate based on what the other people say. This is
particularly true if our first estimate is too far above or below the average
estimate of the group. Asch was able to show similar effects of group norms
on a task in which people had to identify which two of four lines were the
same length. You or I could easily pick out the identical lines because
they were quite obvious. However, when other people enter the picture,
things are not as straightforward. Unknown to the person making such a
judgment, the other people in Asch's study were working with the experimenter. There were times when all his assistants made an obviously incorrect choice. When this happened, participants also made an incorrect
choice about one-third of the time.

As you can easily see, the norms that others establish may influence
our perceptual judgments. The effect is not limited to changes in spots of
light or line estimates. Daily, each of us judges such things as: "Can we
trust the other group?" "What do these data mean?" "How would you

interpret her behaviors?" "How hard a grader is Professor Jones?" "Is it safe to walk around the downtown streets at night?" When we discuss such things with other people, a variety of experiences, attitudes, and opinions are shared and agreed upon. Such discussions lead to the development of perceptual norms. Once a norm is formed, it is hard for any of us to disagree with the group.

Do such norms actually change our perceptions, or do we simply refuse to disagree publicly? Both outcomes occur in our lives. There are probably times when we privately accept the information or interpretations supplied by the group. There are other occasions when we express in public things that we do not privately believe or accept. Herbert Kelman has called the former process *conformity* and the latter *compliance*. Conformity occurs when we accept the group's interpretation because it is personally appealing or rewarding. Compliance occurs when we accept a group's opinion or perception because it will lead to a favorable reaction from other people. Thus, when we conform to group norms, we are likely to continue performing those behaviors or holding those opinions and perceptions in the absence of the group. When we comply with group norms, we are likely to do such things only when the group is present. Is the adherence to group norms in the Sherif and Asch studies a case of conformity or compliance?

Norms influence the decision-making process in groups. All groups make decisions regarding the types of goals or activities to pursue. To ensure that appropriate decisions are made, a group needs norms that encourage individuals to discuss and share openly ideas and information. When such norms do not exist, a group is likely to run into problems.

Irving Janis describes the negative effects of group norms on decision making in a process he calls *"groupthink."* Groupthink occurs when members of a group begin to think alike, exert pressures on other members to follow them, and ignore or refuse to gather opinions from people outside the group. During the presidency of John Kennedy, a plan was formed and unsuccessfully carried out to raid Cuba. It has since become known as the Bay of Pigs fiasco. One of the factors involved in the invasion's failing were norms that developed in Kennedy's advisory group. The norms forced people to think alike and not to disagree with each other. Consequently, people complied with these norms but afterward admitted they had harbored doubts that were not expressed.

Groupthink is not limited to presidential advisory groups. It is possible for a group that we are members of to develop such tendencies. The conditions that encourage the development of norms favoring groupthink are listed in Table 8-1. Think of a social or work group to which you be-

Table 8-1

Factors Promoting Groupthink

- Group members tend to feel that the group is strong enough to do anything it wants to do.
- The group is seen by members as containing individuals who will not make a bad collective decision.
- The group places a high degree of emphasis on getting everyone to agree before an action is carried out.
- Ideas and potential courses of action are seldom discussed with people outside the group.
- The group does not consider many alternative opinions or courses of action before reaching a decision.
- Outside experts are not invited to meet with the group to discuss its plans.
- People do not openly express their doubts and concerns about the group's plans.
- The leader often gives the group his or her own position on an issue before discussion occurs.

Based on a discussion of groupthink factors by Irving Janis in *Sanctions for Evil,* N. Sanford and C. Craig (Eds.), Jossey-Bass Publishers, 1971, and used with permission.

long and decide which factors appear to apply. If one-half or more of the items apply to your group, the group may be headed in the direction of groupthink. If this is the case, attempting to believe or perform just the opposite of what is stated in each item will lessen the chances for groupthink. Perhaps your group ought to discuss the extent to which it is susceptible to this problem.

The Roles We Play

Did you ever think of yourself as an actor? You may not have starred in a play, but one way to view our daily interactions is to see our environment as a stage with each of us playing different parts. The parts we play are called *roles.* In various group settings, you and I may find ourselves playing the roles of students, teachers, parents, brothers, sisters, storeclerks, or any number of other things. Roles allow us to structure our relationships with other people and are a normal part of our daily interactions. Because they have particular privileges, obligations, and responsibilities associated with them, they prescribe certain guidelines for our behaviors. These guidelines are learned through our past experiences with a given role, our perceptions of the expectations others have for our behaviors in a situation, and specific instructions people give us about how to behave. As a student, several of your role guidelines include attending class, studying, asking questions, and discussing course content. As a teacher, I must structure the course format and content, make assignments, give presentations, assign grades, and write examinations. I do such things based on my past experiences as a teacher, my present expectations for how a teacher behaves, and the rules and regulations of my college. How did you learn your student role?

Each of Us Interprets the Same Role Differently

Although basic role guidelines exist, not all students, teachers, parents, or bosses behave in exactly the same manner. Each of us has a different personality. Consequently, our interpretation of a role will vary, in the same way that several actors will interpret the same stage role differently. We act out a role in ways that make it comfortable for us to meet the demands of a

situation. As students, you can see how this process occurs by reviewing the descriptions of student learning styles in Chapter 4. Competitive and collaborative styles, for example, represent two of the ways you might interpret and play your student role. Depending upon the demands of a particular course, you probably find yourself and others capable of playing a number of variations on the role of student. Similar variations in the role of a teacher also exist. Richard Mann has described several, and they are listed in Table 8-2. As you can easily see, there are several ways a teacher's role might be interpreted. Most of your instructors probably show several of the characteristics described in Table 8-2 in their classroom behavior.

Table 8-2

Variations in Teacher Roles

Expert

Transmits information, the concepts and perspectives of the field. Leans toward scholarly preparation of classes and is most comfortable in the role of presenting material and answering questions.

Formal Authority

Sets goals and procedures for reaching goals. Defines structure and standards of excellence for evaluation of student performance.

Person

Wants to convey that teachers are people with a full range of human needs and skills. Tries to be self-revealing. Encourages students to be warm and open.

Facilitator

Attempts to promote growth and creativity in students' own terms. Wants the student to overcome obstacles to learning and tries to respond to student needs.

Socializing Agent

Attempts to clarify goals and career paths for students beyond the course. Tries to help prepare students for the field. Acts as a guide and gatekeeper for the inner circle of the field.

Ego Ideal

Wants to convey the excitement and value of intellectual inquiry in a given field of study. Acts as a model for student to follow once they enter the field.

Teacher style descriptions are based on styles identified by Richard Mann and are adapted from *The College Classroom: Conflict, Change and Learning,* John Wiley & Sons, New York, 1970 and used with permission.

EXERCISE 8-3: VARIATIONS IN TEACHER ROLES

To obtain a closer view of how the same role is played differently, think about your instructor in this class and in one other that you are currently taking. On a sheet of paper, rank order the extent to which your teachers engage in these behaviors. Place a 1 if the description is most like a particular teacher and a 6 if it is least like that instructor. Rank order the other descriptions as 2, 3, 4, and 5. What similarities and differences do you notice in how each person acts as a teacher? What variations in the role of a teacher as expressed in Table 8-2 do you personally prefer? Do you think each instructor's perceptions of his or her role would match yours? Why not share your observations with your teachers?

Each of Us Plays Several Roles in Our Daily Interactions

As we move among different groups and social situations, we find ourselves asked to do a variety of things. In a day's time I play the roles of father, teacher, researcher, writer, committee chairman, and department head. Life can get complicated at times, but there are positive aspects to playing multiple roles. Martin Shepherd suggests that to grow and develop, we must portray several roles. We should, however, be able to switch roles without appearing rigid and with a certain degree of spontaneity. People usually accept us in our various roles if we do not appear to be putting on an act. When we play multiple roles well, we add a certain amount of variety, interest, and excitement to our lives.

What are the different roles you play daily? Which do you perform better than others? Which of your roles do you like most? Which do you like least?

Unfortunately, playing multiple roles can also produce a certain amount of tension and frustration. These feelings occur because of the stresses involved in doing too many things and because of conflicts associated with our different roles. *Role conflicts* arise when we must make difficult choices about how to behave in particular roles. They can occur in three ways.

We have more than one role relationship to a person or group. I recently found myself in a rather awkward situation. I was a consultant to a group in which several of the members were personal friends of mine. These same people were the source of the group's problems. My dilemma was how to behave toward them. Should I behave as a consultant or as a friend? Would I jeopardize my friendship if I made inputs to the group regarding their behaviors? Pretend that you are the parent of a son or daughter who is also a member of a tennis team you coach. Your child misses two consecutive practices without telling you. Would you discipline the child in your role of coach or as a parent?

People disagree on how a role other than their own should be played. In one of my recent classes, I asked the students for their preferences regarding course content for the second semester. About half of them wanted me to lecture on concepts and theory, and the other half wanted me to design small group experiences and stress applications. I became rather frustrated over what they said. Assume that you and your best friend have had a series of angry encounters. You discuss this problem with several people. Your father says to stop talking to your friend, your mother says to try to work things out, and your favorite teacher suggests ignoring your friend for three weeks. What would you do?

Other people play their roles in ways that are incompatible with our own. Normally, people in roles related to our own behave in ways that are compatible with us. Thus, husband-wife, brother-sister, and student-teacher behaviors often complement each other. Sometimes, though, the roles become incompatible because the individuals define the role differently. Their behaviors present problems for us. During the late 1960s the women's liberation movement began and attempted to redefine the role of women in our culture. Almost overnight, some husbands found their wives deciding to define and play their roles differently. Wives no longer wanted to do all the cooking, change all the diapers, or spend their days cleaning house. Husbands who retained a traditional definition of the father-husband role found the "liberated" wife-mother producing stress and conflict in the relationship.

To see how such conflicts develop, assume that you are a student who has a dependent and a competitive learning style as discussed in Chapter 3.

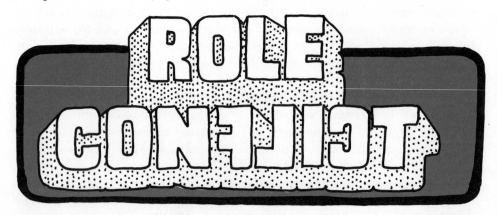

Your teacher takes a facilitative and person orientation toward his or her role. Is there likely to be any tension in your relationship, and why is this likely to happen? What role would the teacher have to play to become more compatible with a dependent and competitive student learning style? Use the information in Table 8-2 to form a response.

There are four ways to deal with role conflicts. Theodore Sarbin and Vernon Allen suggest four things that you and I can do when faced with a role conflict. *We can redefine the role so that the conflict is eliminated.* This method is the one I used to handle the problem with my class. I decided not to stress either theory or applications. I compromised and did a little of each. *A second approach is to end the relationship.* I decided to discontinue my relationship as a consultant to the group that had several of my friends as members. *A third alternative is to attend to one role and not let the other bother you.* The parent who is also a tennis coach might find this approach to be an appealing solution. It is probably better to behave as a coach and treat the child as just another team member. *Finally, we can simply grin and bear it.* There just may not be a satisfactory solution.

Are you experiencing any tension or frustration with one or more of your roles? Is it due to any one of the three causes of role conflicts we have listed? Are any of the four solutions suggested here applicable?

Leadership

Have you ever been in charge of a group? Have you ever closely watched a leader to see how he or she behaved? *Leadership* is a process of providing guidance and direction to a group. Based on your experiences and observations of this process, you probably appreciate how difficult it is to give guidance and direction. It is a rather complicated process and one that has received a great deal of attention from social scientists. Let us look at several principles that emerge from the research literature. We can use this information to understand the process better and to help us increase our potential as leaders.

Leadership is a process of interpersonal influence. To understand leadership, we must see it in the context of our needs to influence other people. Each of us has needs to influence other people, and we express these needs in settings that range from selling raffle tickets to helping our friends select a course to take in school. Leadership represents the use of interpersonal influence to help members achieve the goals and directions of the group.

How are leaders able to influence people? According to John French and Bertram Raven, there are five ways in which this influence occurs. They are listed in Table 8-3. We often find combinations of these sources of power used. A boss who says, "I am in charge here. Do what I say or else you will be fired" is using a combination of *legitimate* and *coercive* power. A parent who tells a child, "Please do me a favor by helping me clean the bathrooms. Then I will give you some money for the movie" is employing *referent* and *reward* sources of influence. A classroom teacher who says, "Based on my experience, the Jones book has the best analysis of this theory. If you read it, I will not give you a low grade" is using *expert* and *coercive* power. French and Raven suggest that people appreciate and respond better to attempts at influence made on the basis of expert and referent power. The extensive use of legitimate, reward, and coercive bases of influence is not as well liked or effective.

Think of someone you know who holds each of the following leadership positions. What sources of influence described in Table 8-3 do they use

Table 8-3

Five Ways in Which People Influence Each Other

Expert power

Influence over other people is derived from the knowledge or expertise one person has in an area. Others recognize this expertise and follow the suggestions that the person makes.

Referent power

Influence over other people occurs because a close interpersonal relationship exists. People are likely to listen to someone whom they feel close to or otherwise like.

Legitimate power

Influence occurs because of the position an individual holds as the formal head of a group. Group members recognize and respect the individual's right to make demands on them.

Reward power

Influence is derived from an ability of one person to dispense rewards.

Coercive power

Influence is derived from an ability of one person to punish others.

Based on a discussion of social power which appears in *Studies in Social Power*, D. Cartwright (Ed.), Institute for Social Research, Ann Arbor, 1959, and used with permission.

most often? How effective are they as leaders? How do they influence other people?

a. classroom teacher
b. parent
c. coach of a team
d. committee chairperson
e. a boss you have worked for

Leaders and their subordinates do not differ extensively on the personal traits or characteristics they possess. Much of the early research on leadership was concerned with identifying common traits that leaders possessed. Presumably, if they were identified, the selection and training of people for leadership positions might be enhanced. Unfortunately, the research literature does not show large differences between leaders and their followers. Marvin Shaw suggests that even though the correlations between personal characteristics and leadership ability are not large, a few generalizations are possible. He suggests that leaders, when compared with their followers, often have more enthusiasm, initiative, and persistence toward task completion. They are often more sociable and have a higher verbal ability than those under them. Are any of these things true of people you know in leadership positions?

Before you decide to sharpen these skills to increase your personal leadership potential, there are several things to remember. The generali-

EXERCISE 8-4: SELECTING A LEADER

To illustrate the problems in selecting a leader based on personal characteristics, read and follow the instructions in the following problem:

Suppose that once, as a result of a marine disaster, the following eight people found themselves in a lifeboat with 20 others, mainly children, a thousand miles from the nearest land and off the shipping lanes, with food and water sufficient in terms of normal consumption to sustain them for five days. There are two sets of oars, a small sail, and a compass.

Mr. Gold, age 40, a self-made man, the owner and director of a million-dollar company which has been built during the past 15 years. He is extremely tough and is well organized when forced to confront a problem.

Mrs. Gold, age 32, a social psychologist, who is also the president of the American League of Woman Voters. She is sometimes anxious in crisis situations but they seem to give her more energy.

Rev. Price, age 50, one of the country's most prominent religious leaders and pastor of one of the largest churches in New York City. His wife is missing in the disaster. He is low keyed and able to put people at ease.

A Soviet sea captain, age 59, who cannot speak English. His foot is badly hurt and he is in constant pain. He is extremely knowledgeable about the sea and is able to work with people.

Mr. Washington, age 29, promoter of various black activities on the West coast. Served as a medic in Vietnam. Is a very responsible person who shows a great deal of initiative.

Mr. Pope, age 60, a wizened little man without his teeth, a deckhand with 45 years at sea. He has an unusual ability to organize the components of a problem for obtaining a solution.

Mr. Smith, age 55, an official of the Teamster's union, battled his way up from the picket lines as an organizer. He is enthusiastic about the things he does and enjoys talking with people.

Miss Gordon, age 35, a prominent motion picture star. Enjoys sailing and good times but seldom allows her feelings for people to interfere with what she wants to do.

The sea is calm. The immediate emergency is over. The problem is now survival. Which of these eight people would be the best choice for a position of leadership, how would the person use this position, and why do you think his or her personal characteristics are important for acting as a leader?

Why did you select the person you did? Do you think that other people will agree with you? Check your selection and the reasons for it with typical responses my students make on page 269. Why do you think it is hard for everyone to agree on a single person? What does this say about predicting leadership based on the personal characteristics of people?

zations do not have a strong data base. Furthermore, such traits may be more important for obtaining a leadership position than for actually exerting leadership. Finally, can you be trained to show enthusiasm, initiative, or any other trait? This is certainly a debatable question.

A colleague of mine in the theater department claims that enthusiasm can be developed. He believes that effective classroom leadership depends

---

Typical Answers to Exercise 8-4

At some time or other, my students have picked everyone on the lifeboat as a possible leader. The most popular choices seem to be Mr. and Mrs. Gold, Mr. Washington, Mr. Smith, and Miss Gordon. The typical reasons given for each selection are listed here.

Mr. Gold. His background suggests that he takes initiative and is able to organize people. He is likely to just tell people what to do. Since the situation is bad, they are likely to follow him if his advice is sound.

Mrs. Gold. She probably understands people and how groups operate. She is likely to ask people to talk about what is happening and what needs to be done. She would find out who has skills that would help the survivors and ask them to perform those tasks.

Rev. Price. People are likely to need spiritual guidance in such a situation. He could help calm people through prayer and get them to cooperate with each other. He might simply ask people to pray for their safe recovery and then ask them to discuss what needs to be done to ensure survival.

Soviet sea captain. Because of his position, he obviously has the skills and abilities to get people through. Due to his injury and inability to speak English he could have problems communicating. Yet it is possible that someone else on board speaks Russian and could interpret. He might become a leader by stating who he is and what skills he has.

Mr. Washington. His knowledge of medicine and body care are invaluable to people in this situation. He might begin by attending to the injured and asking others to help him. People will begin to depend upon him; he is likely to be well liked and they would follow his directions on other tasks.

Mr. Pope. He understands the sea and his knowledge would be very useful. He might exercise leadership initially by telling people he knows of similar situations and that he understands what needs to be done.

Mr. Smith. He is likely to just take over. He is tough and he might simply tell people that they need to work together to survive. He would ask people what they can do and direct them to use their skills.

Miss Gordon. She is likely to use her image as a movie star to exert influence on the group. People probably know about her, they may like her and be willing to listen to her ideas. Not allowing feelings to interfere with what she wants to do could be helpful in an emotional situation. She is probably able to make the tough decisions.

Table 8-4

Theory X and Theory Y Assumptions about People

Theory X

The average human being has an inherent dislike of work and will avoid it if possible.

Because of the human characteristic to dislike work, most people must be coerced, controlled, directed, or threatened with punishment to get them to put forth adequate effort toward the achievement of organizational objectives.

The average human being prefers to be directed, wishes to avoid responsibility, has relatively little ambition, and wants security above all.

Theory Y

The expenditure of physical and mental effort in work is as natural as play or rest.

External control and the threat of punishment are not the only means for bringing about effort toward organizational objectives. People will exercise self-direction and self-control in the service of objectives to which they are committed.

Commitment to objectives is related to the rewards people get for their achievement.

The average human being learns, under proper conditions, not only to accept but to seek responsibility.

The capacity to exercise a relatively high degree of imagination, ingenuity, and creativity in the solution of organizational objectives is widely, not narrowly, distributed in the population.

Under the conditions of modern industrial life, the intellectual potentialities of the average human being are only partially utilized.

Theory X and Y assumptions are based on **Douglas McGregor,** *The Human Side of Enterprise,* McGraw-Hill, New York, 1960, and are used with permission.

upon the teacher's enthusiasm. Before each class he locks himself in his office and jumps up and down, waving his arms and shouting, "I'm enthusiastic, I'm enthusiastic!" So far, he has been unsuccessful in getting others to join him in building their enthusiasm.

The behavior of leaders is often influenced by their assumptions regarding the characteristics of people under them. In Chapter 1, we saw that different assumptions regarding human behavior affect our understanding of its causes. They also influence our behavior toward other people. As a classroom leader, if I assume that students are very dependent and need direction, that they are not able to take initiative or to complete a task in a responsible fashion, then I will behave in a certain manner. I am likely to provide specific directions, have them check with me before doing anything, and constantly watch what they are doing.

Our assumptions may be incorrect. If they are, two things may occur. One is that tension and frustration will be introduced into our interactions. People may resent the way we treat them. A second is that a self-fulfilling prophecy will occur. We will reward people for behaviors that fit our expectations. They in turn will begin to behave in a manner consistent with our assumptions, and we will find our views confirmed.

A dramatic demonstration of this point was made by Robert Rosenthal. He told grade-school teachers that, based on tests he had administered, certain children in their classes were brighter and more likely to succeed than others. In reality, he randomly selected the children he had labeled. There was no reason to expect that as a group they were actually brighter than the other children in class. Rosenthal found that when the teachers assumed the children would perform better, they did. Apparently the teachers paid more attention to these children and communicated enthusiasm about their ability. The children in turn tried to do well and otherwise responded in ways that matched the teacher's expectations.

Douglas McGregor has developed two viewpoints that people in leadership positions often hold about those under them. He describes these as *Theory X* and *Theory Y* views of people. A description of each appears in Table 8-4. It is unlikely that any one of us makes either one or the other set of assumptions exclusively. More likely, each of us makes combinations of both assumptions.

EXERCISE 8-5: THEORY X AND THEORY Y

To gain some feeling for how a specific viewpoint influences a leader's behavior, respond to each situation that follows as you think Theory X and Theory Y leaders might. Check your responses with typical reactions that my students have to each situation (see page 274).

Situation 1: You are a parent of a 10-year-old boy. He refuses to do chores around the house. You sit down with him one day to discuss his behavior. What would you say if you took a Theory X position? A Theory Y position?

Situation 2: You are the manager of a shoe department in a large store. Your department is growing and you have two new employees assigned to your area. This is their first day on the job and you want to discuss their job responsibilities in the department with them. What would you say if you took a Theory X position? A Theory Y position?

Based on your responses and those of my students, you probably found that Theory X assumptions lead to one-way communication with one person handing down instructions and decisions to others. Theory Y actions involve two-way communication processes and obtain the involvement of others in goal setting, planning, and decision making. What assumptions do some of the people you know in leadership positions make? What assumptions do you prefer?

Leadership should reflect a concern for accomplishing a task and meeting the interpersonal needs of people. While contemporary writers like Kenneth Benne, Edgar Schein, and David Singer stress how important both task and interpersonal needs are to a group, it is impossible for any one person to ensure that these needs are met. The formal leader of a group cannot do all these things. This fact means that you and I, as leaders or as members of a group, must be concerned with both aspects of our group's functioning. When we begin to look at task structure and interpersonal relations as leadership functions, we need to look at leadership as something that is shared by all members of the group.

How can we do this? To begin, we need to be aware of behaviors that will assist our groups in meeting their task and interpersonal needs. We have to use those behaviors, and we must encourage other people to use them. Table 8-5 describes several of the things that can be done to help with task and interpersonal maintenance functions. As you can easily see, the procedures suggested in this table are rather straightforward and are not difficult to use. However, there is a tendency in many groups to ignore the interpersonal maintenance functions and to concentrate on tasks. Research shows that when interpersonal needs are not met, members are often dissatisfied with the group's output and the quality of work suffers. It is important for us to try to overcome this bias when we participate in a group.

EXERCISE 8-6: TASK AND INTERPERSONAL MAINTENANCE BEHAVIORS

As a check on your understanding of the behaviors associated with each function, read the following interactions. Use Table 8-5 and identify the specific type of task or interpersonal maintenance behavior that is shown. Write each response on a separate sheet of paper. Think of the reason for your response. Check your responses with those presented on page 275. How well do your responses agree with the suggested answers? Could there be other interpretations of the behaviors that are also correct?

Situation 1: A student-faculty curriculum review committee meeting

    Professor Carter: It's good to see so many familiar faces on the commit-
tee. This committee should be able to suggest needed changes in our
curriculum. I'd like to suggest we start by examining the required
courses. (_____)

    George: Do we have any information about the strengths and weaknesses
of these courses? (_____)

    Professor Jones: Wait a minute, I think that we are getting too far ahead
of ourselves. Before we look at anything we need to look at the department goals. (_____)

    Professor Carter: I don't see why we need to do that. At every faculty
meeting problems with our core of required courses have been raised.
(_____)

    Sally: I'm not sure that Professor Carter and Professor Jones are pro-
posing two different things. (_____) I think that we
can look at our department goals in the context of how our required
courses allow us to achieve them. Would that be all right with the
two of you? (_____)

    Professor Carter: I have no objection to that. However, I would like to
hear what the other members of the committee have to say about that
idea. (_____)

Situation 2: A family discussion regarding a vacation trip

    Father: Where should we go on our vacation trip this year?

    Mother: We picked the spot last year. I thought we agreed to allow Ted
and Sue to pick it this year. Is that correct? (_____)

    Ted: Dad and Sue are nodding their heads so I'm sure you are right. I'd
like to spend some time on the beach. I hear that southern California
has several lovely spots. (_____)

    Sue: Oh, Ted, you always want to go to the beach. Last year we went to
the lake and you hardly stepped into the water. What a waste of time
that was. Why don't we visit Washington, D.C., and see some of our
national monuments? (_____)

    Ted: I'd like to hear what Mom and Dad have to say about both ideas.
(_____)

    Father: Let me see if I understand what the two of you are saying. Ted,
your preference is to get near the ocean and Sue, you would like to
sightsee.

    Mother: I'm not sure why we could not do both. Washington, D.C., is not
too far away from some lovely East coast beaches. We could spend
some time in both places. (_____)

    Sue: I like that idea. That means we will probably split our time equally
between the two settings? (_____)

    Father: I would think we could spend an equal amount of time in each
place. That solution would make me feel quite good about things.
(_____)

    Ted: That is all right with me. Thanks, Mom and Dad, for helping us get
this thing settled. (_____)

Typical Answers to Exercise 8-5

Situation 1

> *Theory X:* Look, I am tired of your behavior. You need to help out around here. From now on, you will not be permitted to watch television or get any spending money unless you help with chores. This is the way it is going to be and I do not care to discuss it any further.

> *Theory Y:* I've been feeling a little angry about your not pitching in and helping out around the house. What seems to be bothering you? Let's talk about it and see if we can figure out what to do about the problem together.

Situation 2

> *Theory X:* It's good to have you both here. We will get along just fine if you remember that I am totally responsible for what happens around here. I'm going to give each of you assignments for work on the sales floor and in the stockroom. I expect things to be done well, and remember that your commissions and bonuses depend upon how well you work.

> *Theory Y:* It's good to have you both here. I would like the department to continue growing and I think that each of you can contribute. Let's discuss some of the things that need to be done in the department. I would like your ideas on how to handle things and what you think you would prefer to do. It's important for each of us to do some of the things we want to do.

Decision Making in Groups

"I could have made a better decision than that group. You just have to wonder how competent they are. Can you believe what they did? Every time that management group gets together they make decisions that prevent us from doing our job. My six-year-old could have made a better decision." In my experiences, such statements are a common reaction to group decisions. I have seldom met people who are completely satisfied with the decisions made by groups to which they belong. On the other hand, it is not necessarily true that a single individual will make a better decision. Both group and individual decisions reflect a wide range of quality and acceptance by others. Irving Lorge suggests that the existence and degree of superiority of group versus individual decision making depends on a number of situational and task factors. Groups tend to be more effective than individuals when: an emphasis is placed on a good or early answer; errors are costly in terms of money, time, or other group resources; labor is cheap so that the group can afford the time spent in group discussions; and each member of the group will be affected by the decision.

Situation 1	Task or Maintenance Behavior	Reason for Labeling the Response
Professor Carter:	Initiating	He is trying to get the group to get off the ground.
George:	Seeking information	Apparently he likes the idea but wants more information first.
Professor Jones:	Initiating	She does not like the first suggestion and wants an alternative starting point for the group.
Professor Carter:	Giving information	He is stating a reason for pursuing his original idea.
Sally:	Harmonizing	She is trying to show them that they are not in conflict.
	Compromising	She is suggesting a solution that will mesh both responses.
Professor Carter:	Gatekeeping	Before proceeding he wants to make sure that others have a chance to respond to the suggestion. He wants to keep the communication channels open.

Situation 2:		
Father:	Initiating	Wants to start the discussion.
Mother:	Consensus testing	Based on previous discussion she thought a decision had been reached. She is testing to see if that is the case.
Ted:	Giving information	He has an idea and wants to share something he knows about it.
Sue:	Giving information	She is stating her preference for a vacation spot.
Ted:	Gatekeeping	Wants to keep communication channels open and get other points of view.
Father:	Summarizing	He is making sure that he understands what has been said by restating the alternatives.
Mother:	Compromising	She is suggesting a solution that combines both suggestions.
Sue:	Clarifying or elaborating	She is stating her understanding of the solution and elaborating on the time implication of what they will do.
Father:	Expressing feelings	He is indicating his positive reaction to the solution.
Ted:	Recognizing individual contributions	He is showing his appreciation to his parents for their inputs.

Table 8-5

Task and Interpersonal Maintenance Behaviors

Task Functions

Seeking information: Groups must often obtain additional information to function properly. This process includes requesting facts, seeking relevant information regarding a group concern, and asking for suggestions or ideas. *Examples of such behavior include:* "What did we say the target population for our advertising campaign was?" "What is accomplished in the Student Affairs Office?" "Do we have any background information on this problem?"

Presenting information: Groups need various facts, concepts, and opinions to accomplish a task. This function is served when members provide relevant facts, state beliefs, or offer suggestions or ideas. *Examples of such behavior include:* "When the Phillipses took a vacation, they used the Ajax Travel Agency." "You should use Chapter 10 in the text to find a solution to the last problem." "I found that the same thing was true. As far as I can tell so has everyone else." "Here are the sales figures we need to begin working."

Clarifying or elaborating task concerns: Discussions are seldom as clear as they could be. Attempts by people to interpret or reflect ideas, clear up confusions, and indicate alternative approaches are important behaviors. *Examples of such behavior include:* "Let's see if we can understand the problem better if we look at it from another point of view." "Before we go any further, I wonder if everyone would state how they see the issues raised." "Let me see if I can put things into a broader perspective."

Initiating a discussion: There are times when a group cannot get started on a task. There is a need for tasks or goals to be proposed, problems defined, or procedures and ideas for attacking a problem suggested to get discussion started. *Examples of such behavior include:* "Let's raise money by holding a raffle." "I think we could solve the problem if we broke into subgroups for a short period of time." "I think that the problem is one of getting those two divisions to cooperate with each other."

Summarizing: Many ideas are generated in discussions. It is quite easy to forget what was said. Related ideas must be pulled together or things must be condensed and restated. *Examples of such behavior include:* "Based on what Mary and Jill said, raising money and keeping the board of directors happy are things we must attend to." "George, your position is that we need to test-market the product in the Midwest."

Consensus testing: A group needs to monitor its progress toward reaching a decision and should check periodically on how much agreement has been reached. *Examples of such behavior include:* "It sounds to me like we are going to build a new plant. Is that how the rest of you see it?" "Have we reached a decision?" "Can we go on to the next point?"

Table 8-5 (continued)

Interpersonal Maintenance Functions

Harmonizing: Conflicts or differences in opinion often arise in the process of working together. Such disagreements often need to be discussed. People should be encouraged to explore their differences. *Examples of such behavior include:* "Ellen, I think that you should allow Ed to make his point." "Sam and Jim, I don't think that you are as far apart on this issue as you think. Let's look at the things that you agree upon." "Pete, I have the feeling that Betty said something with which you disagree."

Gatekeeping: Everyone in a group should participate or at least have the opportunity to do so. Communication channels must remain open to facilitate participation. *Examples of such behavior include:* "Ed, you have not reacted to the issues. What do you think about the concerns that were raised?" "Todd, you and George have said a lot in the past 30 minutes. I wonder if we could hear from some of the other people before our meeting time is over?" "Joan, let's hear from you first and then let's let George and Martha respond."

Compromising: Two or more points of view are often possible when a single course of action is needed. Sometimes two or more positions must be meshed. This can occur by suggesting minor modifications to alternative proposals or offering to change one's own position. *Examples of such behavior include:* "Jane, I wonder if you would consider a combination of what Ed and Jim said as a possible remedy?" "Ernie, if I don't push for all the department heads to come to the meeting, will you agree to the basic plan I suggested?"

Expressing individual and group feelings: Members' emotional feelings regarding issues and each other influence discussions. There are times when such things must be expressed to clear the air and promote further dialogue. *Examples of such behavior include:* "Jim, I sense that you are angry at us for making such a decision. It would help me if you could tell me what your concerns are." "I am happy about the direction we are taking. It should help us achieve our goals."

Recognizing individual contributions: People often need to feel that their inputs are appreciated and useful to the group. Reinforcing such contributions is important for people to maintain interest in the group's activities. *Examples of such behavior include:* "I really appreciate the things you just said. It helped me to see things a bit differently." "I would like to thank Ellen for taking care of the details on that last conference we held." "Most of you seem to like the ideas that Ted presented. What are the specific things you enjoyed?"

A member's satisfaction with the group's decision-making process will improve if members spend time discussing whether a group decision is necessary or desirable. Sometimes individuals or subgroups who have special competencies are better suited to making a particular decision. If necessary, they can report their findings and suggested actions to the larger group for approval. In trying to appear democratic and involve everyone, many groups will demand that everyone participate in all aspects of the process. This is not always necessary. A helpful suggestion is for someone to say, "Before we tackle this problem, let's spend a few minutes talking about the best way to reach a decision or develop alternative courses of action." Could you use this suggestion in a group to which you belong? What do you think would happen?

Factors within a group can impede its decision-making effectiveness.

EXERCISE 8-7: FACTORS WHICH INTERFERE WITH GROUP DECISION MAKING

Even if a group has clearly determined the issues that must be decided by the total group, sometimes things do not go well. There are a number of factors that occur in groups that can impede decision making. These are listed in Table 8-6 in the form of a checklist. Think of a group to which you belong and rate your group on each item. Any item that receives a rating between three and five is likely to indicate a problem area. Why do these factors interfere? Can you think of some things that you or the group might do to overcome each problem? Would encouraging people to pay more attention to task and maintenance functions be of any assistance?

There are advantages and disadvantages to any decision-making process. What is the best way for a group to discuss an issue and reach a decision? In my experience, a single "best" way to make decisions does not exist. There are advantages and disadvantages to almost any method that groups use. Voting and *consensus,* in which people discuss issues until an agreement is reached, are the most typical decision-making formats employed. When groups vote on issues, they usually allow a majority of the members to decide what course of action to take. The discussion of an issue preceding the vote may be quite informal or may follow Robert's Rules of Order. Allowing members to vote after some discussion is often a fast and efficient way to reach a decision. A major disadvantage is that voting often divides the group into "winners" and "losers." I have heard "losers" talk about the group's decision as something "those other people agreed to do." A voting strategy runs the risk of low ownership and hard feelings on the part of some members for the decision. This is particularly true if an inadequate discussion of ideas and alternatives precedes the vote.

Consensus decision making occurs when the group has discussed an issue until everyone is in essential agreement with a course of action. After

Table 8-6

Factors Which Interfere with Decision Making

```
      1        2        3        4        5
   +--------+--------+--------+--------+
   Never         Sometimes        Always
```

Group members:

_____ Do not have the interpersonal communication skills needed to discuss issues adequately.

_____ Do not trust each other.

_____ Are not concerned about the welfare of other members in the group.

_____ Tend to argue for their own positions rather than trying to find common areas of agreement.

_____ Do not volunteer their ideas in group discussions.

_____ Compete with each other to see who has the "best" ideas.

_____ Use threats and bluffs to get their way in discussions.

_____ Fear the consequences of their decisions; that is, they tend to worry excessively about what other people will think about what they do.

_____ Have conflicting loyalties. Their decisions in this group affect their ability to work in other groups.

_____ Use decision-making procedures that are too rigid.

_____ Find that their personal needs and goals are excluded from the decisions and directions the group wants to follow.

---

talking about an issue, someone will say, "I feel as if we have reached a decision. Is it worthwhile to continue our discussion?" This does not mean

that everyone gets what he or she wants. People must at least partially agree with the components of the decision. Compromises are thus inevitable and necessary. They should occur, however, based on a discussion and understanding of alternative points of view. People should not be forced to accept an idea or course of action. To reach a consensus is going to take time. Generally speaking, it takes more time than does a voting process. Its major advantage is that a larger number of alternatives and ideas is explored and each member feels a sense of ownership for the group's product. Table 8-7 presents five ways of helping a group reach consensus.

What personal experiences have you had with voting or consensus decision making? Which do you prefer, and why? Could some of the suggestions for reaching consensus be used to enhance discussions in groups that vote? Suppose a group had a limited amount of time to discuss issues and was using a consensus process. Even after discussion, a decision could not be reached in the time allotted. Would voting then be a helpful way to make the decision?

Conflict and Group Life

I am sure you have experienced *conflict* in a group setting. It may have occurred among members of your group or between your group and another. Conflicts occur because people or groups have a difficult time selecting among alternatives (e.g., what selling strategy to take, where to spend a vacation) or because people or groups find themselves in opposition on some issue (e.g., we want to build the factory on Site A but our competition wants that site

Table 8-7

Suggestions to Assist a Group in Reaching Consensus

---

1. Try to approach the task on the basis of logic. Listen to what others have to say and try to see the advantages and disadvantages in what people are saying.
2. Do what you can to help ensure that everyone has a chance to voice an opinion. Remember that silence does not necessarily mean that a person agrees with what is said.
3. Avoid changing your opinion only to reach agreement and to avoid conflict. Try to support solutions with which you are able to agree at least to some degree.
4. Do what you can to help the group avoid a heavy reliance on reducing its conflicts by majority votes or trading one thing against another to reach a decision.
5. View differences of opinion between yourself and others as helpful rather than a hindrance to decision making. Try to see what is useful about an idea before deciding to reject it.

as well). Different people have different attitudes toward conflict. Some see it as representing a loss of control or irrational or otherwise unnatural behavior in which civilized people do not engage. Consequently, it is something to be avoided. Another viewpoint is that conflict adds energy to our interactions and can promote growth or change within and between groups. Both views are to some extent accurate and justified.

Conflict is an inevitable part of group life. A group that has never experienced a conflict is rare. We might want to question how well such groups are actually functioning. Research by Raymond Hill and Brendan Reddy shows that there are certain advantages to groups that are somewhat incompatible and have moderate levels of tension. They are likely to become more productive and to help their members grow and develop better than are groups that appear to be in harmony.

A great deal of conflict within or between groups usually interferes with interpersonal relationships. One outcome is that a group may not be able to function. A colleague of mine recently consulted with a classical music quartet. Over a period of years, they were finding that they were having a difficult time agreeing on what music to play and how to play it. The tension was so great that one day they simply could not agree on where to practice or what they should practice. They simply were not able to make a decision. A second outcome of great tension, when it occurs between groups, is that the groups may find themselves involved in a *win-lose conflict*. They are competing for the same thing and only one group may obtain it. The situation might involve a share of the market for a product, members being recruited into an organization, or even the territory and resources of another country.

EXERCISE 8-8: SOURCES OF GROUP CONFLICT

Table 8-8 lists several sources of conflict within and between groups. Think of two occasions when groups to which you belonged or knew about were in conflict. Try to select an example of a conflict within a group and one between two or more groups. Before reading further, list the cause or causes of each conflict and briefly describe what occurred.

A high degree of conflict between groups changes their functioning and their perceptions of each other. Members of groups in conflict develop norms that encourage people to think and behave alike. These behaviors are understandable, since they help a group mobilize its energy to compete with the other group. However, such behaviors also help to prolong the conflict. Here are some examples of what can happen:

a. Each group becomes more closely knit and able to evoke greater loyalty in its members. People feel closer to the group and are willing to do more for its interests. "I don't care what happens to me, I'm for the group and what it is doing!"

b. A concern with task increases and interpersonal issues are often put aside. "If we stop now to deal with how you and George feel about this, we will never get anything accomplished. We need to take some action now and not waste our time worrying about the decision."

c. Leadership patterns often change from democratic to autocratic. "I've decided what we need to do. Listen carefully because I'm going to give each of you assignments to carry out."

d. Each group sees itself as representing truth and justice and the other group as somewhat evil. The feeling is that one group is right and the other is wrong. "We did absolutely nothing to them to get such behavior in return. I cannot believe how nasty they were to us. We have no choice but to retaliate."

e. Each group feels that it has the right to take certain actions but does not feel that the other group has similar rights. Recently our university had a collective bargaining process for the faculty. The administration and faculty representatives were often in conflict during the negotia-

Table 8-8

Five Common Sources of Conflict Between and Within Groups

Different Goals

All groups are goal directed, yet not everyone agrees on what goals to pursue. Within a group, family members might disagree on whether or not to take a vacation or build a room addition. When given a choice by their instructor, students may not be able to choose between a term paper and a final exam as a terminal course project. Between groups, two nations may have an interest in an underdeveloped country. One wants to help by giving it money to stimulate its economic development. The second nation simply wants to overthrow its government and take it over.

Different Methods Proposed to Reach a Common Goal

There are usually alternative approaches to achieving almost any goal. Consequently, people or groups get into a conflict over the best way to accomplish a goal. Family members might argue over flying or driving to a vacation spot. Students might disagree over whether to tell their instructor they want a multiple choice or an essay exam. Two nations may want to help another build its armed forces. One gives it long-term loans to buy weapons from the lender nation; the other gives it weapons and technical assistance free of monetary cost. A company needs to finance a new plant. One group wants it to raise money by selling bonds. A second group wants it to use part of its profits from the sale of a product.

Different Methods to Distribute Resources

People, materials, and money are usually in limited supply. How to distribute them is often a problem for groups. A family might find that it has a limited amount of money in savings, and members might disagree on how it should be spent. A group of students working on a project may disagree on who should do what part of the project. The State Department and the Department of Agriculture might not agree on what countries to send wheat to and how often to send it.

Different Expectations

There are times when people or groups expect different things from each other. The role conflicts described earlier fall into this category. Between-group examples include various family groups disagreeing on expectations of who is going to sponsor a family reunion. A marketing division and research and development division may have different expectations on when a product will be ready for sale.

Threats to Self-Esteem, Identity, or Security

Within a group, attempts of people to attack each other verbally, to force members out of the group, or to prevent a person from participating will lead to conflict. Such behaviors will make members defensive and increase the level of tension and frustration in the group. Between groups, attempts of nations to invade another's territory, engage in terrorism, or cut off needed resources like water, fuel, or food will lead to conflict.

Table 8-9

Procedures for Resolving Conflicts within and between Groups

Superordinate Goals

There are times when a common goal will assist in resolving a conflict. If the groups or individuals can agree on a goal they can pursue together, past differences may attenuate. Working toward a common goal establishes a spirit of collaboration and understanding which may then transfer to working on other problems. A friend of mine and his neighbor used to argue over their property lines. One day his house caught fire and his neighbor assisted him in putting it out. They forgot their past differences during that episode. Each felt so good about helping avert a tragedy that they found themselves discussing the property line issue more effectively in the future.

Withdrawal

One or both parties decide to back away from the issues or situation. In effect, they both agree to leave things alone, or one party withdraws. A local bank wanted to build a branch office near a residential neighborhood. A citizens' council went to court to block construction. Since the bank was relying on business from the neighborhood, it decided not to antagonize the residents and located the branch elsewhere.

Compromise

One party agrees to do something if the other party agrees to do something else. My wife and son got into an argument over watching television on Saturday morning. She thought he spent too much time on Saturday mornings watching television and wanted him to stop entirely. They agreed that he would watch less if she took him to the zoo or somewhere else for the remainder of the morning.

Avoidance

Both parties feel that nothing can be done. Consequently, they decide to live with and make the best out of the situation. A personnel department and a production department of a company were in conflict because of hiring policies. Each blamed the other for the state of affairs. Eventually each decided simply to leave things as they were.

Third-Party Intervention

A consultant is often used to assist the parties work out their differences. Faculty within an academic department often were not able to talk to each other without becoming angry. A consultant was employed and she assisted them in talking about their concerns and appreciating each other's points of view.

Table 8-9 (continued)

Erecting Buffers Between People or Groups

The United Nations is often asked to intervene between two nations in conflict. A neutral buffer zone is erected and patrolled by UN troops. The intent is to keep the two sides apart. Two tenured professors I know seldom discussed their differences with each other. They used the department head as an intermediary to convey what each felt about the other.

Create a Structure

Sometimes an organizational structure will resolve a conflict. One college had its education, psychology, sociology, and anthropology faculty in a single department. Conflict among the groups was resolved by creating four separate and autonomous departments.

Taking a Problem-Solving Attitude

This works well if people are willing to talk about things about which they agree and disagree. It is essential that they want to solve the conflict and are willing to make compromises. Groups can do this alone or they may need a third party. Two groups of students in my class proposed to do the same project. Resources were available for only one group to do it. I asked them to meet and come up with a mutually agreeable solution. They were able to do this quite well.

---

tion process. The faculty union hired the best attorney it could find. However, several of the faculty representatives said to me, "We can't believe what the administration has done. Do you know that they hired the toughest labor relations attorney they could find? Now what does that tell you about their intentions to settle this quickly?"

Look again at the example of a conflict between two or more groups that you listed earlier in this section. Which of the five factors we have just described apply? What effects did they have on the group? Is it possible for such factors to be at work among people within a group? That is, have you ever noticed whether individuals in conflict perceive their positions as right and others as wrong, whether they become more autocratic and demanding, whether they look after their self-interests or fail to see how their behaviors produce reactions in other people?

There is no single or best way to resolve a conflict. Conflict resolution means that the parties reach a mutually satisfactory agreement for handling the issues that concern them. Muzafer Sherif, Robert Blake, and Jane Mouton suggest a number of ways that conflicts may be resolved. These are described in Table 8-9.

SUMMARY

Much of our daily interaction takes place in groups. There are certain group processes that are common to any group. They include such things as the establishment and attainment of goals, the adherence of members to group norms, and the ways in which members assume various roles, leadership is exercised, decisions are made, and conflict is managed. Our knowledge of these processes can help us develop skills to enhance our participation and to improve the group's functioning.

Establishment and attainment of goals. This is an important part of a group's activity. To do it well, members need to participate actively in the development of goals and activities. In addition, the goals and activities ought to relate to the task needs of the group and the personal needs of its members. When both of these criteria are met, members will feel a higher degree of ownership and satisfaction with the group's goals and activities.

Group norms. A norm represents a shared idea regarding how a particular behavior should occur. Norms may be formal and outlined in verbal or written rules or informal and simply followed because of past experience or custom. Both types of norms help to provide boundaries for the behaviors of group members. The boundaries may restrict behavior or encourage a wide range of permissible behavior. Norms can affect our perceptions of other people, groups, objects, and the process by which decisions are made. When a person accepts the group's interpretation of an event because it is personally appealing or rewarding, we call the process conformity. However, when an individual accepts a group's opinion or perception because it leads to a favorable reaction from the members, this is called compliance. When we conform to group norms we are more likely to retain our ideas or perceptions in the absence of the group.

The roles we play.   Roles allow us to structure our relationships with other people because they prescribe guidelines for our behaviors.   Even though basic role guidelines exist, each of us interprets the same role differently. We act out a role in ways that are comfortable for us in keeping with our personalities and the demands of the situation.   As we interact in different groups we find ourselves asked to play several different roles.   The ability to play multiple roles can add a certain amount of variety, interest, and excitement to our lives.   On the other hand, it can produce a certain amount of tension and frustration.   There are stresses involved in doing too many different things, and role conflicts can occur.   Role conflicts arise when we must make difficult choices about how to behave in particular roles or what role to play in a situation.   They can be resolved by redefining the role so that the conflict is eliminated, ending the relationship in which the problem exists, attending to one role and not the other, or simply living with the conflict.

Leadership.   Every organized group has at least one person who is expected to guide and direct its activity.   Leadership is a process of interpersonal influence whereby a leader tries to get group members to attain the group's goals.   Leaders exert influence based on the knowledge they possess (*expert power*), how much others like them (*referent power*), the position they hold in the group (*legitimate power*), or their ability to reward or punish others (*reward and coercive power*).

Research on leadership suggests that leaders and their subordinates do not differ extensively in the personal traits or characteristics they possess. Furthermore, the behavior of leaders is often influenced by the assumptions they make regarding the characteristics of people under them.   Incorrect assumptions introduce tension and frustration into a relationship or produce a self-fulfilling prophecy—that is, we treat people in ways that are consistent with our assumptions and they then behave accordingly.   Douglas McGregor's Theory X and Theory Y are often used to categorize the types of assumptions leaders make.   Theory X assumptions view people as disliking work and needing to be coerced, controlled, and directed to accomplish anything.   Theory Y assumptions see people as wanting to take initiative and interest in their work and being able to exercise self-direction and self-control.   Finally, group leadership must be concerned with tasks and with maintaining interpersonal relationships.   Task functions are those behaviors that assist in setting goals, solving problems, and making decisions.   Interpersonal maintenance functions are behaviors of members that assist the group with the relationship concerns of its members.

Decision making in groups.   There are advantages and disadvantages to group versus individual decision making.   Groups tend to be more effective than individuals when an emphasis is placed on a good or early answer, errors are costly in terms of money, time, or other group resources, and labor is cheap so that the group can afford the time spent in discussion. Not every decision must be made by the entire group, but members' satisfaction with the decision process will improve if some time is spent discussing whether a group decision is necessary or desirable. Most groups reach decisions by voting or consensus. Voting is an efficient way to reach decisions, but it often splits the group into "winners" and "losers." Consensus occurs when the group discusses an issue until everyone is in essential agreement. It takes more time than voting but yields a higher level of member ownership for the decision.

Conflict and group life. Conflict occurs because people or groups have a difficult time selecting among alternative goals or activities or because they find themselves in opposition on some issue. It is an inevitable part of group life and can often help a group function if it exists at moderate levels. A high degree of conflict simply escalates the tension within the group or between groups. Groups in conflict tend to see themselves as right and the other group as wrong and they become more closely knit. Leadership patterns become more autocratic, and the group sees itself as having the right to do certain things that are illegitimate for the other party.

THINGS TO DO

1. Think of yourself and one other person who holds a similar role. This might be someone in your class, your family, or some other group to which you belong. How did each of you learn your role? What are the common behavior guidelines that both of you seem to follow? In what ways do you behave differently? Try playing the role as the other person does for a day or two. Think about how you feel and how other people behave toward you.

2. At the next meeting of a group that you attend pay attention to the following things: (a) The way that the group leader behaves. What principles of leadership discussed in the text are present? (b) What conflicts are present in the discussion? How are they handled? (c) How are decisions made? What are the advantages and disadvantages of the procedures used? (d) What you could do to make future meetings more effective. Consider that giving members information based on your observations and discussing it often leads to change in how the group operates.

3. As a classroom exercise, have several groups try to pick in order the two people who are most likely to rise as leaders in the lifeboat example in this chapter. Each group must reach a decision. Half of the groups should use a

majority vote and the other half a consensus process. Discuss the advantages and disadvantages of each.

4. Read a description of a conflict in a newspaper or national news magazine. What is the cause of the conflict and what procedures seem to be used to settle it? What might be done to reach an agreement? Refer to Tables 8-8 and 8-9 for information that might assist you here.

5. As a classroom exercise, ask your instructor to rank order the variations in teacher roles that he or she plays, as in Table 8-2. Then obtain the mean rankings from each member of the class. Discuss the reasons for any similarities or differences in perceptions.

6. Based on what you have read in this chapter, pretend that someone asks you for advice on the best way to run a meeting. What would you say, and what principles discussed in the chapter would you suggest be used?

REFERENCES AND OTHER INTERESTING THINGS TO READ

ASCH, S. E. Opinions and social pressure. *Scientific American,* 1955, *193,* 31–35.

BENNE, K., and SHEATS, P. Functional roles of group members. *Journal of Social Issues,* 1948, 2, 42–47.

BLAKE, R., and MOUTON, J. *Building a Dynamic Corporation Through Good Organization Development.* Reading, Mass.: Addison-Wesley, 1969.

CRANO, W. D. *Conformity Behavior: A Social Psychological Analysis.* Homewood, Ill.: Learning Systems Company, 1975.

DAVID, J. H. *Group Performance.* Reading, Mass.: Addison-Wesley, 1969.

FORD, B. The good samaritan syndrome: Why some people help and some don't. *Science Digest,* October, 1973.

FRENCH, J., and RAVEN, B. The bases of social power. In Cartwright, D. (Ed.), *Studies in Social Power.* Ann Arbor: Institute for Social Research, 1959.

HANEY, C., and ZIMBARDO, P. G. The blackboard penitentiary: It's tough to tell a high school from a prison. *Psychology Today,* June, 1975.

HILL, R. Interpersonal compatibility and workgroup performance. *Journal of Applied Behavioral Science, 11,* 1975, 210–219.

JANIS, I. L. Groupthink among policy makers. In Sanford, N., and Craig, C. (Eds.), *Sanctions for Evil.* San Francisco: Jossey-Bass, 1971.

KELMAN, H. C. Compliance, identification, and internalization: Three processes of attitude change. *Journal of Conflict Resolution,* 1958, 2, 51–60.

KOLB, D. A., RUBIN, I. M., and McINTYRE, J. *Organizational Psychology: An Experiential Approach.* Englewood Cliffs, N.J.: Prentice-Hall, 1971.

LIEBERMAN, M. A., YALOM, I. D., and MILES, M. Encounter: The leader makes the difference. *Psychology Today,* March, 1973.

LORGE, I., FOX, D., DAVITZ, J., and BRENNER, M. A survey of studies contrasting the quality of group performance and individual performance. *Psychological Bulletin,* 1958, *55,* 332–337.

LUFT, J. *Group Processes: An Introduction to Group Dynamics.* Palo Alto, Calif.: National Press Books, 1970.

MANN, R., ARNOLD, S., BINDER, J., CYTRYNBAUM, S., NEWMAN, B., RINGWALD, B., RINGWALD, J., and ROSENWEIN, R. *The College Classroom: Conflict, Change and Learning.* New York: John Wiley & Sons, 1970.

McGREGOR, D. *The Human Side of Enterprise.* New York: McGraw-Hill, 1960.

REDDY, B. Interpersonal affection and change in sensitivity training: A composition model. In Cooper, C. L. (Ed.), *Theories of Group Processes.* New York: John Wiley & Sons, 1975.

ROSENTHAL, R., and JACOBSON, L. *Pygmalion in the Classroom.* New York: Holt, Rinehart and Winston, 1968.

SANFORD, G., and ROARK, A. D. *Human Interaction in Education.* Boston: Allyn and Bacon, 1974.

SARBIN, T. R., and ALLEN, V. L. Role theory. In G. Lindsey and E. Aronson (Eds.), *The Handbook of Social Psychology.* Vol. 1. Reading, Mass.: Addison-Wesley, 1968.

SCHMUCK, R., and SCHMUCK, P. *Group Processes in the Classroom.* Dubuque, Iowa: Wm. C. Brown, 1971.

SHAW, M. *Group Dynamics.* New York: McGraw-Hill, 1971.

SHERIF, M. Superordinate goals in the reduction of intergroup conflict. *American Journal of Sociology,* 1958, *63,* 349–356.

SHERIF, M. A study of some social factors in perception. *Archives of Psychology,* 1935, *27,* No. 187.

SHERPARD, M. *The Do It Yourself Psychotherapy Book.* New York: Peter H. Wyden, Inc. 1973.

SINGER, D. L., ASTRACHAN, B. M., GOULD, L. J., and KLEIN, E. B. Boundary management in psychological work with groups. *Journal of Applied Behavioral Science,* 1975, *11,* 137–176.

SWINGLE, P. G. *Social Psychology in Natural Settings.* Chicago: Aldine Publishing Co., 1973.

CHAPTER AIMS

A. After reading this chapter, the reader should be able to explain:

1. How to define a problem so that the source of the problem is located and it suggests more than one solution.

2. How the use of an idea tree, metaphors, brainstorming, attribute listing, a checklist, and searching for rules facilitates the development of alternative ideas for a solution.

3. Two ways to develop criteria for selecting and evaluating possible solutions to a problem.

4. The way that problem avoidance, prematurely evaluating ideas, and having a group leader make content inputs into a problem discussion interfere with group problem-solving activity.

5. One way that problem avoidance, premature evaluation, and a leader's making content inputs can be overcome as negative influences in group discussions of problems.

B. While reading this chapter, the reader should be able to use the information:

1. To complete each of the exercises in the text.

2. To begin to think of and to develop ways of using the information in daily interactions.

9

Individual and Group Approaches to Problem Solving

GLOSSARY

Functional fixedness. A tendency to assume that a familiar object (e.g., a knife) cannot be used for something else (e.g., a screwdriver).

Heuristic. A "rule of thumb" or general approach to finding a solution. Dividing fractions by the least common denominator is an example of a heuristic.

Means-end analysis. A heuristic that describes our working a problem by reducing the difference between our present state and what we want to do. We use this heuristic when planning a trip to another city.

Problem. Anything for which we do not have a ready response.

Remote associations. A less common response to a stimulus. *Grass* is a very common association to the stimulus *green*. *Thumb* is a less common association.

Set. A tendency to approach problems with a somewhat rigid and persistent way of thinking.

Solution. A combination of new or existing ideas that will work in a given situation.

Subgoal hierarchy. A heuristic that describes our working a problem by reducing it into smaller units. Solving each subunit leads to a complete solution.

Working backward. A heuristic that describes our working a problem by formulating a solution and then developing the steps that are needed to obtain the solution.

Problems, Problems, Problems!

"What shall I wear today?" "Do we have enough money to build a house?" "Now that I've taken this toaster apart, I wonder where these two springs belong." "What should I do with my life for the next five years?" "I'm constantly busy. Is there any way I can better manage my time?" "How can I get Joe to take an interest in me?" "These math problems are sure tricky. I wonder what the next step in this one is?" "Why does my reflection appear backward in a mirror?" "Is it possible to draw a figure that adequately represents a square circle?" "If the universe is increasing in size, into what is it expanding?" "How can our company get a larger share of the market?"

Have you ever had similar thoughts? They represent a few of the issues that my students, colleagues, and friends have attempted to answer. Many of our daily activities are exercises in problem solving. A *problem* is anything for which we do not have a ready response. Its *solution* represents a combination of new or existing ideas that will work in a given situation. Our environments pose a variety of issues for which we must create and invent some solution. We might work alone or in group settings. In either case, problems motivate us to spend a considerable amount of our time and energy in seeking answers.

Have you ever thought about how you try to solve problems? I find

that most people have some consistent set of procedures that they employ. Some analyze problems and try to base a solution on a careful analysis of each part. Others use a shotgun approach—rather than spend time in analyzing a situation, they think of several possible solutions with the hope that one will work. A few people begin to analyze a problem, decide it is too difficult, and then quit. I am sure that you could add to this list. As you can see, our everyday strategies are quite variable and are likely to have a wide range of effectiveness.

Regardless of the strategy used, most of us have experienced some difficulty in our ability to solve problems. I know that I am sometimes frustrated with some of my attempts. Have you ever felt this way? Fortunately, a large body of literature exists on how to enhance our problem-solving skills. Contrary to what many people believe, it is possible to improve upon our current abilities. To accomplish this end, we need a strategy that will facilitate our problem-solving efforts and lead us in a systematic fashion toward a solution. It should contain suggestions for thinking about the various components of a problem in ways that will not interfere with finding an answer. One such method includes carefully defining the problem, generating a range of alternative ideas for solving it, and then selecting and evaluating the best solution. Let us take a closer look at what is involved in each of these steps. The remainder of this chapter will examine in detail this approach to solving issues. Understanding this information will assist you in developing a wider range of approaches to problems and in building your confidence to solve them.

A Problem-solving Strategy: Carefully Define the Problem

Unless we adequately define our problem, we are not going to obtain a solution. Perhaps this is an obvious point, yet the research on problem solving suggests that this is something most of us do inadequately. *A good problem definition properly locates the source of the problem and states it in ways that suggest more than one solution.*

Locating the problem simply means knowing what part of the environment is most likely responsible for the issue. Two of my recent experiences illustrate this point. A neighbor had a series of strange experiences. Every time he drove past a new radio station, his car radio temporarily stopped working. It only happened on that street and occurred just as he drove past the station. He complained to the station manager that something they were doing was interfering with his car radio· He was quite irate and the station spent several hours checking equipment and its effect on various car radios. Apparently, my neighbor's radio was the only one that failed to function near the station. Eventually a repairman checked his radio and discovered a loose connection. Several small potholes in the street produced enough vibration to cause his radio to stop functioning at that location. My neighbor incorrectly located the problem with the station and not with his own radio.

A client recently told me that they were having a problem keeping the washroom on his floor of the office clean. It was used by both visitors to the building and his staff. Towels, soap, and water were everywhere. They decided to issue washroom keys to the staff and have the visitors use the public washroom downstairs. Unfortunately, the washrooms remained as messy as ever. They incorrectly located the problem with visitors and not with the staff. Once they properly located the problem and issued washroom rules to the staff, the appearance of the washroom improved. Have you ever located the source of a problem inappropriately? What action can you take to avoid doing this?

In addition to locating the source of a problem, we must define the problem in ways that do not restrict our efforts toward finding an answer. Remember that we want to obtain the most effective solution to a problem. *We can hinder our efforts if we define a problem in very general terms or if we define it so that it includes a specific solution.* A good problem definition should suggest things we can do to find more than one alternative solution. Please do Exercise 9-1 before reading further.

Examples b and e illustrate how a very general definition may hinder our solving the problem. Examples a, c, d, f, g, and h show the effect of including a solution in the problem definition. It is possible that such solutions may be quite satisfactory. However, we are better off if we initially spend time thinking about the issues of dirt separation, heat retention, and money raising. It is quite possible that other interesting solutions may occur from such thinking.

EXERCISE 9-1: RESTATEMENT OF PROBLEMS

The following problem statements illustrate the above issues. Restate each problem along the lines suggested in this paragraph. The first two are done for you. Suggested responses appear on page 296.

a. What is the best product we can make to give a dog a bath?
   Restatement: What is the best way to separate the dirt from the dog?
b. My car will not work.
   Restatement: My engine will not start.
c. What is the best way to improve a furnace thermostat so that the rooms in a house have the same temperature?
d. How can I develop a videotape presentation to show the other students in class how to develop pictures?
e. I'm not feeling well.
f. What type of raffle should we have to raise money for the club?
g. What is the cheapest way to fly to Los Angeles?
h. How much of a pay raise should I give George to get him to work harder?

A Problem-solving Strategy: Generate a Range of Alternative Ideas for Solving the Problem

After properly defining a problem, we should seek a number of ideas for alternative solutions. Seeking alternative ideas will increase the chances that we will discover an appropriate and perhaps even an innovative solution. I find that people often have to force themselves to do this, for two reasons: First, we have tendencies to select the first thing we think of or some other very common response when faced with a problem. Second, we often use rather rigid and persistent assumptions when looking at an issue. Both factors interfere with our finding answers to issues.

Selecting the first thing we think of or some other common response

---

Suggested Answers to Exercise 9-1

c. *Restatement:* What is the best way to keep the same amount of heat in each room of a house?

d. *Restatement:* What is the best way to visually show students how to develop pictures?

e. *Restatement:* My stomach aches and I'm running a fever.

f. *Restatement:* How can we raise money for the club?

g. *Restatement:* What is the cheapest way to travel to Los Angeles?

h. *Restatement:* What is the best way to motivate George?

---

has a great deal to do with our past experiences. You will remember from our discussion in Chapters 3 and 4 that one aspect of our learning involves the association among various stimuli and responses. Because certain responses are often practiced and reinforced in the presence of particular stimuli, they are most likely to occur. It is probable that any problem with which we are confronted will have stimuli with which we are already familiar. We then respond with an action that has been most often associated with these stimuli in the past.

There are times when such responses will help us solve problems—balancing our checkbooks or deciding what clothes to purchase or how to deal with an angry friend. There are also times when problems demand less common responses. Selecting a common response will only interfere with the process. A neighbor of mine has a gas gauge on his car that does not work. Four times in the past three months his car has stalled because it was out of gas. "I've been meaning to get it fixed," he told me on several occasions. Last week his car stalled on a country road. Based on his four previous experiences, his first reaction was that the car was out of fuel. He walked two miles to a gas station and returned with a gallon of gasoline. The car still did not start. He then decided to look under the hood and found a loose wire dangling from the distributor. Connecting the wire allowed him to solve the problem. Initially, selecting a common response had interfered with obtaining a solution.

A related issue is that we often use rather rigid and persistent assumptions when looking at an issue. The term *set* is used to describe such reactions. Again, based on our past experiences, we assume that only certain things are possible. As we noted in Chapter 1, our behaviors then have a tendency to conform to our assumptions. A good example of this tendency is a set we use that assumes familiar objects cannot be used in different ways. This is called *functional fixedness.* What happens is that we fixate on the common use of an item. Recently, my wife needed a screwdriver to tighten the handle on a cabinet in which we keep the silverware. She be-

THEY SPENT ALL NIGHT WORKING ON THE SAFE, AND THE COMBINATION WAS WRITTEN ON THE SAFE DOOR!

came frustrated since we did not have a screwdriver that was thin enough. I took one of the knives from the cabinet and asked her to see if the tip might work. It did and the problem was solved. Thinking of a knife as something to cut things with or to spread butter on bread interfered with viewing it as a screwdriver. Have you ever had a similar experience?

Are the issues of set and selecting the first thing you think of or some other response interfering with your ability to solve problems? Are you currently satisfied with the range of ideas you generate to solve problems? If not, the suggestions in the following paragraphs will help you increase your ability to develop ideas for solving a wide range of issues.

Form an idea tree. Many problems have a number of possible answers among which the actual solution is sure to be found. A three-letter anagram puzzle (e.g. BTI) has six possible combinations of the letters. To find which of the six is a solution, we can form an *idea tree* similar to the one in Figure 9-1. As you can easily see, an idea tree simply groups possible solutions in an orderly fashion. In this case, answers having B, T, and I as the first letter were listed together.

EXERCISE 9-2: DEVELOPING AN IDEA TREE

Pretend that you are a member of a Parent Teacher Association that needs to raise money. They have asked you to prepare a report for the next meeting regarding some of the directions they might take. Complete the idea tree in Worksheet 9-1 to show a range of possibilities. Check your responses with those suggested in Figure 9-2.

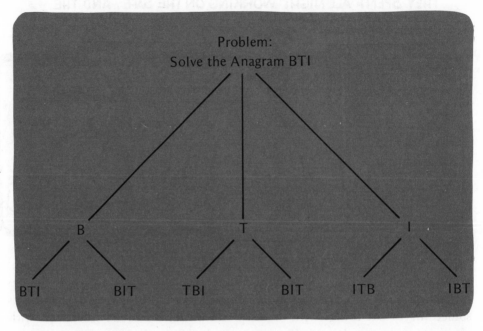

Figure 9-1
An idea tree for a three-letter anagram puzzle.

Use metaphors. Often the use of a metaphor or an analogy to represent the problem or some part of it is helpful. All we need do is consciously ask ourselves what object, person, place, or thing is similar to our problem and/or already solves it in ways that we might adapt. A number of interesting discoveries have ocurred in this way. The French physician Laennec was interested in finding a method for listening clearly to the human heart. One day, he noticed two small boys playing with a long board. They were passing signals along the piece of wood. As one youngster tapped his end with a rock, the second child pressed his ear to the other end. The transmission of sound through a medium gave Laennec the idea for producing the stethoscope. During World War II, the U.S. Navy was interested in developing a device for detecting objects in the ocean depths. People on the deck of a ship or in a submarine are effectively blind to anything at a great depth. In thinking about this problem, someone noted that a bat has a similar difficulty. Although blind, it is still able to locate insects and other objects by the use of high-frequency sound waves. This analogy formed the basis for the development of sonar.

William Gordon and George Prince have developed procedures to train people in forming metaphors to assist their problem-solving activities. Getting people to think in such unconventional ways often leads to innovative solutions to problems. Three ways these authors suggest to form metaphors

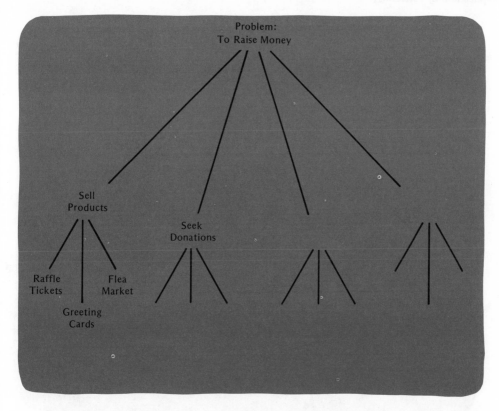

Worksheet 9-1

appear in Table 9-1.   How can metaphors help you with a problem you currently have?

Brainstorming.   This method for generating ideas was developed by Alex
Osborn to help groups solve problems.   His goal was to create an atmosphere in which a large quantity of ideas would be produced.   He believed
that out of a large number of ideas a new combination of previously unrelated things might occur.   The rules for brainstorming by yourself or in a
group setting are quite simple.[1]   They are: (a) List as many ideas as you
can within a specified time period (e.g., 15 to 30 minutes).   (b) Do not be
overly concerned about how practical the ideas are.   Simply list them.
(c) Defer any evaluations or criticisms of your ideas until after the listing
period is over.   Otherwise you are likely to prematurely eliminate useful
ideas.   (d) After the listing period, try to combine and improve the ideas
generated so that they will be more useful to you.   (e) After completing
(d), eliminate the ideas that you feel are not useful, cannot be improved, or

[1] Based on rules for brainstorming developed by Alex Osborn and described in *Applied
Imagination*, Scribner's, 1963, and used with permission.

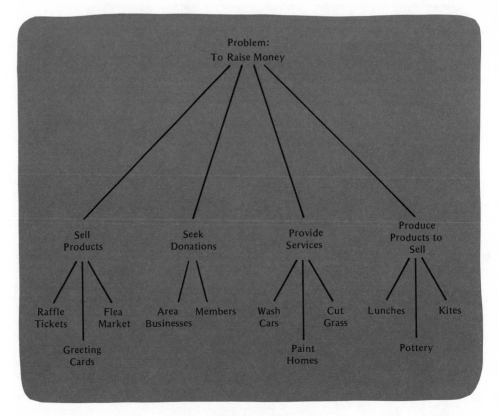

Figure 9-2
An idea tree for the money-raising problem. Keep in mind that this tree can be extended even further. For example, are there any other ways that money can be raised in new categories or under those already listed? In addition, the types of raffles, greeting cards, or lunches can also be expanded. Some idea trees may never be complete as long as we are resourceful and imaginative in our thinking.

are simply too undesirable. Before reading further, please complete the problem in Exercise 9-3.

Attribute listing. Robert Crawford has noted that new ideas occur by the improvement of characteristics or attributes of existing things or by the transference of such attributes from one situation to another. By breaking some problems into their components, it is possible for us to generate ideas that will lead to a solution. Automobile designers solve their problems in this way. They break the characteristics of an automobile into categories like body size, color, shape, horsepower, seating capacity, and decoration. They then make improvements in each of these characteristics from one

Table 9-1

Three Ways to Create Metaphors

Fantasy analogy

To use a fantasy analogy, simply think of an ideal but far-fetched solution to the problem. You then follow the implications of your fantasy to see where it leads you. You might ask, for example, "Could the problem solve itself?" After all, who ever heard of a problem solving itself? But what if it could? How would it do it? Someone probably answered these questions to develop a self-sealing tire, a no-frost refrigerator, a self-cleaning oven, and permanent-press slacks.

Direct analogy

Here you need only think of something that is similar to the problem you have. The development of the stethoscope and sonar mentioned in the text are examples of direct analogies. To see how this works, think of the following metaphors: How is a beaver chopping through wood similar to a typewriter? In what ways is a human eye similar to a camera? How is an automobile mechanic working on a car similar to a doctor working on a patient? Do you think interesting insights into making a better typewriter or camera or diagnosing medical problems might result from forming such analogies?

Personal analogy

You form a personal analogy when you literally make yourself a part of the problem. Could you think of yourself as a beam of light, a pump in a washing machine, a person on death row, or a molecule? What does it feel like and how would you react? Sometimes useful ideas regarding the solution to an issue can occur when we do this. Consider the problem of separating the dirt from the dog mentioned earlier. Pretend that you are a piece of dirt attached to the dog. As a piece of dirt, how do you cling to the dog? What sensations do you have? How do you feel when you get wet? How do you feel when the wind blows? What are you afraid of? How do you interact with other pieces of dirt? What would chase you away from the dog? Based on your responses to each question, what are two ideas you now have for separating the dirt from the dog?

Synopsis of pp. 45–53, 41–44, 37–41 in *SYNECTICS: The Development of Creative Capacity* by William J. J. Gordon. Copyright © 1961 by William J. J. Gordon.

EXERCISE 9-3: BRAINSTORMING

To illustrate how brainstorming works, do the following: Spend five minutes listing as many uses as you can for a toothpick. Assume that you are a toothpick manufacturer who is trying to increase the size of the market for toothpicks. Follow the rules for brainstorming and select what you think are two or three of the best ideas for increasing the market. A sample of the responses from some of my students appears on page 302.

Sample Answers to Exercise 9-3

Pick your teeth
Build toy houses
Hold food together
Clean small crevices
Put cotton on end and clean ears
Self-defense weapon
Fill small cracks in wood and paint
*Apply glue to model airplanes
Tack paper to bulletin boards made out of cork
Use for designing architecture models
Glue together, color, and make pieces of art out of them.
*Play a game of pick-up sticks
Build toy ships out of them
Tie a match to the end of one to give you an extended matchstick
Bookmarker
Put ink on the end and use to draw thin lines
*Teach a child to spell by using them to form letters and words
Picking up dead bugs from the floor
Pipe cleaners

---

* These are the ideas that my students think have the potential of increasing the number of toothpicks sold.

year to the next. Creating a television series often involves the transfer of characteristics from one situation to another. Rival television producers transfer the characteristics of a hit show and use them to form a "new" series. Although this solves their production problems, it tends to leave a number of police, medical, western and comedy shows looking quite similar.

The improvement or tranference of attributes to generate interesting ideas is quite easy to do. We begin by listing the attributes of the situation. Alternatives to the listed attributes are then formulated. Finally, we pick various combinations of the alternative attributes and try to imagine an interesting solution to the problem. Table 9-2 illustrates this process for the problem of designing a new credit card. The blank spaces indicate categories for which you should generate your own ideas. Remember that as long as you can identify the basic characteristics of any problem, you can use this technique.

Use a checklist. A checklist is a series of questions that directs your attention to components of the problem. Your responses to such questions generate a series of ideas that might assist you. Table 9-3 gives an example of a checklist that I have used. Based on the type of problems you face, you

Table 9-2

An Example of Attribute Listing

Problem: Design a new format for a credit card.

Attributes:

Rectangle	Plastic	Raised letters and numbers	Multi-Colored	_____

Alternatives:

Square	Metal	Concave letters and numbers	Black	_____
Circle	Glass	No letters and numbers	White	_____
Triangle	Wood			
_____	____	Magnetic impression for ID numbers	_____	_____
_____	____	_____	_____	_____
		_____		

Select Different Combinations of Alternative Attributes

Circle,	Metal,	Magnetic ID,	White
_____,	____,	_____,	_____

What solution (s) *are suggested?*

A credit card that looks like a quarter. Identification information is put on a magnetic code. Available amount of credit could be coded as well. Card is dropped into a coin slot apparatus which is connected to a central computer. Credit check could be run and the purchase price automatically subtracted from the amount of available credit.

Your solution:

_____

EXERCISE 9-4: USING A CHECKLIST

To see how a checklist can help, read Table 9-3 while thinking of the problem of getting more people to use your area's mass transit system. Answer those questions you feel are applicable to this issue. How helpful was the checklist?

Table 9-3

A Checklist for Stimulating Ideas

Answer the following questions in relation to the problem you have. Remember that not all of the questions may be applicable. Skip those that are nonapplicable to your issue.

1. List the attributes and characteristics of your problem.

2. How can some of the following things be changed?
   - Physical dimensions (larger, shorter, taller, smaller, wider, borders)
   - Social dimensions (number of people, communication patterns, leadership, norms, roles, goals)
   - The way things are ordered (right-left, up-down, first-last)
   - The time element (faster-slower, longer-shorter)
   - The cost (more-less, high-low)
   - The texture (rough-smooth, hard-soft, wet-dry, heavy-light)
   - The function (do more, do less)

3. What parts of the problem can be:
   - rearranged
   - reversed
   - combined
   - minimized
   - magnified
   - substituted for by something else
   - altered
   - completely eliminated

4. How can you do the following:
   - change the physical environment
   - produce new learnings
   - go against tradition
   - change the values people have
   - make use of emerging future trends
   - change attitudes and opinions

5. Based on the ideas you thought of, what are two or three possible solutions to the problem? Which one do you like best? Which one do you like least? What are the reasons you have for your selection?

---

might want to modify it and add additional questions that would help stimulate your thinking.

Look for and apply rules. Before reading further, please solve the problem in Exercise 9-5.

EXERCISE 9-5: APPLYING RULES

Complete each of the following series of numbers.

a. 2, 4, 6, 8, 10, _____.
b. 1, 3, 7, 15, 31, _____.
c. 3, 5, 9, 17, 33, _____.
d. 5, 17, 53, 161, _____.

The correct responses were 12, 63, 65, and 485 respectively. Did you finish each of them correctly? How were you able to determine the last item? To complete each series you had to discover the rule used to construct it. The rules for each series were: (a) add 2 to each digit, (b) double each digit and add 1, (c) double each digit and subtract 1 and, (d) triple each digit and add 2.

For some problems, looking for rules will yield ideas for possible solutions. Discovering such rules often makes obtaining a solution rather efficient. In the example, you could have continued the series for as long as your time, energy, and interest permitted. Furthermore, if you encountered a similar series you could have tested the rules presented to see if they were appropriate.

There are several ways that we can obtain rules to help us in our daily affairs. For certain types of problems (e.g., playing a card game, a sport, or chess) the rules are given to us and we simply apply them as well as we can. Other problems demand that we discover the rules which underlie them. These include situations such as that presented in Exercise 9-5, a scientist trying to describe the molecular structure of a new compound, a traffic engineer attempting to develop a model for the flow of traffic, and a student solving a difficult math problem. Finally, based on our experiences, we bring to a problem certain general rules which give us ideas for seeking a solution. Such approaches are often termed *heuristics* or "rules of thumb." To solve the problem of moving the football and scoring, a coach uses several "rules of thumb" which include not punting on the first down, running the ball on short yardage, attacking the weakest part of the opponent's line, and maintaining possession to keep the ball away from the other team.

Herbert Simon and Allen Newell have identified three heuristics that can assist us in generating ideas for solutions. They include a *means-end analysis, working backward,* and *subgoal hierarchies.* A means-end analysis involves our seeing the problem in terms of reducing the difference between our present state and what we want to do. Problems of traveling from one place to another use this approach. If I wanted to travel from Los Angeles to New York, I would ask myself, "What is the best way for me to reduce the distance between these two places?" Thus, I might consider and evalu-

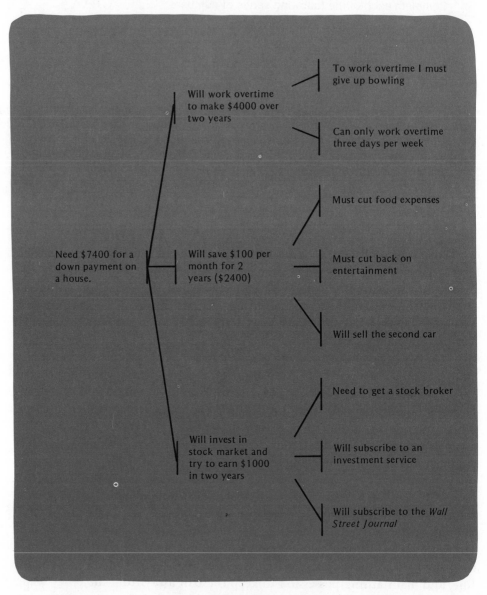

To work overtime I must give up bowling

Will work overtime to make $4000 over two years

Can only work overtime three days per week

Must cut food expenses

Need $7400 for a down payment on a house.

Will save $100 per month for 2 years ($2400)

Must cut back on entertainment

Will sell the second car

Need to get a stock broker

Will invest in stock market and try to earn $1000 in two years

Will subscribe to an investment service

Will subscribe to the *Wall Street Journal*

Figure 9-3

An example of a problem that used the heuristic of working backward. An outcome or solution is first suggested, and then one tries to determine what things have to happen to obtain a solution.

ate any combination of automobiles, airplanes, or other methods of travel.

Working backward is used when we basically know what we want as an outcome to the problem. We then ask ourselves, "What were the steps we needed to take to get us here?" This method helps us obtain ideas for reaching a solution that we already have in mind. An example of this approach appears in Figure 9-3.

Finally, we form subgoal hierarchies when we reduce the problem into smaller units. An example of this is how we solve the problem of obtaining a college degree. We look at the total amount of time and course credit it takes, and we then break it up into convenient units. That is, our ideas for obtaining a degree are seen in terms of so many course credits in particular areas each term. When our ideas for each term are put together, we have a solution to the problem.

A Problem-solving Strategy: Select and Evaluate a Solution Based on the Ideas Generated

If you followed the advice in the last two sections you may have more than one potential solution to a problem. You will find yourself asking whether there is any way to determine the best solution. It is hard to give a response that will apply to every situation. *However, a general guideline is to select a response that meets the criteria you have for a solution.*

How do I establish such criteria? There are several ways. Some problems have pre-established criteria for determining the best answer. The problems you encounter in mathematics, statistics, and laboratory work in school have certain guidelines already established. The criteria may be based on some theory, the types of results most other people obtain, or the preferences of your instructor. Once you know such things, you can select the response that best meets those criteria. Most of the time things are not that clear. How do you know the best way to redesign a credit card? What are the most important safety features to design into an automobile? What is the most effective method for disciplining a child? Again, our alternative solutions must be assessed against a set of criteria. However, you may need to establish the criteria. Your answer to the questions that appear in Table 9-4 will help you do this for a wide range of problems. Keep in mind that not all the questions apply to every problem you might have and you may even think of other questions to ask.

The questions in Table 9-4 are not helpful only in selecting among several alternative solutions. There are times when you may suddenly find yourself with a single response to a problem. Whether you should explore

EXERCISE 9-6: SELECTING A SOLUTION

Review the alternative ideas you developed for exercises 9-2, 9-3, 9-4, and 9-5. Apply the questions in Table 9-4 to those ideas. Is there another problem that you are currently thinking about for which the questions in Table 9-4 might help you generate a solution? Use the questions and see how helpful they were to your problem.

other avenues can be determined by answering such questions. Furthermore, don't be complacent about a solution once you have formulated and/or used it. How well it acutally works in practice is an important criterion. Try to collect and use feedback on how well it seems to work. *Do not get locked into a solution forever.* Modify it and even consider dropping it if circumstances warrant.

Think of a problem for which you have more than one possible answer. Pick the questions in Table 9-4 that you feel are most relevant to your problem. How well does each solution match the criteria suggested by the questions? What are some additional criteria you might use?

Table 9-4

Questions Which Help Establish Criteria for Selecting
among Alternative Solutions

1. Think of the situation in which your problem exists. There are likely to be things that work in favor of your solving the problem (e.g., money, time, assistance from friends). What are they? There are also things that work against you. What are they? How well does each solution increase the positive aspects of the situation? How well does it decrease the negative aspects of the situation?

2. Imagine that the problem is solved. What does each solution allow you to accomplish that you could not accomplish before?

3. What are two things which the solution must absolutely handle?

4. Will each solution create other problems that are worse? What are they likely to be?

5. Do any criteria already exist that can be used?

6. Is each solution better than what already exists?

7. Do you need a short- and/or long-term solution? What does each solution provide?

8. What are the monetary costs of each solution? Can you afford them?

9. What are the monetary benefits of each solution?

10. What are the psychological costs of each solution (e.g., tension, anger, anxiety)? Can you afford them?

11. What are some of the psychological benefits that are important to you (e.g., better relationships, less anxiety, comfort)? What does each solution seem to provide?

12. What deadlines do you have to work against? How would each solution allow you to meet those deadlines?

13. How much time, energy, and other resources are involved in implementing each solution? Will you have enough of such things? Which solution gives the most impact relative to the time, energy, and resources involved?

14. Are other people likely to accept each solution?

15. Does each solution lead to an improvement in the quality of what is currently done? How does this occur?

16. If you had to leave a solution to someone else in your last will and testament, which one would you leave, and why?

Group Issues in Problem Solving

Most of us have had experiences solving problems in group settings. Our discussion in previous sections is certainly relevant to group problem-solving efforts. Groups have certain advantages over individual efforts in resolving issues. Information can be pooled from individual members and shared with others. Even though they take longer, groups make fewer errors and obtain a higher number of correct solutions.

Having read the chapters on interpersonal communication and group processes, you also realize that putting people together in groups may present certain problems. Such things as one-way communication patterns, interpersonal conflict, hidden agendas, pressures to conform, and a lack of personal communication skills will certainly affect a group's problem-solving ability. In addition to such factors, the following actions may also impede a group's attempts to resolve an issue.

Problem Avoidance

Working on problems takes time and energy. Unless it is something the group absolutely has to do, there are tendencies to avoid it. When you begin to hear the following statements from group members, avoidance tendencies are probably present: "Our people won't like it; let's forget it." "It's too early to begin thinking about that issue. Let's wait awhile." "We better not deal with that issue. The membership is likely to scream." "Look, things have always been done this way. Why do we need to change things now?" "This issue cannot be separated from several others. We cannot solve it without dealing with the rest." "This issue exists everywhere. Why should *we* worry about it?"

Do any of these responses sound familiar? When they occur in groups to which you belong, there are several things that you can do to get the group to deal with the issue. *Ask people to clarify why they feel as they do.* My experience suggests that when asked this question, most people lack an adequate reason or have not really thought about their concern. They recognize it and often reduce their concern. *Show how the problem relates to the group's goals and activities.* People are more willing to deal with an issue if it is relevant to what the group is already doing. This is best done by pointing out several specific implications of the problem for the group's ability to obtain its goals or continue its ongoing activity. For example: "We cannot ignore the problem. The decrease in sales after Christmas means that we will have to borrow more money to meet our short-term debt. This will prevent us from getting our new product line out on time." How could these suggestions assist you?

Evaluating Ideas Prematurely

I'm sure you have suggested an idea only to have someone quickly pick it apart. This norm often exists in groups. It is a problem because the time taken to discuss and evaluate an idea often means that fewer alternatives are raised. It also makes people defensive. When someone disagrees with another person's ideas, it tends to raise emotions and makes people defensive and less likely to listen to alternative points of view. The premature evaluation of ideas leads to less flexibility in exploring new solutions.

One way to overcome this issue is to set a time limit for generating ideas and remind people that the discussion of specific alternatives will occur later. I have found that frequent reminders are necessary. Comments during the listing of alternative ideas should be limited to brief comments regarding definition or clarification. Any member of a group, including its leader, could be responsible for controlling the discussion. How comfortable would you feel controlling the discussion in a group to which you belong?

A leader tries simultaneously to make content inputs and to monitor the group's process. Norman Maier suggests that the ideal use of a group leader's skills is to organize and integrate the group's problem-solving activity. *This is best done if the leader does not contribute ideas regarding the solution or products that are produced.* Maier believes that a leader's role in solving problems is to concentrate on the group process. Therefore, a leader would see that communication channels are open and that conflicts are dealt with and would use communication skills such as summarizing and paraphrasing extensively. The other members of the group would contribute ideas and work on putting the solution together. The leader would only facilitate such interactions.

There are good reasons for this suggestion. Maier's research shows that a leader's ideas are given more weight than they should be by members.

This leads the members to spend more time discussing the leader's ideas and ignoring others and may interfere with obtaining a gool solution. Furthermore, effective problem-solving groups need someone to organize and facilitate their interactions. It is hard for a leader to contribute ideas and also keep the group's interactions moving well.

Most group leaders, however, are not willing to stop participating. To do so takes a certain amount of trust in others and a willingness to give up some control and influence. In my experience, group leaders want their ideas considered and are not willing to chance that someone else will come up with a similar idea.

As members of groups, there is something we can do about this issue. We might suggest that the responsibility for attending to the group's process rotate among various members. Thus, the leaders can participate and the interactions will be monitored by someone else. When this is done, the person responsible for monitoring the process must make sure that the group does not extensively defer to the leader's input.

SUMMARY

Our daily environments pose a variety of problems for which we must create and invent some solution. Whether we work alone or in groups, most of us could benefit from improving our ability to problem solve. Understanding how to improve this ability involves considerations of formal problem-solving strategies and the barriers that exist to group efforts.

A formal problem-solving strategy that is often effective involves the following components:

Carefully define the problem. A good problem definition properly locates the source of the problem and states it in ways that suggest more than one solution. Locating the problem simply means knowing what part of the environment is most likely responsible for the issue. Once we have located it, we must define our problem in ways that do not restrict our efforts to obtain an answer. We will hinder our efforts if we define a problem in very general terms or in ways that include a specific solution. A good problem definition should suggest things we can do to find more than one alternative solution—for example, redefining the problem "how to develop a product that will give a dog a bath" into "how to separate the dirt from the dog."

Generate a range of alternative ideas for solving the problem. Seeking alternative ideas for solutions increases the chances that we will find an appropriate and perhaps even an innovative solution. To generate these alternatives we must overcome tendencies to make rigid assumptions about what is possible and to select the first idea we think of or a very common response.

Several procedures will help us overcome these tendencies. They include:

a. *Forming an idea tree.* Here we simply list all or most of the possible solutions before selecting one of them.

b. *Using metaphors.* Sometimes forming an analogy to some object, person, place, or thing that is similar to our problem may help. This is ˏ particularly true if our analogy represents something that solves our problem in ways that we might adapt.

c. *Brainstorming.* This involves a procedure whereby we initially list all the ideas we can think of without making value judgments about them. Having done this, we then try to eliminate the ideas that are not useful, cannot be improved, or are simply too undesirable.

d. *Attribute listing.* New ideas are often improvements on characteristics or attributes of existing things or simply the transfer of such attributes from one situation to another. By studying the attributes of a problem we can often generate new ways to solve it by combining new or existing attributes in interesting ways.

e. *Developing a checklist.* Sometimes it is desirable to have a series of questions that will help us imagine new ways of looking at a problem. Working through such a list of questions often generates ideas for a solution.

f. *Looking for and applying rules.* Some problems are best solved when certain rules are used. Heuristics or "rules of thumb" often help us obtain ideas for solutions. Common heuristics include a means-end analysis, working backward, and subgoal hierarchies.

Select and evaluate a solution based on the ideas you have generated. There are times when it is difficult to determine the best answer. A general guideline is to select a response that meets the criteria you have for a solution. Sometimes the criteria are given to us; sometimes we must create them.

When working in groups, we need to be aware of how our interpersonal and group processes affect our problem-solving abilities. Of particular concern to problem-solving groups are tendencies for members to try to avoid the problem, evaluating ideas prematurely, and having a leader who tries to make both content and process inputs simultaneously. A leader is most effective if his or her role of monitoring the group's process is separated from making content inputs on a problem. A leader's ideas often carry more weight in such discussions and may interfere with the group's seeking alternatives. Groups can overcome this concern by having the leader refrain from making content inputs or have other members monitor the group's process to ensure that the group does not spend an undue amount of time on the leader's ideas.

THINGS TO DO

1. Keep a daily log every 15 to 30 minutes of how you spend your time. Do this for a couple of days. Use the information in the chapter to answer the following questions: Are you using your time effectively? How can you get the most out of the time you spend on various activities?

2. Pretend that beginning tomorrow, you will no longer be able to function as a student, in the job you have, or in the leisure activities that you enjoy. What are the things that you would do to replace your current activities? Could you integrate some of these things into what you are currently doing?

3. Use the ideas in the chapter for generating alternative ideas to solve the following problems:
   a. You have just inherited $100,000. What is the safest way to invest that money to yield the highest rate of return?
   b. Design a more effective mousetrap.
   c. How can you complete your college program in half the time?
   d. How can you complete the work you do on the job in half the time?

4. What are some of the personal barriers that you feel prevent you from becoming a more effective problem solver? List each barrier and think of two things that you can do to overcome it. Have a friend or classmate join you in this activity. Share your ideas and ask your friend or classmate to react to what you said and to add to your list. Do the same thing to your friend's list.

5. You are hired by a calendar manufacturer to design two cubes (six sides on each cube) so that every day of the month (01 to 31) can be shown. How would you arrange the digits on each cube so that this can be done? Use the ideas in the chapter to help facilitate your solving this problem.

REFERENCES AND OTHER INTERESTING THINGS TO READ

ADAMS, J. *Conceptual Blockbusting: A Guide to Better Ideas.* San Francisco: W. H. Freeman and Company, 1974.

BARRON, F. *Creative Person and Creative Process.* New York: Holt, Rinehart and Winston, 1969.

CAMPBELL, D. T. Blink variation and selective retention in creative thought as in other knowledge processes. *Psychological Review.* 1960, *67*, 380–400.

CRAWFORD, R. P. *Techniques of Creative Thinking*. New York: Hawthorn Books, 1954.

DAVIS, G. A. *Psychology of Problem Solving*. New York: Basic Books, 1973.

DE BONO, E. *New Think: The Use of Lateral Thinking in the Generation of New Ideas*. New York: Basic Books, 1968.

DE BONO, E. *The Five Day Course in Thinking*. New York: Basic Books, 1967.

DUNCKER, K. On Problem Solving. In W. Kessen and G. Mandler (Eds.), *Thinking: From Association to Gestalt*. New York: John Wiley & Sons, 1964.

FORD, D., and NEMIROFF, P. Applied Group Problem-Solving: The Nominal Group Technique. *Annual Handbook for Group Facilitators*. La Jolla, Calif.: University Associates, 1975.

GORDON, W. J. *Synectics*. New York: Harper & Row, 1961.

GUILDORD, J. P. Creativity: Its Measurement and Development. In S. J. Parnes and H. F. Harding (Eds.), *A Source Book for Creative Thinking*. New York: Scribner's, 1962.

KOBERG, D., and BAGNALL, J. *The Universal Traveler: A Soft-Systems Guide to Creativity, Problem-Solving and the Process of Reaching Goals*. Los Altos, Calif.: William Kaufmann, 1974.

MAIER, N. R. *Problem Solving and Creativity: In Individuals and Groups*. Belmont, Calif.: Brooks/Cole, 1970.

MAIER, N. Assets and Liabilities in Group Problem Solving. *Psychological Review*, 1967, *74*, 239–249.

MALTZMAN, I. On the Training of Originality. *Psychological Review*, 1960, *67*, 229–242.

McKIM, R. H. *Experiences in Visual Thinking*. Monterey, Calif.: Brooks/Cole, 1972.

MEDNICK, S. The Associative Basis of the Creative Process. *Psychological Review*. 1962, *69*, 220–232.

NEWELL, A., SHAW, J., and SIMON, H. Elements of a Theory of Human Problem Solving. *Psychological Review*, 1958, *65*, 151–166.

OSBORN, A. F. *Applied Imagination*. New York: Scribner's, 1963.

OSHRY, B., and HARRISON, R. Problem-Analysis Questionnaire. *Annual Handbook for Group Facilitators*. La Jolla, Calif.: University Associates, 1975.

PRINCE, G. *The Practice of Creativity*. New York: Collier Books, 1970.

SCHEERER, M. Problem Solving. *Scientific American*, 1963, *208*, 118–128.

SIMON, H. A., and NEWELL, A. Human Problem Solving: The State of Theory in 1970. *American Psychologist*, 1971, *26*, 145–159.

WERTHEIMER, M. *Productive Thinking*. New York: Harper & Row, 1945.

WICKELGREN, W. *How to Solve Problems: Elements of a Theory of Problems and Problem Solving*. San Francisco: W. H. Freeman and Company, 1974.

A. After reading this chapter, the reader should be able to explain:

1. How expert, statistical, personal, cultural, and personal effectiveness criteria are used to define our ability to adjust.

2. Three things that normally produce stress in our lives.

3. Four ways in which anxiety can develop.

4. How particular coping and defense mechanisms are used to deal with stress and anxiety in our daily lives.

5. Two differences between coping and defense mechanisms.

6. The effects that a positive and a negative self-concept have on our behaviors.

7. How talking to a close friend, relative, or professional person is likely to help us with a problem.

8. What assumptions of personal choice and responsibility for our actions suggest for our attempts to adapt to events in our lives.

9. Four principles for saying no in an assertive fashion.

10. Five rights that we have in interpersonal relationships and what we need to do to obtain them.

B. While reading this chapter, the reader should be able to use the information:

1. To make appropriate responses to the exercises in each section.

2. To begin to use the information in some of the issues faced in daily life.

10

Adapting to a Complex Environment

GLOSSARY

Adjustment. Refers to the adequacy of the personal and interpersonal processes that we use to adapt to our environment. There is no way to define a good or poor adjustment without the use of certain biases that we and others have for what represents appropriate behaviors.

Anxiety. An emotional state of feeling fearful, apprehensive or worried in the absence of a real danger to our physical well being. Such feelings represent an unrealistic fear.

Approach-approach conflict. A difficulty in choosing between goals that have equally attractive or desirable consequences for us—for example, having a difficult time choosing between two movies that we think are equally good.

Approach-avoidance conflict. Conflict in which one or more goals have both attractive and unattractive consequences for us. An example of a simple approach-avoidance conflict involving a single goal is deciding whether to attend a movie that you might like but that has a high admission fee. An example of a multiple approach-avoidance conflict involving two goals is having to decide which of two jobs to take. Job A pays more but demands time away from home. Job B involves no travel but pays less.

Avoidance-avoidance conflict. A difficulty in choosing between goals that have equally unattractive or undesirable consequences for us—for example, having to decide between two required courses when we don't like either.

Behavioral therapy. Psychological therapy that assumes that people have learned to behave as they do. Goal of therapy is to help people learn new and more adaptive patterns of behavior. Behavioral therapy is generally not concerned with the underlying causes of the behavior.

Client-centered therapy. Psychological therapy that places emphasis on the potential of the patient or client for developing insight into his or her problems. The therapist's inputs are kept to a minimum.

Coping mechanisms. The ways in which we consciously try to adapt to stress and anxiety in our lives. They are characterized by thoughts and behaviors that are oriented toward searching for information, problem solving, seeking help from others, recognizing our feelings, and establishing goals and objectives.

Defense mechanisms. Our automatic and unconscious attempts to adapt to stress and anxiety in our lives. They try to protect us from stress and anxiety by hiding unpleasant thoughts and emotions from us.

Psychoanalytic therapy. Psychological therapy that tries to help patients gain a deep understanding of the role of unconscious conflicts, past and current thoughts and feelings, and how various defense mechanisms contribute to their problems.

Repression. An important defense mechanism which automatically forces unpleasant thoughts and feelings into our unconscious minds. The inability of repression to work adequately leads to an attempt to use other defense mechanisms to handle the unpleasant thoughts and feelings. A failure of repression to work well is a prime factor in the development of neuroses and psychoses and other, less severe adjustment problems.

Stress. An emotional state of tension which is often characterized by feelings of frustration, hostility, or aggression.

Unconscious impulses. The ideas, feelings, attitudes, and conflicts of which we are not consciously aware. However, they still influence our behaviors. An example is a young boy telling his mother that he likes his baby brother while consistently doing things to irritate the baby or to make it cry.

Defining Normal Adjustment

Look, Doc, you've got to listen to me. No one believes my story. My new neighbor is an alien from another planet. He's here to spy on us and neutralize our thought patterns. He's got this machine that stops people from thinking. When the invasion comes, it will stop our leadership from thinking of ways to defend our country. I know how effective that machine can be. He used it on me several times. There are times I can't think straight or my mind suddenly becomes blank. Each time this occurs, I walk to my window and he's standing in his doorway. He has a little black box in his hand and I know that it's a thought neutralizer. Something has to be done. I'm the only one who knows how dangerous he is. You believe me, don't you?

How good is this person's *adjustment* to his environment? What reasons do you have for your response? Do you think that other people would agree with your reasons?

With the exception of a few people who believed in flying saucers and visitors from outer space, the consensus among my students was that such behaviors do not represent a good adaptation. Several of their comments were:

TOM: I certainly do not believe in aliens. I feel that I'm a pretty rational person. Anyone who thinks that way has to have something wrong with him. He can't be well adjusted.

CAROL: My father is a psychiatrist and he sees people like that quite often. He tells me that such fears really have no basis in reality. The man probably needs to undergo psychotherapy before he can adapt.

JANE: Of course it's a poor adjustment pattern. If it weren't, everyone else would believe such things. I mean, if you showed that story to people, I bet that 99 percent would agree that his behavior is not normal.

MIKE: In this country, in the latter part of the twentieth century, that kind of behavior just won't do. People are not going to buy that story. Most folks look at you funny if you tell them such things. They might believe him more if he said that a foreign spy lived next door, but a visitor from outer space. No way! He definitely has trouble adjusting.

PHYLLIS: I don't think that he is well adjusted because he is obviously consumed by this fear of others. Furthermore, if he believes that someone else controls his thoughts, he can't feel too good about his own ability to run his life. As a result, he has to have problems getting along with others.

Did you have reactions similar to those of the people in my classes?

There is more than one way to define whether certain behaviors represent an adequate adaptation to the environment. Periodically, most of us judge how healthy, unhealthy, normal, abnormal, poorly adjusted, or well adjusted our own or someone else's behaviors are. We might make this type of judgment after reading about a crime in a newspaper, watching an interview on television, seeing a parent disciplining a child, or reflecting upon our own behaviors in some situation. Our judgments always reflect certain biases in our criteria for defining well-adjusted behavior. Not everyone agrees on what standards to use. You can see this disagreement in the example in the last paragraph. Each of my students thought that the behaviors described represented a poor adaptation. However, their reasons differed. Having various standards presents a major problem for developing an overall definition of adjustment. The different points of view described by my students are to some extent appropriate. Rather than argue about which standards are right or wrong, you and I need to become aware of those that exist, which ones we personally use, and their subsequent advantages and disadvantages. Table 10-1 presents five of the standards that are often used to judge the extent to which our own or someone else's behaviors reflect a normal adjustment.

Table 10-1

Common Standards Used to Define Adjustment

Expert. Every society has people who set standards of behavior for others. They include witch doctors, tribal chiefs, psychologists, psychiatrists, military leaders, ministers, judges, lawmakers, teachers, and business managers. Their standards are often quite rigid and accepted by others without questioning their accuracy. Attempts are made to put people into categories (e.g., lawbreakers, churchgoers, nice people, depressed, neurotic, evil, enemy). How well we and others meet the standards they set describes our adjustment.

Examples: "The really good children in my classes are those who sit still and don't talk to anyone else." "As a practicing psychologist, I can say that anyone who walks around terribly depressed for 12 hours a day has a mental problem." "I want to tell everyone in the congregation that coming to church on Sunday represents a healthy outlook on life." "Robbing a bank is a serious offense. You broke the law and I have no choice but to sentence you to prison."

Comment: Although this standard places the development of standards in the hands of people whom most of us regard highly, their judgments

319

Table 10-1 (continued)

are not always perfect. The standards they set are often the things with which they are personally comfortable. The natural differences in behavior among people are sometimes looked down upon by such experts, particularly when the differences do not conform to the categories they set. Individuals may otherwise get along well but do not go to church every Sunday, they may talk in classrooms, and they are sometimes irritable or sad.

Statistical. Any behavior occurs in different amounts within a society. Thus "normal" or "well-adjusted" behavior is often described as that which occurs most frequently or in some average amount for the population. Behaviors that occur less often or that are too far above or below some "average" for a given group of people by definition represent "abnormal" or "poorly adjusted" behaviors. We often judge behaviors in terms of how frequently they occur or how "average" they are.

Examples: "Everyone else sits in their seats during the game. That guy decides to sit on the grass next to the playing field. What is wrong with him?" "The average number of times a person is married is once in a lifetime. Sam was married two times and divorced two times. You just have to wonder about him." "Beth just bought a home in the eastern part of town. Ninety percent of the people in the office live in that area. You have to believe that she shows good judgment and will get along just fine with people in this organization."

Comment: It is not necessarily true that less frequently occurring behaviors or those above or below some average are indications of adjustment problems. A person who lives on the western part of town may have nothing wrong with her judgments or ability to get along with others. Similarly, a person who has married twice is above the national average, but this does not mean that there is something wrong with him.

Personal. We judge behaviors in ourselves and others in terms of how we personally behave in situations. When behaviors deviate from the way we usually do things we question how "well adjusted" or "normal" they are.

Examples: "Compared to how I usually handle my anger, my hitting Fred was not the right thing to do." "I would never rob a store. There must be something wrong with someone who does that." "I'm pleased with how I handled myself in that interview. I did as well as I did in the other ones." "Sam treated Betty rather well given that she was angry with him. He handled her just as I would, if I were he."

Comment: Our personal standards for behavior may not be the best for others. Similarly, some flexibility in our own behaviors is probably desirable. To judge our actions in terms of how we usually behave in a situ-

Table 10-1 (continued)

ation may not be sensitive to changes in the situation which call for a set of different behaviors. In the first example, if Fred was physically attacking that person, hitting him may have been a good response.

Cultural. Every culture has behaviors that a large number of people engage in and of which they approve. The expected behaviors develop through the customs, laws, norms, and daily interactions which exist in every society. Behaviors which deviate from the cultural patterns are considered "abnormal" or to represent a "poor adjustment."

> *Examples:* "Running Fox is not a good member of this tribe. He refuses to drink the blood of the antelope. There is something wrong with him." "In this town, anyone who has three wives in different parts of the city has got to be nuts." "Sally is a decent person. She treats others with respect and does her best to help out at home."

> *Comment:* Standards for behavior vary from one culture to another. In some cultures drinking the blood of animals to obtain their strength or having more than one wife is perfectly acceptable. In others it is not. "Normal" or "well-adjusted" behavior becomes relative to one's culture.

Personal Effectiveness: The emphasis is on the effects individuals' behavior produces in themselves and in others. Such things as how organized the behavior is, whether it is accompanied by anxiety, and whether it will allow the individual to perform adequately on a long-term basis are important considerations.

> *Examples:* "Ellen is really nervous when she takes exams. I see her hands shaking constantly. It's no wonder she does not do well." "Sam really keeps his cool in a crisis. I have never seen him lose his composure and he performs beautifully." "Betty likes to look at both sides of an issue before making a decision. She certainly avoids the problems our last boss had."

> *Comment:* The degree to which one's behavior produces positive or negative effects for us in our daily interactions is a helpful factor to consider. Sometimes, though, what appears in the short run to be a good adjustment may have negative long-term consequences. For example, always carefully analyzing a problem may interfere in situations which call for a quick decision.

In spite of the problems in defining adjustment, certain groups work with people who are experiencing difficulties in their social relationships. Consequently, psychologists, psychiatrists, judges, social workers, and others formulate definitions which they use to identify and deal with people who are experiencing problems. For example, some of my colleagues take a cultural and personal effectiveness view in describing adjustment. Thus, a well-

---

EXERCISE 10-1: DEFINING ADJUSTMENT

As a check of your understanding of each criterion, reread the responses that each of my students made. Which standards do you think each of them used? Check your responses with those on page 000. Which criteria do you think you use most often when assessing your own or someone else's actions? Which ones are used by your close friends? How similar or different are your and your friends' criteria?

---

adjusted person is someone who engages in behaviors that are appropriate for the culture and a given interpersonal situation. Well-adjusted behaviors, according to this view, also are flexible and subject to changes in the environment, produce no harmful effects on the individual or other people, and do not lead to internal hang-ups or short- and long-term interaction problems. Individuals who deviate from this definition are seen as having adjustment problems.

What do you think about this definition? I suspect that not everyone will agree with it. The important point to remember is that in spite of anyone's need to have a definition, there is *no absolute way* to define a well-adjusted person. Any attempt reflects certain biases regarding the criteria with which we or others are comfortable. The standards are unlikely to be shared by everyone we meet.

Psychological Processes in Adjustment

Not everyone adjusts to a situation in exactly the same way. One person assists in a natural disaster while another loots the homes of disaster victims. Some people admit their shortcomings and mistakes, and some continually place the blame on others. Certain students enjoy asking questions, participating in class discussions, and taking exams; others fear such things. To understand the differences in adjustment patterns among people, we must look at the psychological processes associated with our ability to adjust. A large number of such factors are identified in the research literature; we will examine three. They include our reactions to *stress* and *anxiety*, the types of *coping* and *defense mechanisms* we use, and the nature of our *self-concepts*. Each plays a vital role in determining how we react to the events that occur in our daily lives.

Psychological Processes in Adjustment: Stress

Much of our daily activity is spent in attempting to achieve certain goals. Our goals include a variety of activities, such as driving home from work, eating meals, completing an education, engaging in recreational activities, and planning a vacation. Our inability to accomplish them generally leads to stress. Stress is an emotional state of tension which is often characterized by our feeling frustrated, hostile, or aggressive.

Our inability to achieve our goals generally is due to our personal limitations, factors in our environments that block our goal behaviors, and conflicts in selecting among two or more goals. Personal limitations include such considerations as a handicap or disease or a lack of social or intellectual skills. A neighbor of mine had several opportunities to become a major league baseball player. Unfortunately, he was in a car accident which resulted in the amputation of his right leg. He displays much anger when discussing "what could have been."

Environmental factors include events such as severe storms, famines, fires, and wars. They may temporarily or permanently affect our plans. I remember the stress I experienced when I discovered I had to enter active duty in the Army. This occurred within two months of my finishing graduate school. At the time I was more interested in beginning my professional career as a psychologist. I remember how angry I felt and that on one occasion I shouted and screamed at a clerk in the officer assignment division for "doing this to me." When we experience stress as a result of blocked goals, we are likely to feel frustrated or angry or become hostile toward other people.

Criteria Used in Exercise 10-1

Tom: Personal
Carol: Expert
Jane: Statistical
Mike: Cultural
Phyllis: Personal effectiveness

Finally, we can experience stress due to conflicts in making decisions among two or more goals. Such choices become particularly difficult when the goals are equally attractive or unattractive or when one or more goals have both attractive and unattractive qualities. These situations represent *approach-approach, avoidance-avoidance,* and *approach-avoidance conflicts,* respectively. Each is described in detail in Table 10-2. As you can easily see, our reactions to such conflicts include becoming indecisive, withdrawing from situations, avoiding a decision, and seeking reasons to justify one course of action over another.

EXERCISE 10-2: IDENTIFYING STRESS IN OUR LIVES

Can you think of at least one situation in your own life in which you experienced stress because your goals were blocked by personal or environmental factors? Have you ever experienced stress through one or more of the three types of conflicts described in Table 10-2? How did you resolve that conflict?

Psychological Processes in Adjustment: Anxiety

Have you ever felt somewhat afraid or apprehensive while thinking about an important exam in school, while playing on a team before an audience, after arguing with a friend, before appearing in a school play, or while waiting for your boss to decide if you will get a raise? Such feelings are described as anxiety. *Feeling fearful, experiencing apprehension, or worrying in the absence of some real danger to our physical well being is a normal part of our lives.* In small amounts, anxiety often energizes our behavior. Many actors and sports figures report that it helps them to prepare for their performance, and it usually dissipates once the curtain rises or the game begins. On the other hand, higher levels of anxiety may cause us to withdraw from

Table 10-2

Three Common Conflicts that Produce Stress in Our Lives

Approach-Approach Conflict

This occurs when we must choose among goals which have equally attractive or desirable consequences for us. This might occur when we attempt to choose between two jobs, dinner in one restaurant versus another, or one television program as opposed to another. Such conflicts are usually easy to resolve. *All that we need do is find additional reasons why one job, restaurant or television show is better than the other and automatically the second alternative will seem less attractive.* This is usually easy to do. A particular job may be closer to home, one restaurant has faster service, or one television show is not as long as the other.

Avoidance-Avoidance Conflict

This occurs when we must choose among goals which have equally unattractive or undesirable consequences for us. We might need to choose between taking a required course we don't like and not graduating, or between going to a movie we will not like and staying at home with nothing to do. Such conflicts are often described by phrases such as "caught between the devil and the deep blue sea" and "caught between a rock and a hard place." *Unlike an approach-approach conflict, movement toward either goal increases our discomfort. We find ourselves in a dilemma because thinking of either course of action is uncomfortable. Thus we become indecisive and can't make up our minds or we try to escape or avoid the problem.* We might try to get the college to waive the course requirement for us, or we might decide to engage in some other social activity. This would prevent us from having to select one or the other alternative.

Approach-Avoidance Conflict

This can occur in two ways. A single goal may have both attractive and unattractive consequences for us. On the other hand, two or more goals may have both attractive and unattractive consequences.[a] I might want to spend my savings on a new car, but then I will not have money to take a vacation. On the other hand, I might want to choose between Miami or Denver for a winter vacation. Miami has great night spots and the ocean, but it is hot and expensive. Denver has outdoor sports and skiing, but it is cold and expensive. Such conflicts often leave us unable to make a decision. *There are three ways to resolve such a conflict. We can seek additional reasons for adding to the attractive qualities of one alternative.* Transportation to Denver might be cheaper than to Miami. *Furthermore, we might select a third alternative which has the combined positive characteristics of the alternatives.* We might decide to vacation in Palm Springs so that we can swim, enjoy the outdoors, and ski nearby. *Finally, we might just go ahead and pick one of the alternatives.* The rationale is that "unless I do something my vacation time will elapse and I won't be able to do anything." Thus, remaining indecisive has negative qualities which force us to make a choice.

---

[a] When two or more goals have both positive and negative consequences, this is technically known as a double approach-avoidance or multiple approach-avoidance conflict.

or avoid places which evoke it in us. I have known people who have given up golf, refused to ride in elevators, or dropped courses because of the apprehension associated with them.

High levels of anxiety may also cause physical symptoms which prevent us from functioning effectively. Increases in heart rate and blood pressure, a loss of appetite, sleeplessness, and other noticeable changes in our behavior accompany anxiety. As an undergraduate, I had a roommate who perspired heavily and whose hands and knees quivered when he took math examinations. Math was his major and he was afraid of performing poorly. His physical reactions did not allow him to complete the exams on time and he received low grades. Fortunately, his instructors understood and they gave him other opportunities to retake the exams. This allowed him to show what he could really do and in time his physical reactions ceased.

EXERCISE 10-3: IDENTIFYING ANXIETY IN OUR LIVES

Table 10-3 shows some of the things that my students say make them anxious. Before reading further, think of three things that make you anxious and list them. Did you have any responses that were similar to my students? Are the three that you listed best described as producing low, moderate, or high levels of anxiety in you? How does each affect your ability to function in your daily affairs?

How do our anxieties develop? Several interrelated factors seem to be involved. Several of the more common ones include threats to our self-concept, learning processes, unresolved conflicts, and unconscious impulses which affect our behaviors.

Threats to our self-concept. Each of us has a view of ourselves which we try to protect. We may see ourselves as handsome, pretty, intelligent, a good student, a religious person, popular, or some combination of these and other characteristics. Events may occur which pose a threat to the view we have of ourselves. My roommate in college saw himself as a competent math student. He felt that he was able to understand and work math problems better than anyone else. The difficulties he experienced with certain exam problems were a threat to his self-concept. He felt that a competent math student should not have such problems. This made him extremely anxious about taking exams.

Do you think that a person who has a poor image of his or her skills and abilities might become anxious in situations in which it is necessary to perform well? Would such a person also feel anxious if told that his or her

Table 10-3

Common Sources of Anxiety

- Will I do well on that final exam?
- I'm not sure that my boyfriend likes me.
- I just can't seem to decide on a major.
- I think I may be a homosexual.
- Should I go against my parents' wishes and drop out of school?
- Will I ever get married?
- I just can't face going to that class one more time.
- The thought of insects just makes me feel awful.
- I'm afraid there is something wrong with my sex life.
- I can't decide what job to take.
- I may not have enough money to finish school.
- I'm not getting enough time to relax.
- I've just got to leave home and get an apartment of my own.
- I need to tell my father I dented the fender on the car.
- Will I be able to perform as well in the game tonight as I did last week?
- I'm afraid Suzy will reject me if I ask her out.
- I'm not sure I can finish all the work this course requires.
- People might laugh at me if I stood up in class and gave an answer to a question.
- Working in small groups is something that makes me nervous.
- I need a summer job and don't think I'll find one.
- Will I ever be self-sufficient and not rely on my parents?
- I have to leave my daughter with a sitter during the day but I don't like it.
- My wife and I are not getting along very well.
- I don't think people respect me.
- My boyfriend wants me to sleep with him.
- I can't go to the party, but I think Joe will be mad at me.
- I need to talk to someone but I'm afraid of going to the school counselor.
- I'm afraid I'll forget my lines in the play tonight.
- I'm sure no one will ask me to the homecoming dance.
- I'm not sure what grade I'll get in this class.
- My term paper is six weeks overdue.
- I wonder if my wife wants to divorce me.
- My father has to enter the hospital for a serious operation.
- Will a nuclear war break out in the near future?

---

skills and abilities were really better than originally thought? What reasons do you have for your responses?

Learning processes. We may learn to become anxious in certain situations. There are two ways this learning might occur. Anxiety, like other emotional responses, is classified as a respondent. From our discussion of learning processes in earlier chapters, you know that certain stimuli can directly elicit emotional reactions. To develop anxiety to a stimulus, we must first experience a sudden pain, fear, or other aversive reaction to it. After such an experience, we are likely to find that we are apprehensive and fearful in its presence. One of my students recently crossed a street and narrowly missed getting hit by a bus. She reported that for several weeks after that incident, every time she saw a bus she felt uneasy and apprehensive. This occurred even though the bus was no longer a direct threat to her physical well being.

A second way we might learn anxiety responses is to pick up the apprehension that someone else has about a situation. Albert Bandura describes such a process as *imitation learning*. Many of our behaviors occur because we follow the examples of people whom we feel close to, like, and respect. Such people act as models for our behaviors, including some of our emotional responses. A good friend of mine was anxious about taking a trip by airplane. She had never flown. She told me that her mother is also apprehensive about air travel. Her mother constantly talked about the dangers involved in flying, became extremely anxious when her husband took a business trip by plane, and talked for days about any plane crash that occurred. My friend's anxiety was undoubtedly learned through the example her mother set.

Unresolved conflicts. Conflicts are a normal part of our daily lives. There are times when we fail to resolve a conflict, however, and when this occurs we can experience varying degrees of anxiety. A nephew of mine is thinking about going to college. He told me he wants to attend one school, but his father feels he should attend another. He admits that he feels uncomfortable about doing what he wants rather than following the advice of his father. For the past six weeks he has acted nervous, remained awake at night, and has had thoughts that perhaps he does not want to go to college after all.

Unconscious impulses. We are often quite aware of the ideas, feelings, attitudes, and conflicts which affect our behavior. They are part of our conscious thought experiences. On the other hand, Sigmund Freud said that there are also ideas, feelings, attitudes, and conflicts of which we are not aware. They are called *unconscious impulses*. Although we are not aware of them, they exert an influence on our behavior. Two recent experiences of mine illustrate this point. I recently received a note from the college that granted me my bachelor's degree stating that I owed them $900. Apparently a student loan I had taken out 14 years previously had not been paid. I was embarrassed that I had forgotten about it and wondered about the bookkeeping procedures at the college. I wrote out a check for the amount and returned it with a short note. The note stated that I was sorry for being tardy and appreciated the college's letting me know about my financial obligation. Two weeks later, the check was sent back. I had forgotten to sign it. In thinking about this incident, I realized that I was actually angry at the college and resented having to pay a bill that was so late in coming. However, when I wrote the check, I was not consciously aware of such feelings. Nonetheless, they influenced my actions. Not signing the check was the way that my unconscious impulses of anger and resentment toward the college affected my behavior.

The second experience concerns one of my consulting clients who is the manager of a claims adjustment office for an automobile insurance company. He said that in recent months he had been becoming increasingly nervous about how well he was doing, the efficiency of the office staff, and his prospects for promotion. As far as he and I could tell, there was no real basis for his fears. Things were going quite well. He took a vacation soon after our conversation and gave a great deal of thought to the problem. One day he had an insight. He reported that "All at once I realized how relaxed I was away from the office. Getting away was what I wanted to do all the time. I really didn't like my job. My father forced me into this business. I guess I secretly resented him for doing it. I can remember four years ago when I started working that I had a lot of angry feelings toward my father and the job. But for some reason, I forgot about those feelings until I began to think about my job while on vacation. I realized that with things going so well at the office and the prospect of a promotion, I was afraid to get stuck with a job I basically disliked. That is why I was feeling so anxious all the time." Even though my client forgot about the negative feelings he had toward his father and the job, they became a part of his unconscious thought processes.

We all have unconscious impulses which affect us. With a good deal of careful thought we can sometimes discover what they are. It is possible to do this alone, but there are times when a professional counselor or therapist is helpful.

EXERCISE 10-4: DETERMINING THE CAUSES OF ANXIETY

Earlier in this section you listed three things that make you anxious. Review them and see if you can identify the causes of your feelings in terms of a threat to your self-concept, respondent or imitation learning processes, unresolved conflicts, or unconscious impulses. Is it possible for more than one factor to operate at the same time? Do you think that something other than one of these factors is responsible?

Psychological Processes in Adjustment: Stress and Anxiety Occurring Together

As we saw in the previous two sections, stress and anxiety may occur alone. On the other hand, the two may occur together in one situation. Things which make us apprehensive are also likely to become sources of frustration and tension. A neighbor of mine remarked that he was feeling nervous and frustrated about asking his boss for a large raise. He had made a similar request a year ago and his boss became angry at the request. Because of this unpleasant experience, he is understandably anxious about approaching his boss again. However, he needs the extra money to pay for his wife's medical expenses. His boss stands in the way of achieving this goal and this makes him feel frustrated. Have you ever experienced stress and anxiety in the same situation?

Psychological Processes in Adjustment: Coping and Defense Mechanisms

Why do you think some people readily admit their mistakes and others constantly blame other people or events for causing them? What makes one person get angry and then take it out on everyone around while another individual expresses anger only at the person who caused it? Why are some people able to make fast decisions and others can never make up their minds quickly about anything? Each of these questions reflects the fact that each of us adapts differently to the stress and anxiety which occur in our lives. To gain a better understanding of how both emotions affect our daily interactions, let us take a look at the role of coping and defense mechanisms in helping us to adapt to stress and anxiety.

Coping Mechanisms

Coping mechanisms describe the ways in which we try consciously to adapt to the stress and anxiety associated with various events in our lives. Such events might range from conflicts over a career choice to attempts to adjust to the aftermath of a tornado. Our coping mechanisms are the thoughts and behaviors we have when faced with stress- and anxiety-arousing events that are oriented toward searching for information, solving problems, seeking help from others, recognizing our feelings, and establishing goals and objectives. Several common coping mechanisms identified by T. Kroeber and Norma Haan are described in Table 10-4. The thoughts and behaviors as-

Table 10-4

Coping Mechanisms Used to Adapt to Stress and Anxiety

Coping Mechanism: *Objectivity*

Our ability under stress and anxiety to separate one thought from another or to separate our feelings from the thoughts which accompany them. This allows us to obtain a better understanding of how we think or feel and to obtain a clear, objective evaluation of our actions.

> *Example:* Joe just made an error on the job that will cost his company $3,000. He is afraid of what his boss will say and of losing his job. He sits down to think about what happened, how he is feeling, and how responsible he was for the error. He realizes that his emotions are natural but the error will be discovered and he should take responsibility for it. He then tells his boss exactly what happened and admits he was responsible.

Coping Mechanism: *Logical Analysis*

Our ability to carefully and systematically analyze the problems we face in order to obtain explanations or to make plans to solve them. Our explanations and plans are based on the realities of the situations we face.

> *Example:* Mary is in a hurry to attend a meeting. She needs gas for her car and pulls into a gas station. She sits at the pump for five minutes but no one waits on her. She becomes frustrated and worried that she will be late for the meeting and is concerned that no one is paying attention to her. She thinks to herself, "It looks as if everyone is busy. There are just too many cars here now. If I wait much longer I'll be late for the meeting. I'd better leave now and then I'll have time to stop for gas at the station down the street."

Coping Mechanism: *Concentration*

Our ability under stress and anxiety to set aside disturbing thoughts and feelings in order to concentrate on the task at hand.

> *Example:* Susan has just had a baby that is mentally retarded. All the plans she had for her baby's future before it was born are shattered. She is frustrated and worried about what will happen in the future. However, she is able to make plans for the special care her child will need and does not let her emotions interfere with this task.

Coping Mechanism: *Empathy*

Our ability to sense how other people are feeling in situations which are emotionally arousing. As a result, our interactions take into account the feelings of others.

Table 10-4 (continued)

Example: George and Fred are good friends. They find themselves facing each other in the finals of their tennis club's annual tournament. George easily beats his friend. Fred is disappointed that he lost and is somewhat angry at George. George, on the other hand, is delighted he is the club champ, but not too happy that he had to beat his best friend. Fred says to George, "Congratulations, I thought you played a good game. I can sense that you are happy to win but I also feel that you are not too happy that you had to beat me to win the tournament."

Coping Mechanism: Playfulness

Our ability to use past feelings and ideas and behaviors to enrich the solution of problems or otherwise add some enjoyment to life. The feelings and ideas are appropriate to the situation.

Example: Sam is president of a small company. He and his assistants are having a meeting to discuss their sales for the year. Things did not go well that year and sales are down. Everyone is a little frustrated. Midway through the meeting, Sam picks up the sales reports and with a big grin on his face, he throws them into the air. "What's the use of keeping all this bad news in one place," he laughs. His assistants are amused and Sam finds that his gesture breaks the tension in the room.

Coping Mechanism: Tolerance of Ambiguity

Our ability to function in situations in which we or others cannot make clear choices because the situation is so complicated. We are able to carry on when things are "up in the air" in spite of the tension that is often present.

Example: Barbara is a manager of a department in a discount store. Her department specializes in small gifts from the Orient. Sales in her department are not good and she knows that the store is considering two

Table 10-4 (continued)

options: One is to eliminate her department and the other is to put more money into it to try to increase sales. This decision has been pending for six months. She continues to look for merchandise, thinks of ways to increase business, and keeps appointments with people who sell merchandise for her department.

Coping Mechanism: Sublimation[a]

Our ability to express our thoughts and feelings in socially acceptable ways. The ways we do this are personally rewarding or satisfying to us.

Example: Betty lives on a farm. She is quite isolated from other people and because of her chores has little time to socialize with friends. She finds herself lonely and frustrated by a lack of social contact. She finds that writing poems which have themes of loneliness and people as social beings makes her feel much better.

Coping Mechanism: Suppression

Our ability to consciously forget about or hold in abeyance any thoughts or emotions we might have. We hold them back until an appropriate time or place to express them arises.

Example: Sally wants to buy a new lawnmower. She looks in her checkbook one morning and finds that her husband has already spent the extra money that was there on a new toolbox. She is angry at her husband and frustrated over not being able to purchase the lawnmower. She decides not to call her husband at work to find out why he did that, but waits until they are both home to share her thoughts and feelings with him.

Coping Mechanism: Substitution of Thoughts and Emotions

Our ability under stress to consciously substitute other thoughts and emotions for how we actually think or feel in order to meet the demands of a situation.

Example: Karen is campaigning for a seat in the U.S. Senate. She is tired, frustrated that her opponent has a lead in the polls, and worried that she will not win the election. She knows that she cannot afford to lose any more votes. She speaks at a V.F.W. meeting where the members want to know her position on the amount of sex and violence in movies and what the government can do about it. Privately she enjoys movies that display sex and have violent scenes. To make a good impression, she says, "I think there is too much of it and we need to cut it back. I'm in favor of legislation to put a stop to such things."

---

[a] Sublimation is considered a defense mechanism in traditional discussions of its role in our behavior. However, this view is not shared by some contemporary theorists, such as Kroeber and Haan. They consider sublimation a coping mechanism because it seldom has unfavorable long-range consequences for people and its use is sometimes the result of a conscious choice.

sociated with each mechanism are things that we consciously choose to think of or perform and are flexible enough to adapt to any changes in our daily interactions. Their use generally leads to long-term favorable consequences for us as we adjust to the demands of our environments. We may use them alone or in combinations of two or more.

A personal experience of mine illustrates how several coping mechanisms can work together to help us adjust. Recently I backed out of my driveway and into the door of a neighbor's parked car. I was angry at myself for being so stupid and anxious about what he might think. I just sat there for a minute, tried to relax, and thought about what had occurred. I realized that I had failed to use my rear view mirror. As a result I had not seen his car parked across the street. I concluded that the accident was my fault. I also sensed that my neighbor would be a little upset with me. I knocked on his door, explained what had happened, and offered to pay for the damages.

EXERCISE 10-5: USING COPING MECHANISMS

Before reading further, decide what coping mechanisms described in Table 10-4 you think I used and list them on a separate sheet of paper. Have you ever had a similar situation occur? How did you behave? What coping mechanisms did you use?

Think of two or more interactions you had or observed others having this week in which you or others experienced stress or anxiety. Did you use any of the coping mechanisms described in Table 10-4? Did you see other people using one or more of them?

The coping mechanisms I used included *concentrating* on the problem I faced, *logically analyzing* the causes of the accident and what actions to take, *objectively* deciding that I was at fault, and *empathizing* with the possible feelings of my neighbor. Together they allowed me to handle successfully the stress and anxiety I experienced. I felt I had made a decent adjustment to a rather unfortunate set of circumstances.

Defense Mechanisms

Coping mechanisms generally represent thoughts and behaviors we use to face and deal with the stress and anxiety in our lives directly. Defense mechanisms represent a second way that we attempt to adapt to such things.

They try to protect us from stress and anxiety by the use of self-deception. Defense mechanisms disguise or hide unpleasant thoughts and emotions from us. Several common defense mechanisms are presented in Table 10-5.

Unlike coping mechanisms which we choose to use and which we are consciously aware of, the defense mechanisms occur automatically and we are

Table 10-5

Defense Mechanisms Used to Adapt to Stress and Anxiety

Coping Mechanism: *Objectivity*
Defense Mechanism: *Isolation*

Unconsciously separating ideas and/or emotions that belong together. This keeps us unaware of the illogical nature of our actions and thus reduces anxiety and stress.

> *Example:*   Joe just made an error on the job that will cost his company $3,000. He thinks to himself, "Oh, well, that's the way things go, sometimes." He looks quite relaxed and doesn't report feeling anxious about what occurred.

Coping Mechanism: *Logical Analysis*
Defense Mechanism: *Rationalization*

Using superficial explanations to justify how we behaved or felt in a given situation. The explanations often omit crucial aspects of the situation or are otherwise incorrect. The explanations are used by us to reduce the amount of stress and anxiety we feel.

> *Example:*   Mary is in a hurry to attend a meeting. She needs gas for her car and pulls into a gas station. She sits at the pump for five minutes but no one waits on her. She becomes frustrated and worried that she will be late for the meeting and concerned that no one is paying any attention to her. She leaves the station and thinks to herself, "I really didn't need gas anyway. No time has been wasted since I didn't have to rush to the meeting after all."

Coping Mechanism: *Concentration*
Defense Mechanism: *Denial*

Refusing to acknowledge thoughts and feelings that are unpleasant even though they are supported by convincing evidence.

> *Example:*   Susan has just had a baby that is mentally retarded. All the plans she had for the baby's future before it was born are shattered. She is frustrated and worried about what will happen in the future. She tells other people that her baby's problem is just temporary and will go away as it gets older.

335

Table 10-5 (continued)

Coping Mechanism: Empathy
Defense Mechanism: Projection

Unconsciously attributing objectionable thoughts and feelings to other people to conceal from our conscious minds that the thoughts and feelings are our own.

> *Example:*   George and Fred are good friends.   They find themselves facing each other in the finals of their tennis club's annual tournament.   George easily beats his friend.   Fred is disappointed that he lost and somewhat angry at George.   George is glad that he won, but not happy he beat his best friend.   Fred tells his wife that he thinks that George must be angry at him because he tried to beat him so badly.

Coping Mechanism: Playfulness
Defense Mechanism: Regression

The use of past feelings, ideas, and behaviors to reduce anxiety and stress.   The behaviors are often inappropriate to a situation and often produce more tension if other people are present.

> *Example:*   Sam is president of a small company.   He and his assistants are having a meeting to discuss their sales for the year.   Things did not go well that year and sales are down.   Everyone is a little frustrated.   Midway through the meeting, Sam picks up the sales reports and throws them at his assistants.   He begins to shout and scream that "This is the worst thing that could happen to the company.   I'm sick and tired of what's going on."   He pounds his fist on the table, throws a couple of chairs around, and leaves the room.

Coping Mechanism: Tolerance of Ambiguity
Defense Mechanism: Extreme Doubt and Indecision

Not being able to make up our minds or function in situations in which things are "up in the air."   We don't trust our own judgments or perceptions and hope that someone else will be able to solve the problem or that it will solve itself.   This reduces stress and anxiety because we believe that the responsibility for a solution is not ours.

> *Example:*   Barbara is a manager of a department in a discount store.   Her department specializes in small gifts from the Orient.   Sales in her department are not good and she knows the store is considering two options: One is to eliminate her department and the other is to put more money into it to try to increase sales.   This decision has been pending for six months.   She sits around thinking about whether her job is worth the effort.   She wonders if sales are really that bad and hopes that her boss will be able to figure out a way to save the department.

Table 10-5 (continued)

Coping Mechanism: Sublimation
Defense Mechanism: Displacement

Unconsciously transferring thoughts, feelings, and behaviors to a neutral person or object or to one that is less likely to retaliate. This reduces our stress and anxiety because we don't have to confront the person or situation responsible and can "take it out on someone else."

> *Example:* Betty lives on a farm. She is quite isolated from other people and because of her chores has little time to socialize with friends. She finds herself lonely and frustrated by a lack of social contact. One day at dinner she screams at her mother, "It's all your fault that I have to live out here away from everyone. I'm sick, sick, sick and tired of it."

Coping Mechanism: Suppression
Defense Mechanism: Repression

Unconsciously eliminating unpleasant thoughts or emotions from our memory to reduce the stress and anxiety associated with them. However, they still influence our behaviors.

> *Example:* Sally wants to buy a new lawnmower. She looks in her check-book one morning and finds that her husband has already spent the extra money that was there on a new toolbox. She is angry at her husband and frustrated over not being able to purchase the lawnmower. A couple of minutes later she forgets it and does not mention the incident to her husband when they are at home that evening. However, it is her turn to cook dinner that evening and she overcooks it. She remarks, "Isn't that strange; I'm usually more careful when I cook."

Coping Mechanism: Substitution of Thoughts and Emotions
Defense Mechanism: Reaction Formation

Unconsciously using thoughts and feelings in our behaviors that are the opposite of our true thoughts and feelings.

> *Example:* Karen is campaigning for a seat in the U.S. Senate. She is tired, frustrated that her opponent has a lead in the polls, and worried that she will not win the election. She knows that she cannot afford to lose any more votes. She speaks at a V.F.W. meeting where the members want to know her position on the amount of sex and violence in movies and what the government can do about it. As a child, Karen enjoyed a chance to be aggressive and had a natural interest in sex. However, her parents made her feel anxious and guilty about such things. As a result, she became a pacifist and took a strong public stand on the public display of sexual material. She gives the members a very passionate speech about how ter-

Table 10-5 (continued)

rible sex and violence are in movies and promises to work for legislation to stop it. She also tells them how good it feels to find other people who think as she does on that issue.

Note that the examples used are the same situations described for the coping mechanisms in Table 10-4. This should help you compare the differences between the two mechanisms by seeing how a similar situation is handled by a defense or coping mechanism. Such pairings are adapted in part from an analysis of both mechanisms by Norma Haan, *Psychological Monographs*, 1967, 77, No. 8.

---

not aware of their affecting our behavior. They represent many of our past habits for self-deception. Unlike coping mechanisms, they provide only temporary relief from stress and anxiety and do not lead to adequate long-term adaptations to the problems we face. Although they are not as effective in the long run, we all use them in our daily interactions. Each of us has needs for the short-term relief they provide. We may use them alone or in combinations of two or more.

To get a better insight into how several defense mechanisms might occur together to protect us from stress and anxiety, let us do an instant replay of the accident I described earlier. This time let us assume that I behaved using defense mechanisms. I get out of my car and begin to kick and pound my fists on the fender. Then I run up to my neighbor's house, knock on the door, and when he answers I shout, "What a stupid place for you to park your car. If you hadn't parked in front of your house like that, this accident wouldn't have occurred. My gas pedal must have stuck and that is why I wasn't able to stop. Since you are partly to blame, I expect you to help pay for damages. I'm not about to pay for everything."

EXERCISE 10-6: USING DEFENSE MECHANISMS

Before reading further, decide what defense mechanisms described in Table 10-5 you think I used and list them on a separate sheet of paper. If you have had a similar situation occur in your life, what defense mechanisms did you employ?

Think of two or more interactions that you had or observed others having this week in which stress and anxiety were involved. Did you use any of the defense mechanisms described in Table 10-5? Did you see other people using one or more of them?

The defense mechanisms I used included *displacing* my anger by kicking and hitting the car fender and shouting at my neighbor, *denying* that the accident was my fault and *rationalizing* the cause of the accident as a stuck gas pedal. As you can see, my actions were not oriented to the reality of what occurred. Each mechanism protected me from the stress and anxiety associated with believing that I was at fault. This protection is likely to last only for a short time. My thoughts and actions are not going to lead me to make a long-term adjustment to this problem. There is no way that a legally parked car or its owner is at fault in a collision. My insurance company, the police, and/or the courts would force me to face that reality.

The same situation might find us employing both coping and defense mechanisms. The examples used in the previous paragraphs should not lead you to assume that our behaviors in a given situation are either coping or defensive in nature. In most of our daily interactions we react to stress and anxiety with characteristics of both types of mechanism present. This is particularly true when stress and anxiety are high and we can make a set of complex responses to an event. Backing into someone else's car qualified as such an incident. It is quite possible for me to have kicked and hit the car's fender and rationalized the responsibility for causing the accident as a stuck gas pedal. Yet I might still realize that the accident was basically my fault, sensed that my neighbor would be angry, and offered to pay for everything. My behaviors would have shown a mixture of defense and coping mechanisms. We should not rely exclusively on one type of mechanism or the other to deal with others and events. Most people have both mechanisms present in their behaviors.

EXERCISE 10-7: THE ROLE OF DEFENSE AND COPING MECHANISMS IN BEHAVIOR

For each of the situations described, identify the coping and defense mechanisms described in Tables 10-4 and 10-5 that are present. Check your responses with those given on page 342.

Situation 1: Steve and Jane are responsible for bringing snacks to their garden club's meeting. On the way to the meeting, they stop at a shopping center to buy several things. After loading the snacks in the back seat of the car, Steve asks Jane to come with him to run one more errand. On returning to the car, they find that the snacks have been stolen.

  Jane: The snacks are gone, someone stole them! It's the fault of that darned salesperson; if she had helped us sooner, this would not have happened. (_____)

  Steve: I feel bad about this. I don't think there is any doubt about why it occurred. If I had waited until tomorrow to run this errand or if I had put the snacks in the trunk, this would not have occurred. (_____)

Situation 2: Sam and Pete are discussing their grades on a test. Sam earned an A; Pete got a D.

Sam: Gosh, Pete, you look to me like you are feeling sad. (_____
_____)

Pete: You bet I am. Professor Smith is out to get me. He's been picking on me in class and I'm sure he doesn't like me very much. This D is certainly proof of that. (_____)

Sam: Are you sure of that?

Pete: I have my suspicions. It's funny. I don't really dislike him and I am not angry with him for what he did. (_____)

Situation 3: Ed has had a bad day at the office. He lost two big sales and his boss berated him for losing them. He returns home that night and is greeted by his wife, Margie.

Margie: Hi, Honey! How did everything go today?

Ed: Leave me alone, will you! Everytime I walk in the door you expect me to tell you everything! Get off my back, OK! (_____)

Margie: Why are you shouting at me? (*pounds her fist on the table, kicks the wall, and storms out of the room*) (_____)

Margie (*returns twenty minutes later*): Honey, I'm sorry for losing my temper. You had a hard day and I can see that you are upset. (_____
_____) I have decided to forget about what happened earlier.
(_____) Why don't we have a drink and relax?

Situation 4: Ted and Alice are new members of a law firm. Both have gotten notices that their contracts will not be renewed for another year.

Ted: I'm feeling a bit upset about this. However, I've known for some time that I haven't been doing a good job. (_____)

Alice (*with tears in her eyes*): I'm really not upset. It's only one job. (_____)

Ted: I'm sure you are right. However, I would like to learn from my mistakes here. I think the way I handled clients will have to change. Specifically, I need to do a better job of preparing briefs. That's one thing I had a lot of problems with here. (_____)

Alice: You know, I just don't know where to go or what to do. But I won't worry about it. My friend Howard always has good suggestions. He will find a way out for me. (_____)

Ted: You must have a good friend. I know I don't like this but I need to do something this week. I think I'll call my friend Carol tomorrow and see if she can get me an interview with her firm. (_____)

Alice: You are right. There is no need to blame anyone. I've felt that way all along. I'm going home. (*as she leaves her desk she "accidentally" spills a bottle of ink on the new carpet that was installed in her office*) (_____)

Psychological Processes in Adjustment: The Role of Our Self-concept

Carl Rogers, Gordon Allport, and others have stressed the important role of our self-concept in understanding how we adapt to our environments. Our self-concept is simply our perception or image about who we are. It consists of the thoughts and feelings we have about our skills, abilities, and interests that help to guide and regulate our behaviors. Our behaviors are closely related to this image of ourselves. If I see myself as academically competent, intelligent, having interesting ideas about course content, and able to work alone, I might enjoy and do quite well in my course work. I would want to share my ideas in class, I will not dread taking exams or working on term papers, and I would otherwise look forward to showing my teacher what I can do. On the other hand, if I see myself as academically incompetent, not very intelligent, having uninteresting ideas about the content, and not able to work alone, I will not enjoy or do as well in the classroom. I would not want to share my "uninteresting ideas" in class, and I would fear failing exams and term papers.

How do you see your self-concept in terms of your level of academic ability, intelligence, ideas about course content, and ability to work alone? What effects do you think this has on your classroom behavior?

As you can see, our self-concept has a strong influence on what we think we can accomplish and how we interact. The writings of Martin Covington, Wallace LeBenne, and others show the wide range of effects that positive and negative self-concepts can have on our behaviors. The following represent

Suggested Answers to Exercise 10-7

Situation 1
    Jane: Rationalization
    Susan: Logical analysis

Situation 2
    Sam: Empathy
    Pete: Projection, Denial

Situation 3
    Ed: Displacement
    Margie: Displacement, Regression
    Margie: Empathy, Suppression

Situation 4
    Ted: Objectivity
    Alice: Denial
    Ted: Logical Analysis
    Alice: Doubt, Indecision
    Ted: Concentration
    Alice: Repression

---

some of the relationships that exist between our self-images and our overt behaviors:

- Students who cheat on exams have a rather low self-image of their academic abilities.
- People who have a poor self-concept regarding their ability to influence others are easily manipulated by others.
- Children who have poor images of themselves are more likely to get into trouble with the law.
- People who achieve well in school settings tend to have favorable images about themselves and their abilities.
- Individuals who have a good self-image concerning their skills and abilities accept failures more easily than those who have a poor self-concept. Those with good self-images are more likely to say, "I have failed" and not, "I am a failure."
- A positive self-concept often helps people become less dependent on others for approval of their actions. They are comfortable with their skills and abilities and able to provide themselves with realistic feedback and reinforcement regarding what they have done.
- People with positive self-concepts are less anxious and hold fewer prejudices regarding other races, colors, and creeds.

Our self-images develop from the ways that we are treated by important people in our lives. Our parents, friends, teachers, and bosses have a great deal to do with the formation of our self-concepts.[1] They provide us with feedback and reinforcement on whether our behaviors have met the standards and goals they set. As a result, we begin to find out whether our behaviors are liked, accepted, worthy of respect, and represent a success or failure. Students who are consistently able to meet the standards and goals various teachers have set will feel that they are successful. Children whose parents expect them to do things exactly as they tell them to will feel as if they lack the ability to do anything without outside direction. A salesman who consistently meets the sales quotas his boss sets will earn respect from his boss and peers. He will see himself as a good salesman. Over time this feedback and reinforcement lead us to develop a particular image of ourselves. This image might be uniformly good or poor. More likely, our image is mixed. We see ourselves in a more favorable light in some situations than in others.

Is it possible to change a poor self-concept? This question is something my students often ask me, and it is not easy to answer. There are, however, a couple of things which I have found helpful. To begin to change an image, you need to know what produced it in the first place. Thus, you need to analyze why you feel as you do and then take some actions to correct things.

[1] The terms *self-concept, self-esteem, self-image,* and *self* are often interchangeable in the literature.

EXERCISE 10-8: CHANGING OUR SELF-CONCEPT

Since our self-image is in part related to the feedback and reinforcement we obtain for meeting certain standards and goals, think of an area in your life in which you have a poor self-image. Ask yourself the following questions:

1. *Are the standards and goals that other people set too high for me?*
   If so, you might achieve them if you can negotiate more time to work on them or a change in the goals or standards. A student of mine had a poor image of his ability to write term papers. He consistently received C and D grades on such assignments. As he saw the problem, such assignments were made late in the term and he never got feedback on how well he was doing as he wrote the paper. He decided that it was unfair for teachers to ask him to write A or B papers under such conditions. The next time he received a term paper assignment, he worked a deal out with the teacher. He told the instructor that he felt he could write A and B papers but had not been able to show what he could do. The instructor agreed to give him more time to complete the project and to review early drafts of the paper with him. Needless to say, he

found that both his writing and the image he had of his writing abilities improved. He achieved this improvement by negotiating more time to achieve the goal of writing the paper to an A or B standard. The goal was not to complete one final draft of the paper and have it graded. Rather, he changed it so that several drafts would be written and each would receive comments before a final paper was produced.

2. *Do I really have the skills and abilities to achieve the standards and goals that are set?*

If not, the self-image you have may be accurate. However, you should not feel as if nothing can be done. Before such a conclusion is reached, try to figure out if you can learn what you need. A colleague of mine saw himself as a rather poor teacher. Students often complained about his teaching ability. He decided to find out what aspects of his teaching skills and abilities needed improvement. He worked with an instructional consultant on developing a variety of classroom communication skills. A year later he was pleasantly surprised to hear the favorable comments that students had about his teaching. His self-concept regarding his teaching subsequently improved.

3. *Am I in any way responsible for the poor concept I have of myself? That is, in what ways am I really responsible for the feedback and reinforcement that I get from others?*

We may not be feeling good about ourselves for several reasons. We set personal standards and goals that are too high, we refuse to develop certain skills and abilities, or we contribute in other ways to our poor self-image. A friend of mine complained about how unattractive she thought she was. I suggested she might want to look at her diet and the style of clothes and make-up she selected. In my opinion her diet of candy bars and Cokes for lunch, hastily applied make-up, and baggy clothes did not do anything for her complexion or figure. She took my advice and in six months looked and felt like a different person.

What things to improve your self-image do your responses to each question suggest? What are two actions you could take tomorrow that would help enhance your self-concept? What other actions do you need to take over the next six months to improve things? Write a specific plan of action for what needs to be done, and implement it. If you think it would help, enlist the aid of a close friend to discuss your plan and to help you discuss your progress as you implement it.

Enhancing Your Personal Adjustment

Most of us want to live as full a life as possible. However, there are times when things don't seem to go well for us. We might experience more stress and anxiety than usual. A heavy reliance on defense mechanisms may keep us from obtaining relief from such feelings. We might feel angry or depressed over some event. Finally, we may simply feel sorry for ourselves or otherwise take a poor outlook on our skills or abilities. Such feelings may occur periodically, or they may affect us over long periods of time. When they occur, we are not going to feel as if we are adapting adequately to our environment. Fortunately, there are some things that we can do to enhance our personal adjustment. You may find some of the following suggestions helpful.

Talk to someone. Have you ever noticed how much better you feel after discussing a personal problem with someone? When faced with a personal problem it is often much better to talk about it than to keep it inside. Talking about what bothers us can by itself help release some of the tension we feel. Often a close friend, parent, or relative can be a good listener. He or she may be able to give us advice and emotional support, help us gain insight into our problem, or simply engage us in a good conversation about what bothers us.

If your problems consistently interfere on a long-term basis with your ability to develop good feelings about yourself or to interact with others, talking to a professional therapist or counselor is another alternative. You need not feel ashamed or embarrassed because you want to obtain professional assistance. A variety of counseling and therapy techniques exists, and you should have few problems finding the one that best meets your needs. To give you some idea of the approaches that are available, client-centered, psychoanalytic, and behavioral approaches are briefly described here.

Client-centered therapy places emphasis on the potential of the patient or client to develop insight into his or her problems. Clients explore their attitudes, hopes and fears and are encouraged to discover for themselves how these things affect their social behaviors. The therapist keeps interpretations of what the client says to a minimum. A key part of this process is for the patients to see that they have choices in behavior and that they are responsible for the choices they make. *Psychoanalytic therapy* tries to help the patient gain a deep understanding of the role of unconscious conflicts, past and current thoughts and feelings, and various defense mechanisms in adjustment. The therapist takes a strong role in helping the patient interpret the meaning of what he or she says about past and present life. Such interpretations are designed to help an individual gain insight into the unconscious causes of stress and anxiety. *Behavioral therapy* assumes that people have learned to behave as they do. Consequently, a goal of therapy is to help people learn new and more adaptive patterns of behavior. Patients are encouraged to set goals for their behaviors, to use internal and external reinforcers to control their actions, and to actively monitor their progress in meeting new behavioral goals.

Do you currently spend a lot of time talking about your problems? Have you ever consulted a friend? A professional counselor? How helpful were the people you talked to?

Try not to blame other people or events for your behaviors.   In the final analysis, we are responsible for how we think, feel, and behave. Carl Rogers, Abraham Maslow, and Albert Ellis stress the importance of our accepting the responsibility for our thoughts, feelings, and overt behaviors. This viewpoint suggests that each of us has choices regarding how to behave in various situations in our lives. We decide, for example, to remain in rather than leave a situation, to get angry rather than keeping calm, to downgrade another person rather than being complimentary. No one forces us to do those things. Consequently, it is unfair of us to blame past or present events in our lives and other people for the problems our decisions create for us. This does not mean that past or present events and other people are not relevant to our current problems. We certainly should consider them when thinking about our potential choices. However, the final decision on what to do is ours to make, and past or present events and other people do not force us to make it. We are responsible for the things we do and should accept that responsibility.

There are several ways in which blaming other people and events affects our ability to deal with our problems. One way is that it makes us feel that the people or events must change before a solution will occur or that no solution is possible because certain things have happened and now "there is nothing I can do." A neighbor of mine complains about how much he hates his job. He blames his boss and fellow workers for his poor attitude. He constantly talks about how they must first change before he will feel better about his job. If he saw his negative thoughts and feelings as a choice for which he is responsible, another solution to his problem would be possible. He might ask what things he must do in order to improve the situation.

It also takes time and energy to think and talk about how other people and events cause our problems. This leaves us less time and energy for working on a solution. Furthermore, it adds to our unhappiness because it keeps us from activities we enjoy and which add a little sparkle to our lives. A friend of mine recently broke up with his girlfriend. For four weeks he spent his evenings and weekends feeling angry and depressed and blaming her for how lonely he was feeling. Given the circumstances, his feelings were understandable. Four weeks of such feelings meant that he spent little time working on a solution to his loneliness and he failed to engage in activities he enjoyed like attending movies, playing golf, or quietly reading. This lack of activity contributed to his misery. Had he seen that his feelings were a choice he made and for which he was responsible, he might have spent his time doing other things.

How easy would it be for you or anyone else to accept the point of view expressed in the previous paragraphs? How helpful would the suggestions for choice and responsibility be for you and the problems you face? What do you like or dislike about such a viewpoint?

Exercise your right to say no.   Have you ever done something for someone that you really did not want to do?   In the past, I've let friends drive my car, agreed to teach a course I disliked, sold raffle tickets, gone to dinner parties, and run workshops at times that were inconvenient for me.   Each of these events represented a time I should have said no but failed to do it. I am sure you have had similar experiences.   The result is that we agree and then feel bad, fail to have a good time, or otherwise become anxious and frustrated over our decision.   We probably agreed because we did not want to hurt other people's feelings, we were afraid that they would dislike or reject us, we wanted them to remain our friends, or we felt that we would act in a petty manner if we refused a request.   In reality, no one who is really a friend or otherwise likes and respects us is going to withdraw friendship, not respect us, or feel permanently hurt because we refuse a request.   It is the fear of this happening that keeps most of us saying yes when we should say no.

Saying no more often would probably remove some of the sources of tension from our lives and thus contribute to our overall adjustment. Robert Alberti, Herbert Fensterheim, and Manuel Smith suggest that we have a right to say no and not feel guilty about it.   Each author proposes that we can benefit from becoming more assertive in saying no.   We all must act a bit stronger and be more persistent to obtain this right.   Listed here are four principles I have found useful in helping to say no in an assertive fashion.

1. *Simply say "No" or "I don't want to do it."* Remember that you do not always have to give a reason for your response. In many situations a plain "no" is all that needs be communicated.
2. *Repeat your statement until the other party accepts it.* There really are people who cannot take no for an answer. They usually repeat their requests in the hope that you will change your mind. You must show that you are firm.

   Example Using Principles 1 and 2: Joe always asks Tom to join him for a few beers after class. Tom has accepted in the past because he does not want to disappoint Joe although it interferes with his study time. This time he decides to assert himself.

JOE: Hey, Tom, let's head up to the bar after class.

TOM: Thanks for asking, Joe, but I don't want to do it.

JOE: What's the matter, you sick or something?

TOM: Thanks for asking, Joe, but I just don't want to go to the bar.

JOE: C'mon, it will do you good to go.

TOM: Thanks for asking, Joe, but I don't want to do it.

JOE: OK, I'll see you in class tomorrow.

3. *If someone asks for a reason, give one only if you feel you have information that the other party obviously needs or could benefit from.* There are times when someone might benefit from having the reasons for your decision. Situations in which a pay raise request is turned down, automobile insurance is not renewed, admittance to school is denied, or a parent refuses a child's request to do something are examples of times when an elaboration might help.

   Example Using Principle 3: Sally gets an allowance each week for helping around the house. This week she failed to do her chores on two days. Her father decides to withhold the allowance for this week.

SALLY: Dad, can I have my allowance for the week?

FATHER: No. I'm not going to give you an allowance this week.

SALLY: Why not, Dad? I really need the money.

FATHER: I thought we had an agreement that you would help around the house every day. You decided not to help on Tuesday and Wednesday so I don't think you earned your allowance.

SALLY: I wanted to play a bit longer. Washing the breakfast dishes and making my bed would have interfered with my play time. Won't you reconsider? I'll do better next week.

FATHER: There will be no allowance this week.

SALLY: I don't like it but I can live with the decision.

4. *Do not give a reason if you think the information is unlikely to help the other party or will simply allow them to present a number of counterarguments.* If you are sure that your decision is the one you want to make, then you do not have to give a reason.

   Example Using Principle 4: Mary typically can't refuse a sales pitch. As a result, she buys many things she does not need. A magazine salesman calls on her. She has more magazines than she can read and this time she decides to assert herself. In this case her reasons are unlikely to help the other party and they will only open her up to counterarguments.

SALESMAN: Good afternoon! I'm representing the Ajax Magazine Company and we have a special offer for people in your neighborhood. You can purchase five 10-year subscriptions for the price of two.

MARY: No, thank you; I'm not interested in purchasing magazines.

SALESMAN: Perhaps you don't understand the offer. What reasons do you have for refusing?

MARY: I understand the offer. Thanks for making it. However, I'm not interested in purchasing magazines.

SALESMAN: Surely you can't be against reading and learning more, can you?

MARY: I'm not interested in purchasing magazines.

SALESMAN: Perhaps another time. Good day.

EXERCISE 10-9: SAYING NO TO A REQUEST

Think of a situation in your life in which you have or expect to have a hard time saying no. Pick the principles that you feel will help you. Develop a plan of action to use the principles. Try to imagine yourself in the situation. Practice in front of a mirror saying no and any counterresponses you think the other party is likely to make. Why not put into practice what you have just rehearsed?

Table 10-6

A List of Interpersonal Rights

Each of us has in interpersonal interactions the right to:

- say no to a request.
- not give other people reasons for every action we take.
- stop others from making excessive demands on us.
- ask other people to listen to our point of view when we speak to them.
- ask other people to correct errors they made which affect us.
- change our minds.
- ask other people to compromise rather than get only what they want.
- ask other people to do things for us.
- persist in making a request if people won't respond the first time.
- be alone if we wish.
- maintain our dignity in relationships.
- evaluate our own behaviors and not just listen to evaluations that others offer.
- make mistakes and accept responsibility for them.
- avoid manipulation by other people.
- pick our own friends without consulting our parents, peers, or anyone else.
- let other people know how we are feeling.

Use other interpersonal rights to enhance your adjustment. Table 10-6 describes a few of the other rights that the assertiveness training literature suggests we have in interpersonal interactions. Again, many of us have problems in exercising them because we fear what others will think or we feel guilty about using our rights. As a result, we are prevented from expressing ourselves and enhancing our adjustment. To obtain these rights, we need to let others know what we want in a clear and concise fashion. If necessary, we also need to repeat our requests or state our position until they hear it and take some action.

There are three things to remember when becoming more assertive.

1. Do not behave in ways that are likely to make others overly defensive, angry, or lead them to "turn you off." This will only guarantee that you will not get what you want.
2. Remember that other people have the same rights that you do. You should not try to get what you want by ignoring the legitimate needs and rights of other people.
3. Becoming assertive does not mean that you will get what you want each time. There are times when a compromise is needed or when you will simply fail to get what you want.

The following example illustrates the incorrect and correct way to be assertive in an interpersonal situation.

Situation: George has bought a new television set. He has kept it for two months and problems have developed. The service department of the store is unable to fix it to his satisfaction. He wants it fixed right or his money back. He goes to the store to talk to the manager but asserts himself incorrectly.

> GEORGE: Look, you little #$&¢@#$%. I'm sick and tired of getting cheated out of my money by merchants such as you. This television can't be fixed and you owe me some money. (*makes a request like a bull in a china shop*)

> MANAGER: I'm sorry you feel that way, sir. Let me explain what the store's policy is on returned merchandise. (*uses her right to have others listen to her*)

> GEORGE: I don't care what the policy is. You owe me some money and I want it. (*George repeats request but ignores manager's right to ask other people to listen to her point of view*)

> MANAGER: I think your behaviors are unreasonable and you shouldn't feel the way you do.

> GEORGE: Damn it, I'm angry and I have every right to be. (*George has the right to let others know how he feels, but he does it in ways that are likely to turn the manager off*)

> MANAGER: Look, I'm not giving you your money back and that is final. Good day.

Situation: Instant replay. This time George acts assertive in a more appropriate fashion.

> GEORGE: I've been having trouble getting this television set repaired. Since your service department can't fix it, I want my money back. (*makes a request of another person in a clear and concise fashion*)

> MANAGER: I'm sorry that you feel that way, sir. Let me explain what the store's policy is on returned merchandise.

> GEORGE: Go right ahead. (*allows manager to exercise her right to have people listen to her when she speaks*)

> MANAGER: We do not give refunds simply because of a service problem. If we can't fix it here, we will send it back first.

> GEORGE: I understand what you are saying. However, I want my money back if the factory can't fix it. (*repeats the request since the manager*

has not stated that she understands George's request that a refund must be part of the deal if the television can't be fixed)

MANAGER: I don't like to give a refund. But how about this: If the factory can't fix it, will you take a new set instead? *(uses her right to suggest a compromise)*

GEORGE: That is fine, provided you lend me a set until mine is fixed. *(shows willingness to accept compromise but makes another reasonable request)*

MANAGER: That would be all right with me.

EXERCISE 10-10: USING OUR INTERPERSONAL RIGHTS

Review the rights listed in Table 10-6. Which ones do you feel you fail to use? Pick one or two of them and imagine a personal situation in which they could be used. Develop a plan of action to use those rights. Practice in front of a mirror what you would say and the responses others are likely to make. Put into practice what you have just rehearsed as soon as possible.

SUMMARY

Each of us attempts to judge how poorly or well adjusted our own or someone else's behaviors are. However, there is no single way to assess the adequacy of the ways that we and others adapt to a complex environment. Attempts at defining adjustment always reflect certain biases. Common definitions are based on considerations of how behavior conforms to cultural and expert expectations, statistical judgments of the frequency of behaviors, the personal behaviors that each of us exhibits, and the effects of our behaviors on ourselves and others.

An understanding of our reactions to stress and anxiety, the types of coping and defense mechanisms we use, and the nature of our self-concept are important in understanding our adjustment. Stress is an emotional state of tension which is often characterized by our feeling frustrated, hostile, or aggressive. Our inability to accomplish various goals because of personal limitations and factors in our environment which block our behaviors produces stress. Furthermore, conflicts in selecting among alternative goals also contribute to the tension we experience. Such choices become particularly difficult when two or more goals are equally attractive or unattractive or when one or more goals have both attractive and unattractive qualities. These situations are called approach-approach, avoidance-avoidance, and approach-avoidance conflicts, respectively.

Anxiety is often characterized as a feeling of fear, apprehension, or worry in the absence of any real danger to our physical well being. In small amounts it can often energize our behaviors, but at higher levels it may prevent us from functioning effectively. Anxiety is a normal part of our lives and is produced by threats to our self-concept, learning processes which include classical conditioning and imitation learning, unresolved conflicts, and unconscious impulses.

Coping and defense mechanisms are the components that help us adapt to stress and anxiety. Coping mechanisms represent the conscious thoughts and behaviors we have under conditions of stress and anxiety. They are oriented toward searching for information, solving problems, recognizing our feelings, seeking help from others, and establishing goals and objectives. Their use leads to long-term favorable consequences as we adjust to the demands of our environments. Defense mechanisms try to protect us from stress and anxiety by the use of self-deception. They try to hide or disguise unpleasant thoughts and emotions. Common defense mechanisms include rationalization, projection, repression, denial, and displacement. They provide only temporary relief from stress and anxiety and do not lead to adequate long-term adaptations to the problems we face.

Our self-concept is our perception or image of who we are. It consists of the thoughts and feelings we have about our skills, abilities, and interests that help to guide and regulate our behaviors. A positive or negative self-concept can have a wide range of effects on our behaviors. It develops from the ways that we are treated by parents, friends, teachers, and other important people in our lives. Since such people provide us with feedback and reinforcement, we begin to find out whether our behaviors are liked, accepted, worthy of respect, and representative of success or failure.

Most of us want to live as full a life as possible. However, there are times when things don't seem to go well for us. Each of us runs into a range of minor and major adjustment problems in our lives. Fortunately, there are several things that can be done to enhance our personal adjustment.

Talk to someone. Talking about a problem is often much better than keeping it inside. Discussing a personal issue with a close friend, parent, or relative often helps to release some of the tension we feel. For problems that interfere on a long-term basis with our ability to develop good feelings about ourselves or to interact with others, talking to a professional therapist or counselor is helpful.

Try not to blame other people or events for your behavior.   We are responsible for how we think, feel, and behave.   Other people and events do not force us to think or behave in certain ways.   Our behaviors represent choices that we elect to make.   Blaming other people or events takes time and energy away from working on solutions to problems and detracts from our doing the things we enjoy.

Exercise your right to say no.   Each of us has a right to say no and not feel guilty about it.   Since giving in to the demands of other people often gets us into situations in which we are not happy, refusing some requests would remove a source of tension from our lives.   To do this, we must behave more assertively.

Use other interpersonal rights to enhance your adjustment.   A number of other interpersonal rights exist which can enhance our adjustment.   They include the right to stop other people from making excessive demands on us, to change our minds, to ask other people to do things for us, and to avoid manipulation by other people.   To obtain them, we must let others know what we want in a clear and concise manner.   If necessary, we also need to repeat our requests or state our position until others hear it and take some action.   Asserting ourselves does not always get us what we want.   However, it does allow us to express our needs and desires clearly.

THINGS TO DO

1. Editorials in newspapers and magazines and on radio and television often comment on behaviors of people in the news.   Read or listen to five such editorials and analyze them for the types of criteria described in Table 10-1 that they use to pass judgments on others.   Do certain news sources have biases of one kind or another?

2. Attend a political rally or read a candidate's views and comments in a news source.   What coping and defense mechanisms does he or she use to deal with the stress and anxiety associated with a campaign?

3. It is possible to classify major life stresses according to the degree of stress and anxiety they arouse.   High-stress situations include death of a husband, wife, or close relative, injury to yourself, and marriage.   Low-stress events include a vacation, a change in residence, and trouble with a boss.   In what ways are stress and anxiety produced by each of these events?   That is, what goals could be blocked, what conflicts might occur, and what sources of anxiety are likely to be present?

4. What if you assumed that people are really responsible for the choices they make and that blaming other people or events is a "cop-out?" What implications does such a view have for a person pleading insanity at the time he or she committed a crime? In what ways would our system of laws and penalties for crimes change? How far could you extend such thinking? Do you think that we choose the type of diseases we have and that we could choose to eliminate a disease that affects us?

5. Can you think of ways in which unconscious impulses might influence the behaviors of a professional athlete, a police officer, a teacher, an actor, and a musician?

6. Make a list of your strengths as a person. Think about each one and figure out one way to enhance it. Put your thoughts into practice for two weeks. Afterward, think about how emphasizing your strengths contributes to your ability to adapt.

7. Write a letter to yourself describing the ways in which you fail to exercise the rights described in Table 10-7. Include in your letter the problems this creates for you and how you think it affects what other people think about you. Pick the two things from this list that bother you the most and design an action plan to do something about them.

8. Using the principles described in the chapter for saying no, say no to all requests that others make of you tomorrow. At the end of the day, evaluate how you think this worked out.

REFERENCES AND OTHER INTERESTING THINGS TO READ

ALBERTI, R. W., and EMMONS, M. L. *Stand Up, Speak Out, Talk Back!* New York: Pocket Books, 1975.

ALLPORT, G. W. *Personality: A Psychological Interpretation.* New York: Holt, 1937.

BACH, G. R., and GOLDBERG, H. *Creative Aggression.* Garden City, N.Y.: Doubleday and Co., 1974.

BANDURA, A. *Behavior Modification.* New York: Holt, Rinehart and Winston, 1969.

COOK, H., and DAVITZ, J. *60 Seconds to Mind Expansion.* New York: Random House, 1975.

COVINGTON, M. V., and BIERY, R. G. *Self Worth and School Learning.* New York: Holt, Rinehart and Winston, 1976.

DODSON, F. *The You that Could Be.* Chicago: Follett, 1976.

ELLIS, A. *Humanistic Psychotherapy.* New York: Julian Press, 1973.

EWEN, R. B. *Getting It Together: A Guide to Modern Psychological Analysis.* New York: Franklin Watts, 1976.

FAST, J. *Creative Coping: A Guide to Positive Living.* New York: William Morrow and Co., 1976.

FENSTERHEIM, H., and BAER, J. *Don't Say Yes When You Want to Say No.* New York: David McKay Co., 1975.

FREUD, S. *Introductory Lectures on Psychoanalysis.* London: Hogarth, 1957.

GAYLIN, W. In matters mental or emotional, what's normal? *The New York Times Magazine,* April 1, 1973.

HAAN, N. Proposed model of ego functioning: Coping and defense mechanisms in relationship to IQ change. *Psychological Monographs,* 1963, 77, No. 8.

HERTZBERG, H., and McCLELLAND, D. C. K. Paranoia. *Harpers,* June, 1974.

JOHNSON, D. W. *Reaching Out: Interpersonal Effectiveness and Self-actualization.* Englewood Cliffs, N.J.: Prentice-Hall, 1972.

KIESTER, E., and CUDHEA, D. Albert Bandura: A very modern model. *Human Behavior,* September, 1974.

KROEBER, T. C. The Coping Functions of Ego Mechanisms. In R. W. White (Ed.), *The Study of Lives.* New York: Atherton Press, 1973.

LaBENNE, W. D., and GREENE, B. I. *Educational Implications of Self-concept Theory.* Pacific Palisades, Calif.: Goodyear, 1969.

LANGER, E. J., and DWECK, C. *Personal Politics: The Psychology of Making It.* Englewood Cliffs, N.J.: Prentice-Hall, 1973.

MASLOW, A. *Toward a Psychology of Being.* Princeton, N.J.: Van Nostrand, 1962.

REIF, A. Eric Fromm: On human aggression. *Human Behavior,* April, 1975.

ROGERS, C. R. *On Becoming a Person.* Boston: Houghton Mifflin, 1961.

SARBIN, T. Schizophrenia is a myth, born of metaphor meaningless. *Psychology Today,* June, 1972.

SMITH, M. *When I Say No I Feel Guilty.* New York: Dial Press, 1975.

Index